kimi ni todoke
From Me to You

Vol. 23

Story & Art by
Karuho Shiina

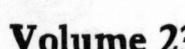

Volume 23

Contents

Episode 92: True Feelings -------------------------- 3

Episode 93: Regret ----------------------------------- 47

Episode 94: Myself ---------------------------------- 91

Episode 95: Thank You --------------------------- 133

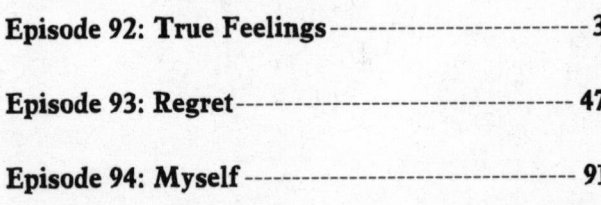

Story Thus Far

Sawako Kuronuma has always been a loner. Though not by choice, this optimistic 16-year-old girl can't seem to make any friends. Stuck with the unfortunate nickname "Sadako" after the haunting movie character, rumors about her summoning spirits have been greatly exaggerated. With her shy personality and scary looks, most of her classmates will barely talk to her, much less look into her eyes for more than three seconds lest they be cursed. Thanks to Kazehaya, who always treats her nicely, Sawako makes her first friends at school, Ayane and Chizu. Eventually, Sawako finds the courage to date Kazehaya.

The time has come for Sawako and her friends to think about their futures after high school. Chizu confesses her feelings to Ryu, and Sawako and Kazehaya continue to work hard towards their goals for after graduation. Meanwhile, Kento and Yano's relationship is at risk of coming to an end. Yano had promised Kento that she would follow him to a university in Sapporo, but she later confesses that she wants to go to a university in Tokyo. Their conversation ends on a sour note as they continue to struggle to tell each other how they really feel.

kimi ni todoke

From Me to You

Episode 92: True Feelings

Karuho Shiina

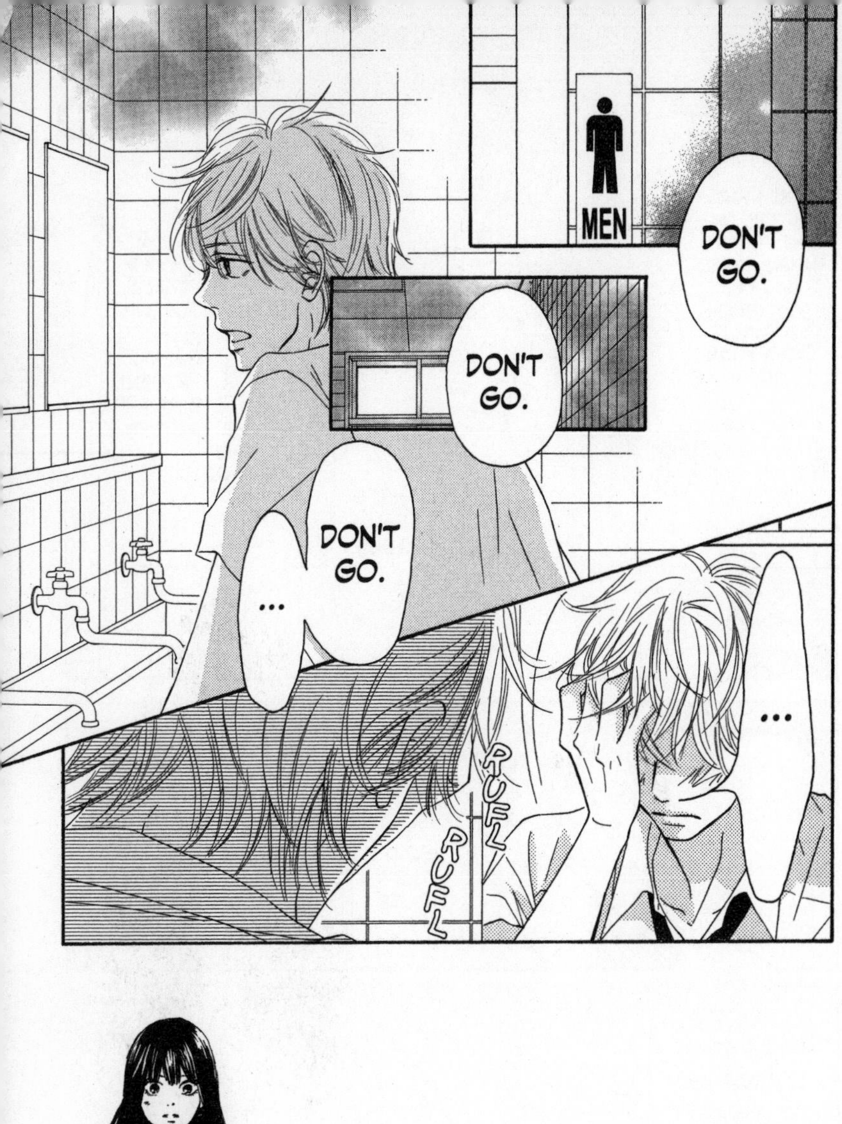
MEN
DON'T GO.
DON'T GO.
DON'T GO.
...
...
RUFL
RUFL

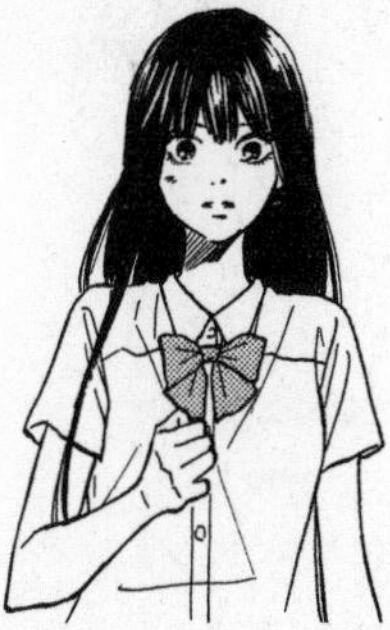

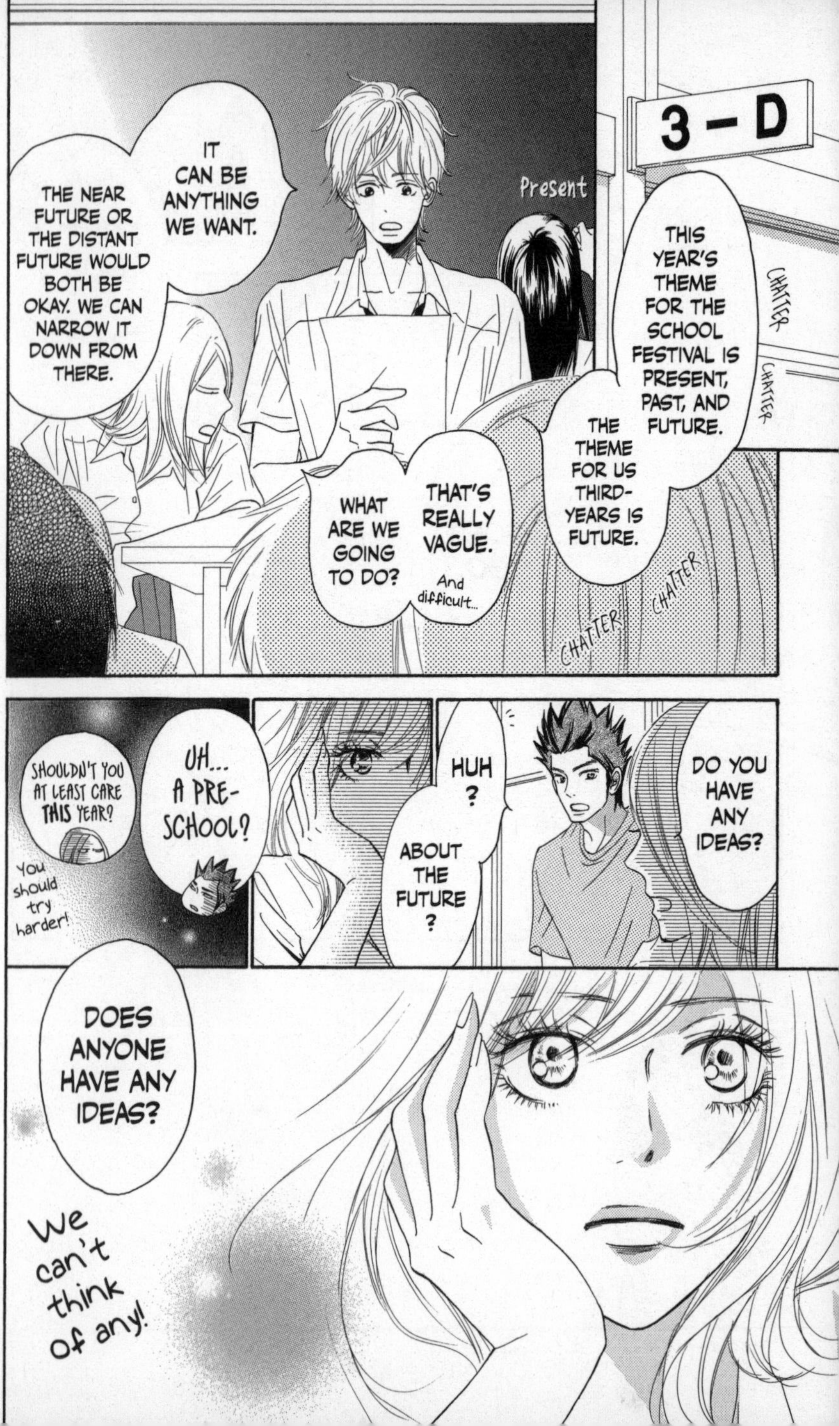
3 – D
Present
THIS YEAR'S THEME FOR THE SCHOOL FESTIVAL IS PRESENT, PAST, AND FUTURE.
CHATTER
CHATTER
THE THEME FOR US THIRD-YEARS IS FUTURE.
IT CAN BE ANYTHING WE WANT.
THE NEAR FUTURE OR THE DISTANT FUTURE WOULD BOTH BE OKAY. WE CAN NARROW IT DOWN FROM THERE.
THAT'S REALLY VAGUE.
And difficult...
WHAT ARE WE GOING TO DO?
CHATTER
CHATTER
DO YOU HAVE ANY IDEAS?
HUH?
ABOUT THE FUTURE?
UH... A PRE-SCHOOL?
SHOULDN'T YOU AT LEAST CARE **THIS** YEAR?
You should try harder!
DOES ANYONE HAVE ANY IDEAS?
We can't think of any!

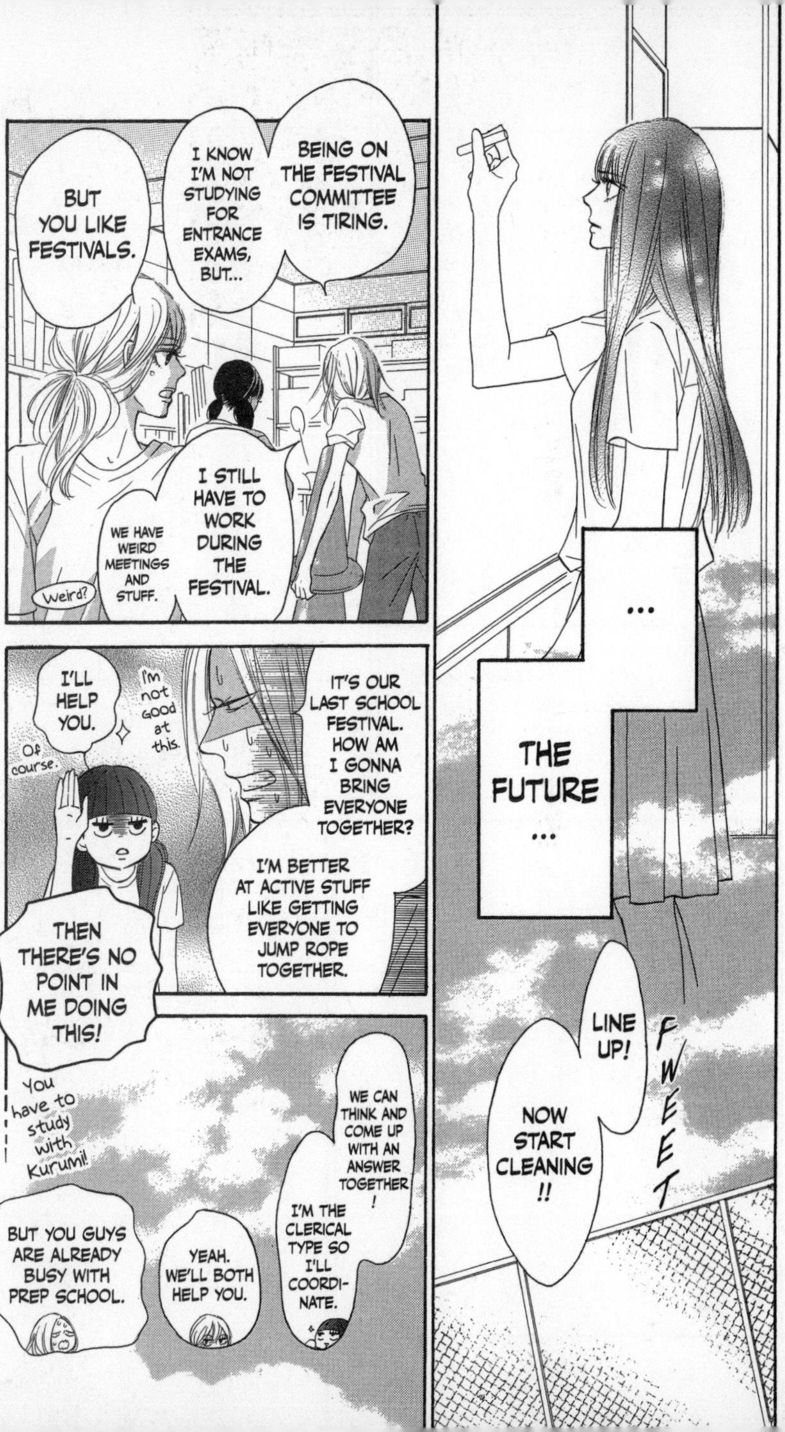
...
THE FUTURE ...
LINE UP!
NOW START CLEANING!!
FWEET
BEING ON THE FESTIVAL COMMITTEE IS TIRING.
I KNOW I'M NOT STUDYING FOR ENTRANCE EXAMS, BUT...
BUT YOU LIKE FESTIVALS.
I STILL HAVE TO WORK DURING THE FESTIVAL.
WE HAVE WEIRD MEETINGS AND STUFF.
Weird?
IT'S OUR LAST SCHOOL FESTIVAL. HOW AM I GONNA BRING EVERYONE TOGETHER?
I'm not good at this.
I'LL HELP YOU.
Of course.
I'M BETTER AT ACTIVE STUFF LIKE GETTING EVERYONE TO JUMP ROPE TOGETHER.
THEN THERE'S NO POINT IN ME DOING THIS!
WE CAN THINK AND COME UP WITH AN ANSWER TOGETHER!
I'M THE CLERICAL TYPE SO I'LL COORDINATE.
YEAH. WE'LL BOTH HELP YOU.
BUT YOU GUYS ARE ALREADY BUSY WITH PREP SCHOOL.
You have to study with Kurumi!

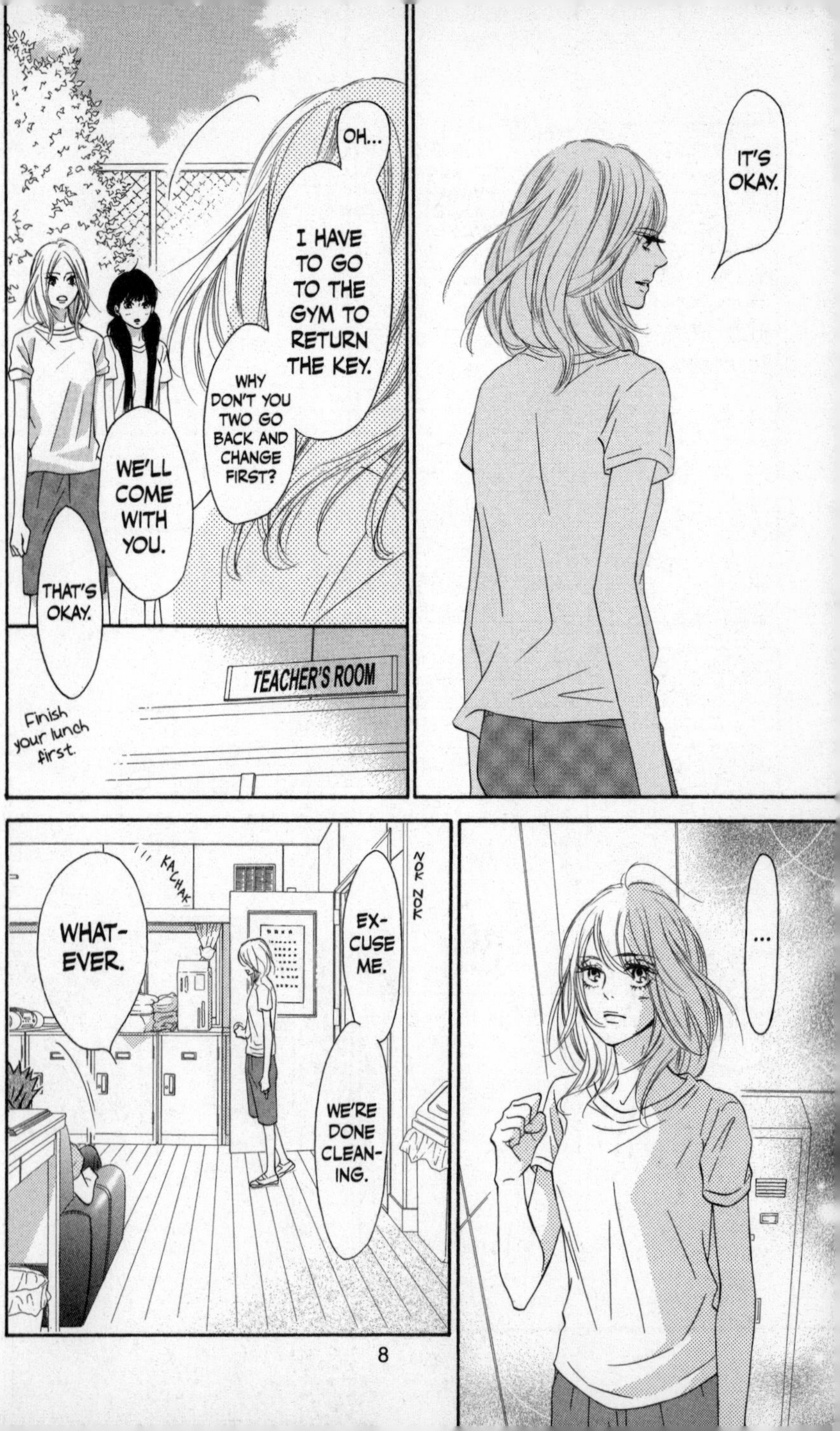
IT'S OKAY.
OH...
I HAVE TO GO TO THE GYM TO RETURN THE KEY.
WHY DON'T YOU TWO GO BACK AND CHANGE FIRST?
WE'LL COME WITH YOU.
THAT'S OKAY.
Finish your lunch first.
TEACHER'S ROOM
...
NOK NOK
EX-CUSE ME.
WE'RE DONE CLEANING.
KACHAK
WHAT-EVER.

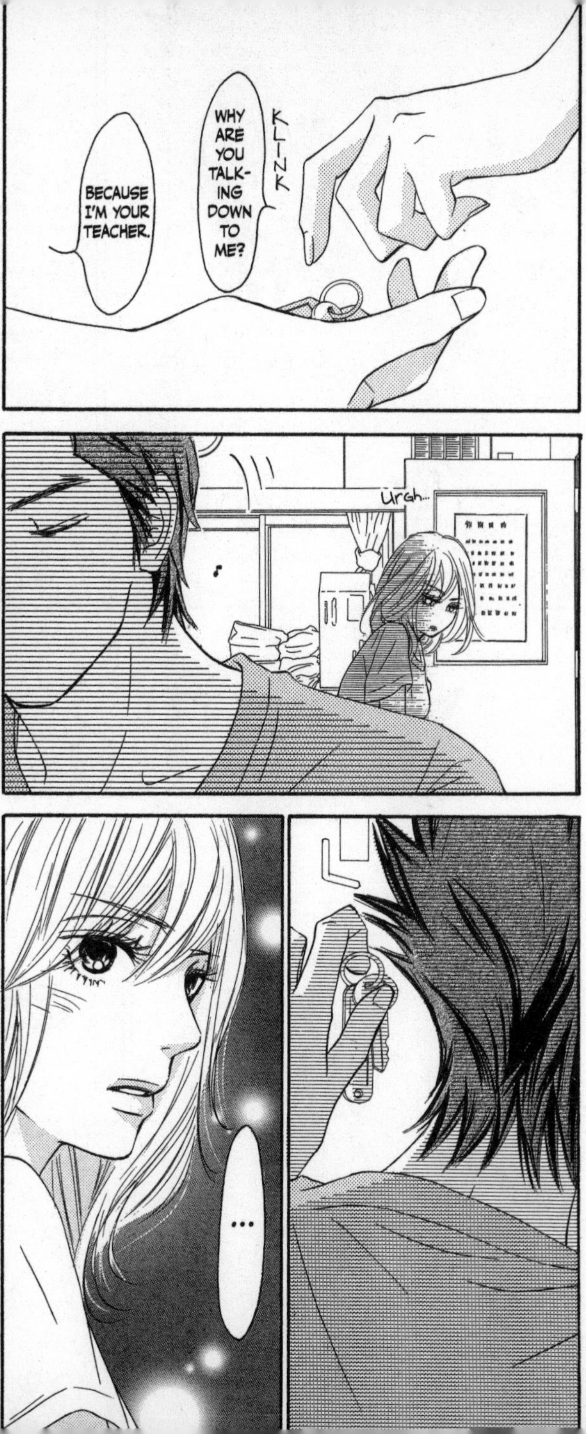
WHY ARE YOU TALKING DOWN TO ME?
KLINK
BECAUSE I'M YOUR TEACHER.
Urgh...
...

KARUPIN on JAPAN 1

Um...I forgot to take my house key with me on the day my husband went away.

Forgot the key...

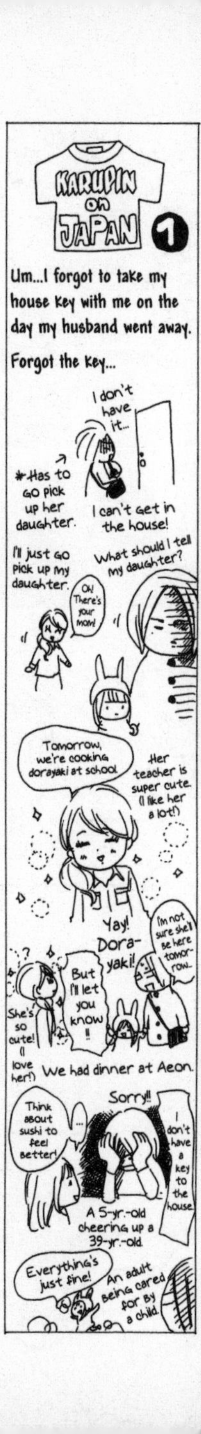
I don't have it...
*Has to go pick up her daughter.
I can't get in the house!
I'll just go pick up my daughter.
What should I tell my daughter?
Oh! There's your mom!
Tomorrow, we're cooking dorayaki at school.
Her teacher is super cute. (I like her a lot!)
Yay! Dorayaki!
I'm not sure she'll be here tomorrow...
But I'll let you know!!
She's so cute! (I love her!)
We had dinner at Aeon.
Sorry!!
Think about sushi to feel better!
...
I don't have a key to the house.
A 5-yr.-old cheering up a 39-yr.-old.
Everything's just fine!
An adult being cared for by a child.

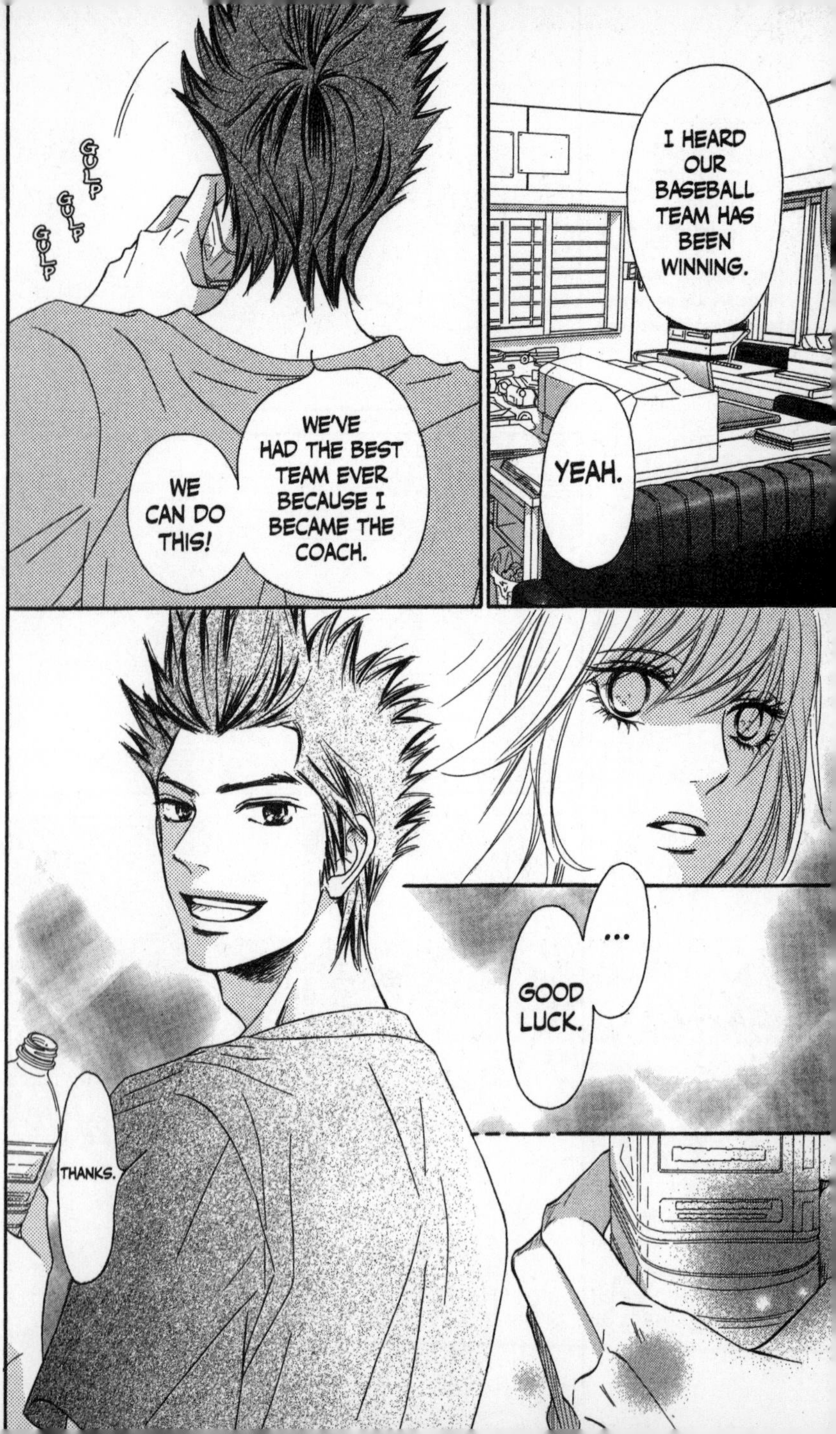
I HEARD OUR BASEBALL TEAM HAS BEEN WINNING.
YEAH.
WE'VE HAD THE BEST TEAM EVER BECAUSE I BECAME THE COACH.
WE CAN DO THIS!
GULP
GULP
GULP
...
GOOD LUCK.
THANKS.

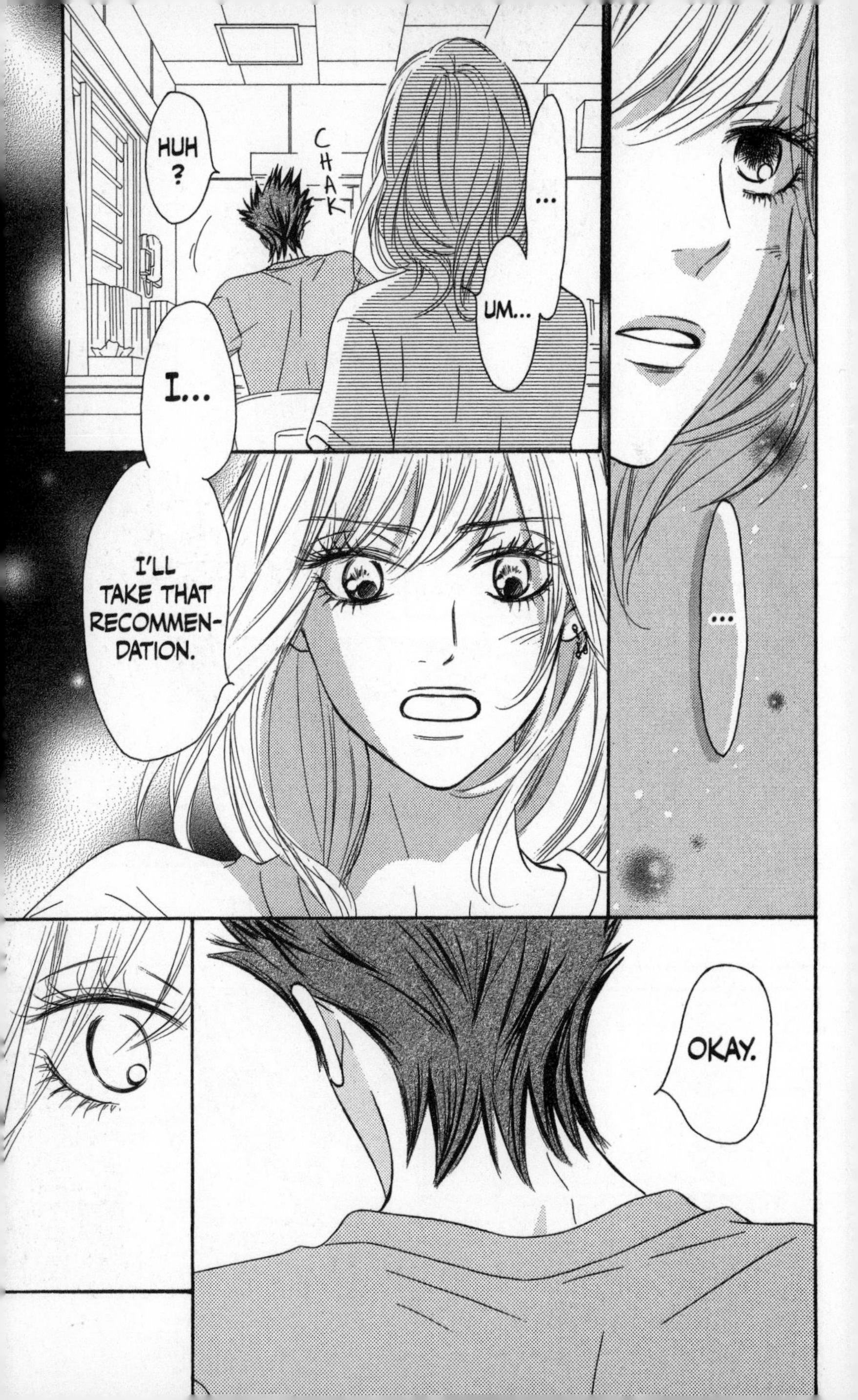
...
UM...
CHAK
HUH?
I...
I'LL TAKE THAT RECOMMENDATION.
...
OKAY.

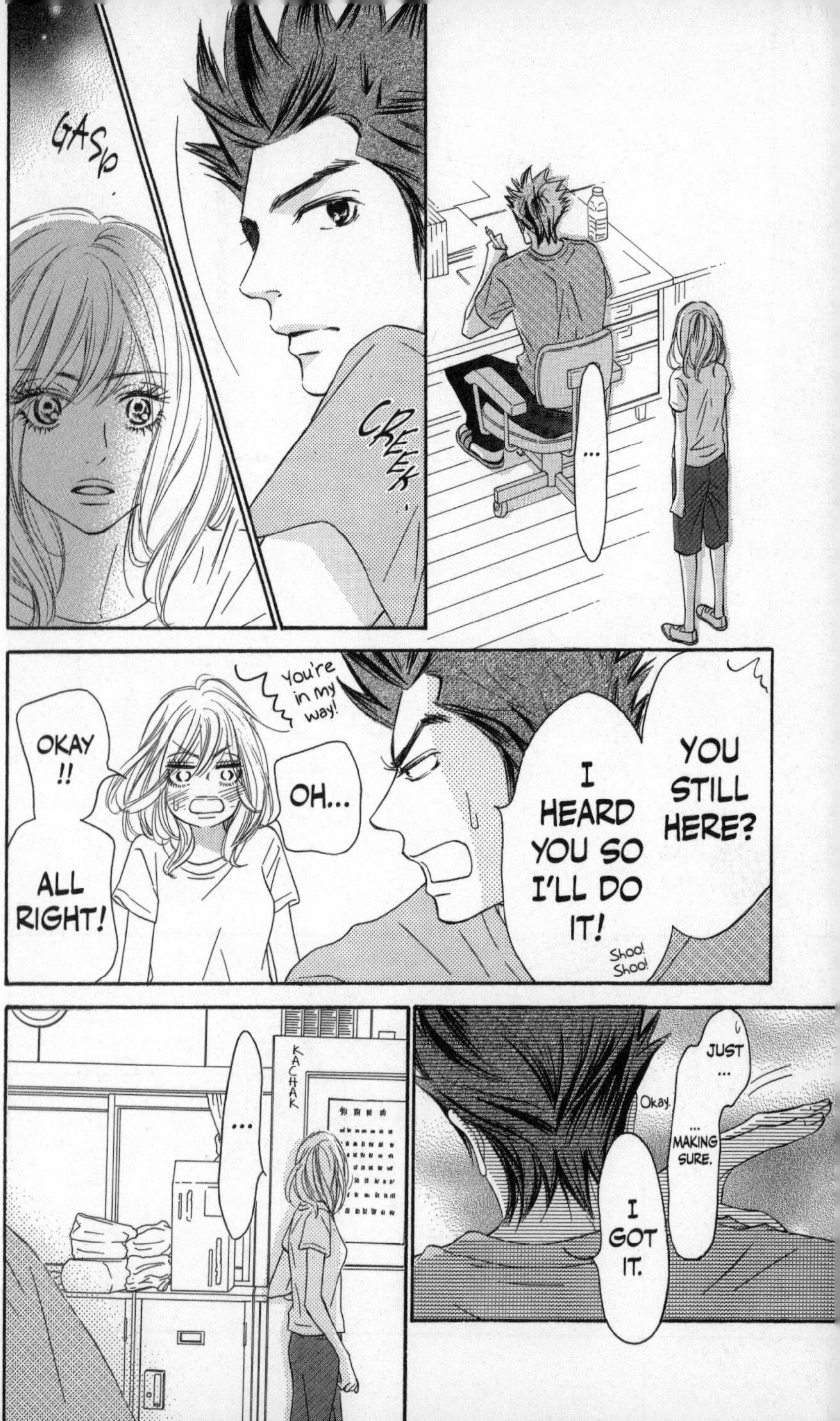
...
GASP
CREEK
YOU STILL HERE?
I HEARD YOU SO I'LL DO IT!
Shoo! Shoo!
You're in my way!
OH...
OKAY !! ALL RIGHT!
JUST ... ... MAKING SURE.
Okay.
I GOT IT.
KACHAK
...

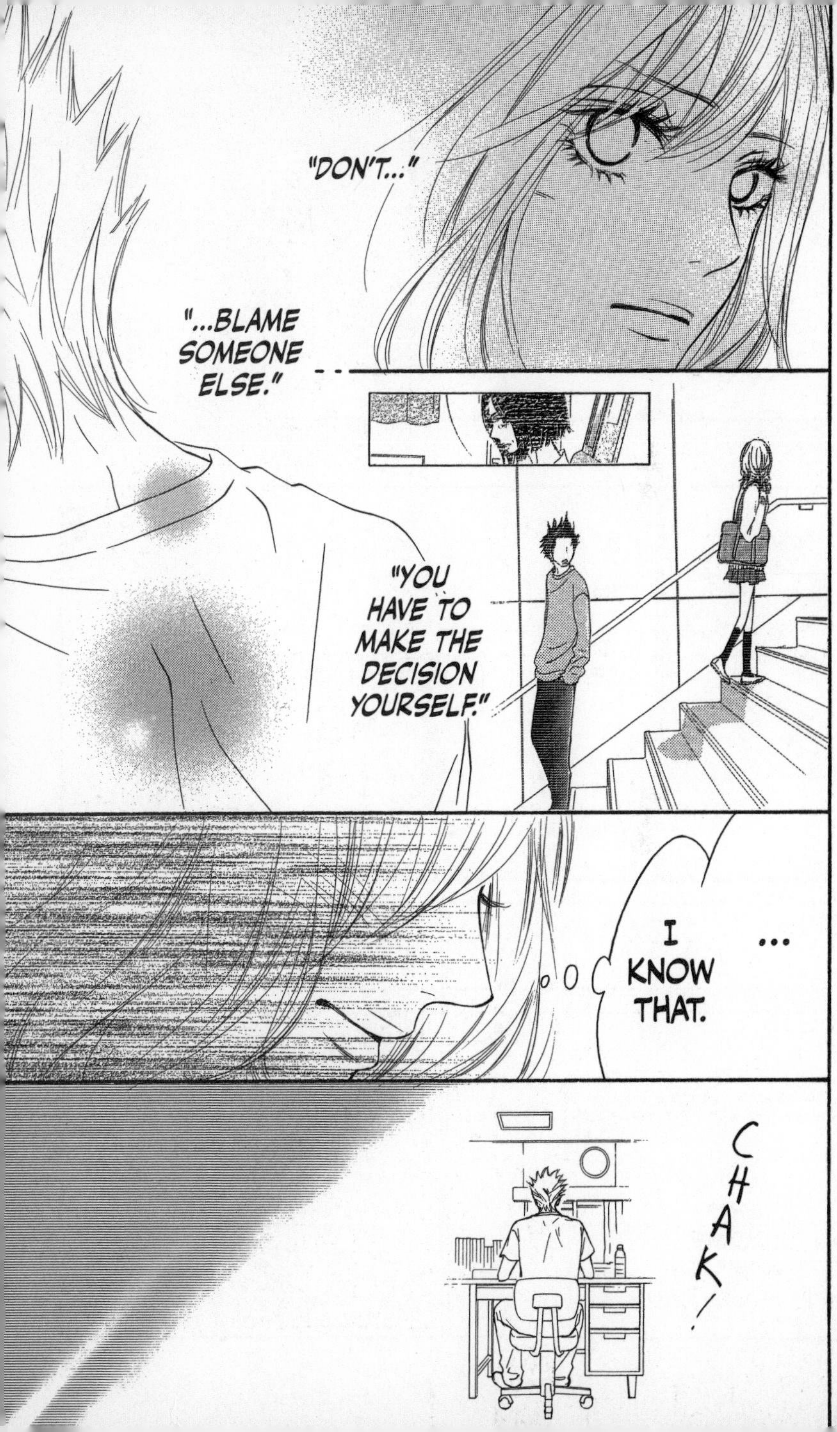
"DON'T..."
"...BLAME SOMEONE ELSE."
"YOU HAVE TO MAKE THE DECISION YOURSELF."
...
I KNOW THAT.
CHAK!

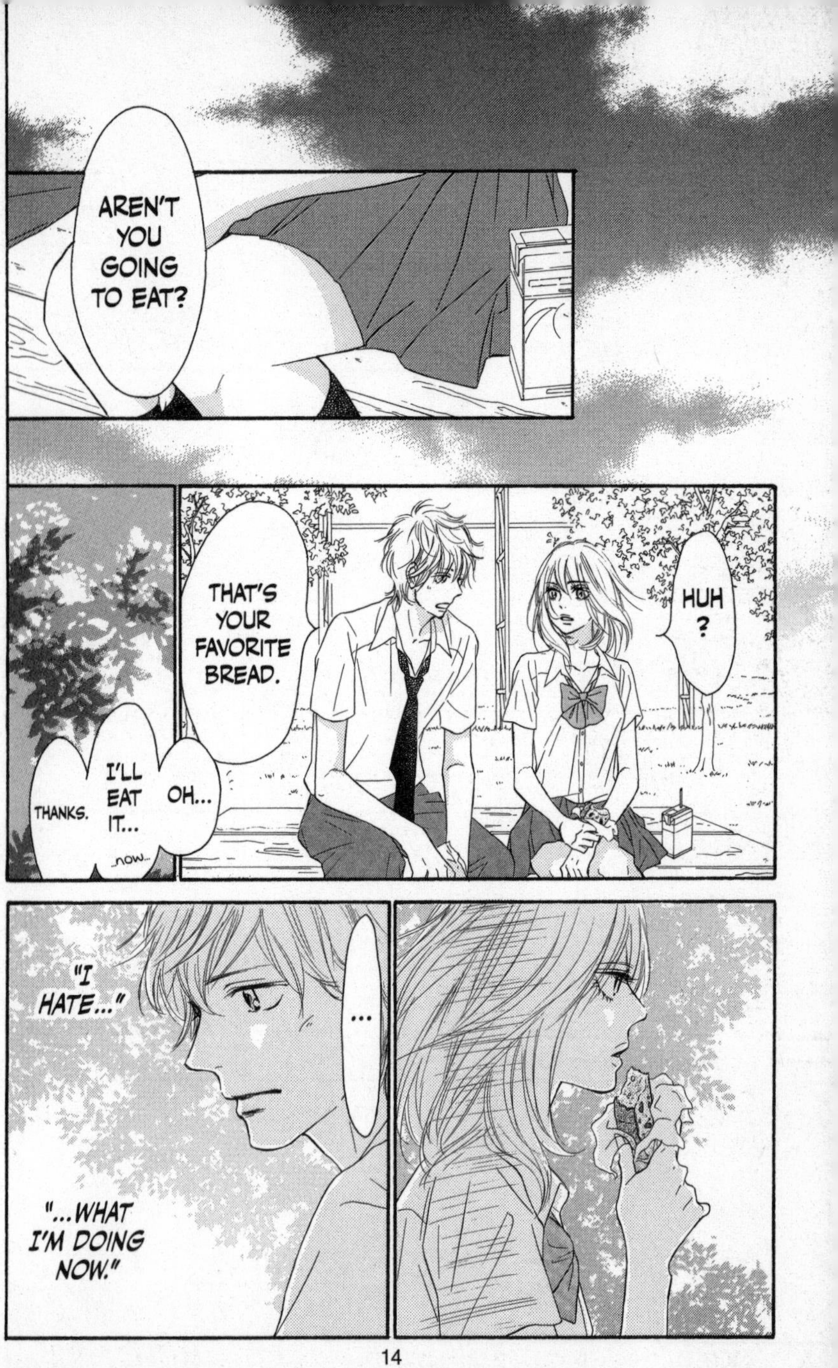
AREN'T YOU GOING TO EAT?
HUH?
THAT'S YOUR FAVORITE BREAD.
OH...
I'LL EAT IT...
...now...
THANKS.
...
"I HATE..."
"...WHAT I'M DOING NOW."

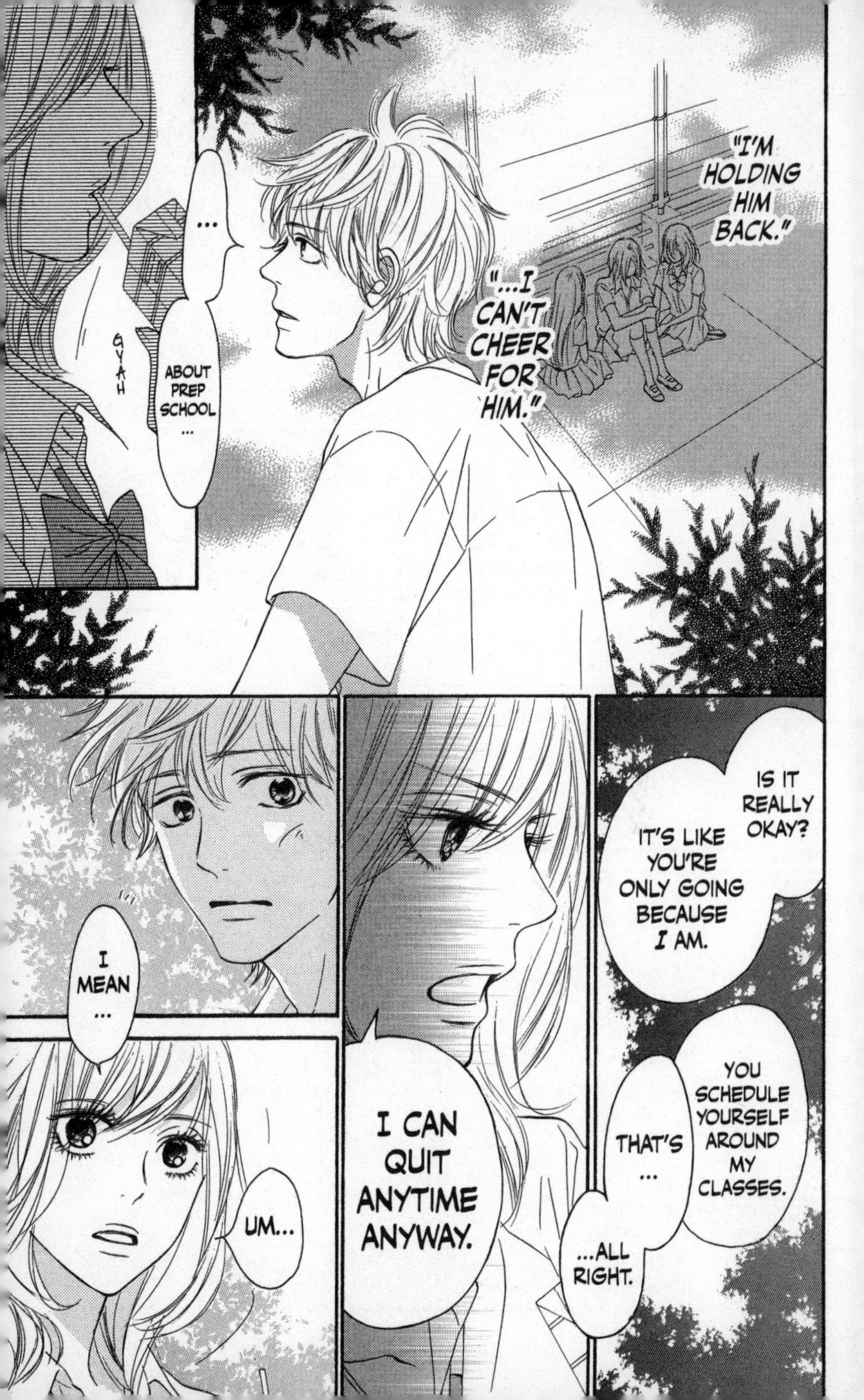
"I'M HOLDING HIM BACK."
"...I CAN'T CHEER FOR HIM."
...
GYAH
ABOUT PREP SCHOOL ...
IS IT REALLY OKAY?
IT'S LIKE YOU'RE ONLY GOING BECAUSE I AM.
YOU SCHEDULE YOURSELF AROUND MY CLASSES.
THAT'S ...
...ALL RIGHT.
I CAN QUIT ANYTIME ANYWAY.
I MEAN ...
UM...

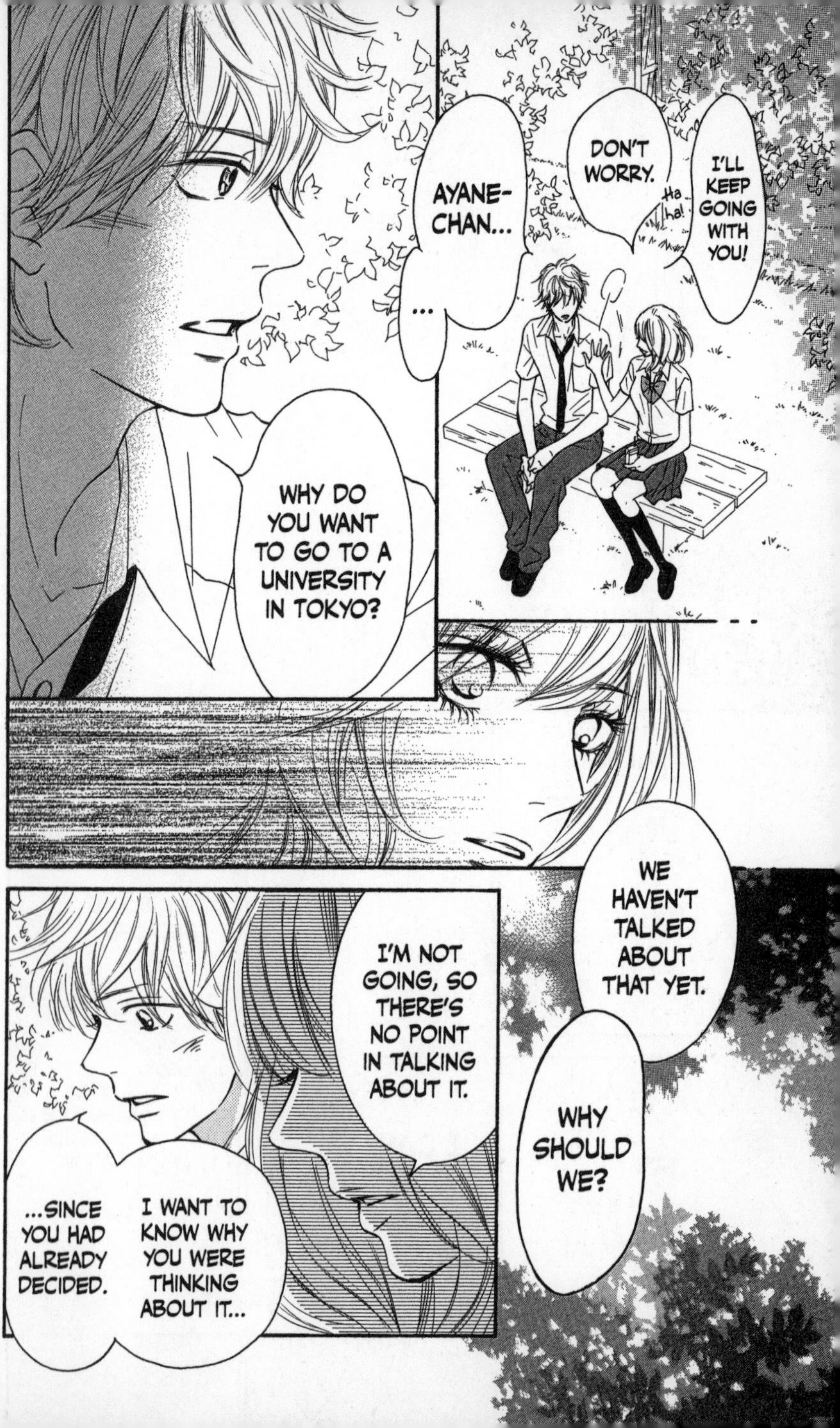
DON'T WORRY.
Ha ha!
I'LL KEEP GOING WITH YOU!
AYANE-CHAN...
...
WHY DO YOU WANT TO GO TO A UNIVERSITY IN TOKYO?
WE HAVEN'T TALKED ABOUT THAT YET.
WHY SHOULD WE?
I'M NOT GOING, SO THERE'S NO POINT IN TALKING ABOUT IT.
I WANT TO KNOW WHY YOU WERE THINKING ABOUT IT...
...SINCE YOU HAD ALREADY DECIDED.

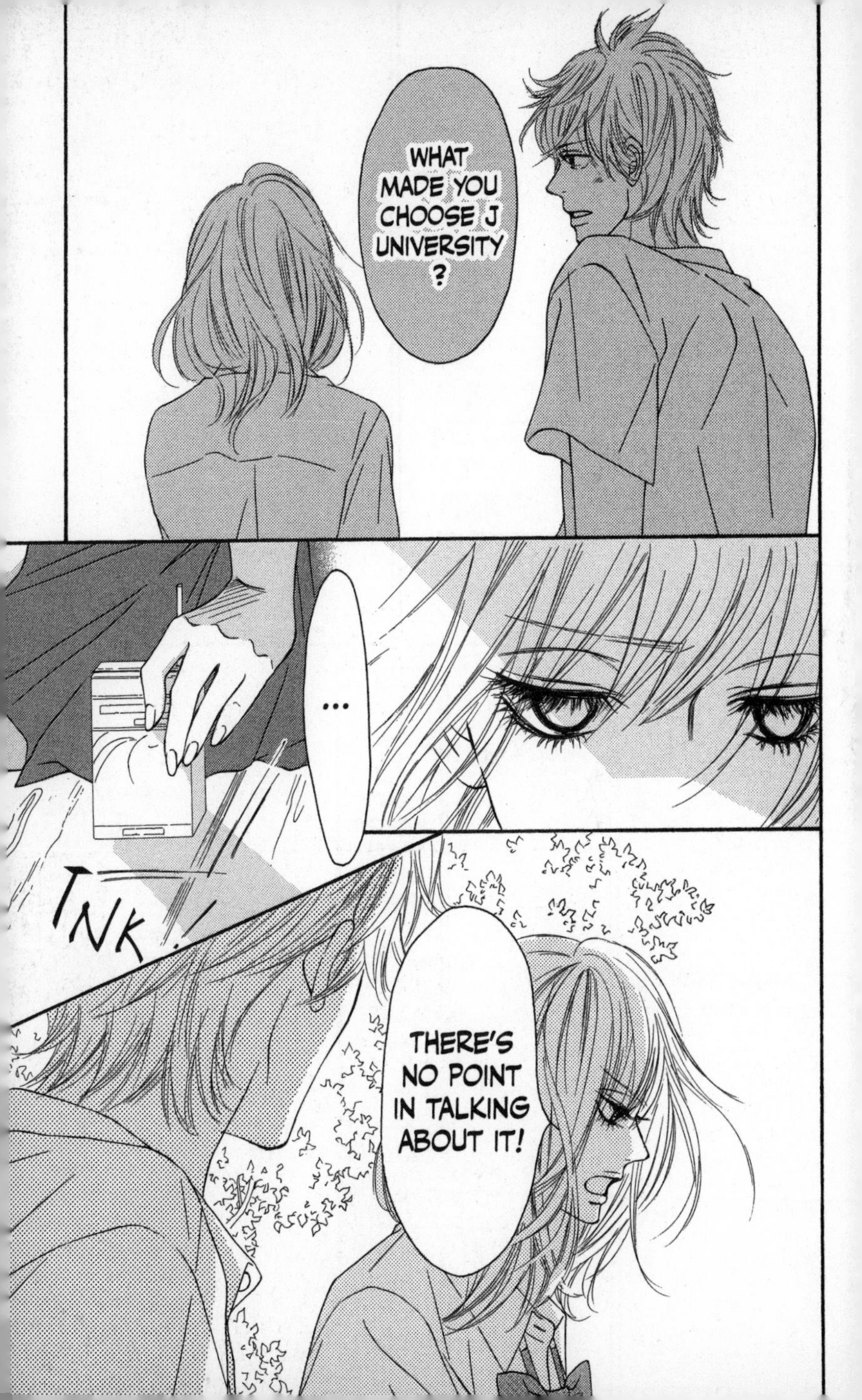
WHAT MADE YOU CHOOSE J UNIVERSITY?
...
TNK
THERE'S NO POINT IN TALKING ABOUT IT!

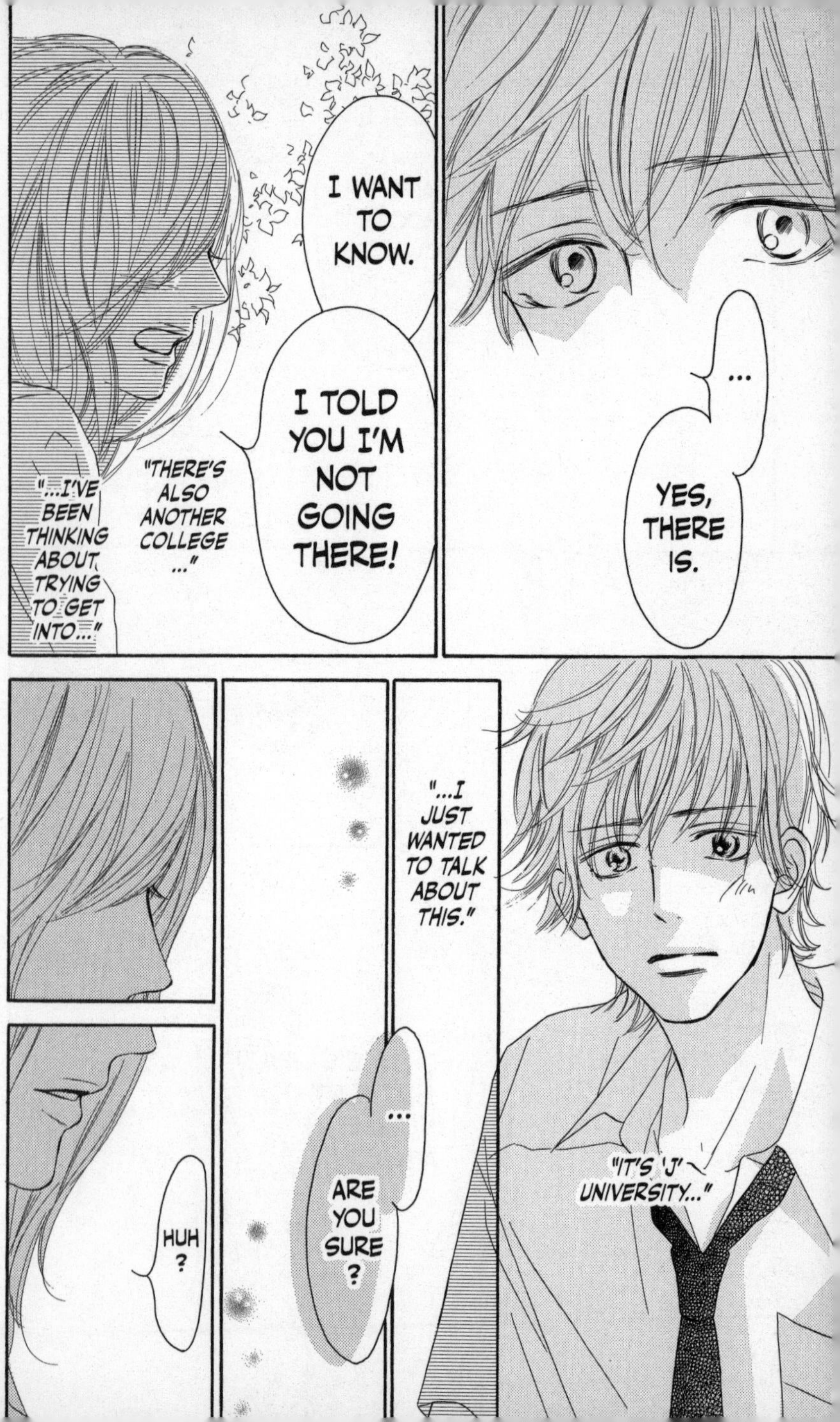
...
YES, THERE IS.
I WANT TO KNOW.
I TOLD YOU I'M NOT GOING THERE!
"THERE'S ALSO ANOTHER COLLEGE ..."
"...I'VE BEEN THINKING ABOUT TRYING TO GET INTO..."
"IT'S 'J' UNIVERSITY..."
"...I JUST WANTED TO TALK ABOUT THIS."
...
ARE YOU SURE?
HUH?

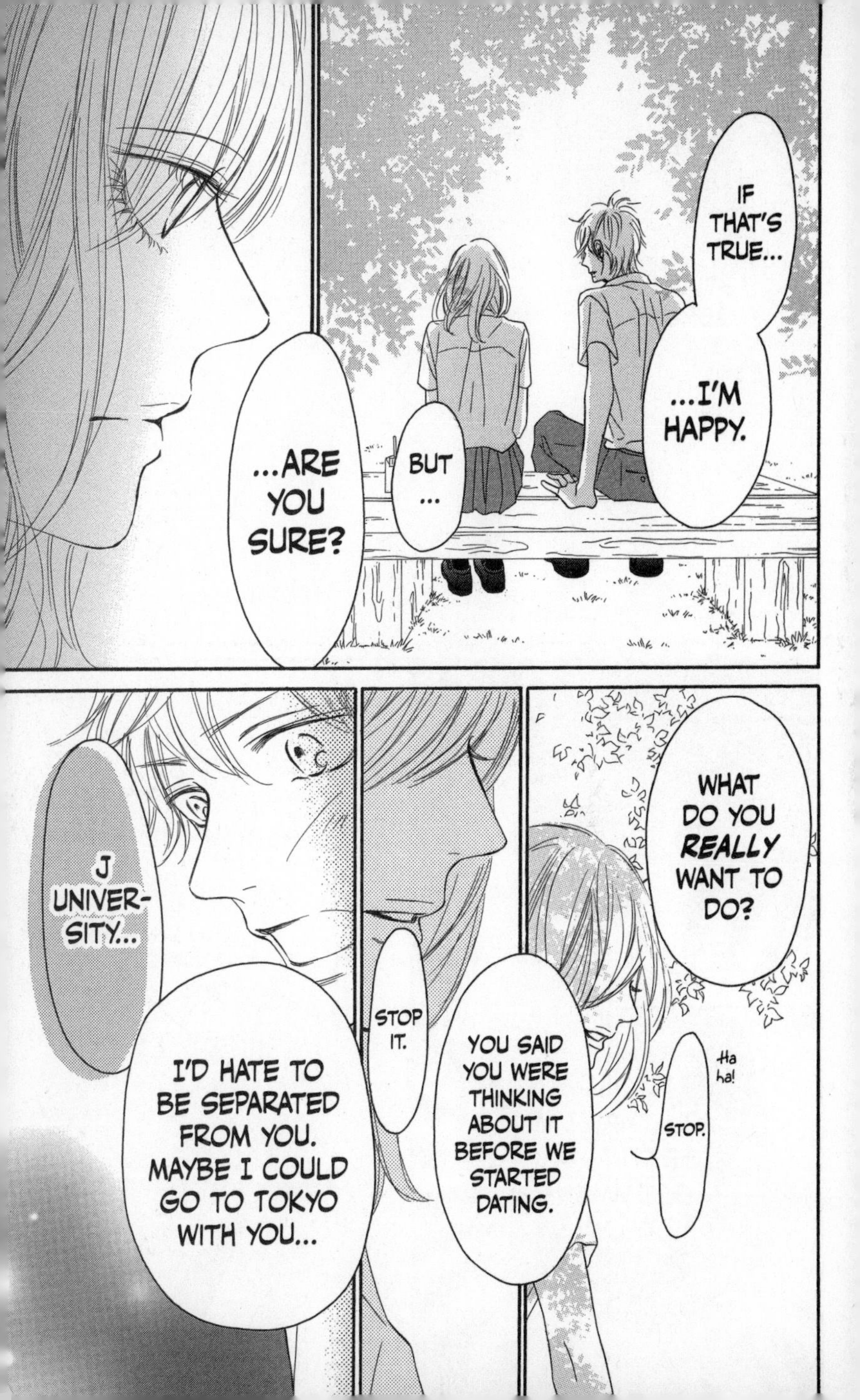
IF THAT'S TRUE...
...I'M HAPPY.
BUT ...
...ARE YOU SURE?
WHAT DO YOU *REALLY* WANT TO DO?
Ha ha!
STOP.
YOU SAID YOU WERE THINKING ABOUT IT BEFORE WE STARTED DATING.
STOP IT.
J UNIVER-SITY...
I'D HATE TO BE SEPARATED FROM YOU. MAYBE I COULD GO TO TOKYO WITH YOU...

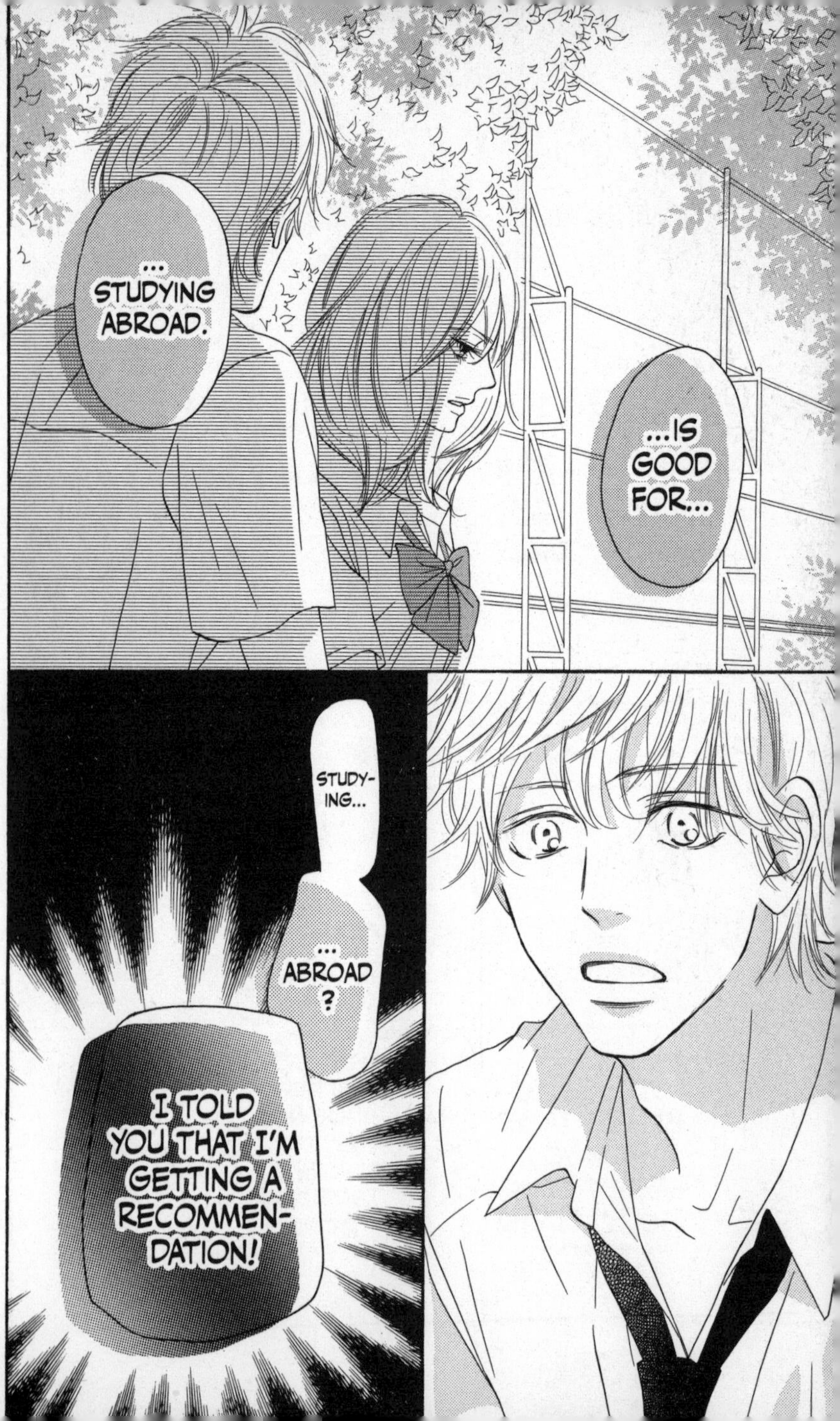
...IS GOOD FOR...
... STUDYING ABROAD.
STUDY-ING...
... ABROAD ?
I TOLD YOU THAT I'M GETTING A RECOMMEN-DATION!

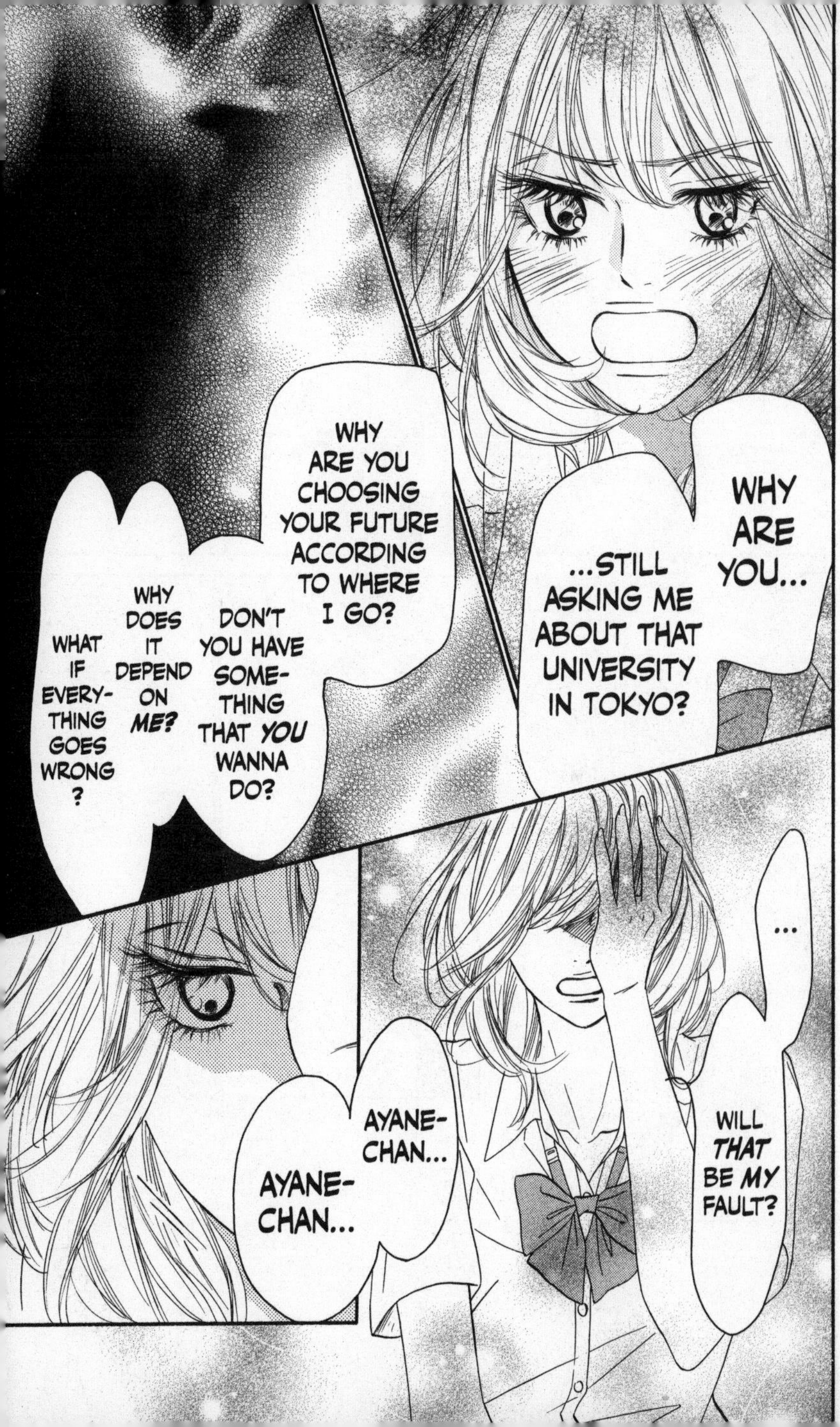
WHY ARE YOU...
...STILL ASKING ME ABOUT THAT UNIVERSITY IN TOKYO?
WHY ARE YOU CHOOSING YOUR FUTURE ACCORDING TO WHERE I GO?
DON'T YOU HAVE SOME-THING THAT *YOU* WANNA DO?
WHY DOES IT DEPEND ON *ME?*
WHAT IF EVERY-THING GOES WRONG?
...
WILL *THAT* BE *MY* FAULT?
AYANE-CHAN...
AYANE-CHAN...

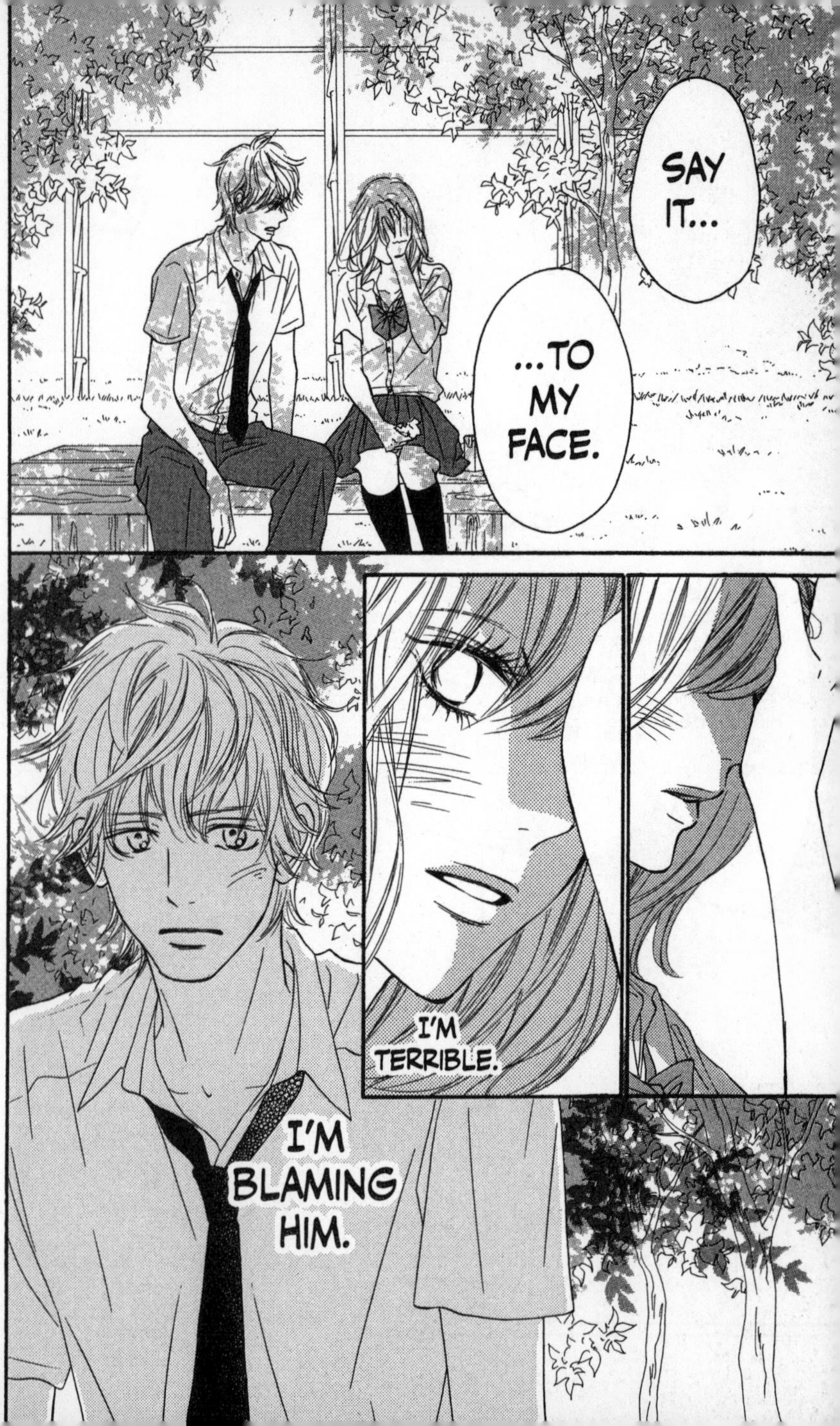
SAY IT...
...TO MY FACE.
I'M TERRIBLE.
I'M BLAMING HIM.

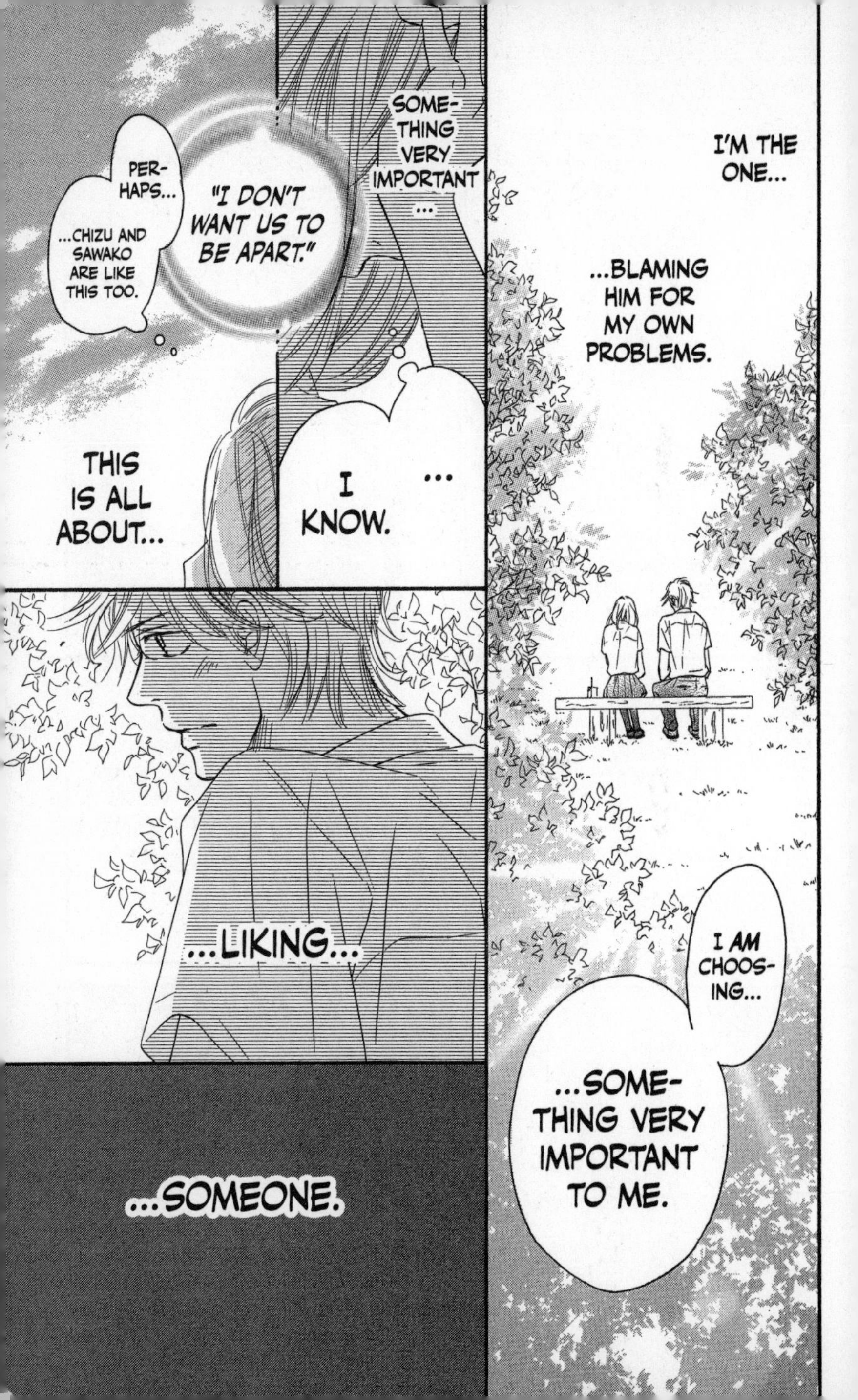
I'M THE ONE...
...BLAMING HIM FOR MY OWN PROBLEMS.
I AM CHOOSING...
...SOMETHING VERY IMPORTANT TO ME.
SOMETHING VERY IMPORTANT...
...
I KNOW.
PERHAPS...
...CHIZU AND SAWAKO ARE LIKE THIS TOO.
"I DON'T WANT US TO BE APART."
THIS IS ALL ABOUT...
...LIKING...
...SOMEONE.

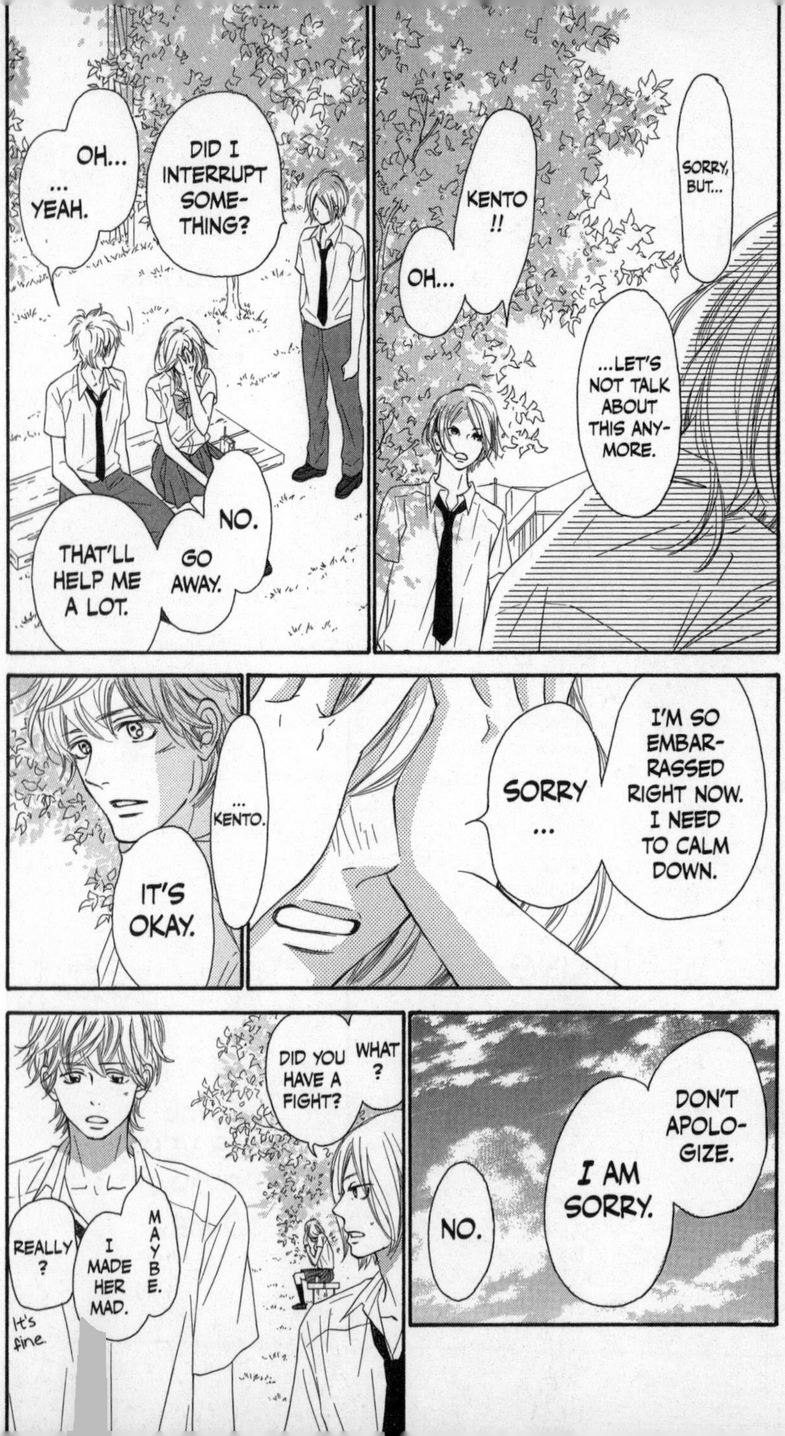

SORRY, BUT...
...LET'S NOT TALK ABOUT THIS ANYMORE.
KENTO!!
OH...
DID I INTERRUPT SOMETHING?
OH... ...YEAH.
NO.
GO AWAY.
THAT'LL HELP ME A LOT.
I'M SO EMBARRASSED RIGHT NOW. I NEED TO CALM DOWN.
SORRY...
...KENTO.
IT'S OKAY.
DON'T APOLOGIZE.
I AM SORRY.
NO.
WHAT?
DID YOU HAVE A FIGHT?
MAYBE.
I MADE HER MAD.
REALLY?
It's fine.

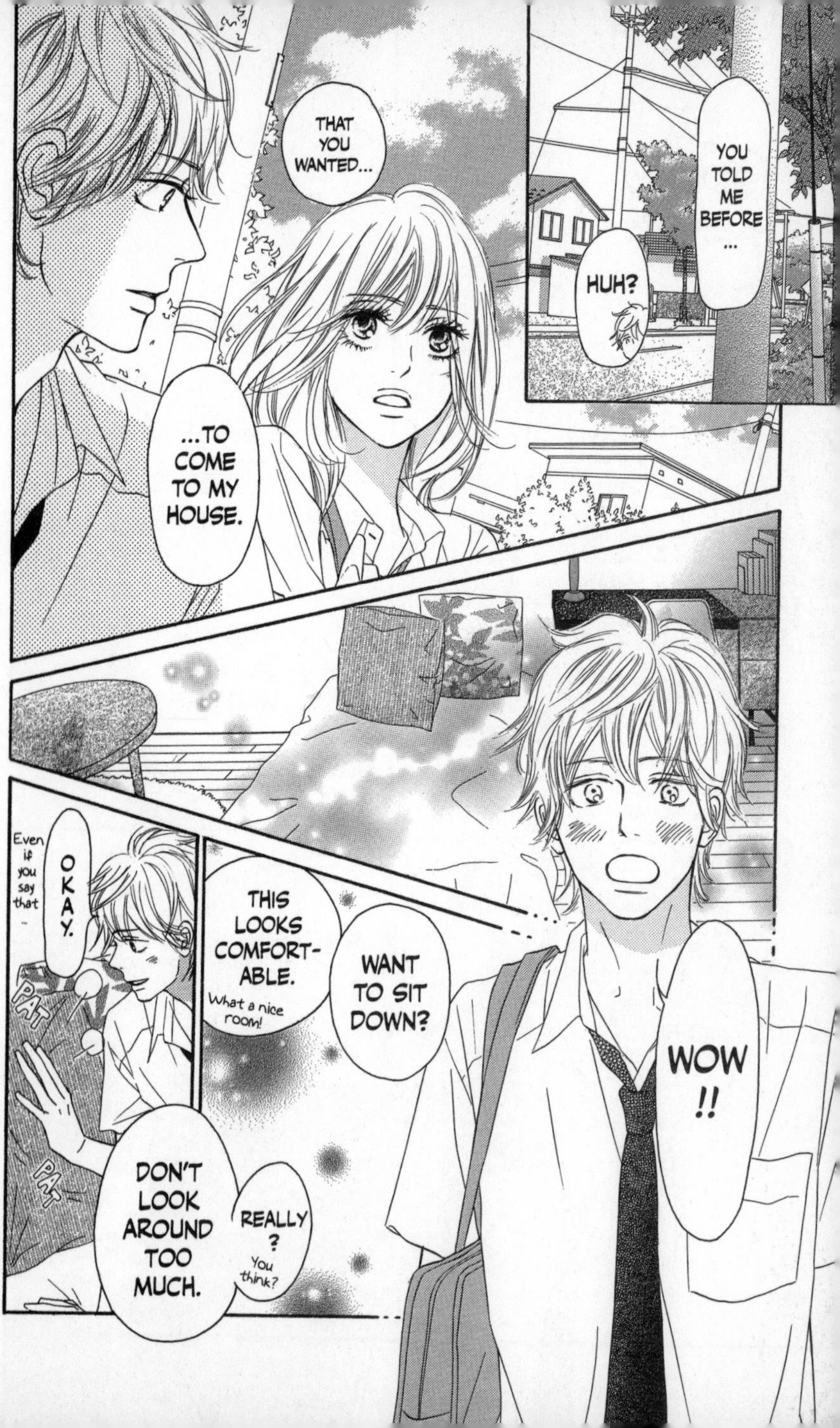
YOU TOLD ME BEFORE ...
HUH?
THAT YOU WANTED...
...TO COME TO MY HOUSE.
WOW !!
WANT TO SIT DOWN?
THIS LOOKS COMFORT-ABLE.
What a nice room!
REALLY ?
You think?
DON'T LOOK AROUND TOO MUCH.
OKAY.
Even if you say that ...
PAT
PAT

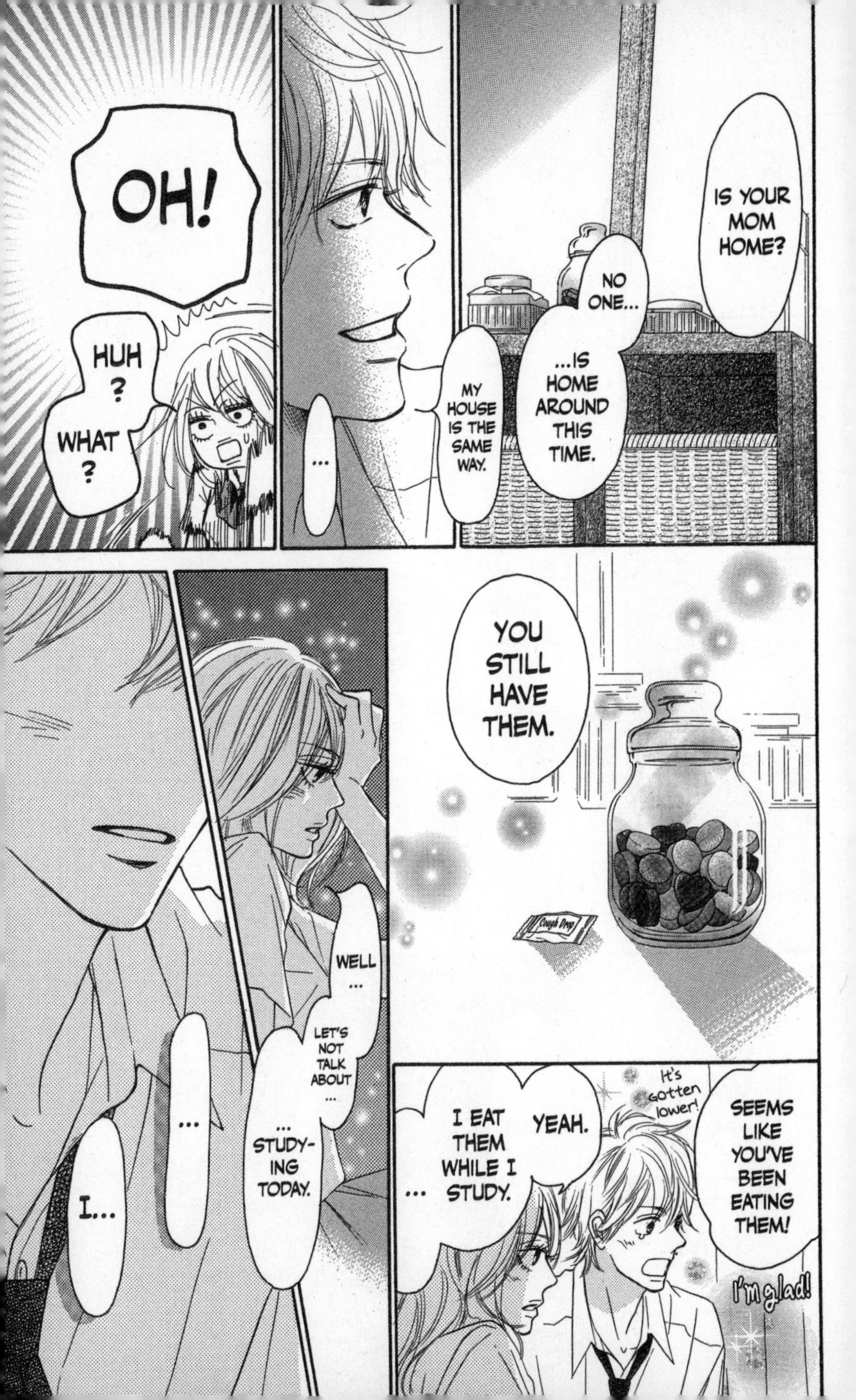
IS YOUR MOM HOME?
NO ONE...
...IS HOME AROUND THIS TIME.
MY HOUSE IS THE SAME WAY.
...
OH!
HUH? WHAT?
YOU STILL HAVE THEM.
Cough Drop
SEEMS LIKE YOU'VE BEEN EATING THEM!
It's gotten lower!
I'm glad!
YEAH.
I EAT THEM WHILE I STUDY.
...
WELL...
LET'S NOT TALK ABOUT...
...STUDYING TODAY.
...
I...

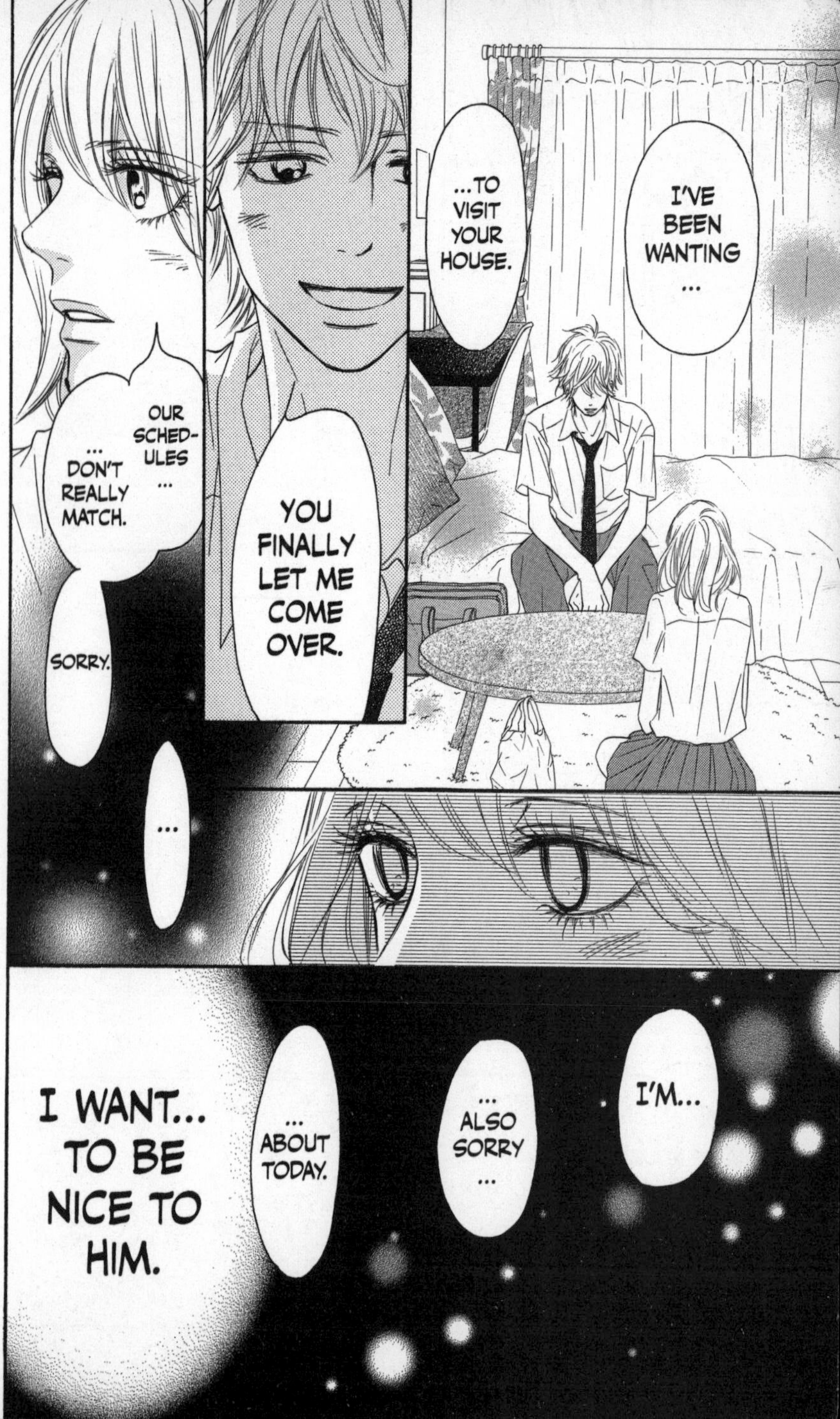
I'VE BEEN WANTING ...
...TO VISIT YOUR HOUSE.
YOU FINALLY LET ME COME OVER.
OUR SCHED- ULES ...
... DON'T REALLY MATCH.
SORRY.
...
I'M...
... ALSO SORRY ...
... ABOUT TODAY.
I WANT... TO BE NICE TO HIM.

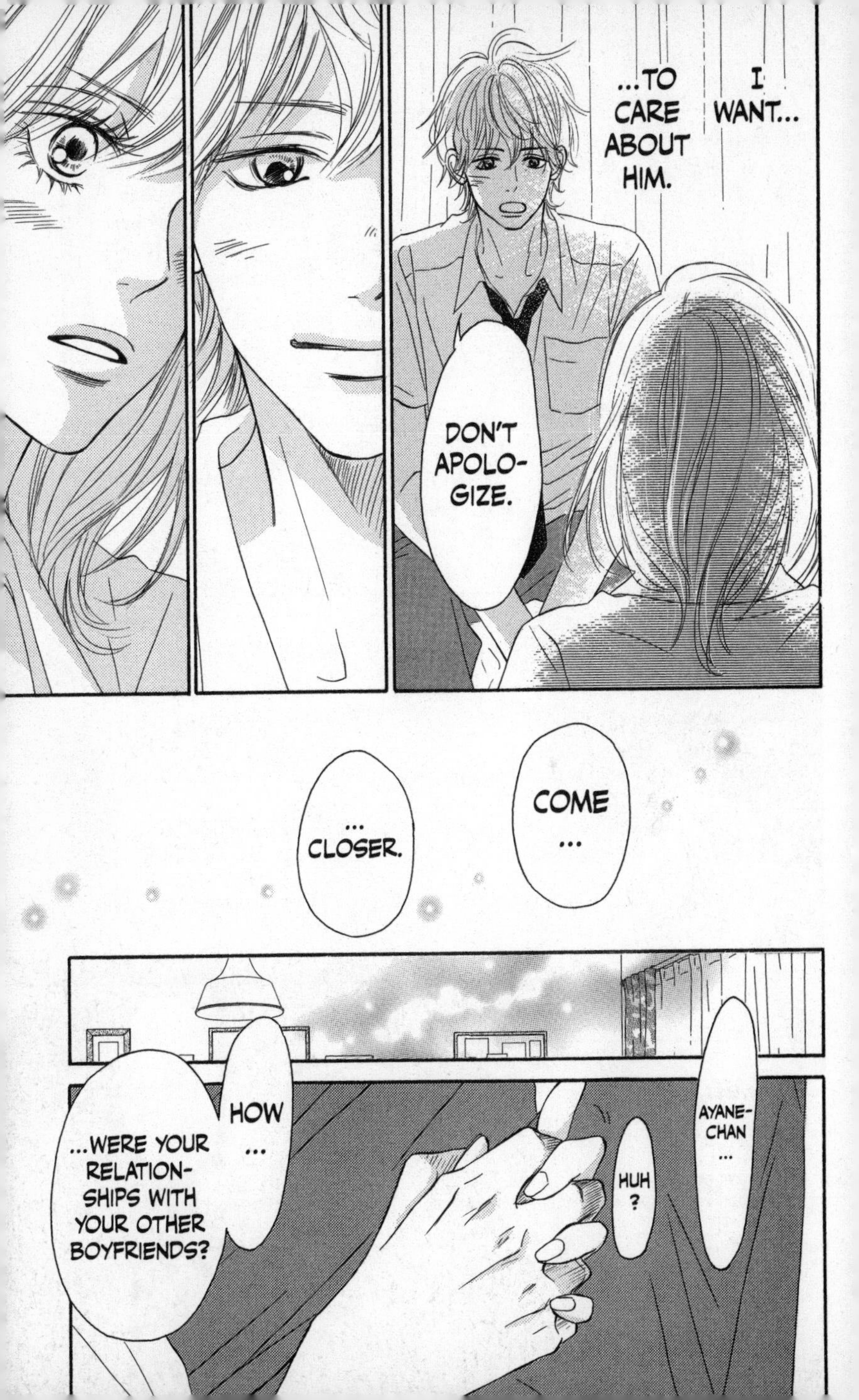
I WANT...
...TO CARE ABOUT HIM.
DON'T APOLO-GIZE.
COME ...
... CLOSER.
AYANE-CHAN ...
HUH ?
HOW ...
...WERE YOUR RELATION-SHIPS WITH YOUR OTHER BOYFRIENDS?

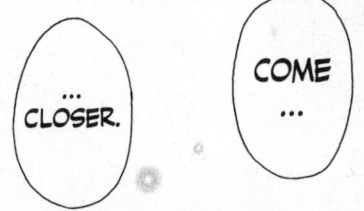

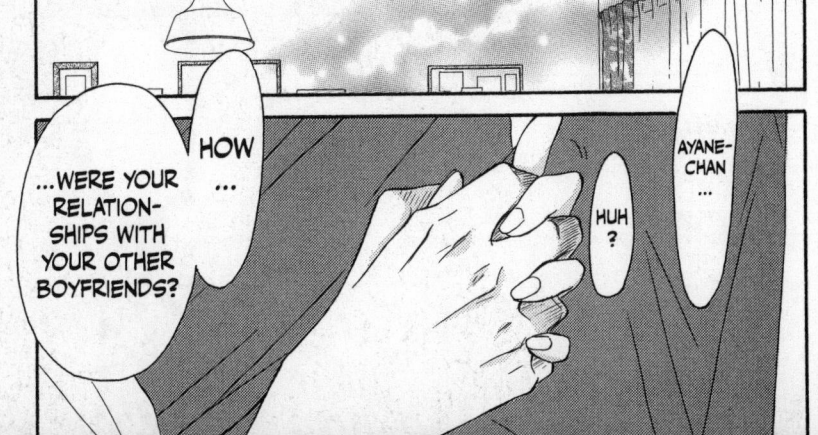

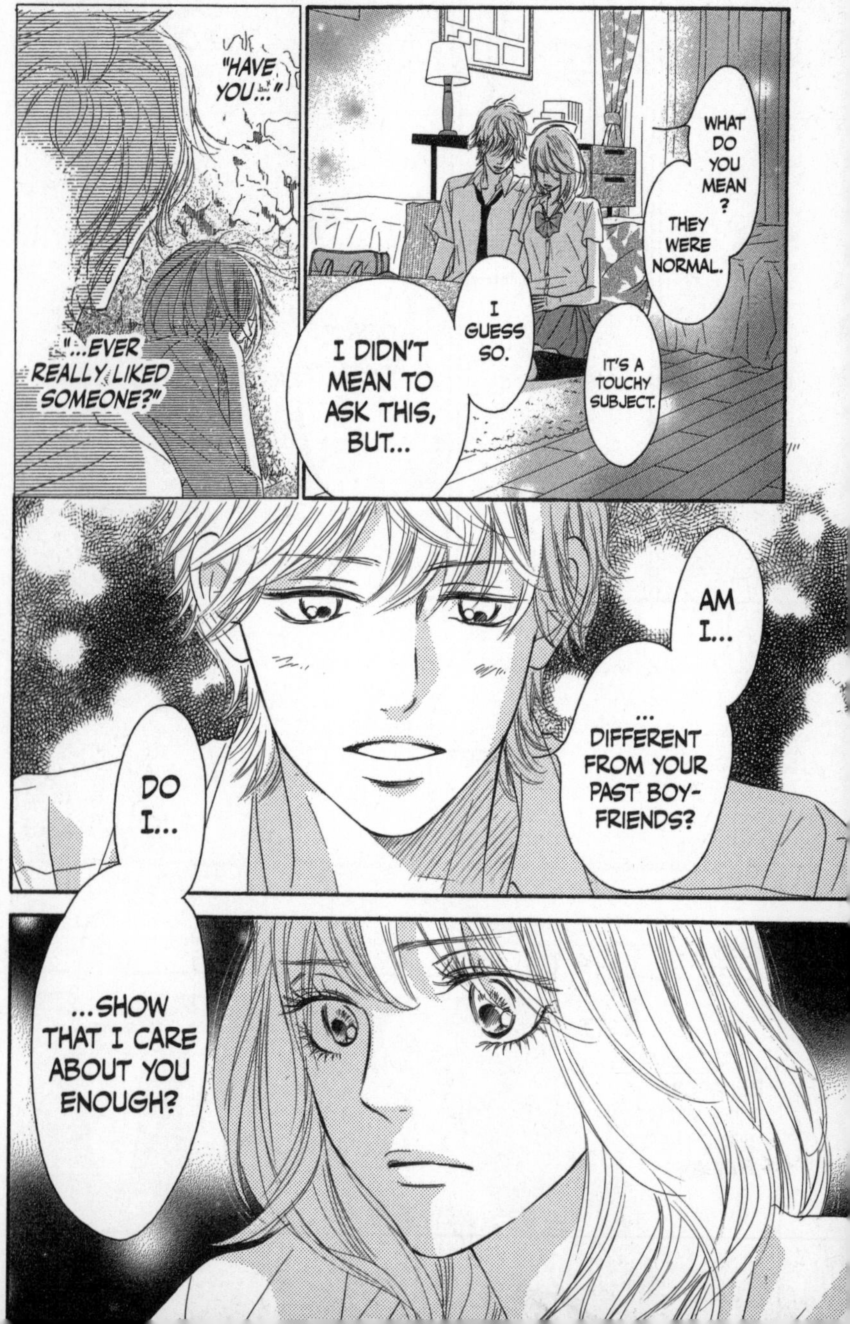
WHAT DO YOU MEAN? THEY WERE NORMAL.
IT'S A TOUCHY SUBJECT.
I GUESS SO.
I DIDN'T MEAN TO ASK THIS, BUT...
"HAVE YOU..."
"...EVER REALLY LIKED SOMEONE?"
AM I...
...DIFFERENT FROM YOUR PAST BOY-FRIENDS?
DO I...
...SHOW THAT I CARE ABOUT YOU ENOUGH?

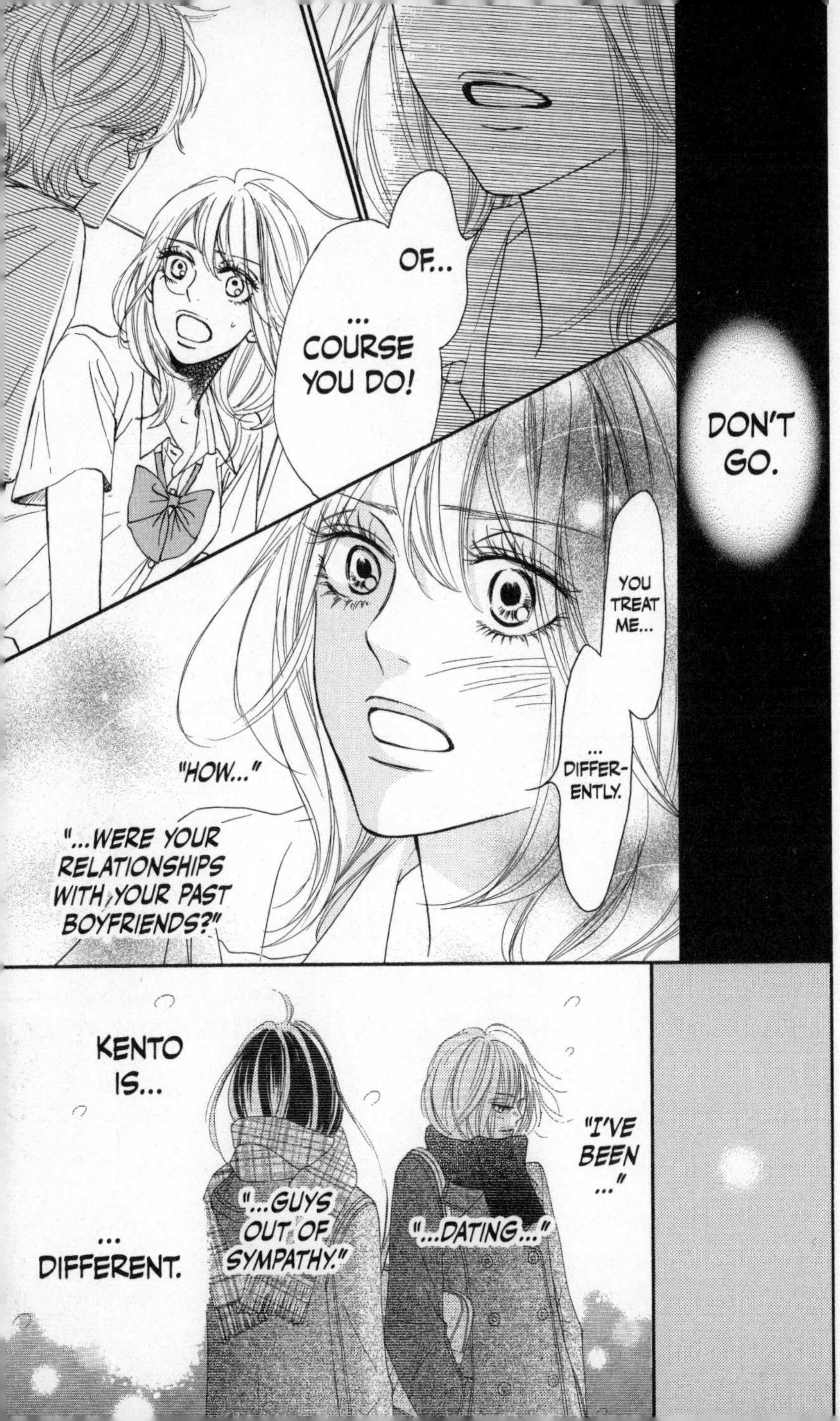
DON'T GO.
OF...
... COURSE YOU DO!
YOU TREAT ME...
... DIFFERENTLY.
"HOW..."
"...WERE YOUR RELATIONSHIPS WITH YOUR PAST BOYFRIENDS?"
"I'VE BEEN ..."
"...DATING..."
"...GUYS OUT OF SYMPATHY."
KENTO IS...
... DIFFERENT.

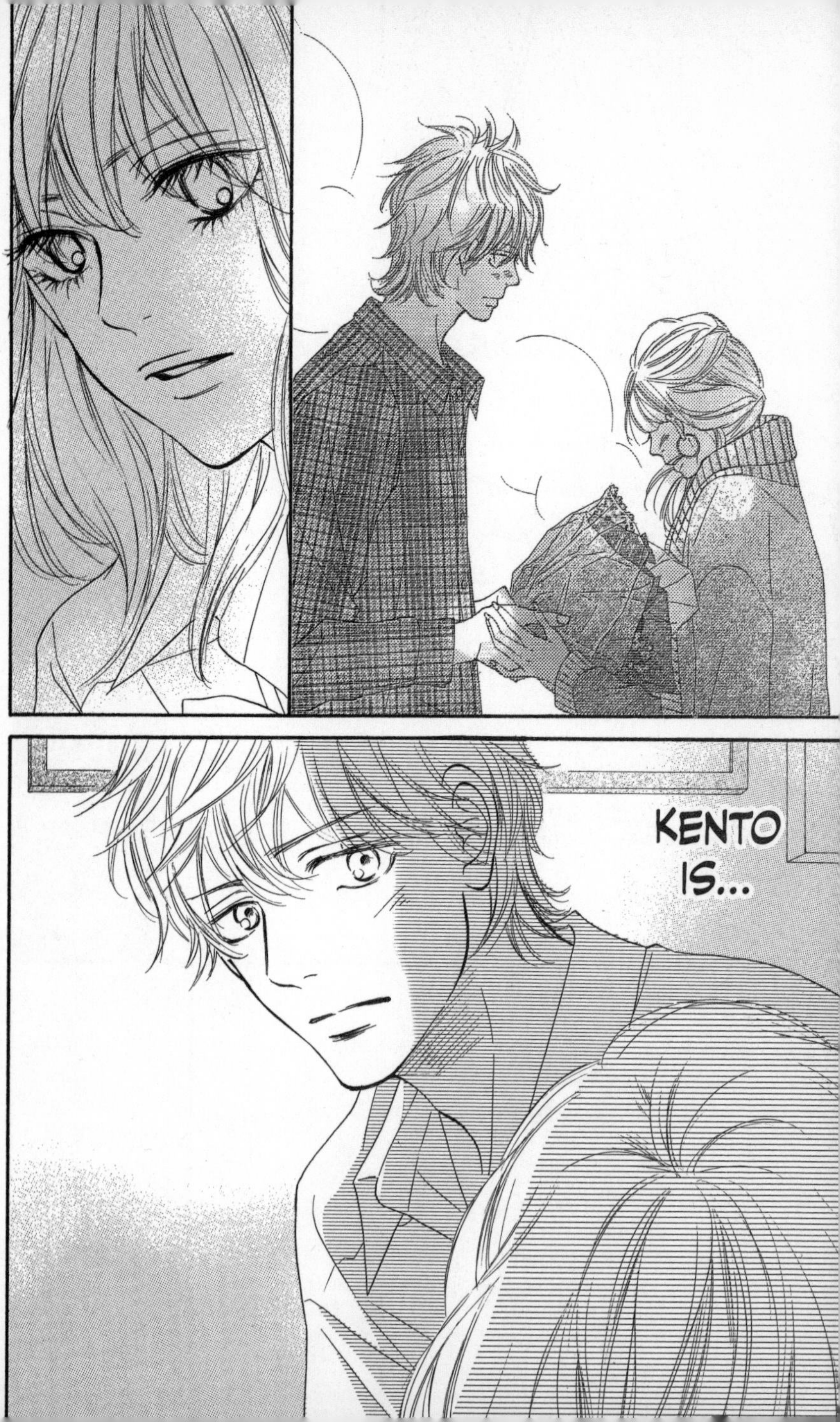
KENTO IS...

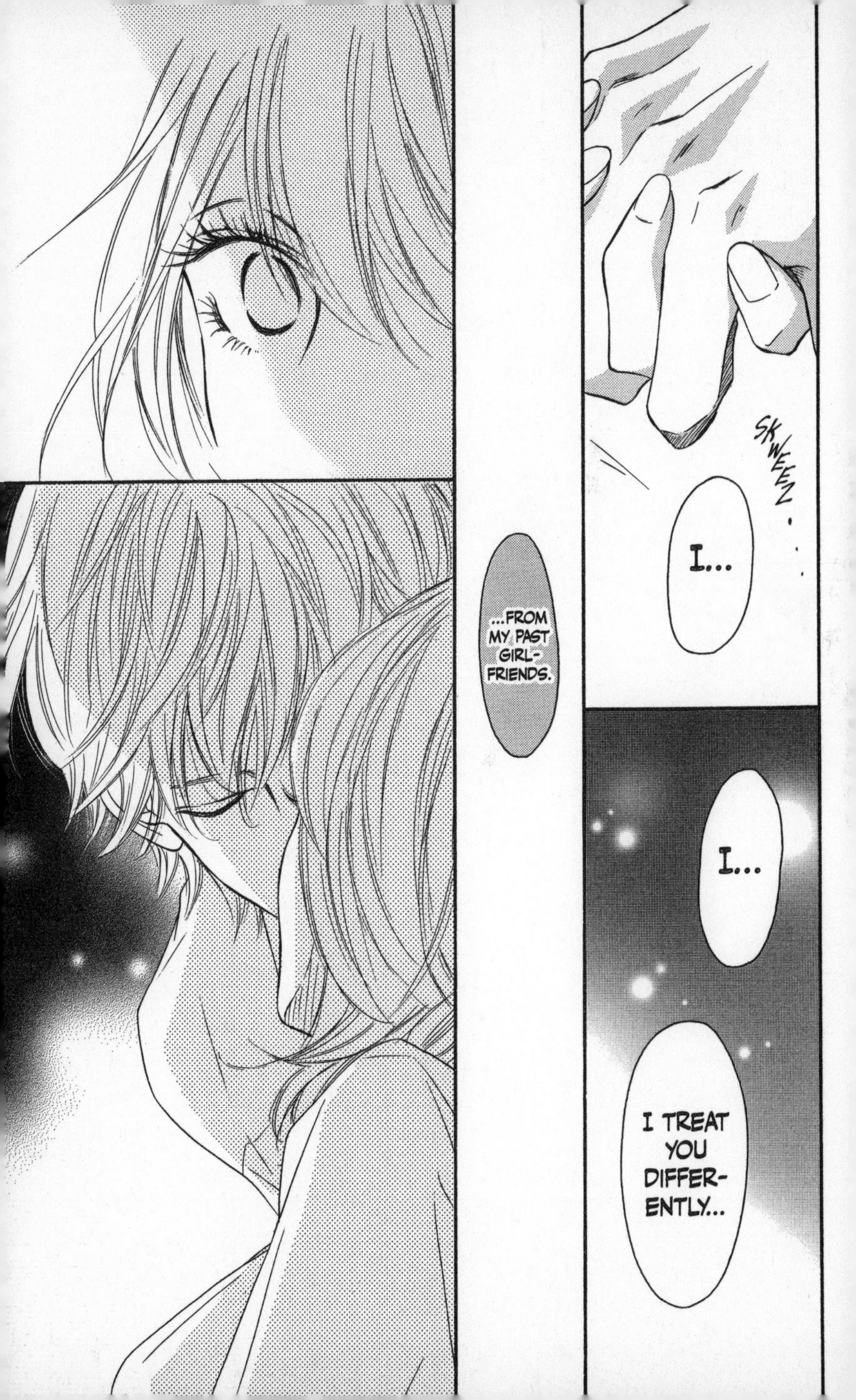
SKWEEN . . .
I...
I...
I TREAT YOU DIFFER-ENTLY...
...FROM MY PAST GIRL-FRIENDS.

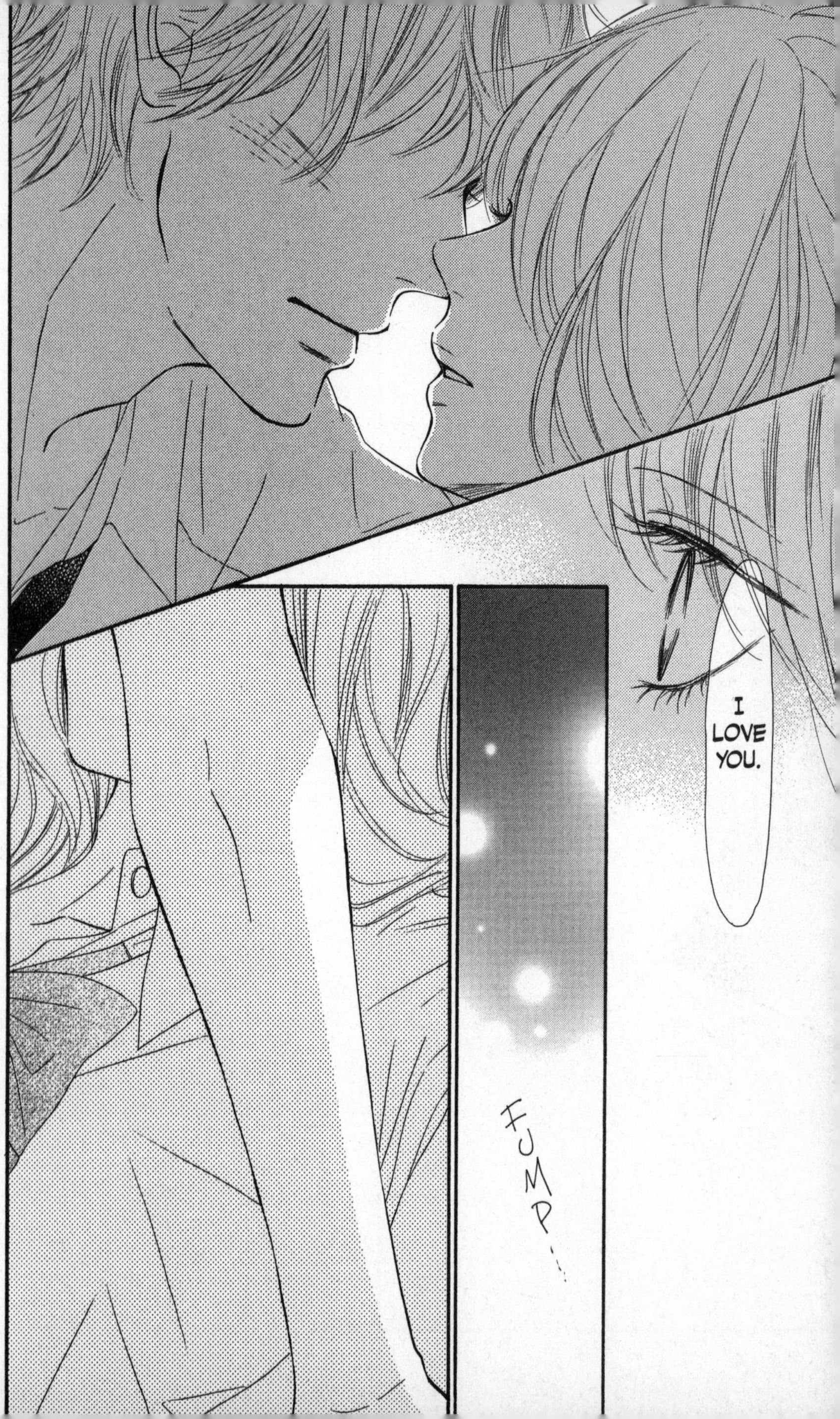
I LOVE YOU.
FUMP...

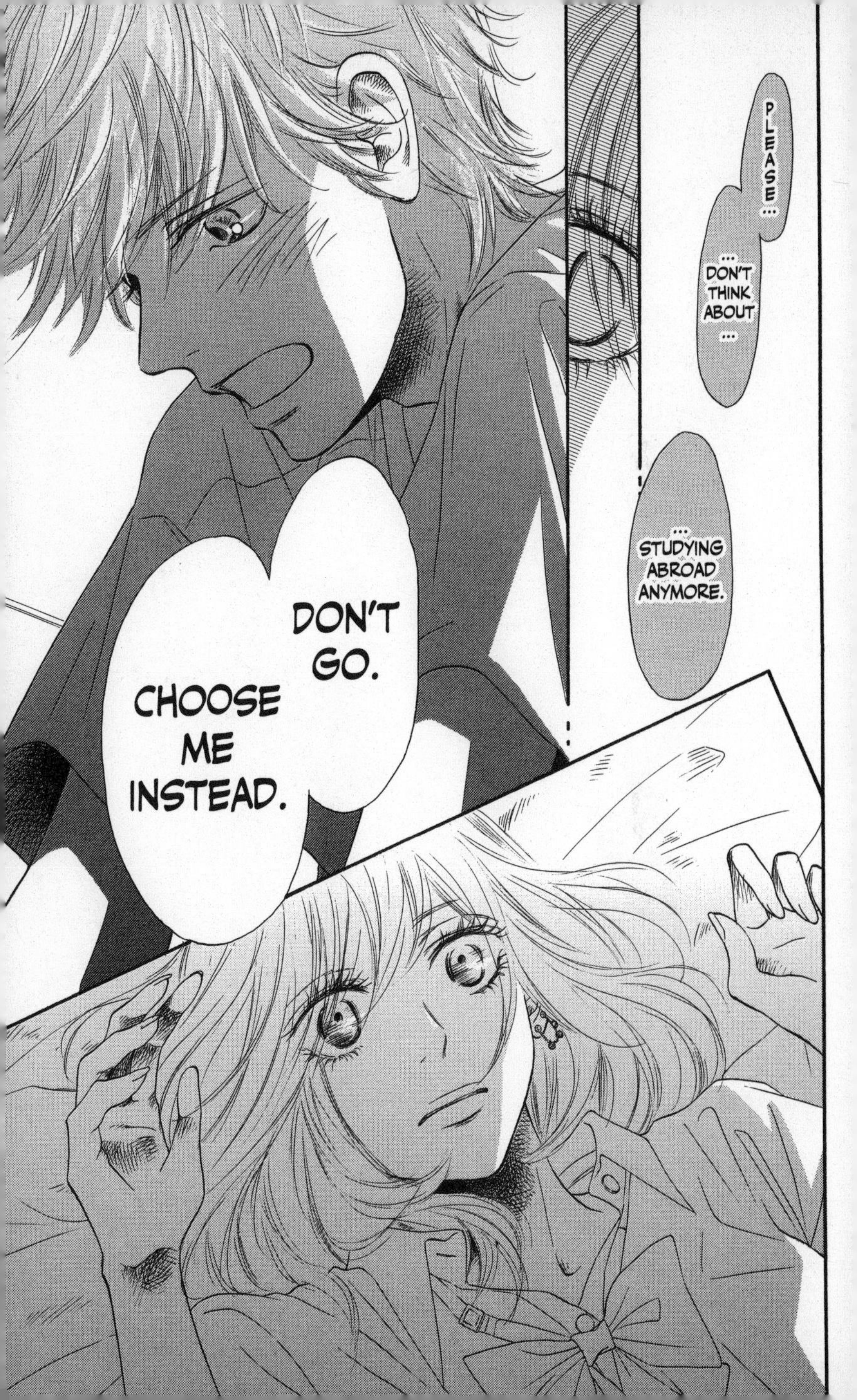
PLEASE...
...DON'T THINK ABOUT...
...STUDYING ABROAD ANYMORE.
DON'T GO.
CHOOSE ME INSTEAD.

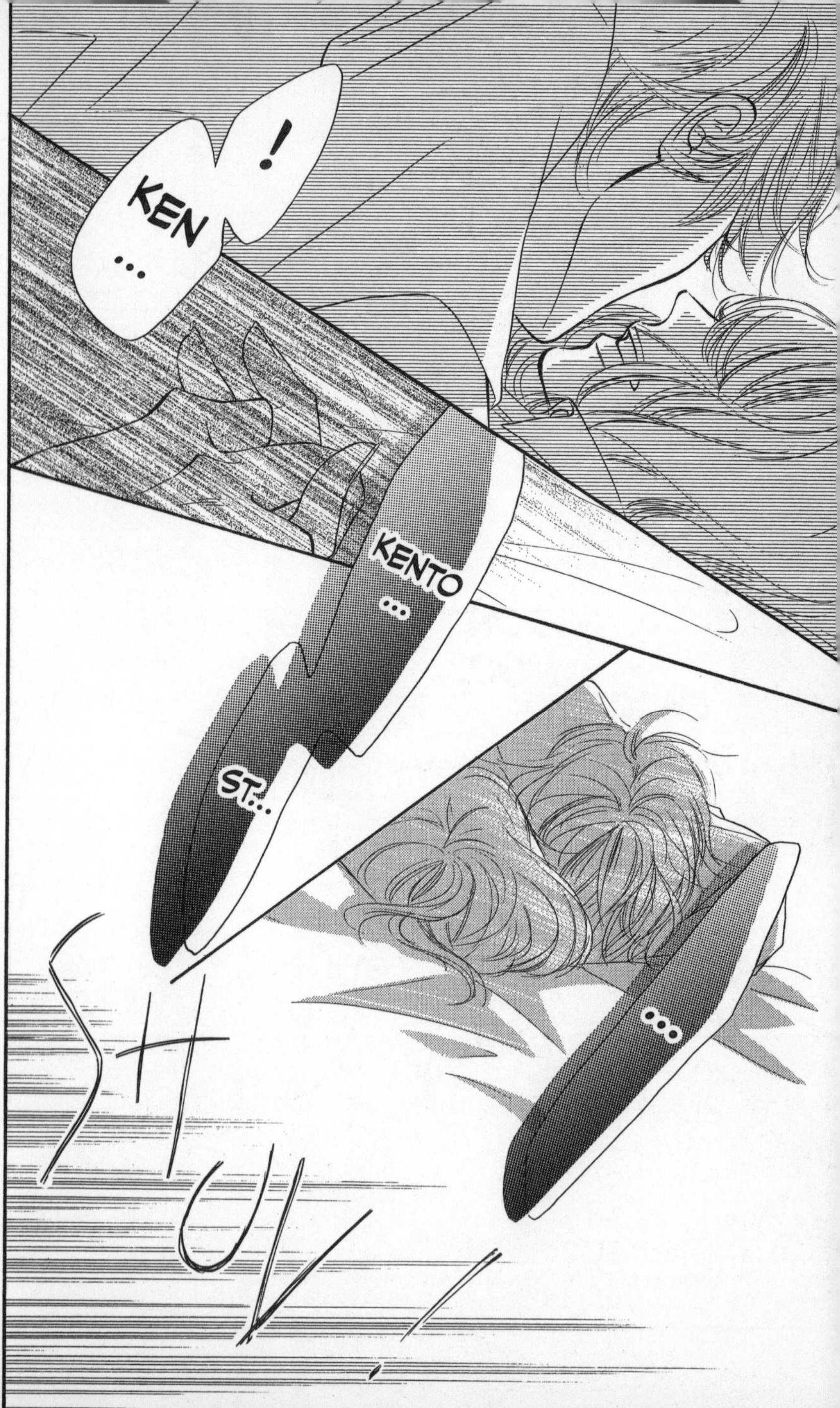
KEN... !
KENTO...
ST...
...
STHUD!!

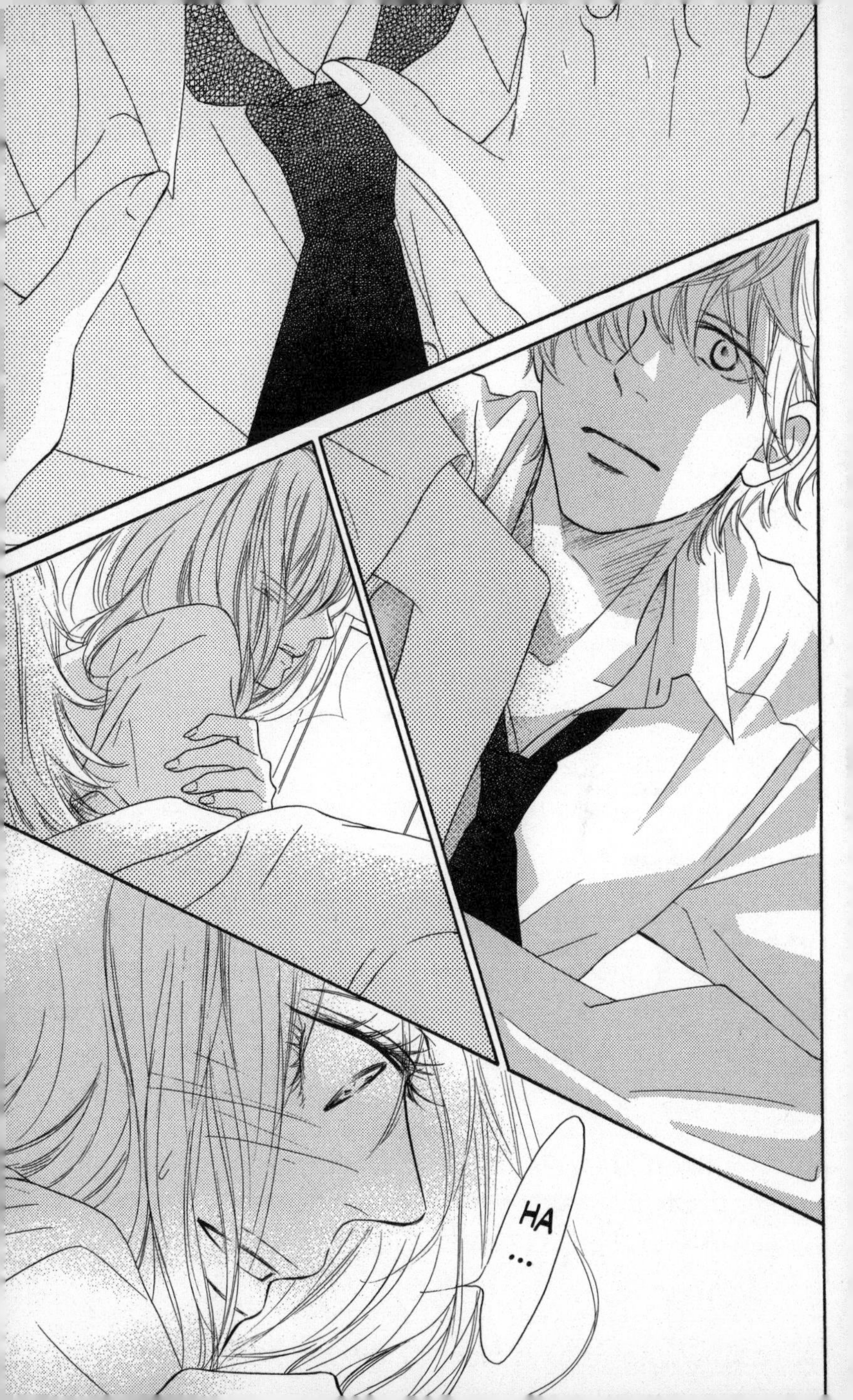
HA ...

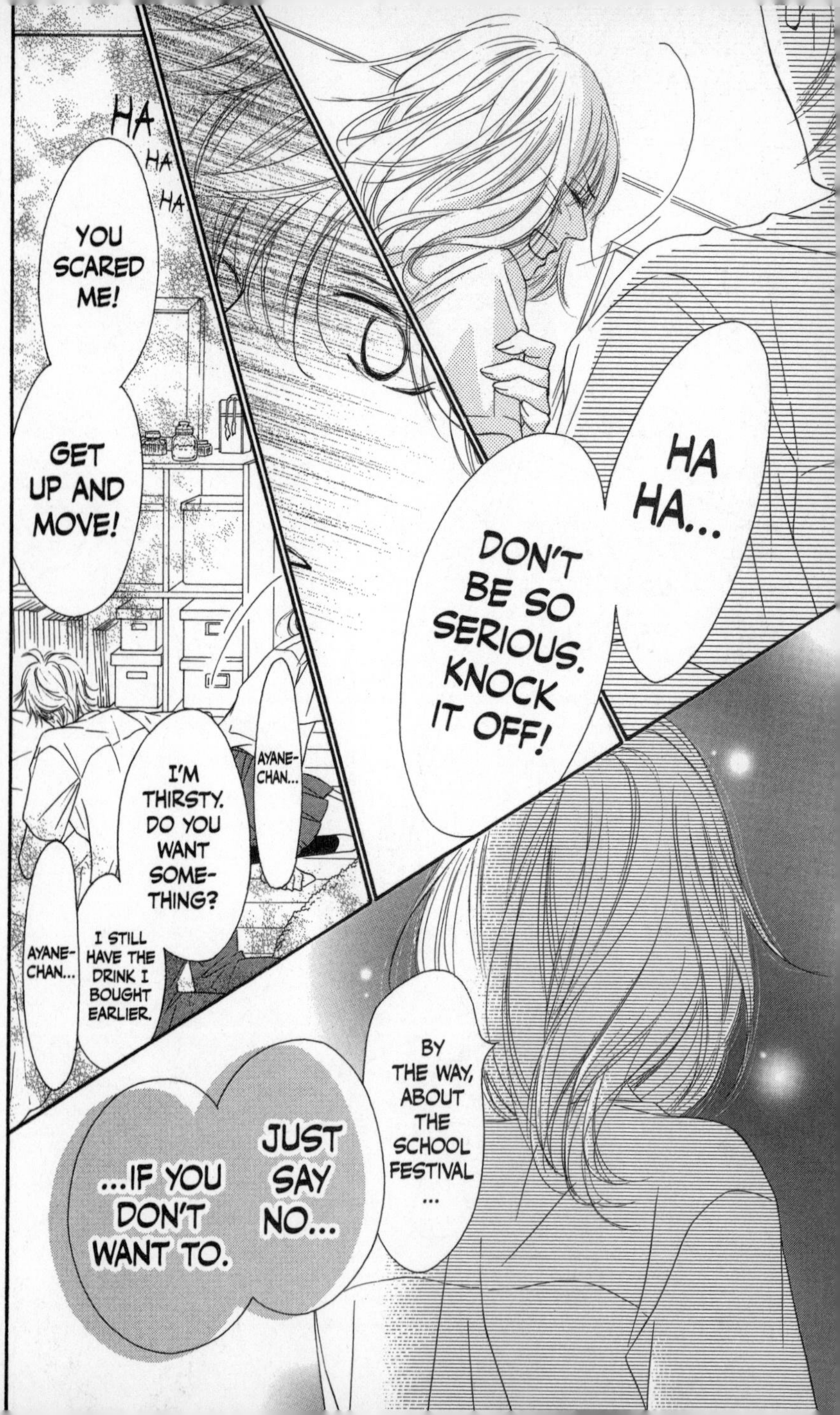
HA HA...
DON'T BE SO SERIOUS. KNOCK IT OFF!
HA HA HA
YOU SCARED ME!
GET UP AND MOVE!
AYANE-CHAN...
I'M THIRSTY. DO YOU WANT SOME-THING?
I STILL HAVE THE DRINK I BOUGHT EARLIER.
AYANE-CHAN...
BY THE WAY, ABOUT THE SCHOOL FESTIVAL ...
JUST SAY NO...
...IF YOU DON'T WANT TO.

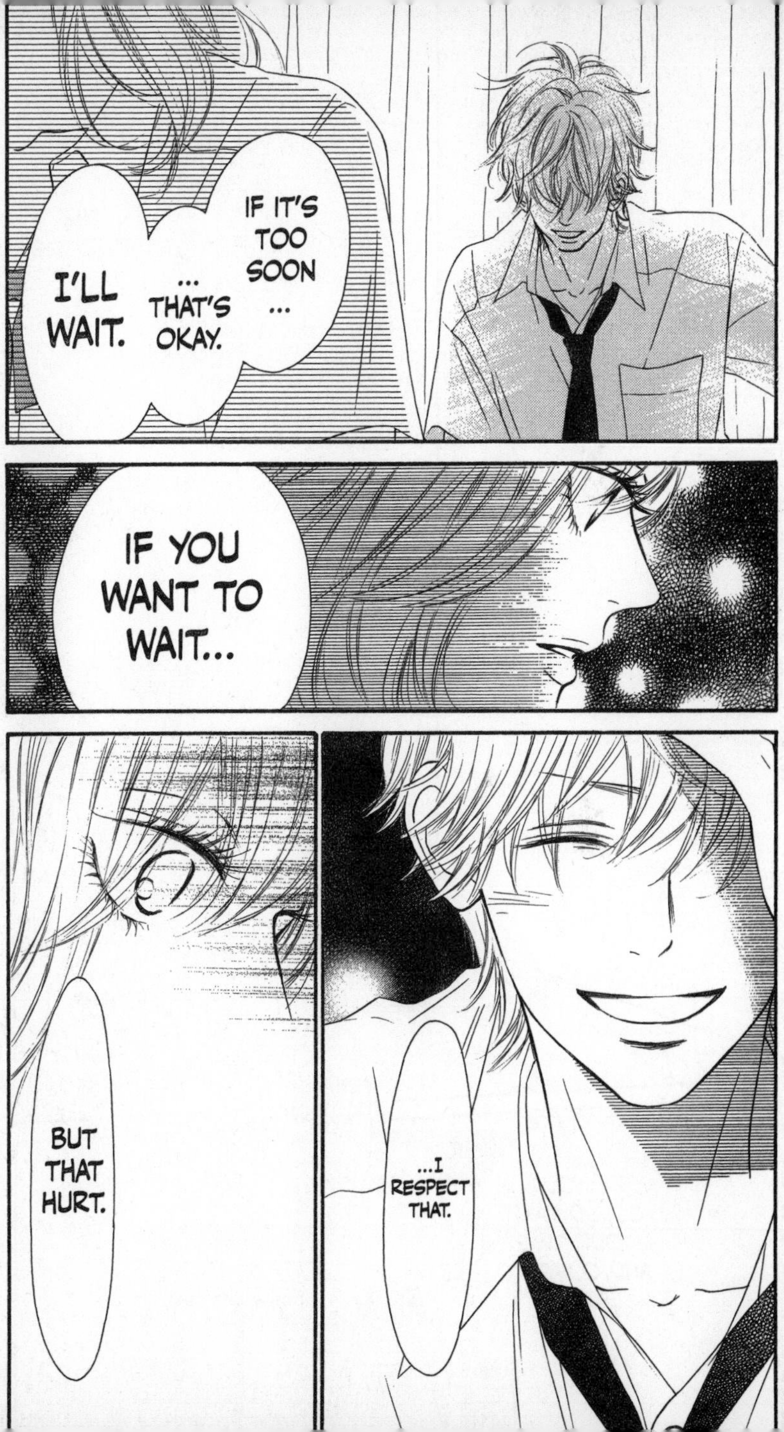
IF IT'S TOO SOON ...
... THAT'S OKAY.
I'LL WAIT.
IF YOU WANT TO WAIT...
...I RESPECT THAT.
BUT THAT HURT.

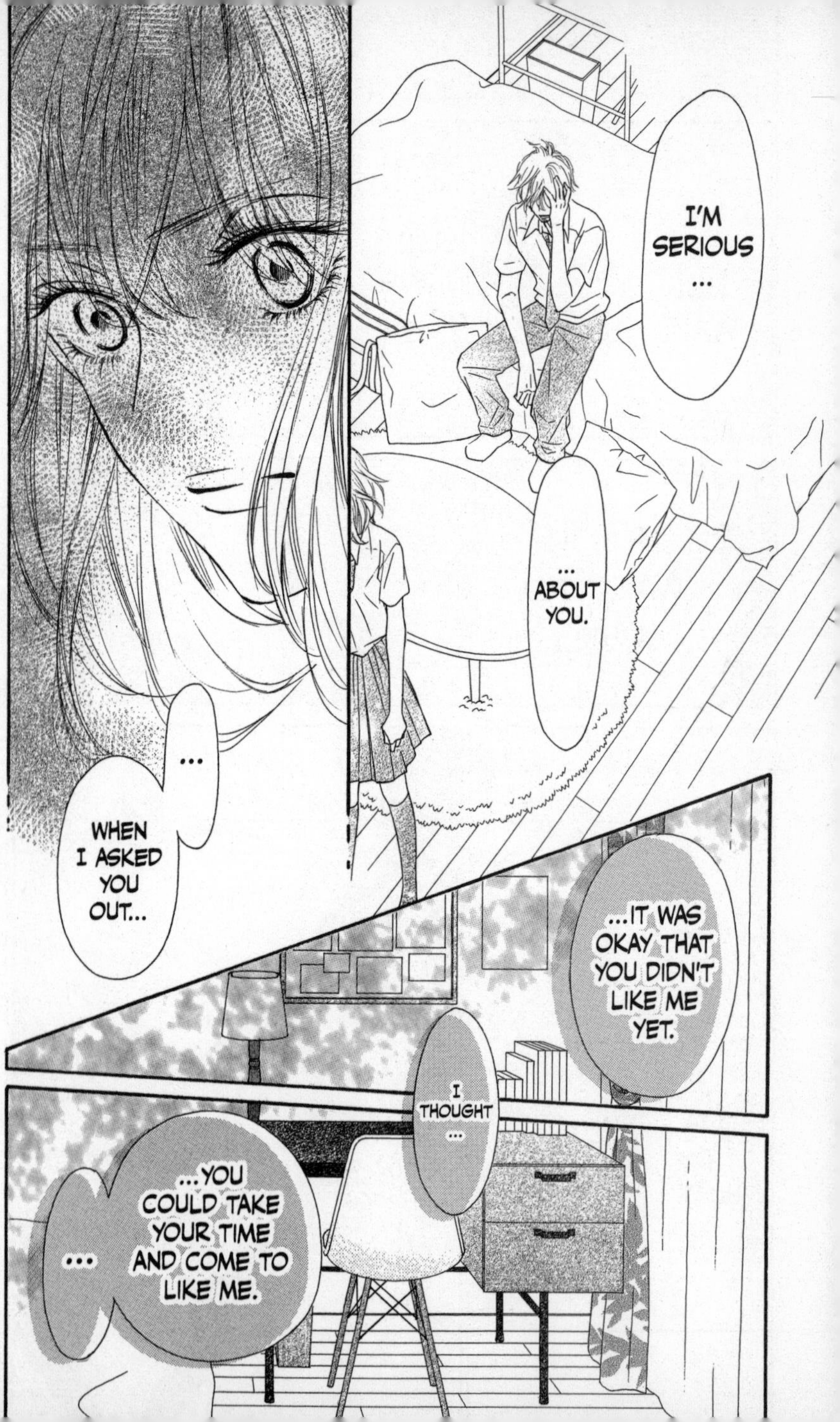
I'M SERIOUS...
...ABOUT YOU.
...
WHEN I ASKED YOU OUT...
...IT WAS OKAY THAT YOU DIDN'T LIKE ME YET.
I THOUGHT...
...YOU COULD TAKE YOUR TIME AND COME TO LIKE ME.
...

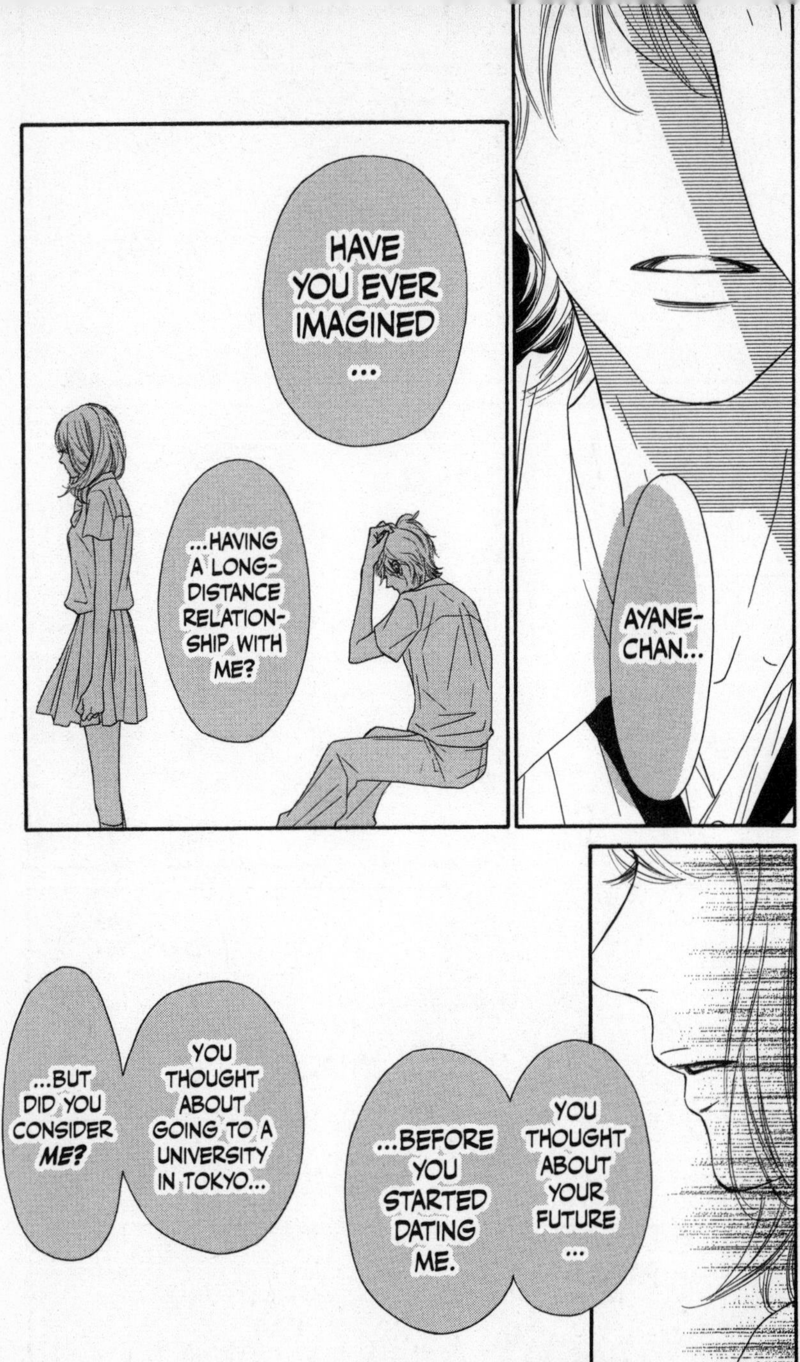
AYANE-CHAN...
HAVE YOU EVER IMAGINED ...
...HAVING A LONG-DISTANCE RELATIONSHIP WITH ME?
YOU THOUGHT ABOUT YOUR FUTURE ...
...BEFORE YOU STARTED DATING ME.
YOU THOUGHT ABOUT GOING TO A UNIVERSITY IN TOKYO...
...BUT DID YOU CONSIDER *ME?*

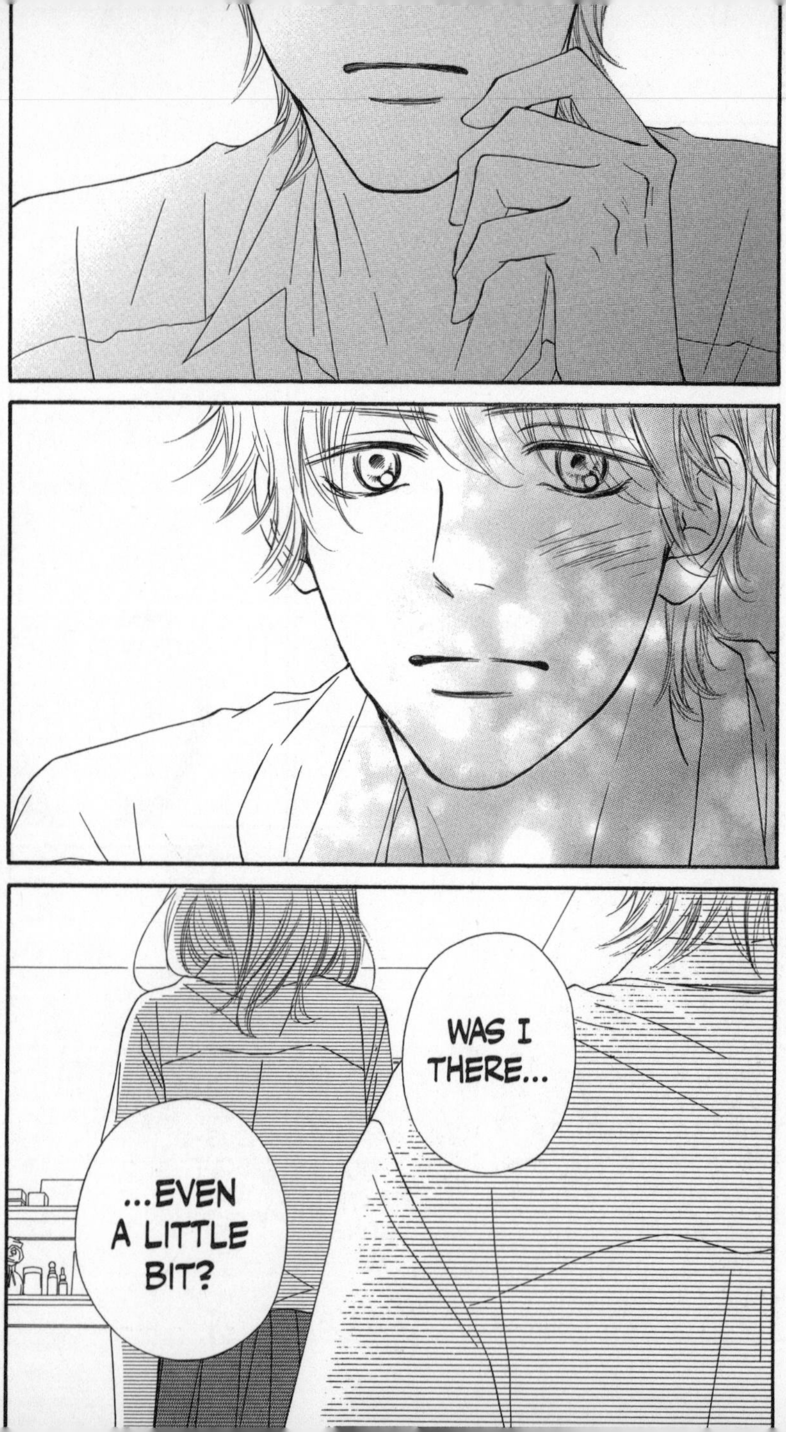
WAS I THERE...
...EVEN A LITTLE BIT?

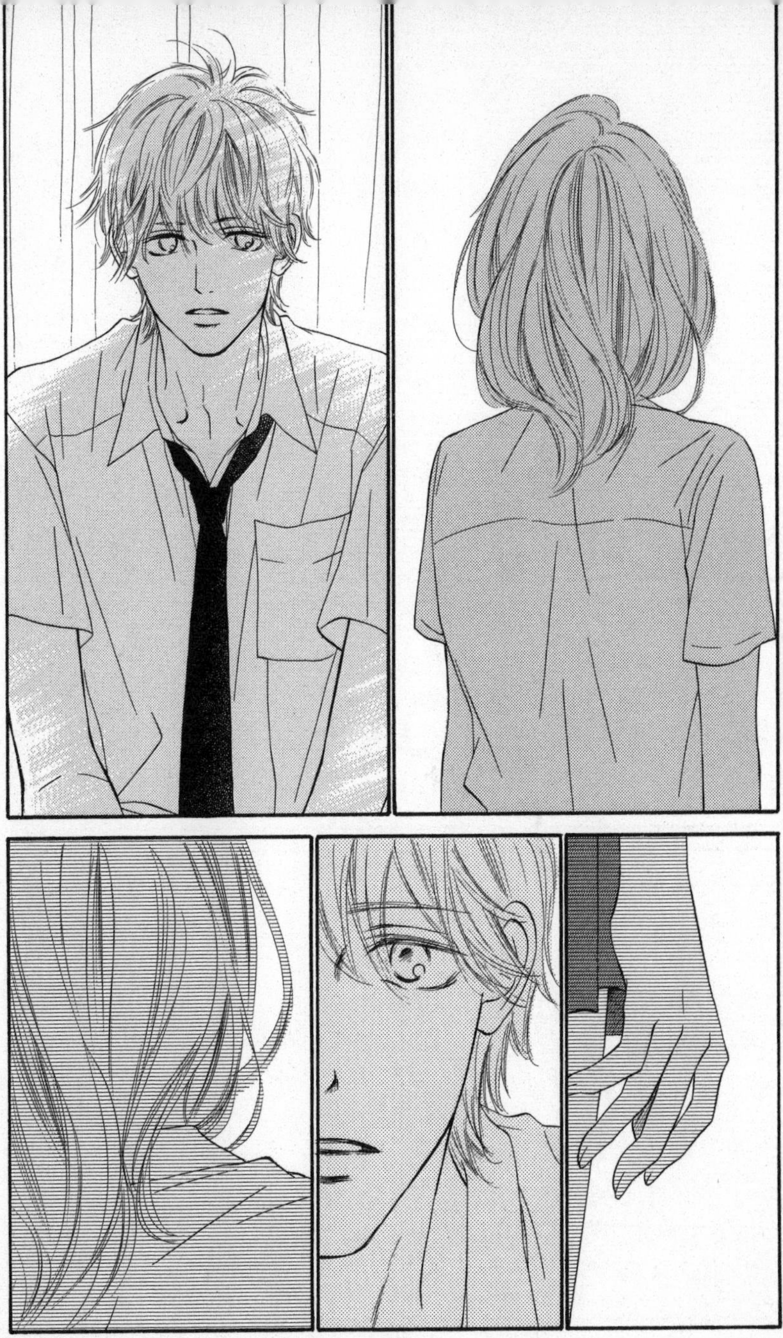

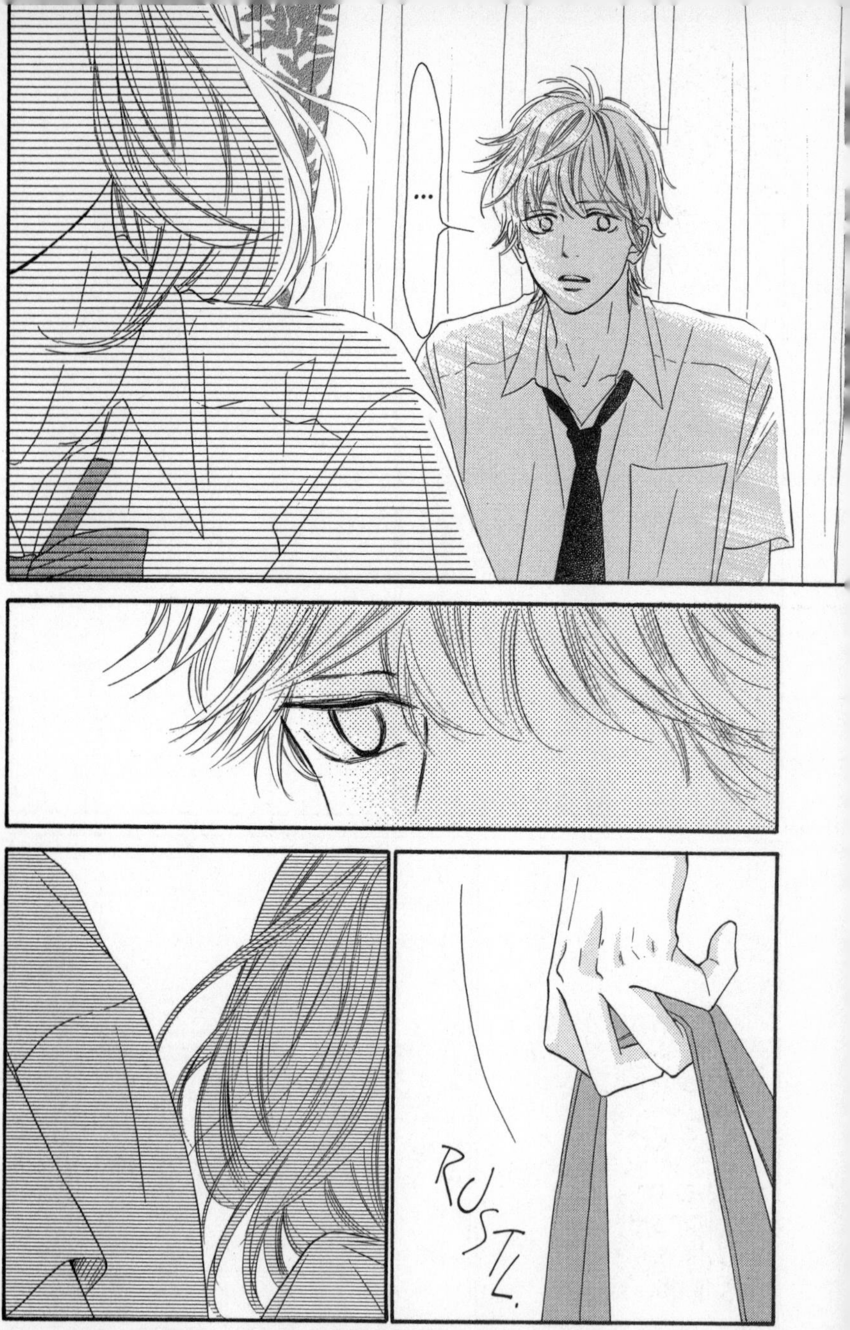
...
RUSTL.

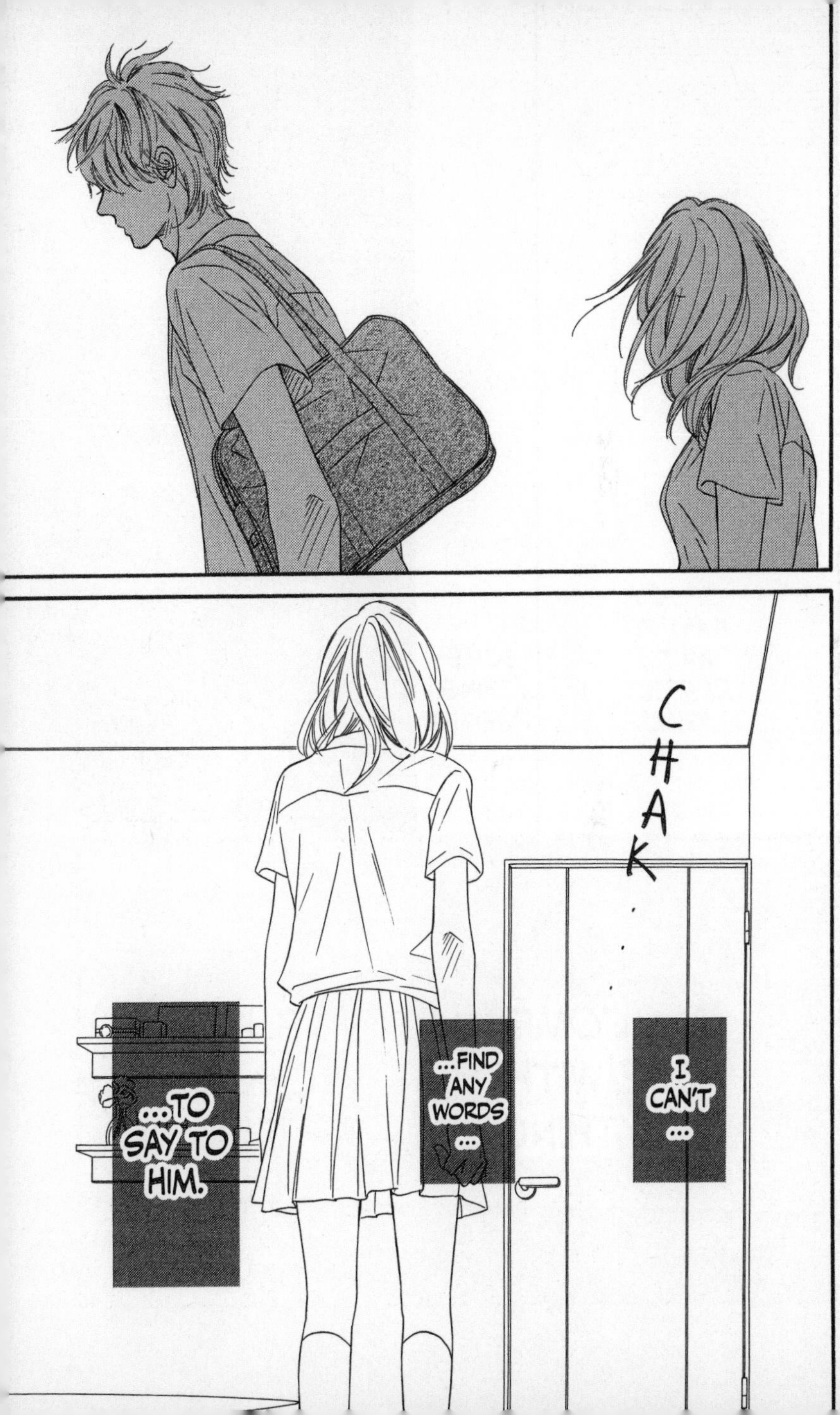
CHAK
I CAN'T ...
...FIND ANY WORDS ...
...TO SAY TO HIM.

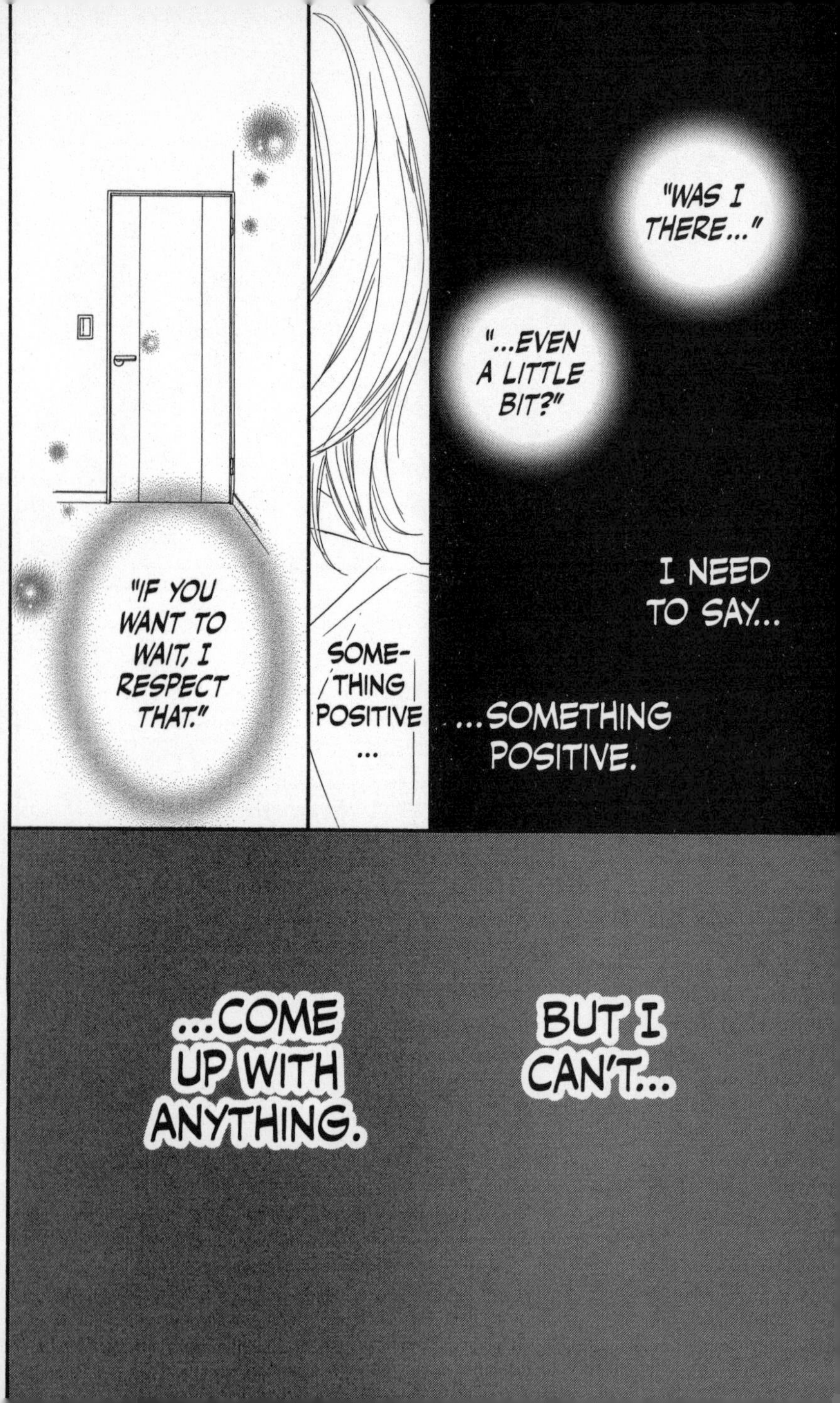
"WAS I THERE..."
"...EVEN A LITTLE BIT?"
I NEED TO SAY...
...SOMETHING POSITIVE.
SOME-THING POSITIVE...
"IF YOU WANT TO WAIT, I RESPECT THAT."
BUT I CAN'T...
...COME UP WITH ANYTHING.

Episode 93: Regret

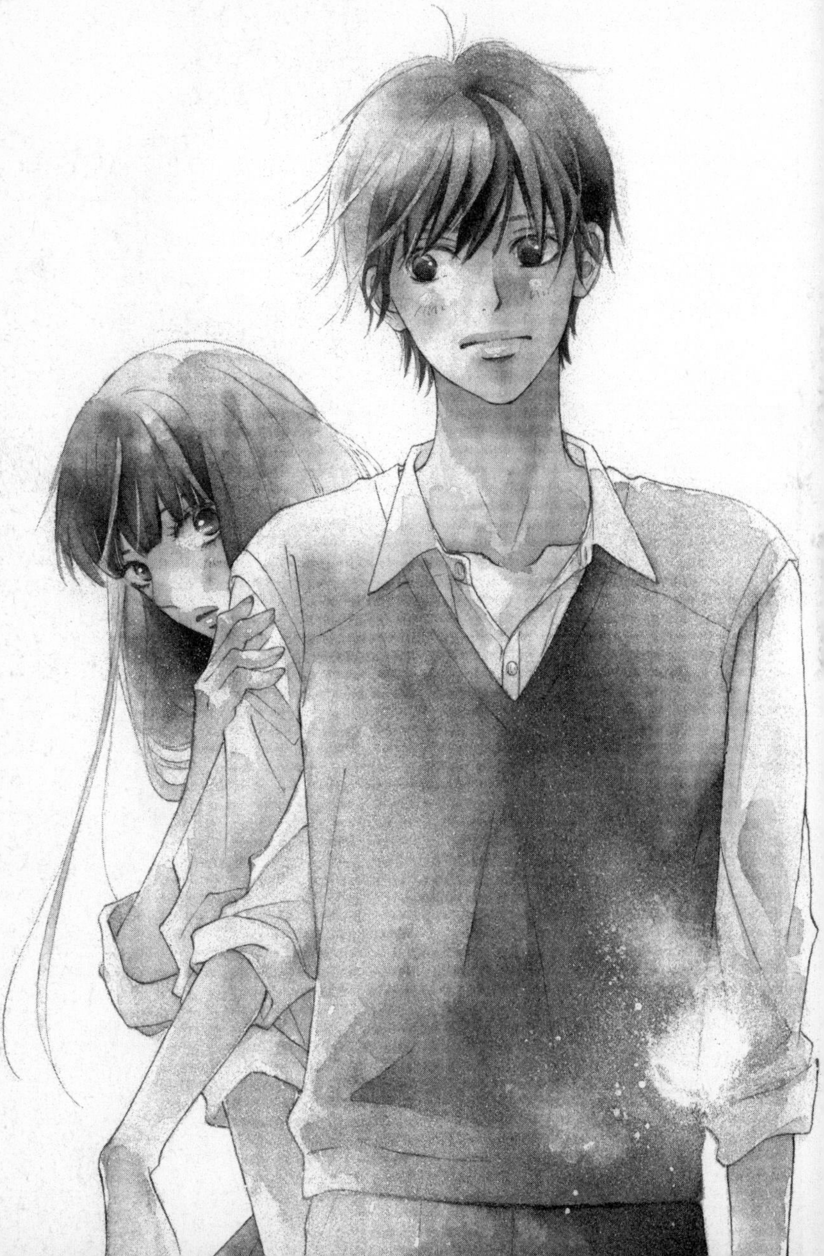

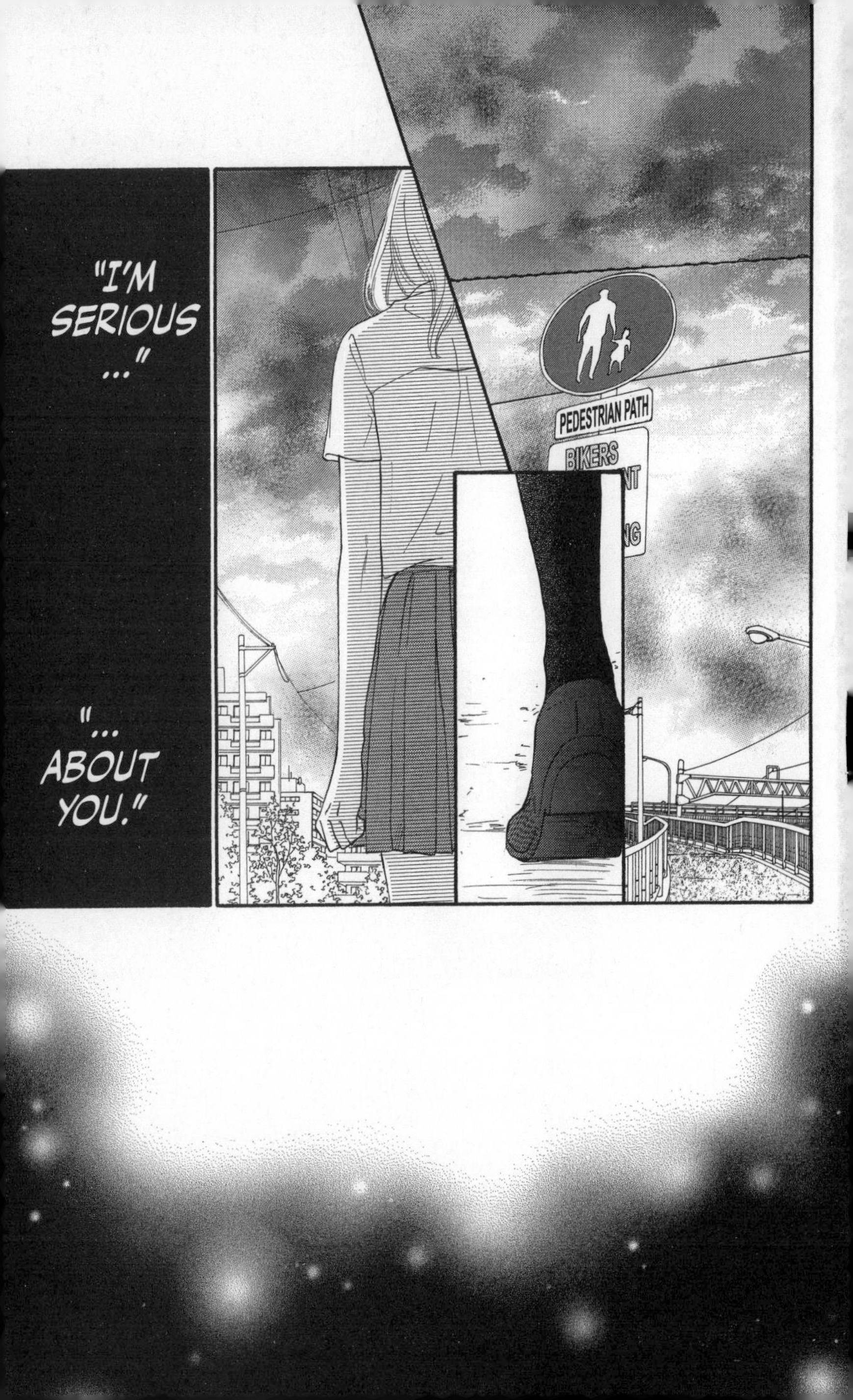
PEDESTRIAN PATH
BIKERS
"I'M SERIOUS ..."
"... ABOUT YOU."

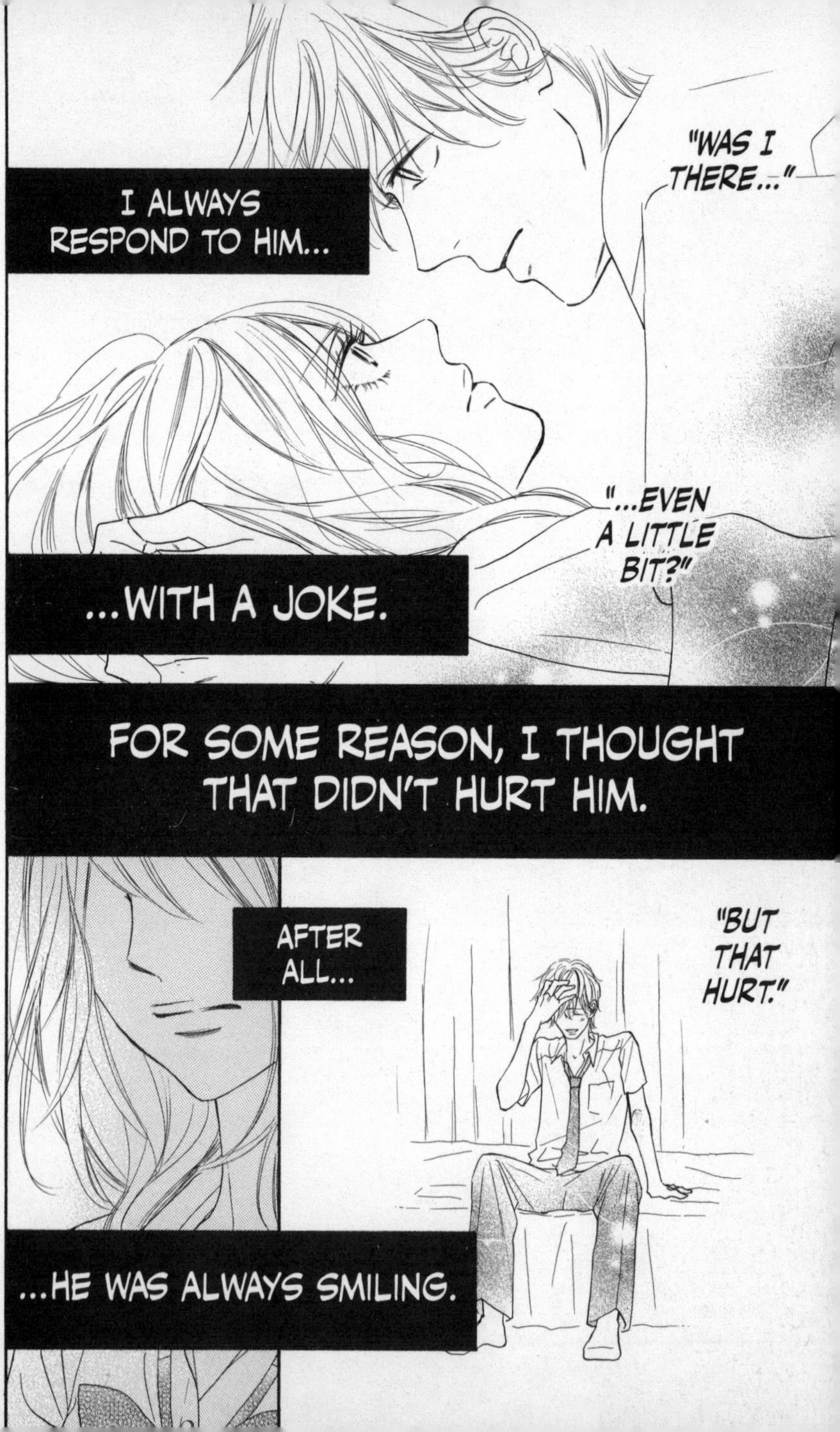
"WAS I THERE..."
I ALWAYS RESPOND TO HIM...
"...EVEN A LITTLE BIT?"
...WITH A JOKE.
FOR SOME REASON, I THOUGHT THAT DIDN'T HURT HIM.
"BUT THAT HURT."
AFTER ALL...
...HE WAS ALWAYS SMILING.

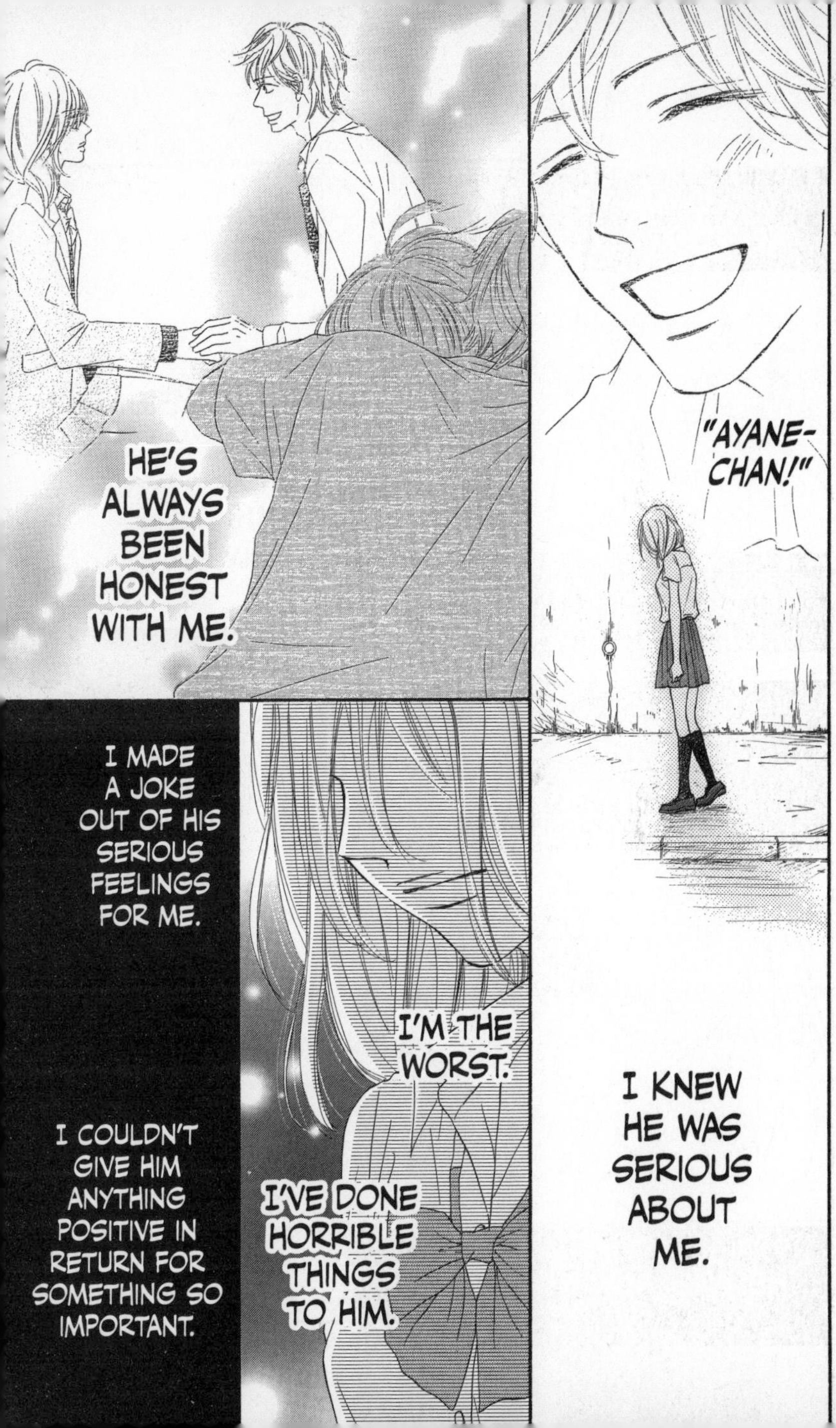
"AYANE-CHAN!"
I KNEW HE WAS SERIOUS ABOUT ME.
HE'S ALWAYS BEEN HONEST WITH ME.
I'M THE WORST.
I'VE DONE HORRIBLE THINGS TO HIM.
I MADE A JOKE OUT OF HIS SERIOUS FEELINGS FOR ME.
I COULDN'T GIVE HIM ANYTHING POSITIVE IN RETURN FOR SOMETHING SO IMPORTANT.

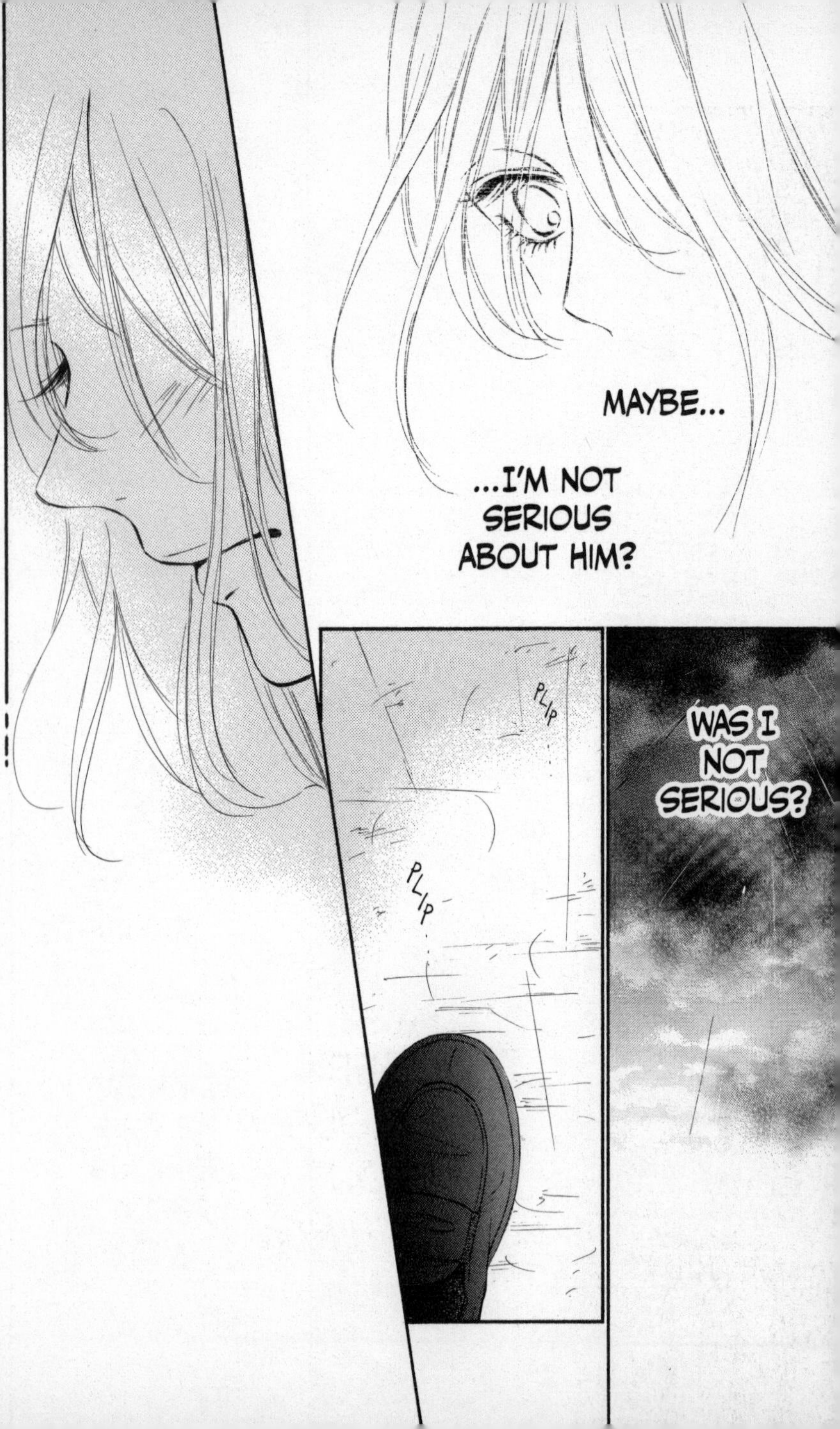
MAYBE...
...I'M NOT SERIOUS ABOUT HIM?
WAS I NOT SERIOUS?
PLIP
PLIP

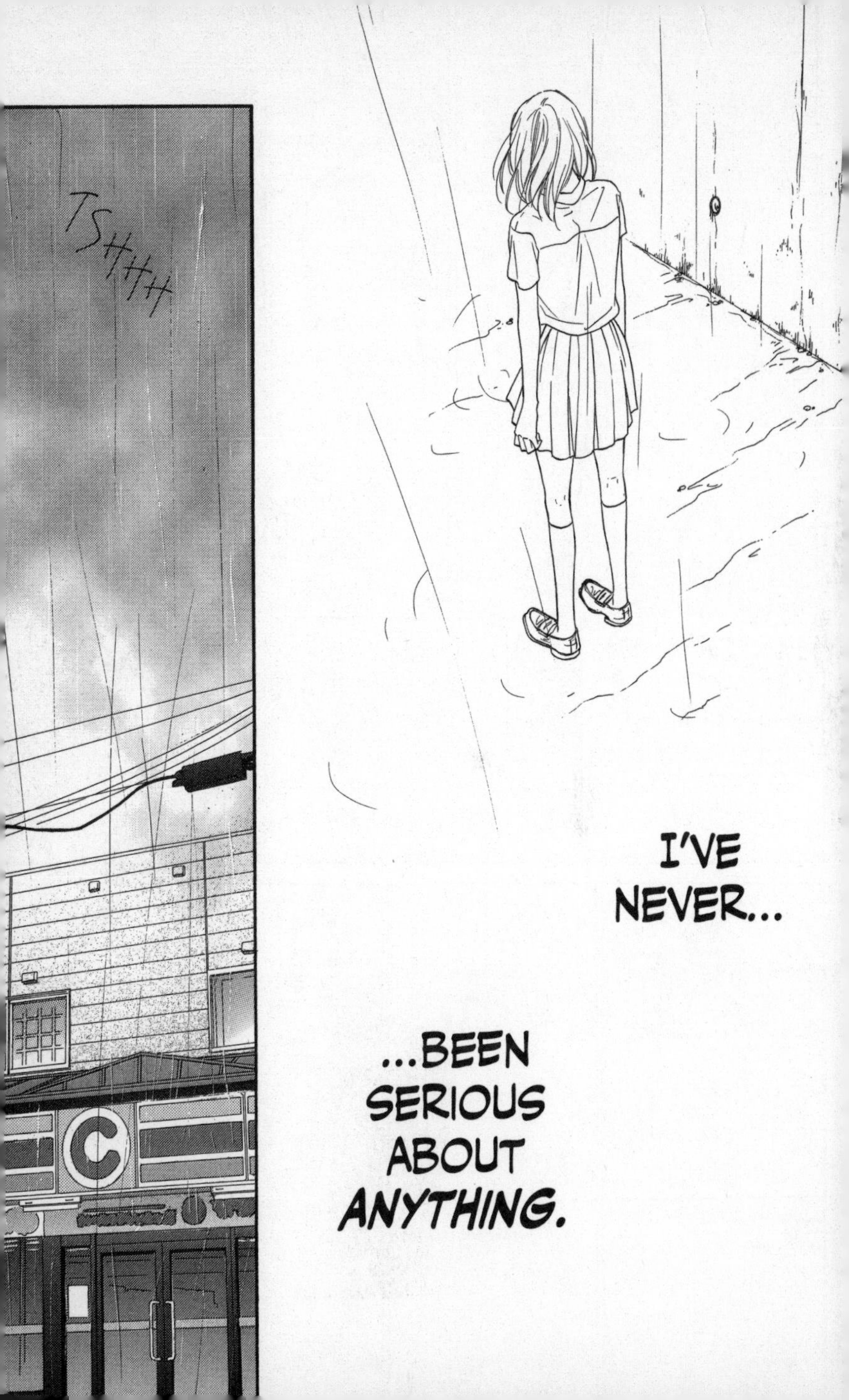
I'VE NEVER...
...BEEN SERIOUS ABOUT ANYTHING.
TSHHHH

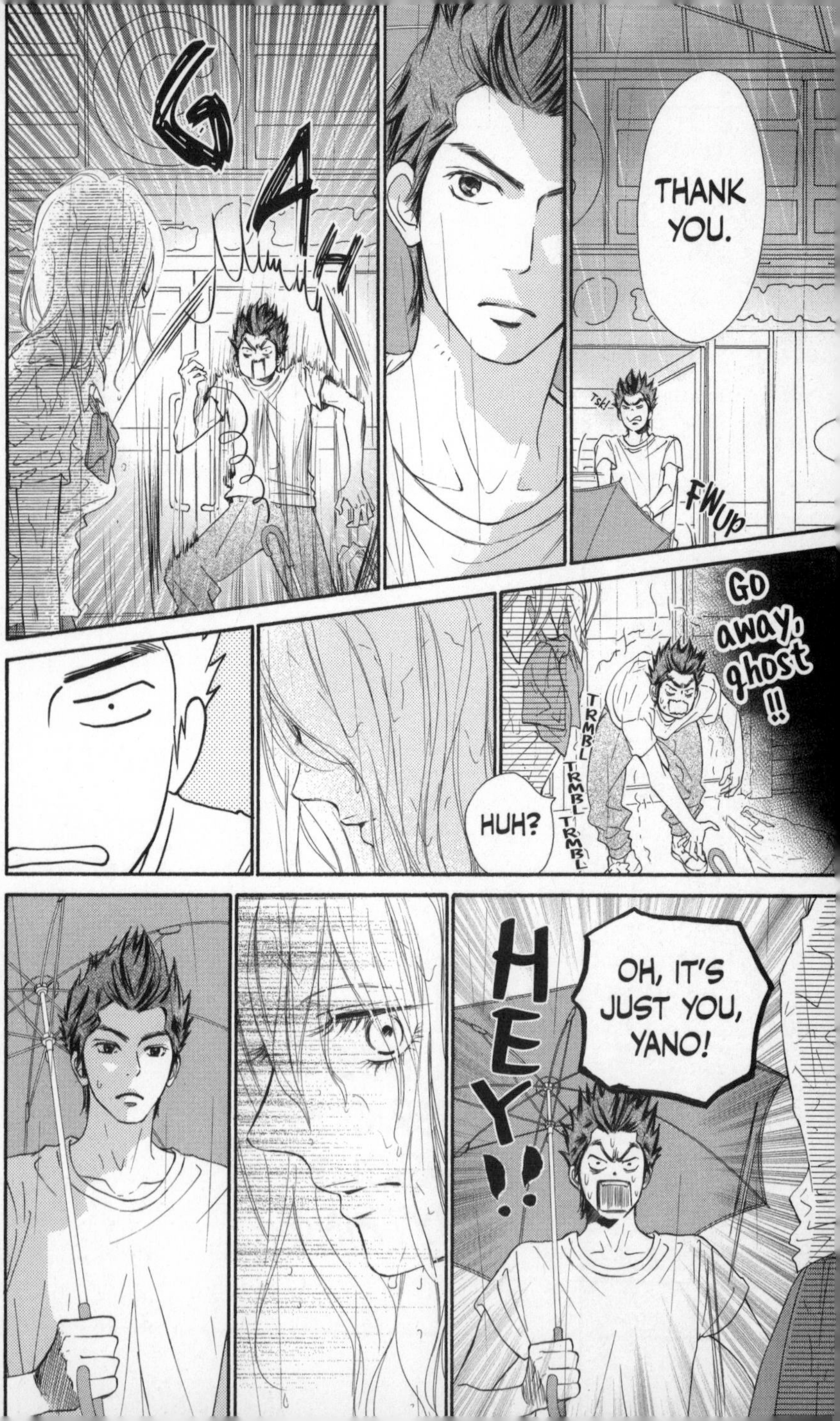
THANK YOU.
Tsk!
FWUp
GAH
Go away, ghost!!
TRMBL TRMBL TRMBL
HUH?
HEY!!
OH, IT'S JUST YOU, YANO!

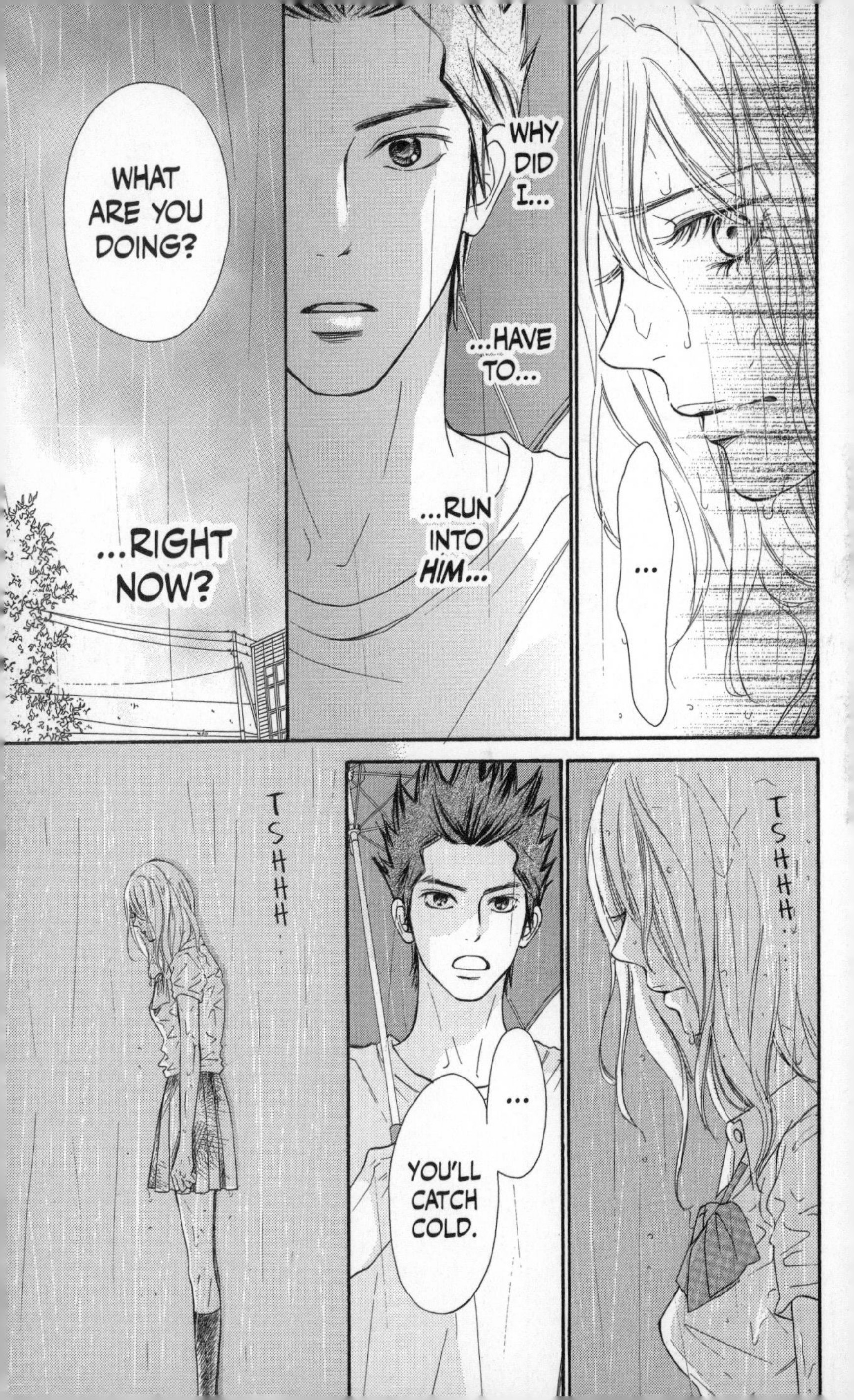
...
WHY DID I...
...HAVE TO...
...RUN INTO HIM...
WHAT ARE YOU DOING?
...RIGHT NOW?
TSHHH...
...
YOU'LL CATCH COLD.
TSHHH...

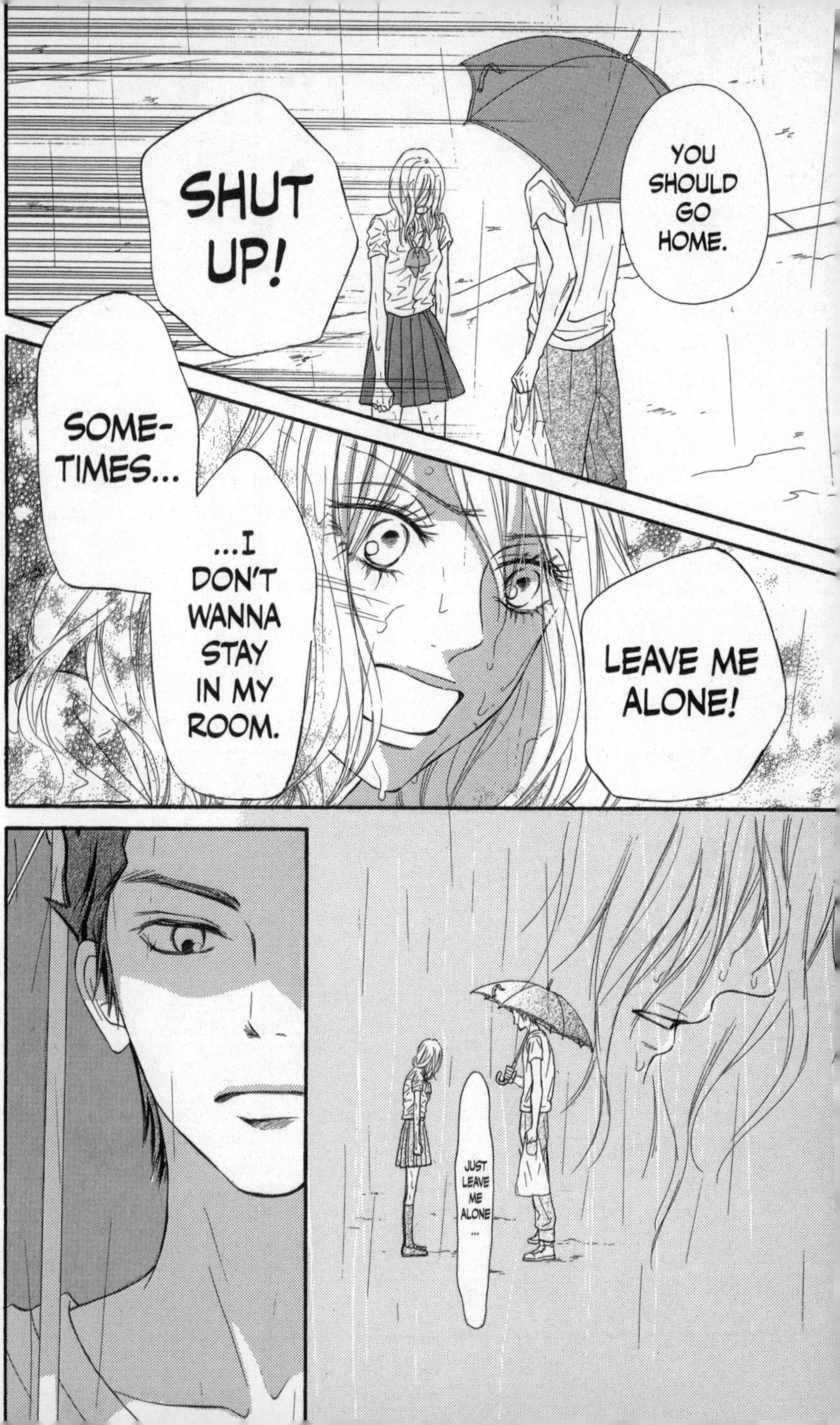
YOU SHOULD GO HOME.
SHUT UP!
LEAVE ME ALONE!
SOME-TIMES...
...I DON'T WANNA STAY IN MY ROOM.
JUST LEAVE ME ALONE...

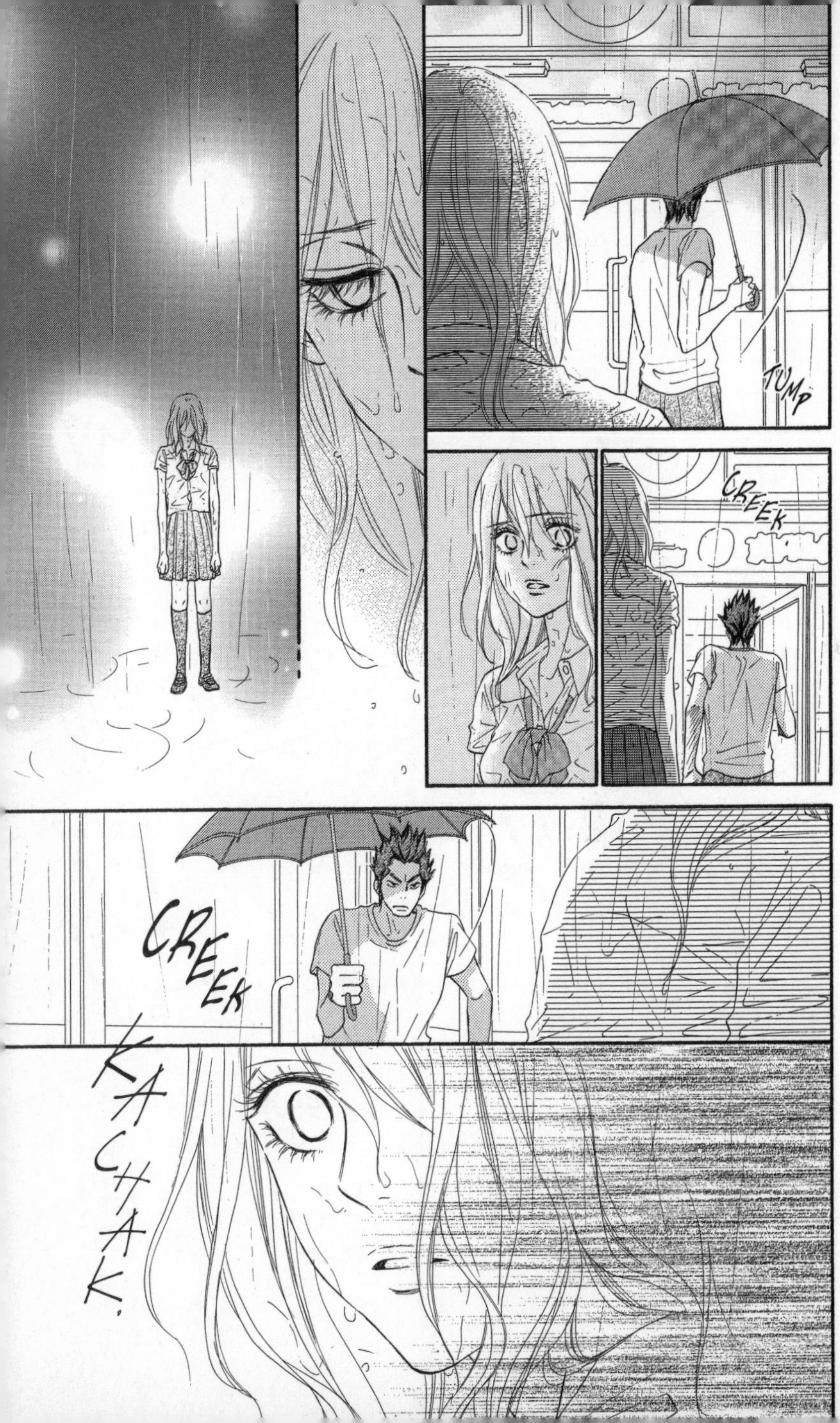
TUMP
CREEK
CREEK
KACHAK.

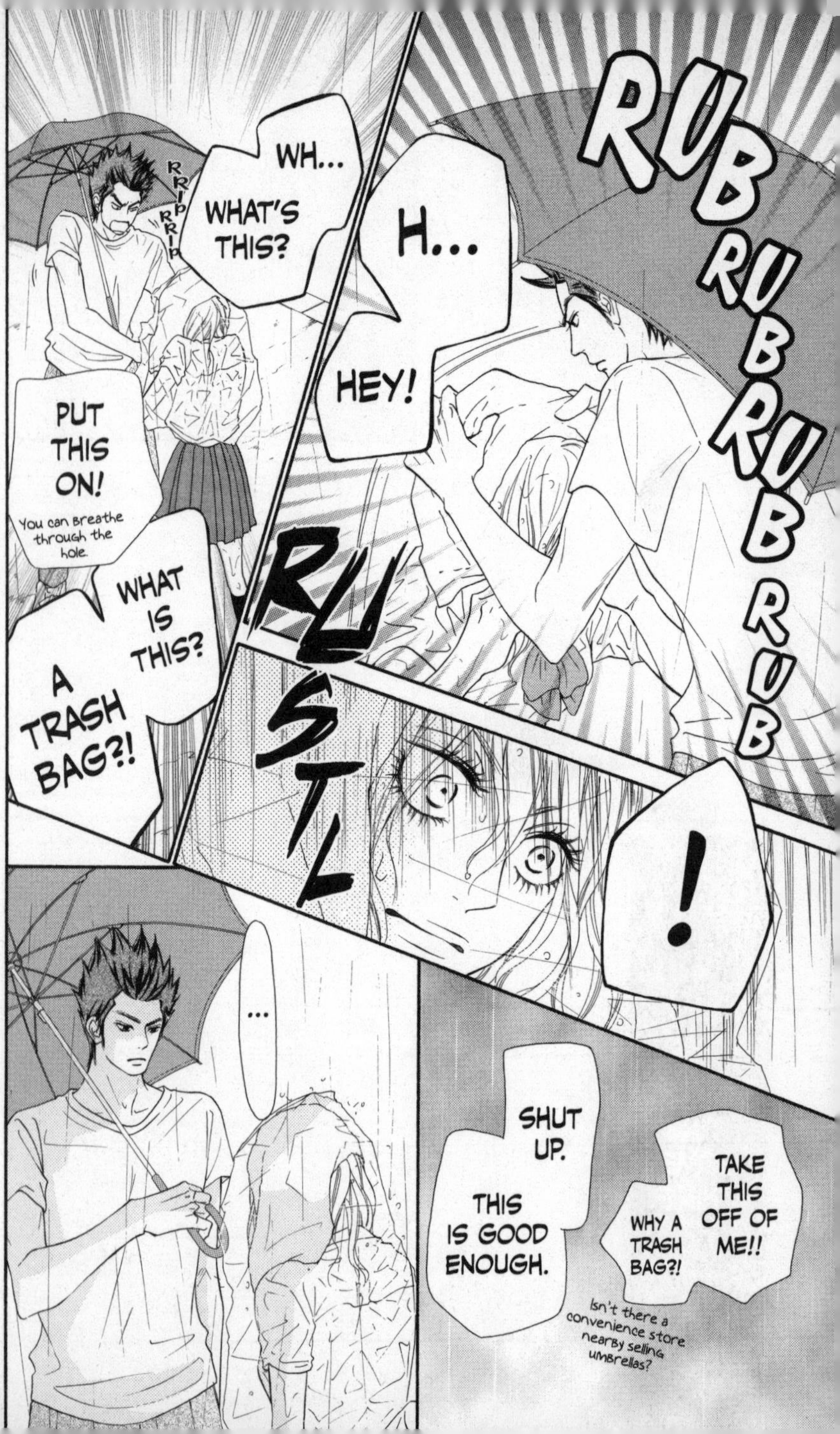
RUB RUB RUB RUB RUB
H...
HEY!
RUSTL
WH...
WHAT'S THIS?
RRIP RRIP
PUT THIS ON!
You can breathe through the hole.
WHAT IS THIS?
A TRASH BAG?!
!
TAKE THIS OFF OF ME!!
WHY A TRASH BAG?!
Isn't there a convenience store nearby selling umbrellas?
SHUT UP.
THIS IS GOOD ENOUGH.
...

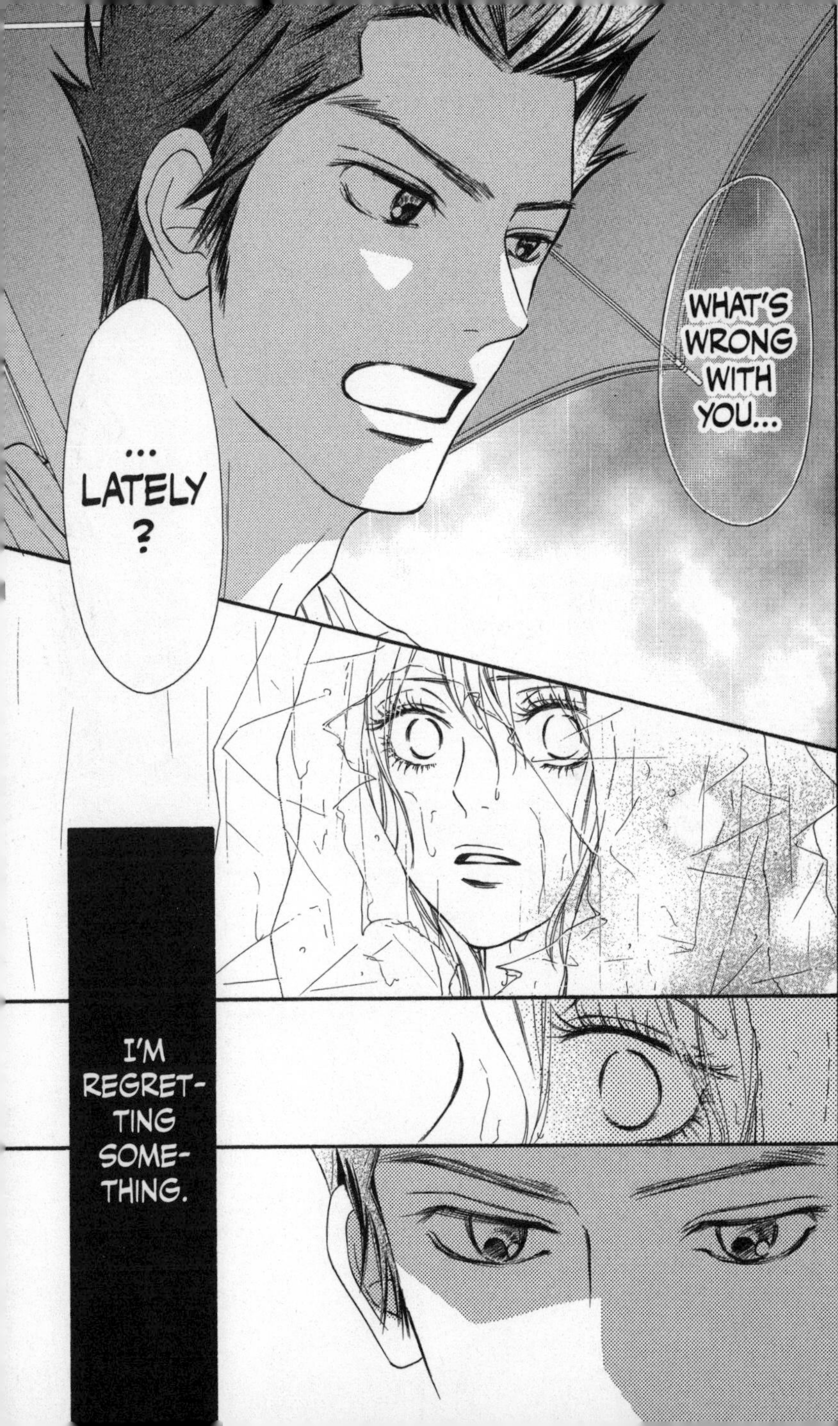
WHAT'S WRONG WITH YOU...
... LATELY ?
I'M REGRETTING SOMETHING.

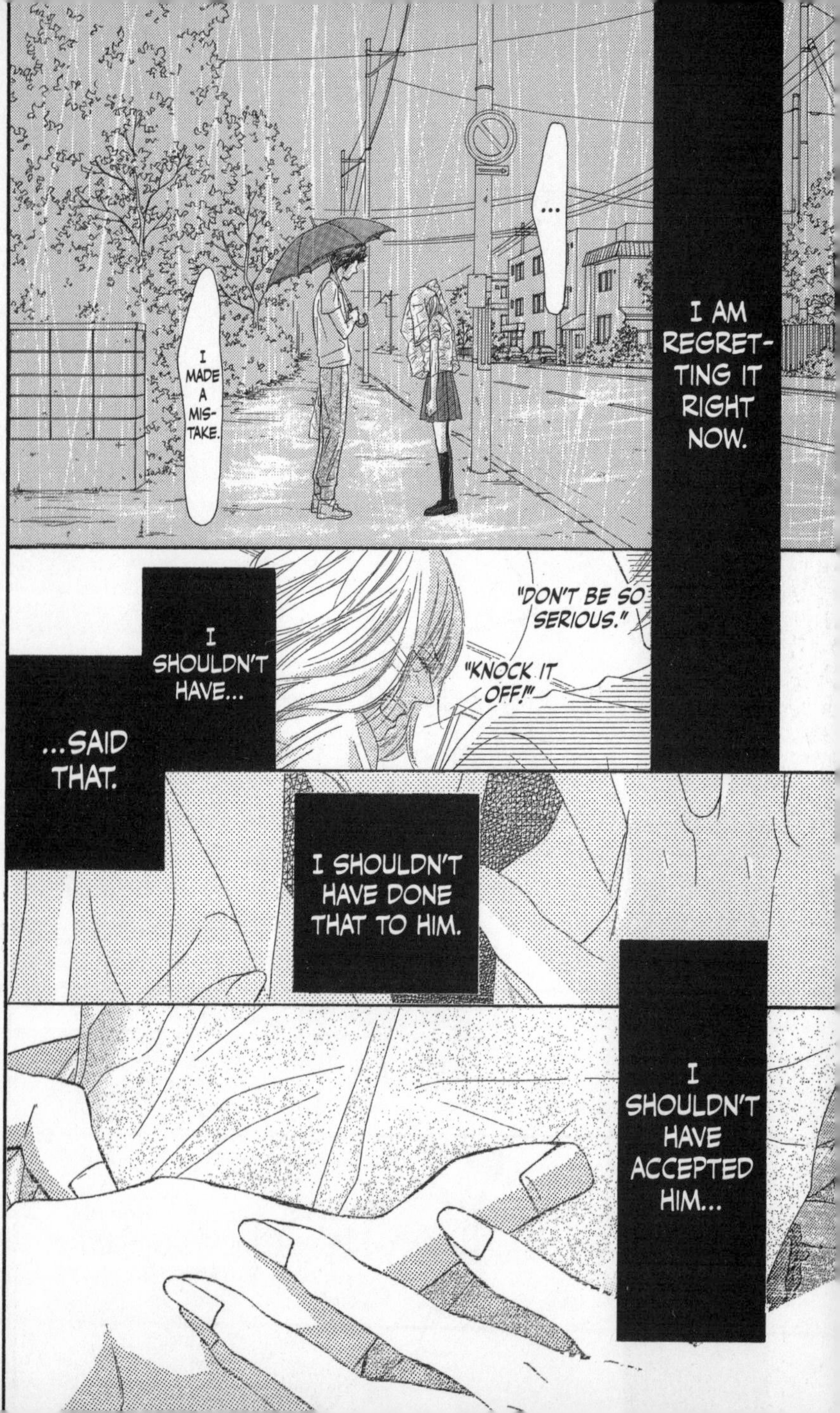
I AM REGRETTING IT RIGHT NOW.
...
I MADE A MISTAKE.
"DON'T BE SO SERIOUS."
"KNOCK IT OFF!"
I SHOULDN'T HAVE...
...SAID THAT.
I SHOULDN'T HAVE DONE THAT TO HIM.
I SHOULDN'T HAVE ACCEPTED HIM...

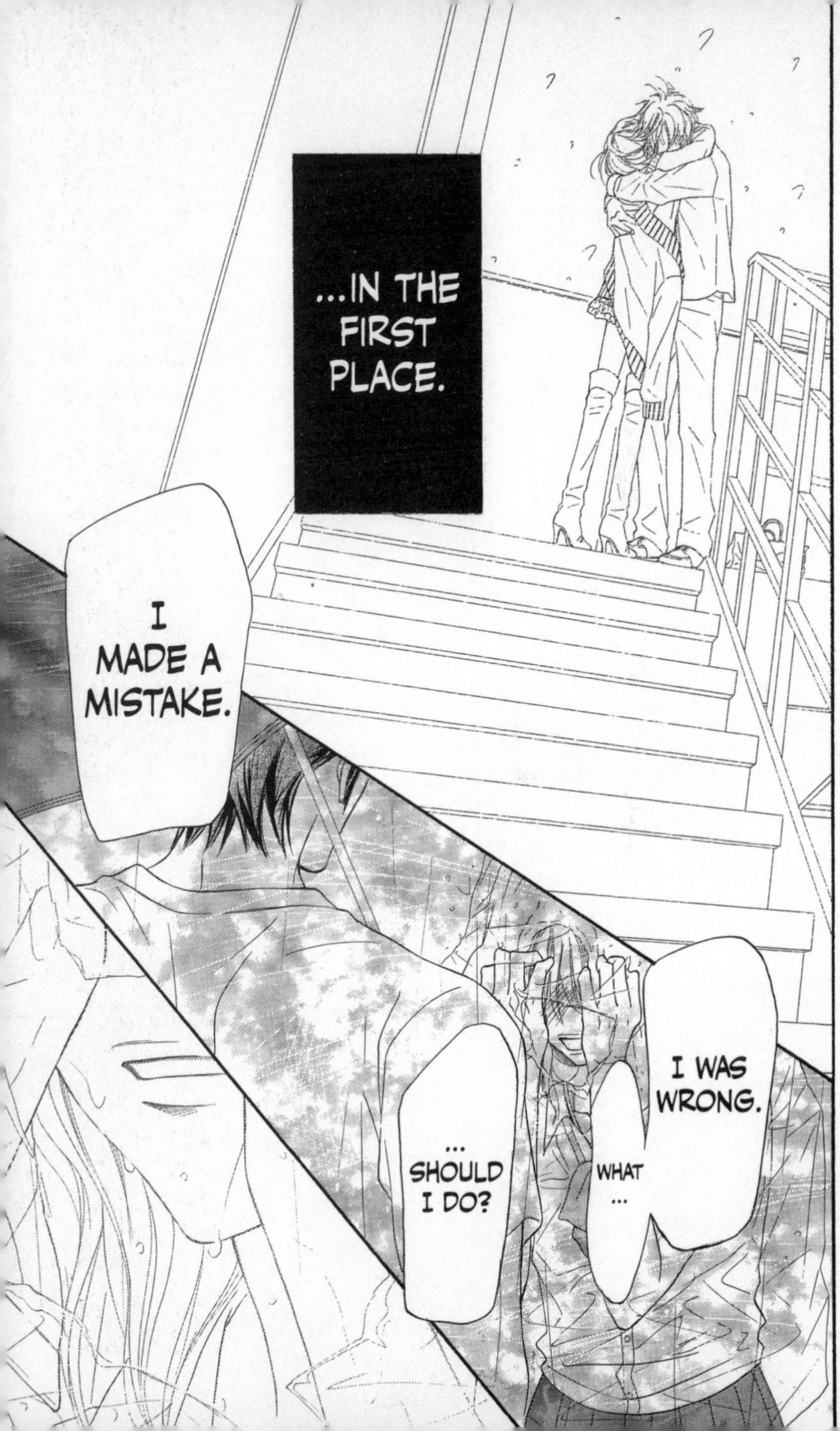
...IN THE FIRST PLACE.
I MADE A MISTAKE.
I WAS WRONG.
WHAT ...
... SHOULD I DO?

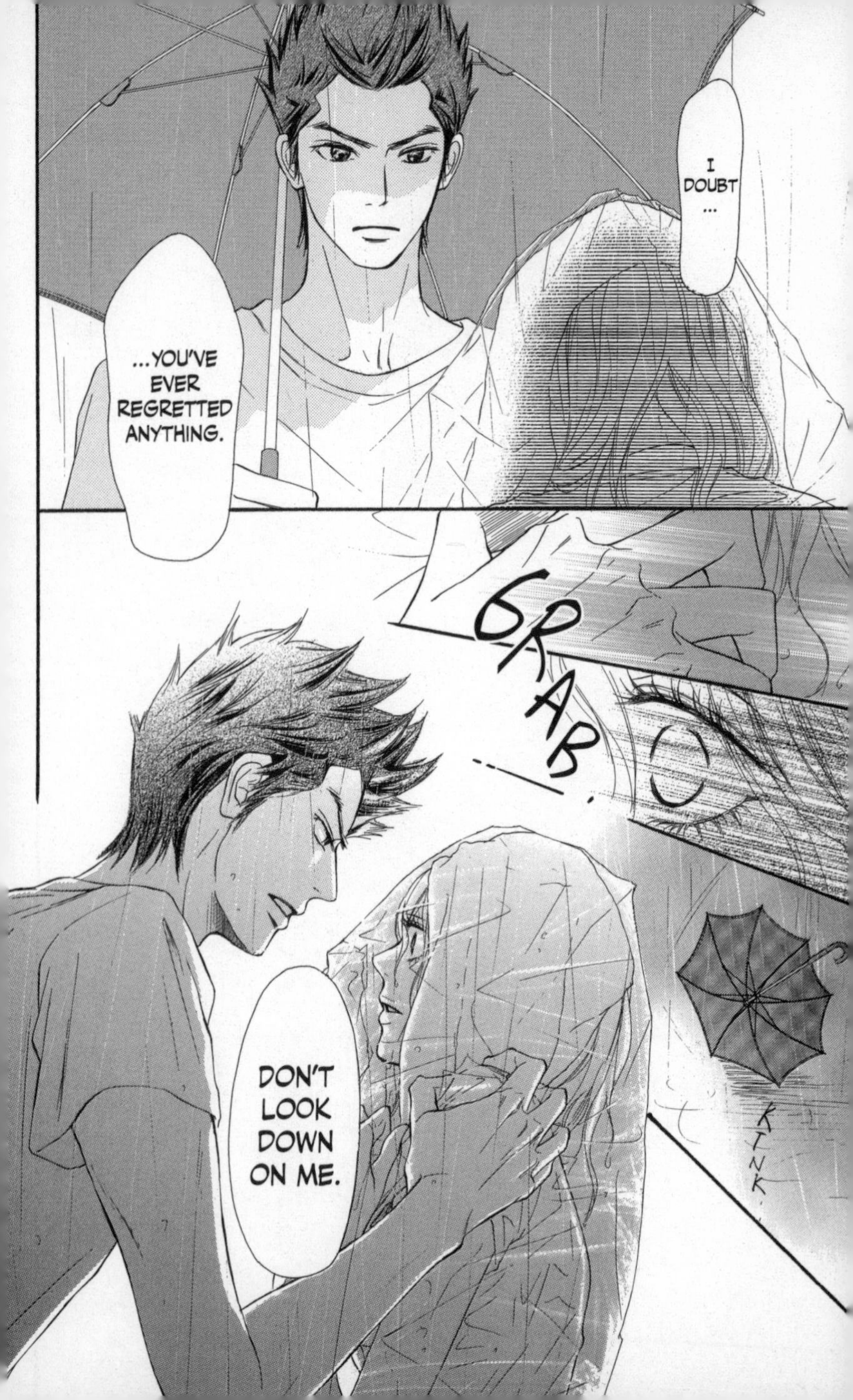
I DOUBT ...
...YOU'VE EVER REGRETTED ANYTHING.
GRAB.
KLINK.
DON'T LOOK DOWN ON ME.

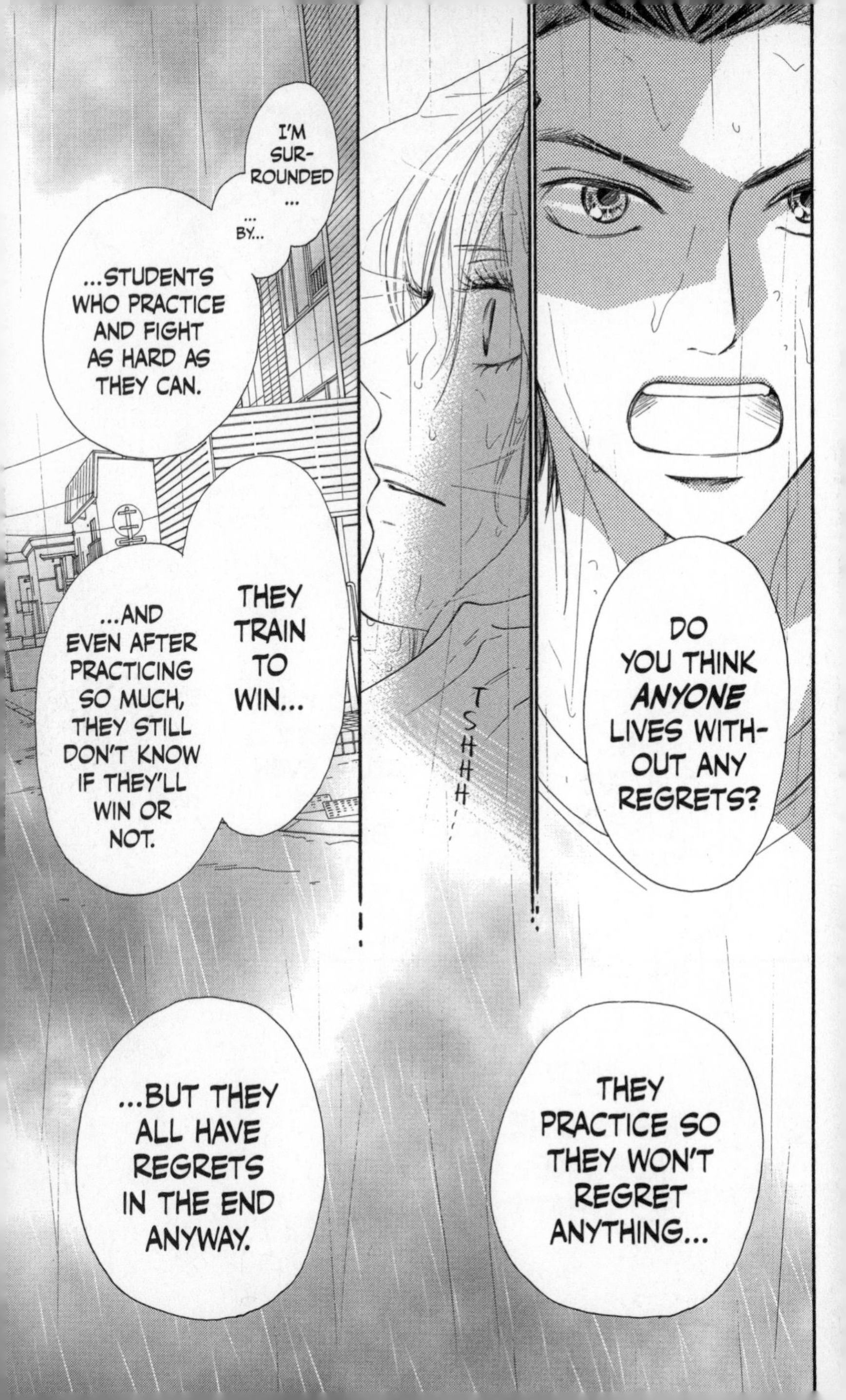
DO YOU THINK *ANYONE* LIVES WITH-OUT ANY REGRETS?
TSHHH
I'M SUR-ROUNDED ...
... BY...
...STUDENTS WHO PRACTICE AND FIGHT AS HARD AS THEY CAN.
THEY TRAIN TO WIN...
...AND EVEN AFTER PRACTICING SO MUCH, THEY STILL DON'T KNOW IF THEY'LL WIN OR NOT.
THEY PRACTICE SO THEY WON'T REGRET ANYTHING...
...BUT THEY ALL HAVE REGRETS IN THE END ANYWAY.

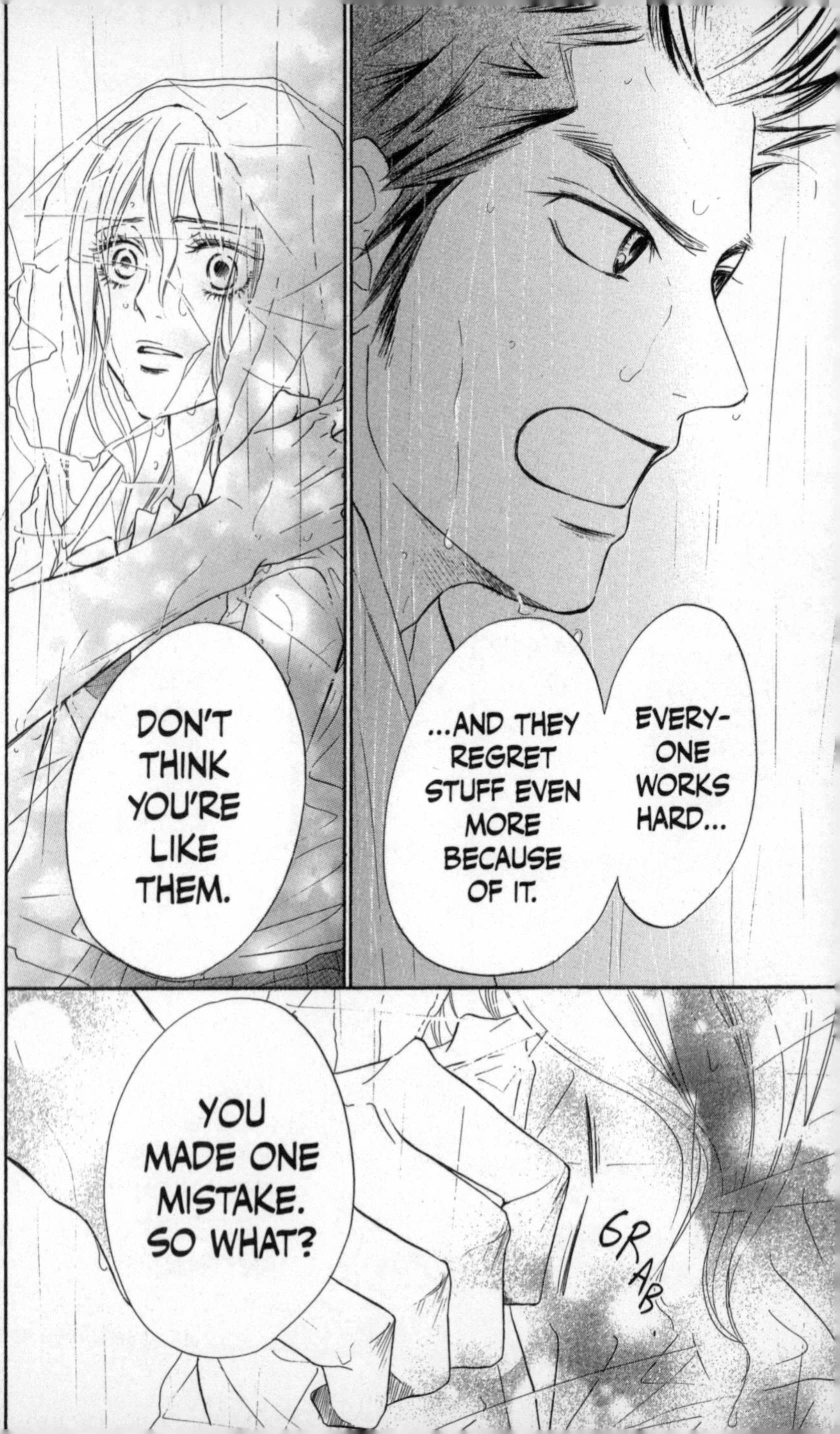
EVERY-ONE WORKS HARD...
...AND THEY REGRET STUFF EVEN MORE BECAUSE OF IT.
DON'T THINK YOU'RE LIKE THEM.
GRAB
YOU MADE ONE MISTAKE. SO WHAT?

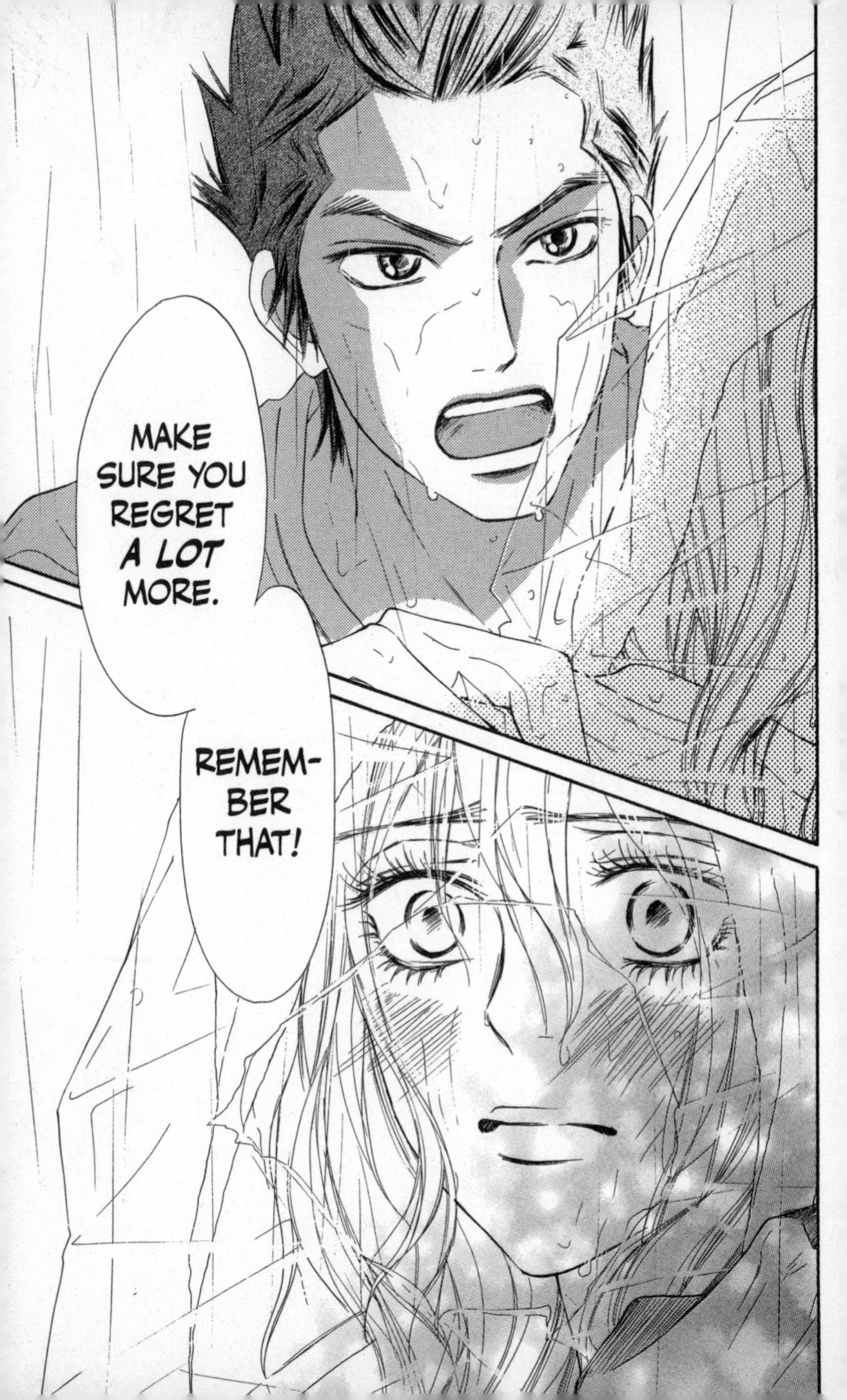
MAKE SURE YOU REGRET A LOT MORE.
REMEM-BER THAT!

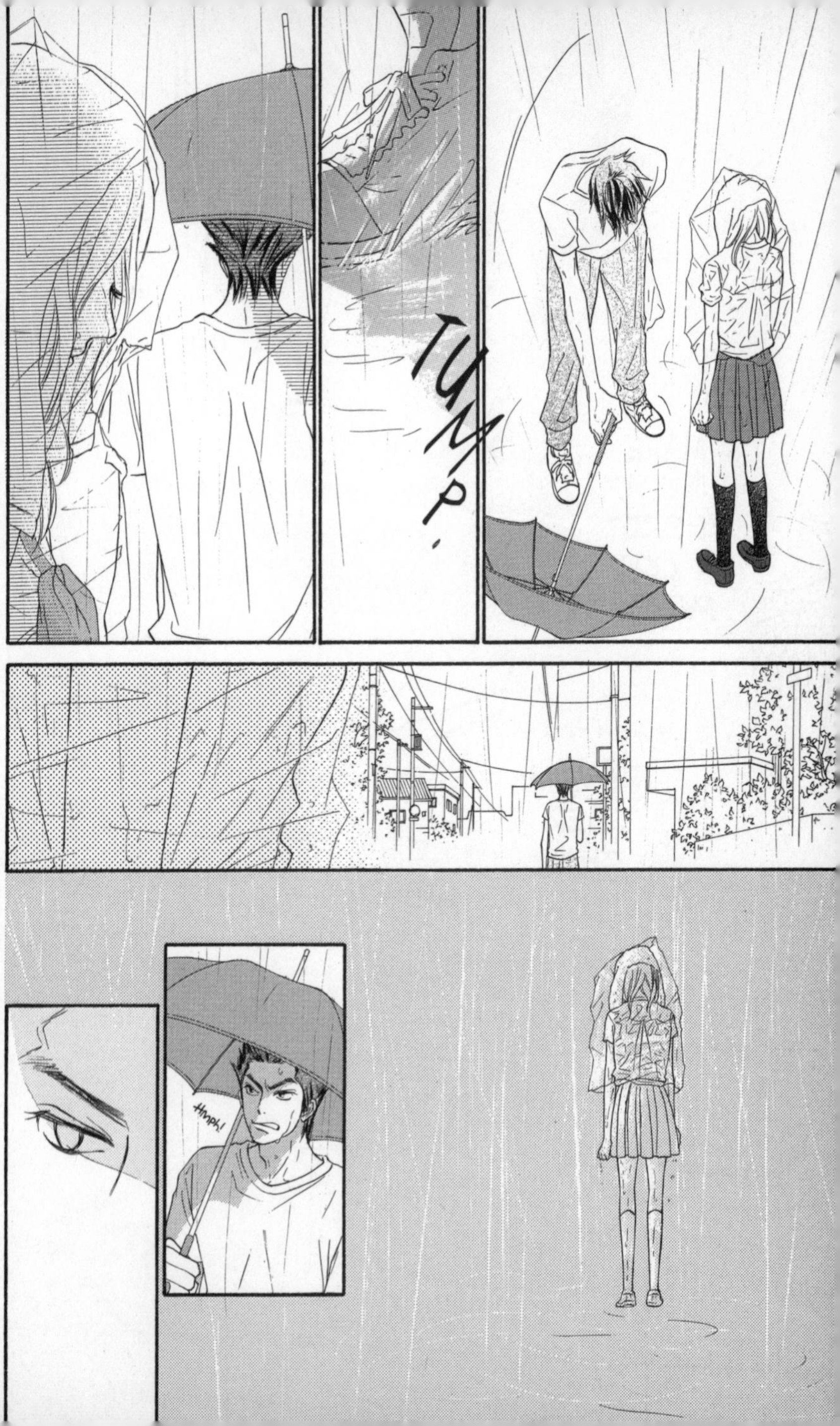
TUMP.
Hmph!

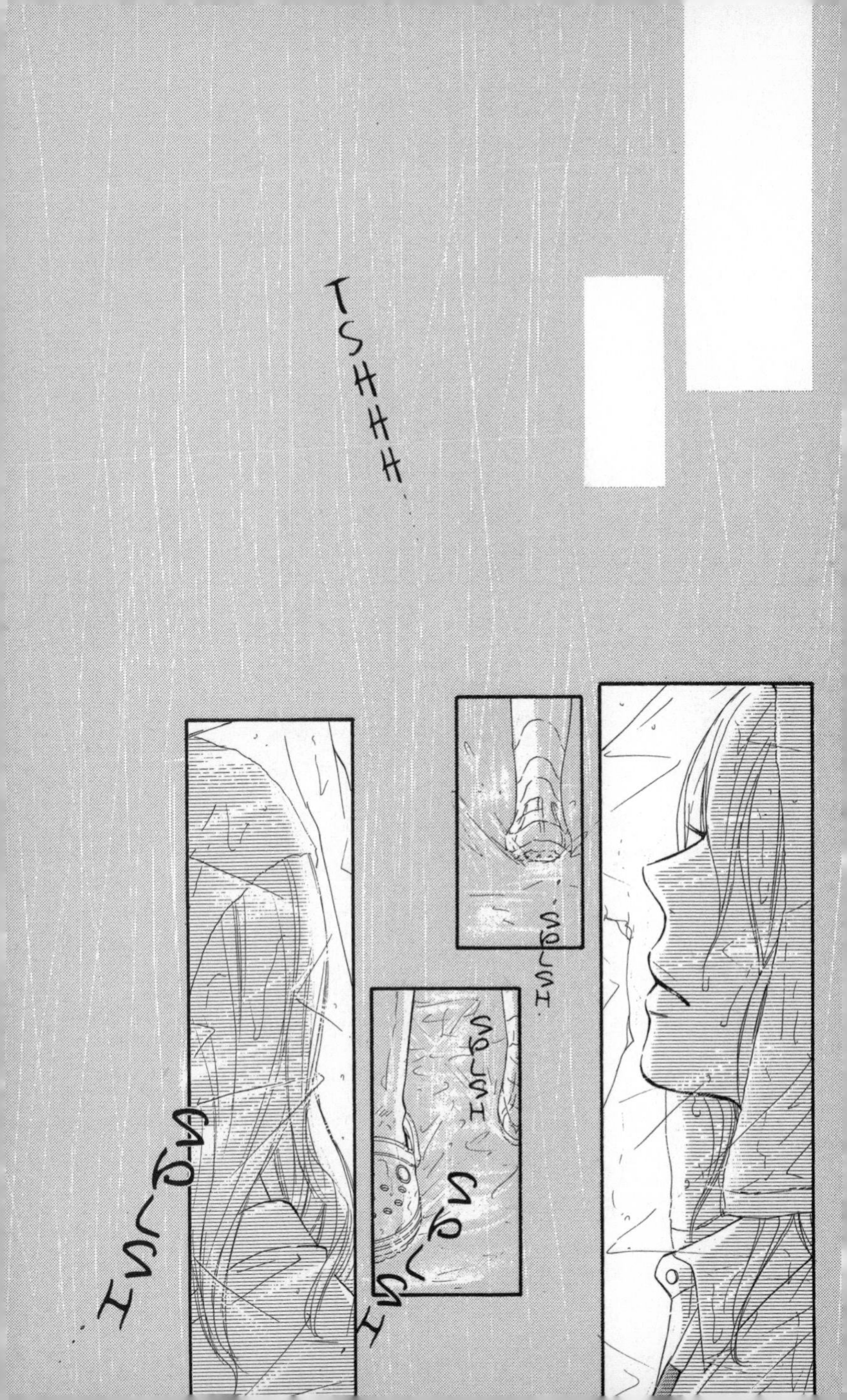
TSHHHH...
SPLISH...
SPLISH
SPLISH
SPLISH...

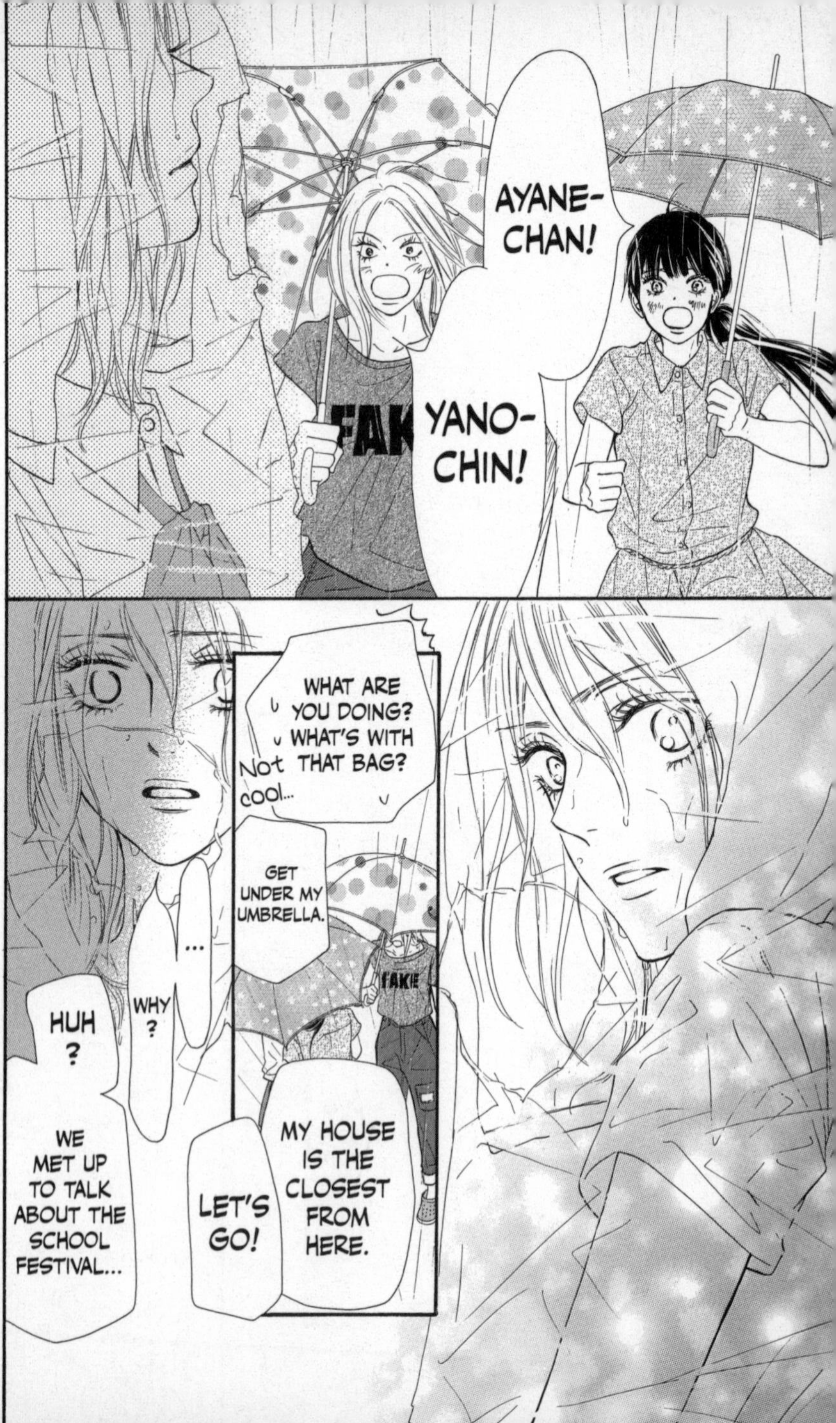
AYANE-CHAN!
YANO-CHIN!
WHAT ARE YOU DOING? WHAT'S WITH THAT BAG?
Not cool...
GET UNDER MY UMBRELLA.
MY HOUSE IS THE CLOSEST FROM HERE.
LET'S GO!
...
WHY?
HUH?
WE MET UP TO TALK ABOUT THE SCHOOL FESTIVAL...

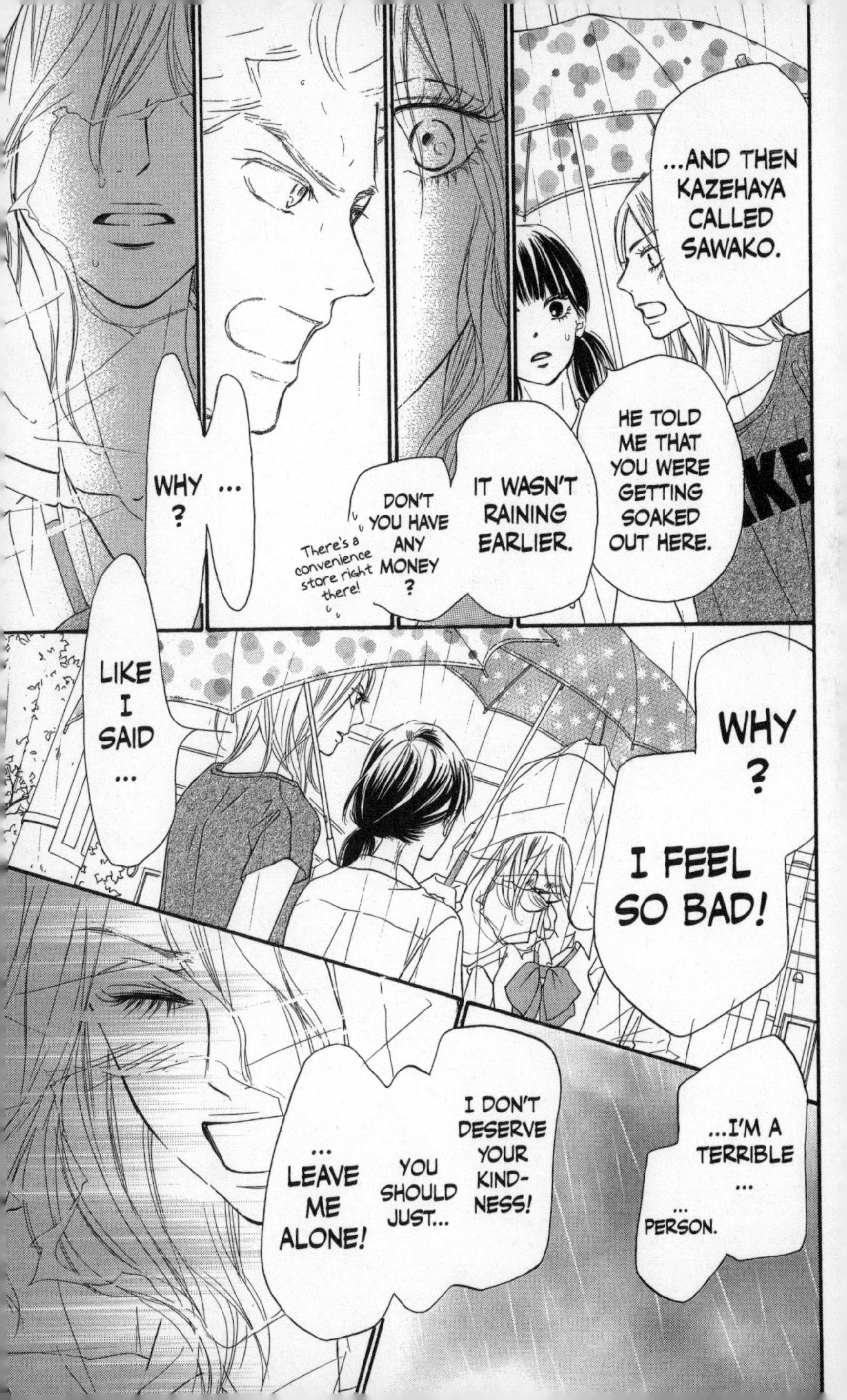
...AND THEN KAZEHAYA CALLED SAWAKO.
HE TOLD ME THAT YOU WERE GETTING SOAKED OUT HERE.
IT WASN'T RAINING EARLIER.
DON'T YOU HAVE ANY MONEY?
There's a convenience store right there!
WHY...?
WHY? I FEEL SO BAD!
LIKE I SAID...
...I'M A TERRIBLE... ...PERSON.
I DON'T DESERVE YOUR KINDNESS!
YOU SHOULD JUST...
...LEAVE ME ALONE!

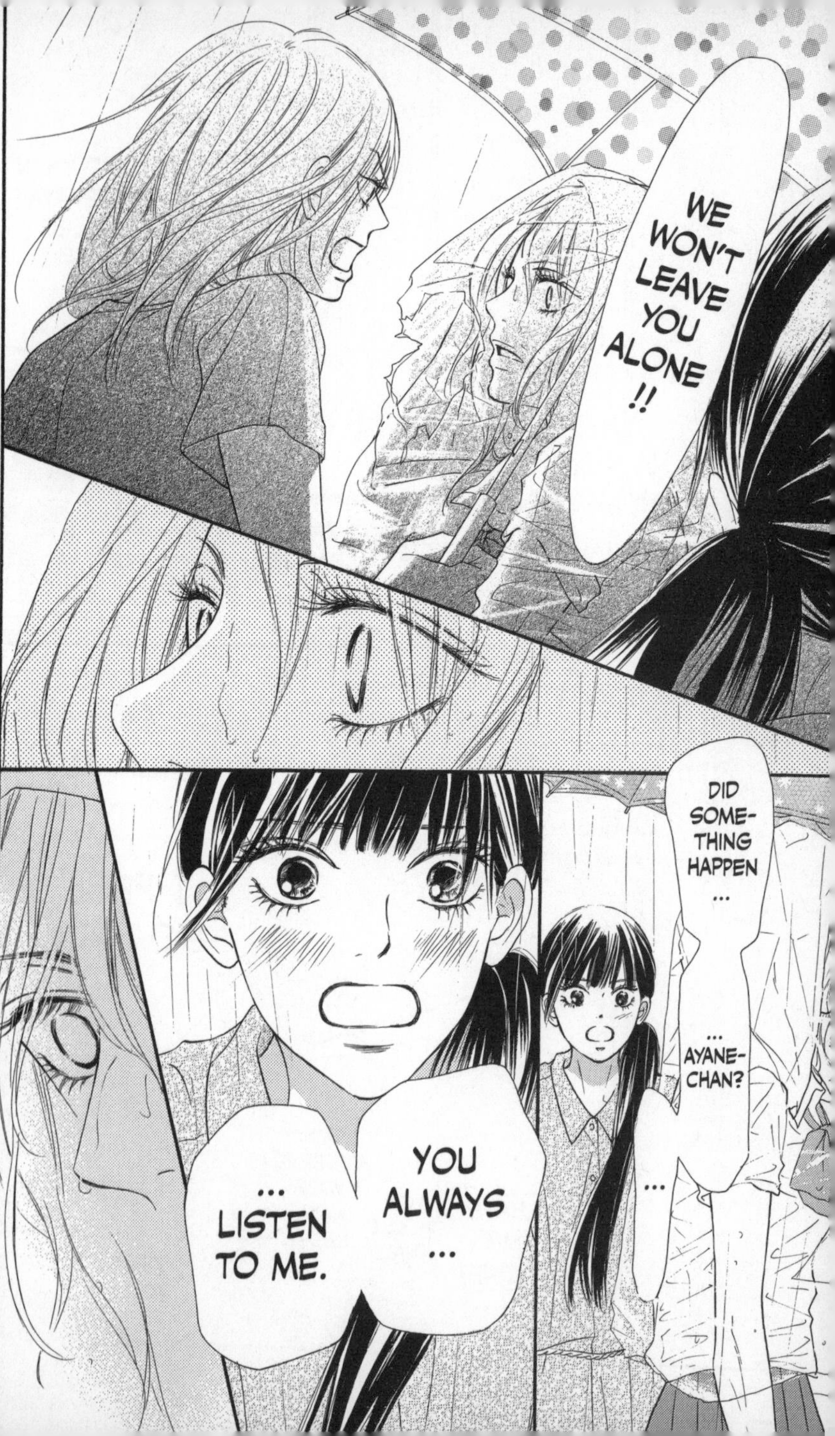
WE WON'T LEAVE YOU ALONE !!
DID SOMETHING HAPPEN ...
... AYANE-CHAN?
...
YOU ALWAYS ...
... LISTEN TO ME.

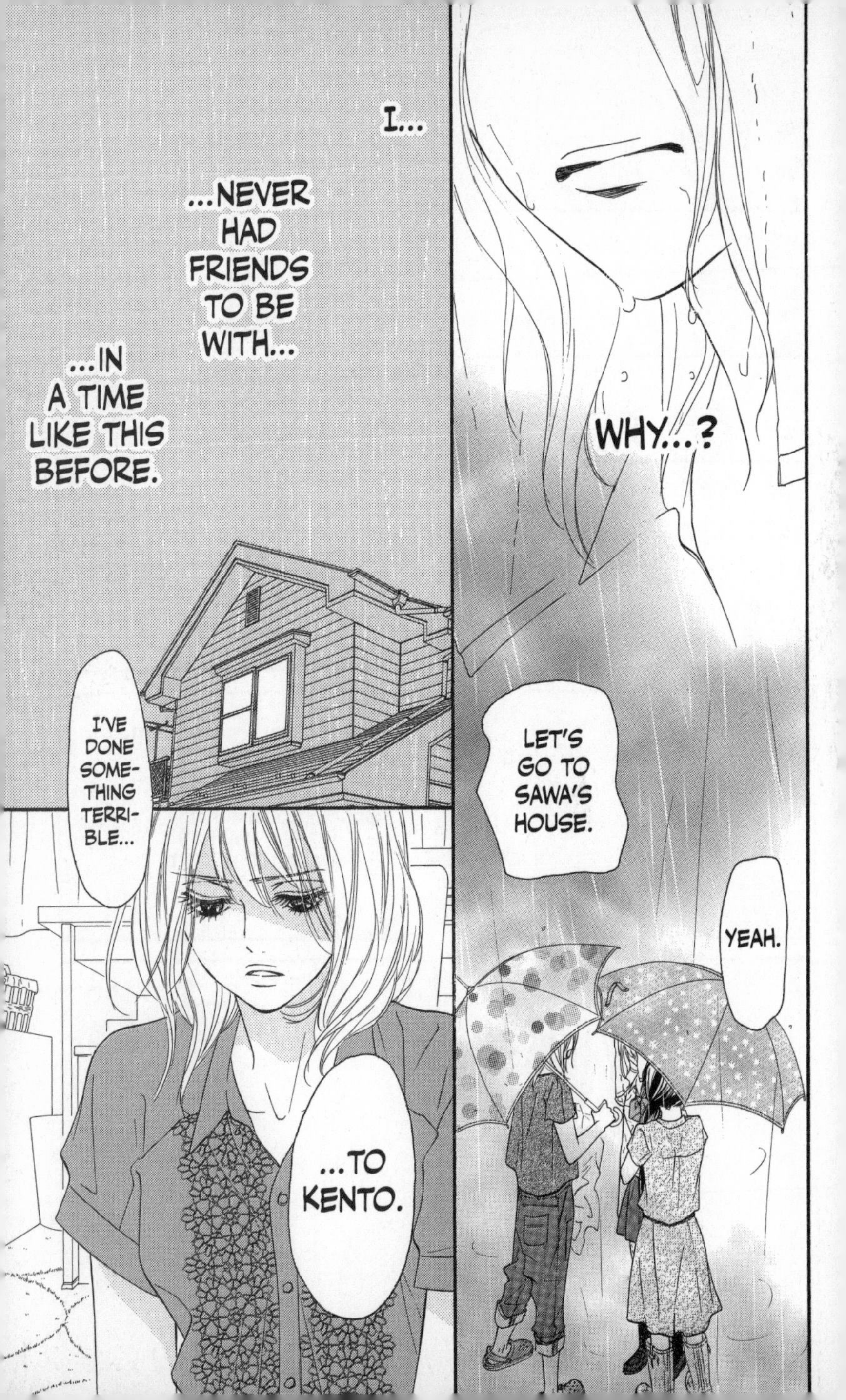
WHY...?
LET'S GO TO SAWA'S HOUSE.
YEAH.
I...
...NEVER HAD FRIENDS TO BE WITH...
...IN A TIME LIKE THIS BEFORE.
I'VE DONE SOMETHING TERRIBLE...
...TO KENTO.

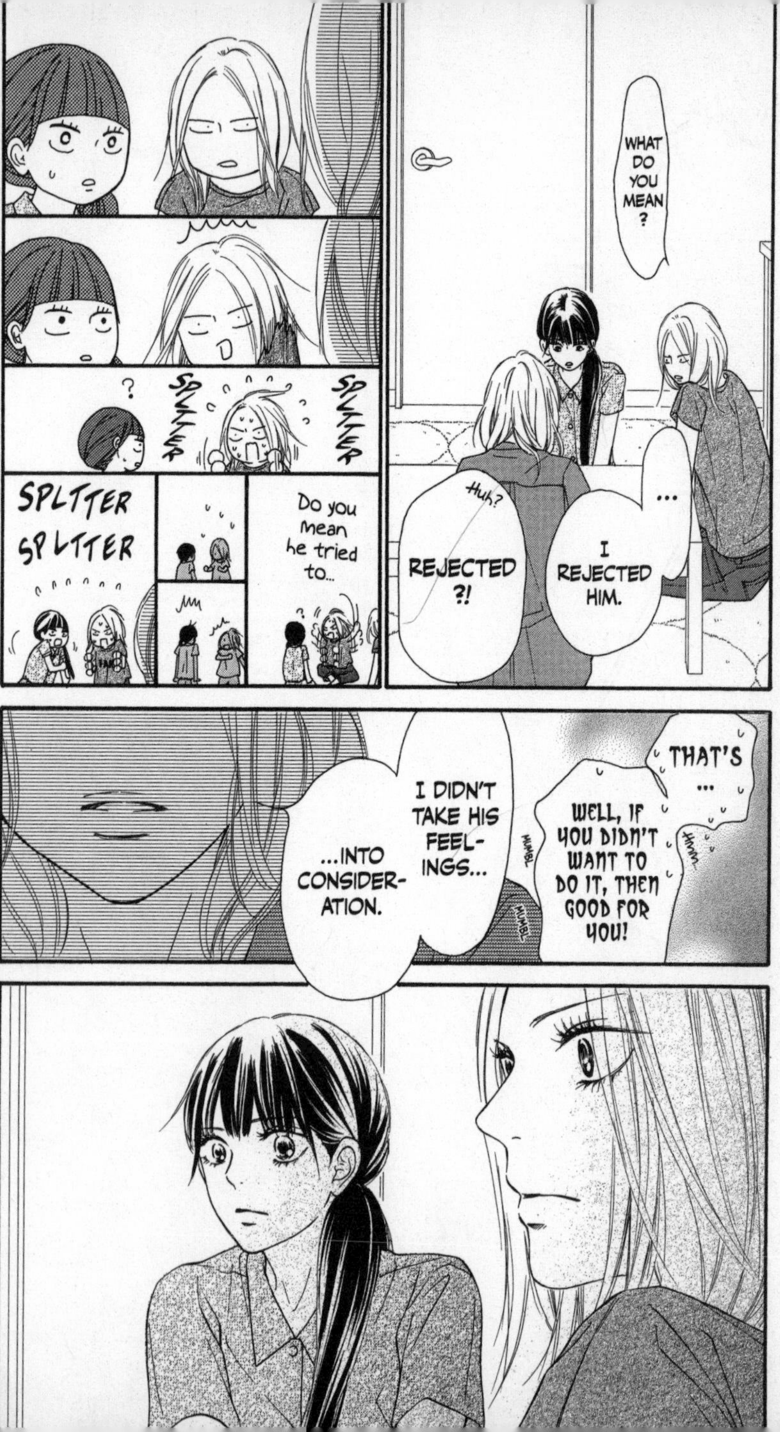
WHAT DO YOU MEAN?
...
I REJECTED HIM.
Huh?
REJECTED?!
SPLTTER
SPLTTER
Do you mean he tried to...
SPLTTER
SPLTTER
THAT'S...
WELL, IF YOU DIDN'T WANT TO DO IT, THEN GOOD FOR YOU!
MUMBL
MUMBL
I DIDN'T TAKE HIS FEELINGS...
...INTO CONSIDERATION.

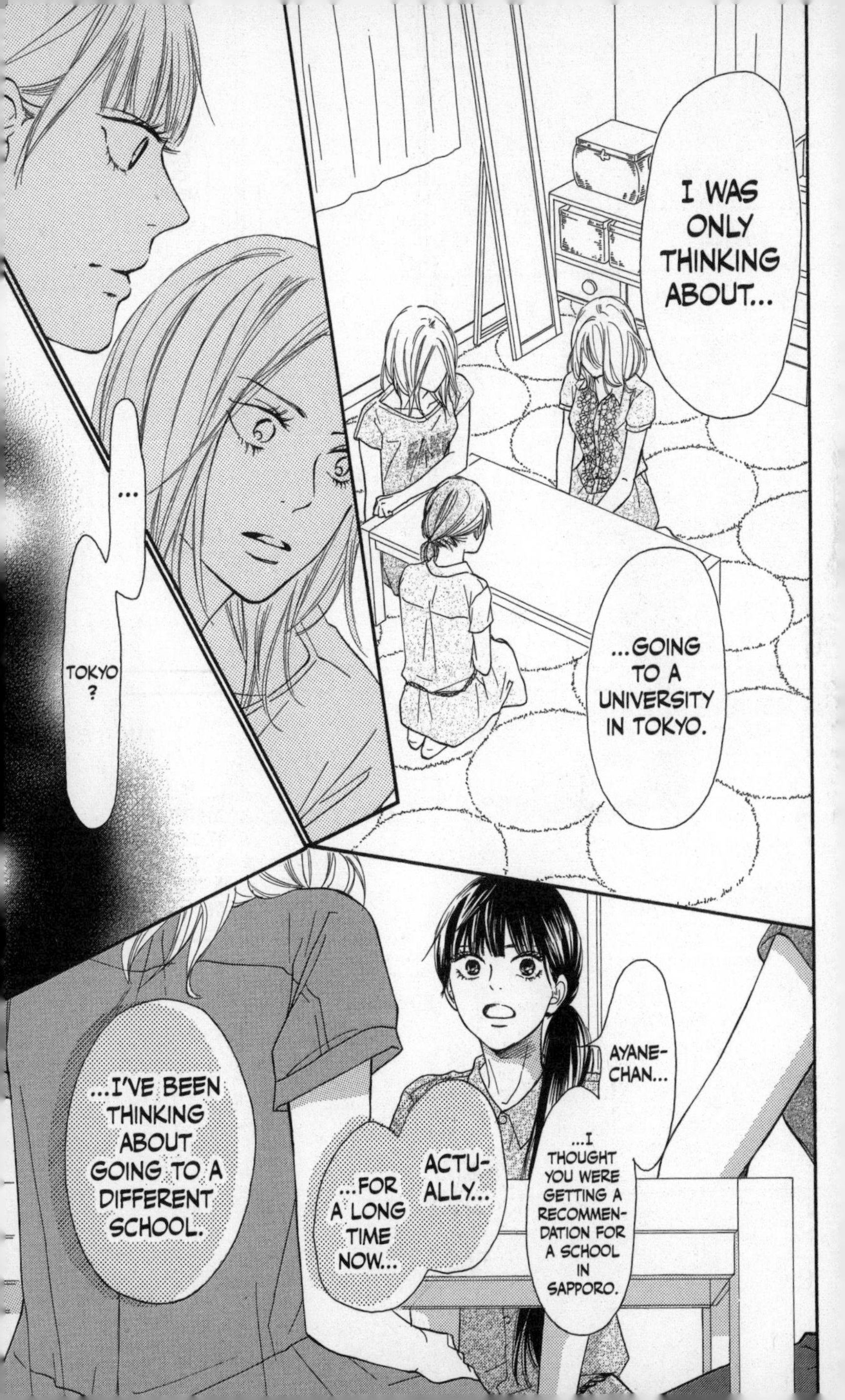
I WAS ONLY THINKING ABOUT...
...GOING TO A UNIVERSITY IN TOKYO.
...
TOKYO?
AYANE-CHAN...
...I THOUGHT YOU WERE GETTING A RECOMMEN-DATION FOR A SCHOOL IN SAPPORO.
ACTU-ALLY...
...FOR A LONG TIME NOW...
...I'VE BEEN THINKING ABOUT GOING TO A DIFFERENT SCHOOL.

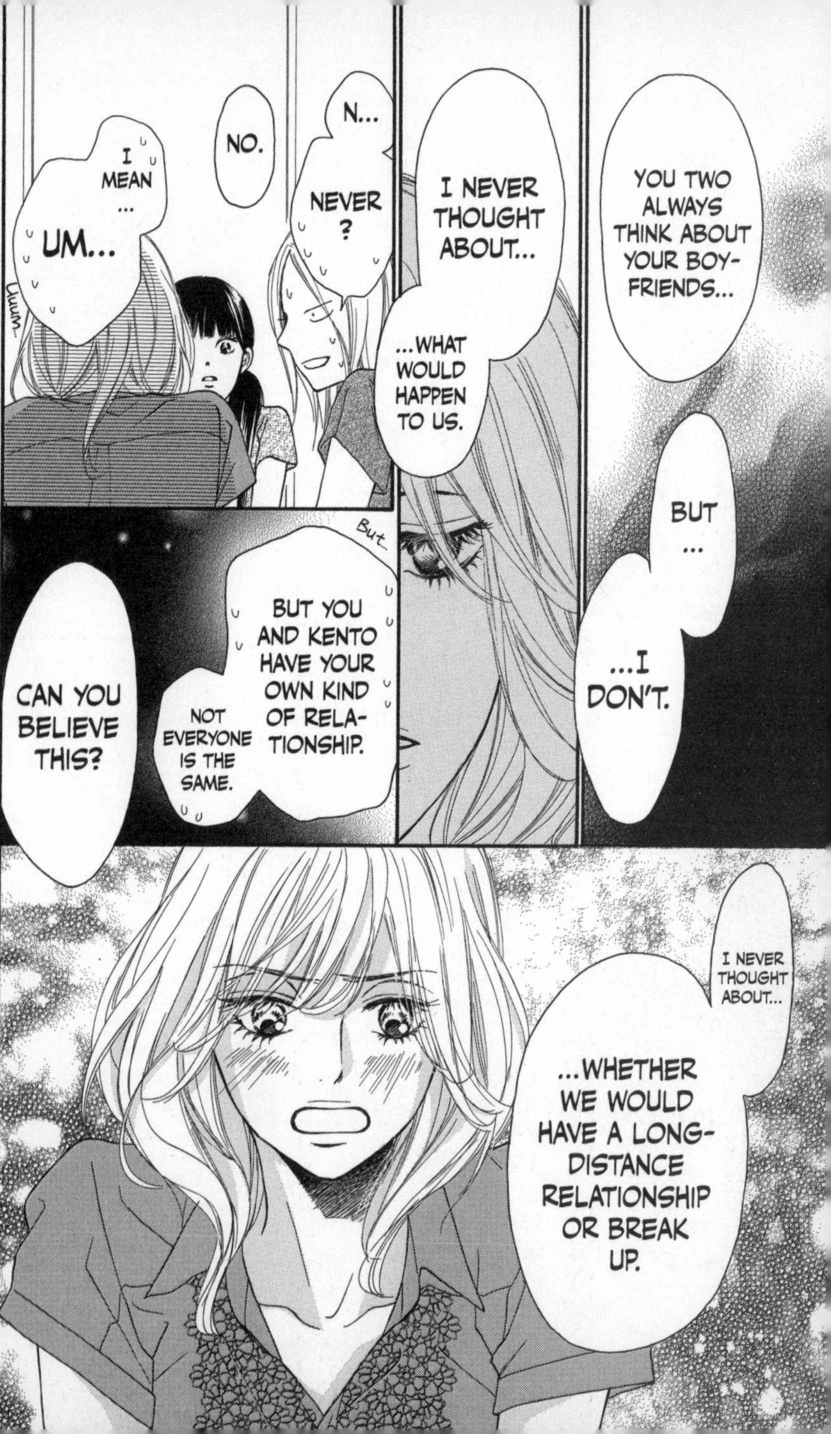
YOU TWO ALWAYS THINK ABOUT YOUR BOY-FRIENDS...
BUT ...
...I DON'T.
I NEVER THOUGHT ABOUT...
...WHAT WOULD HAPPEN TO US.
N...
NEVER?
NO.
I MEAN ... UM...
Uuum...
But...
BUT YOU AND KENTO HAVE YOUR OWN KIND OF RELA-TIONSHIP.
NOT EVERYONE IS THE SAME.
CAN YOU BELIEVE THIS?
I NEVER THOUGHT ABOUT...
...WHETHER WE WOULD HAVE A LONG-DISTANCE RELATIONSHIP OR BREAK UP.

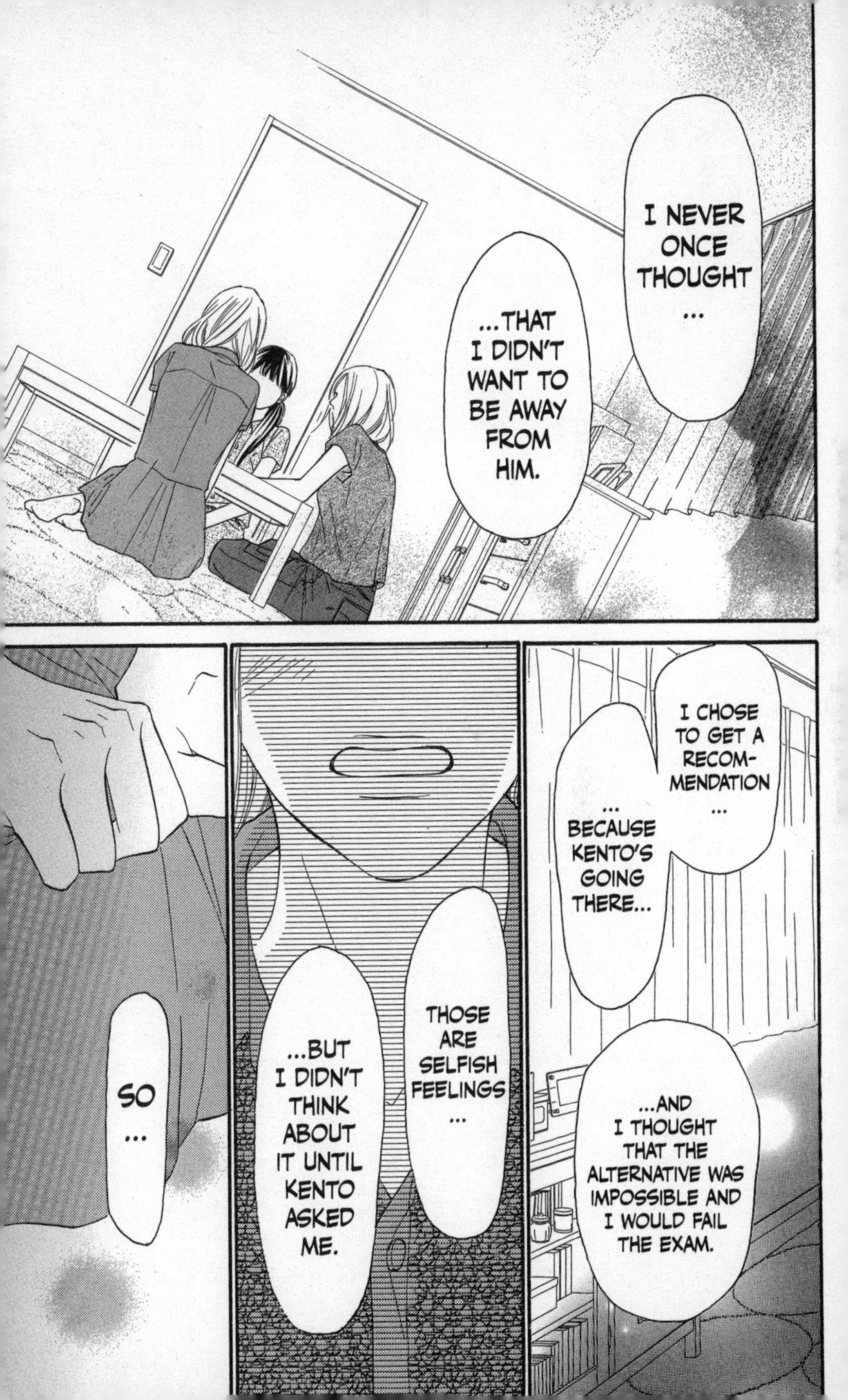
I NEVER ONCE THOUGHT...
...THAT I DIDN'T WANT TO BE AWAY FROM HIM.
I CHOSE TO GET A RECOM-MENDATION...
...BECAUSE KENTO'S GOING THERE...
...AND I THOUGHT THAT THE ALTERNATIVE WAS IMPOSSIBLE AND I WOULD FAIL THE EXAM.
THOSE ARE SELFISH FEELINGS...
...BUT I DIDN'T THINK ABOUT IT UNTIL KENTO ASKED ME.
SO...

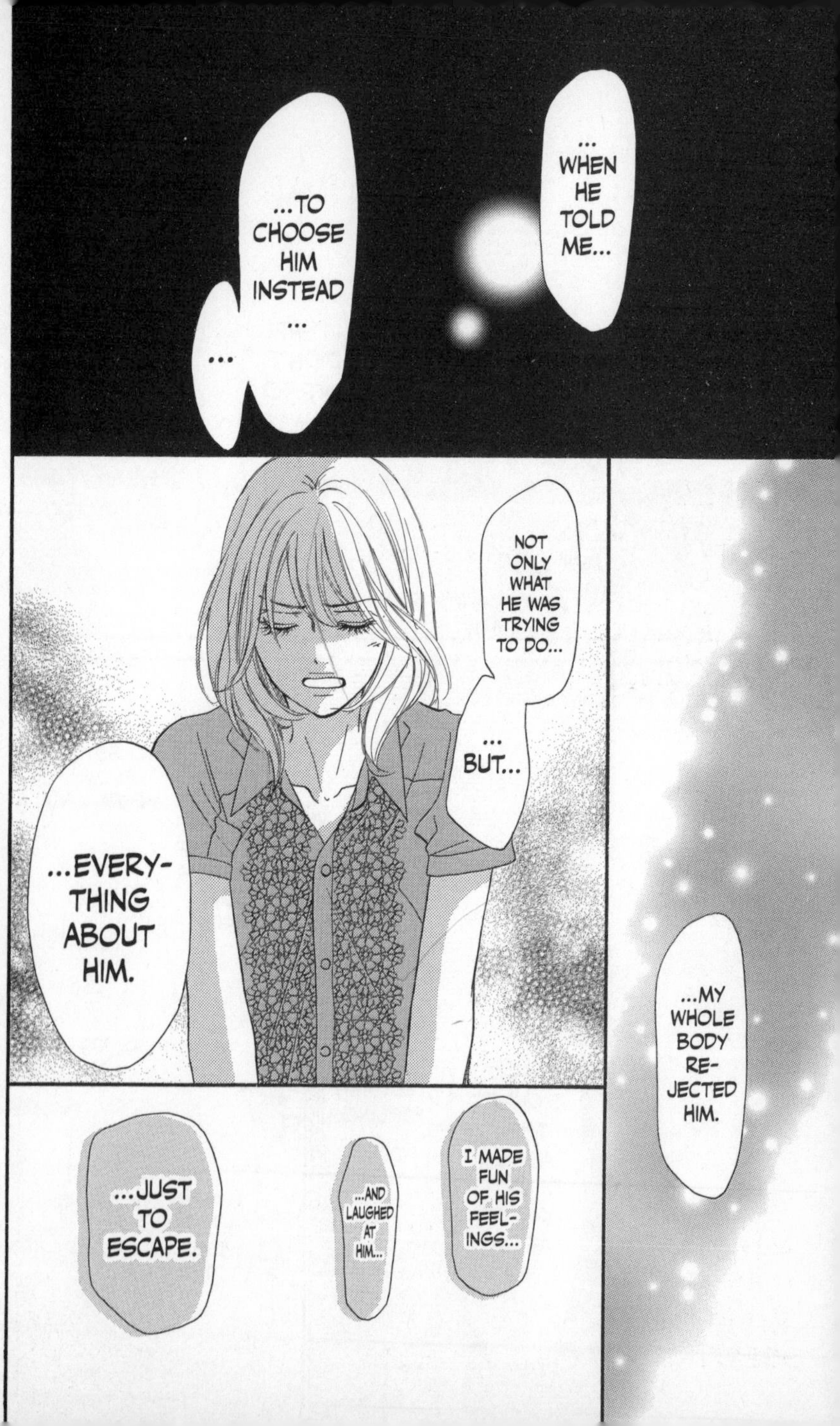

... WHEN HE TOLD ME...
...TO CHOOSE HIM INSTEAD ...
...
...MY WHOLE BODY RE-JECTED HIM.
NOT ONLY WHAT HE WAS TRYING TO DO...
... BUT...
...EVERY-THING ABOUT HIM.
I MADE FUN OF HIS FEEL-INGS...
...AND LAUGHED AT HIM...
...JUST TO ESCAPE.

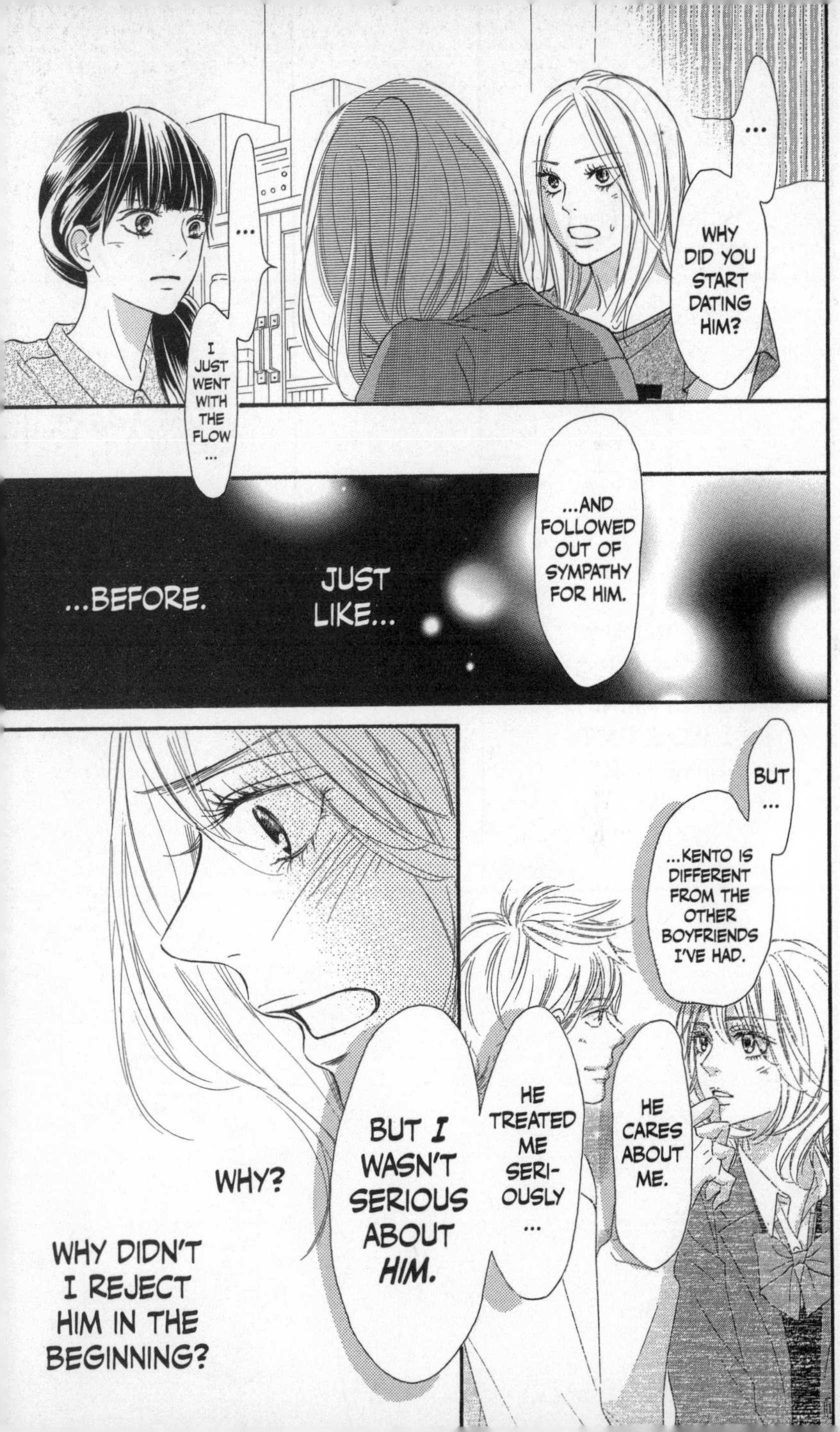
...
WHY DID YOU START DATING HIM?
...
I JUST WENT WITH THE FLOW...
...AND FOLLOWED OUT OF SYMPATHY FOR HIM.
JUST LIKE...
...BEFORE.
BUT...
...KENTO IS DIFFERENT FROM THE OTHER BOYFRIENDS I'VE HAD.
HE CARES ABOUT ME.
HE TREATED ME SERIOUSLY...
BUT *I* WASN'T SERIOUS ABOUT *HIM.*
WHY?
WHY DIDN'T I REJECT HIM IN THE BEGINNING?

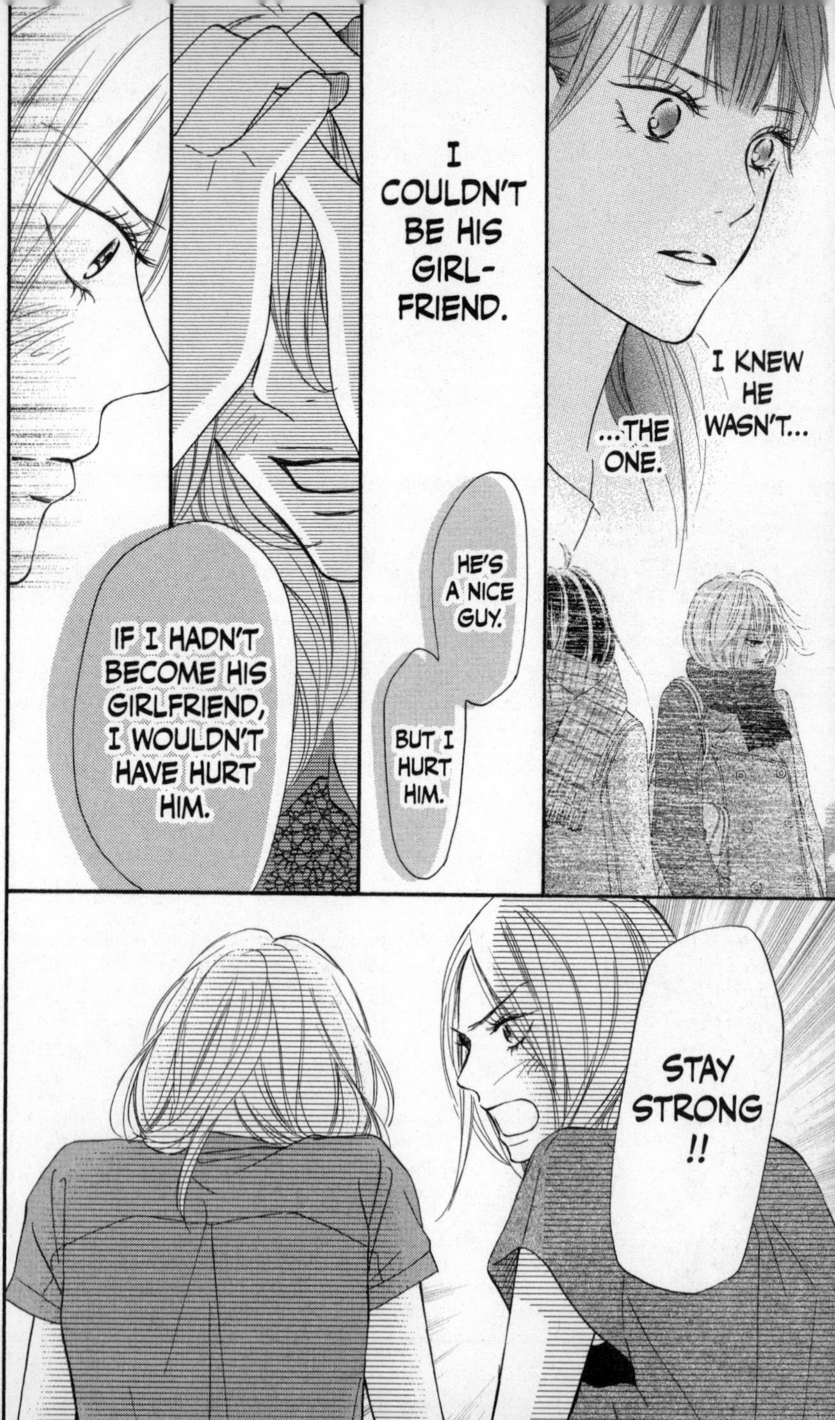
I KNEW HE WASN'T...
...THE ONE.
I COULDN'T BE HIS GIRL-FRIEND.
HE'S A NICE GUY.
BUT I HURT HIM.
IF I HADN'T BECOME HIS GIRLFRIEND, I WOULDN'T HAVE HURT HIM.
STAY STRONG!!

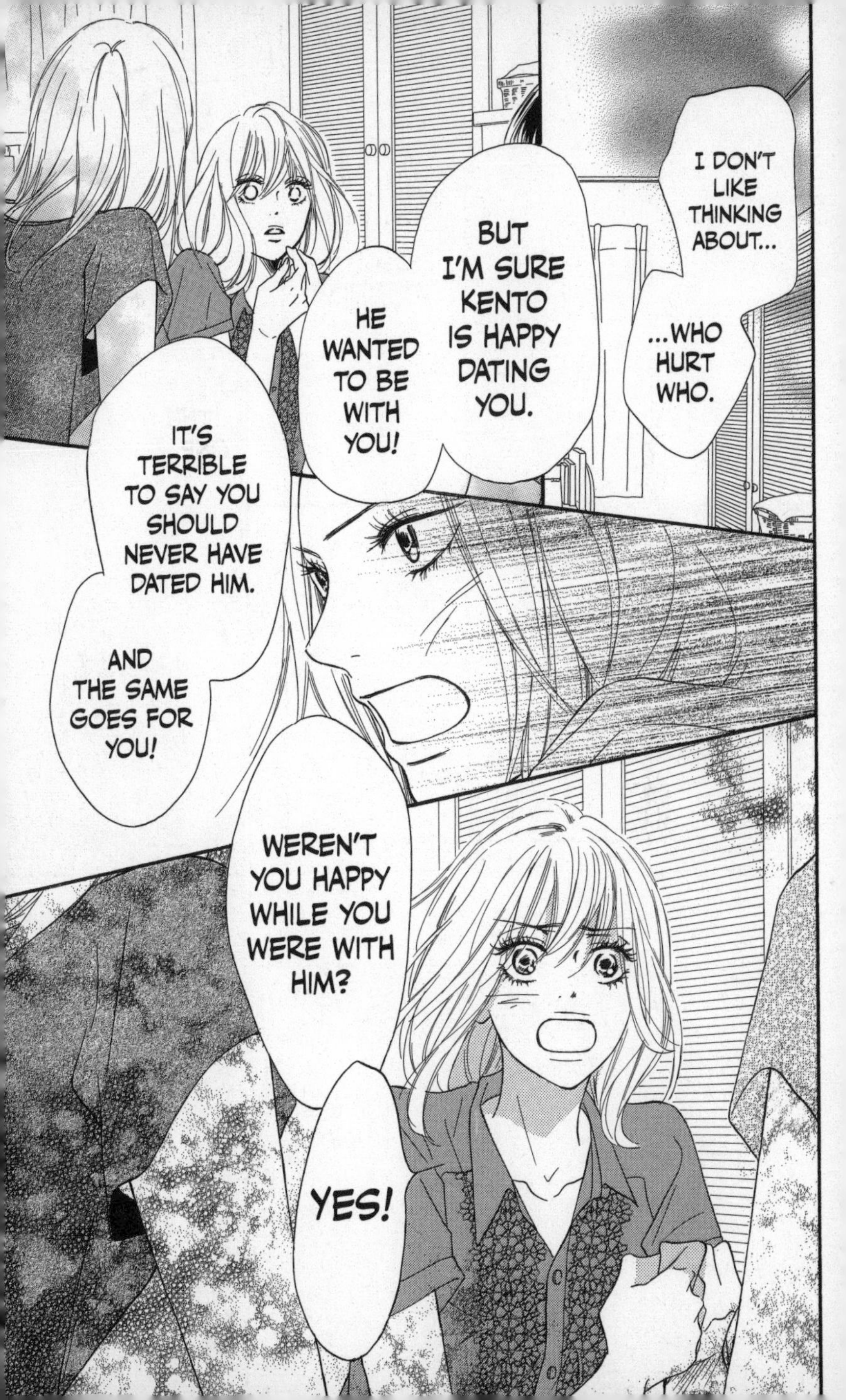
I DON'T LIKE THINKING ABOUT...
...WHO HURT WHO.
BUT I'M SURE KENTO IS HAPPY DATING YOU.
HE WANTED TO BE WITH YOU!
IT'S TERRIBLE TO SAY YOU SHOULD NEVER HAVE DATED HIM.
AND THE SAME GOES FOR YOU!
WEREN'T YOU HAPPY WHILE YOU WERE WITH HIM?
YES!

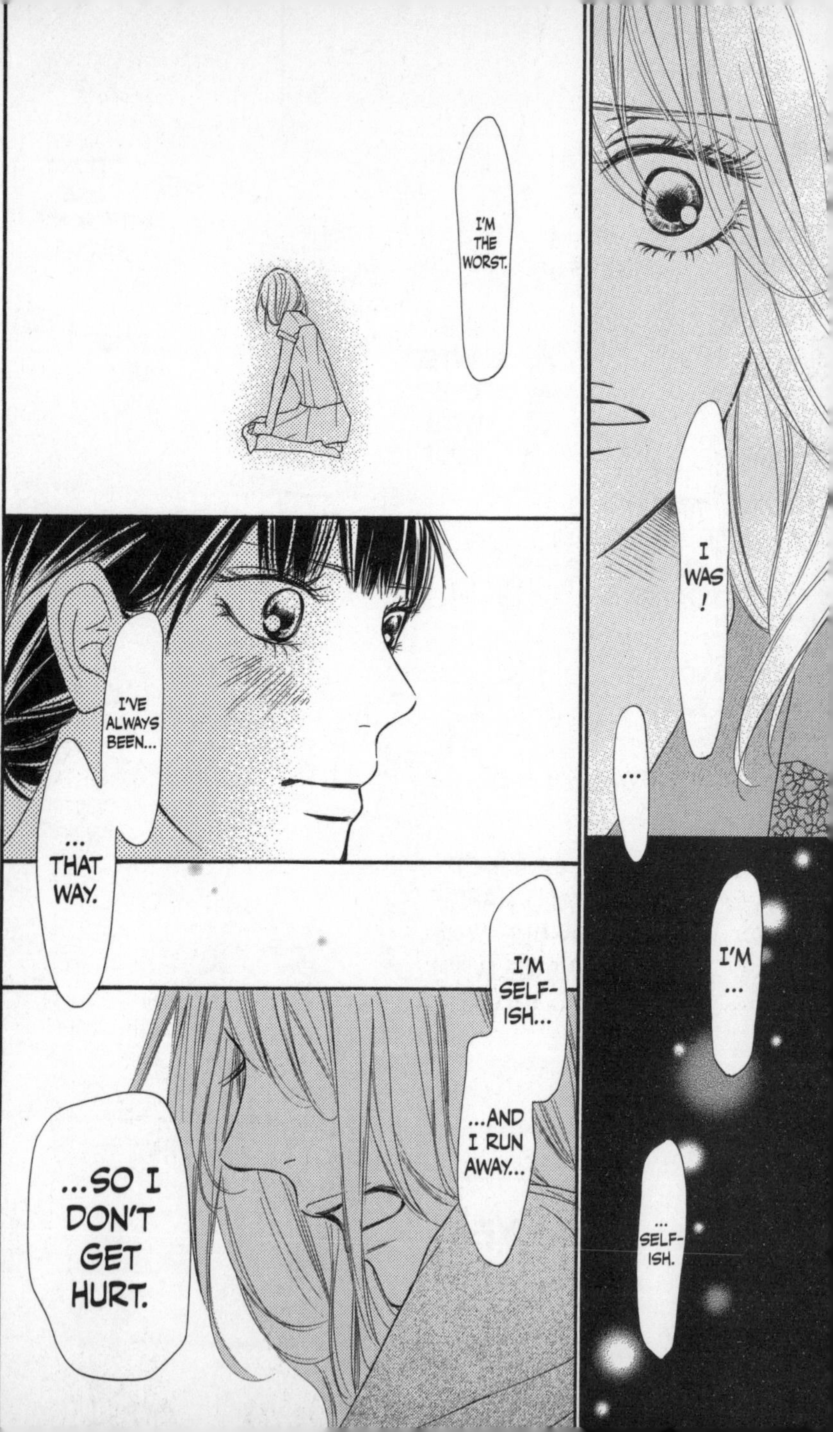
I WAS!
...
I'M ...
... SELF-ISH.
I'M THE WORST.
I'VE ALWAYS BEEN...
... THAT WAY.
I'M SELF-ISH...
...AND I RUN AWAY...
...SO I DON'T GET HURT.

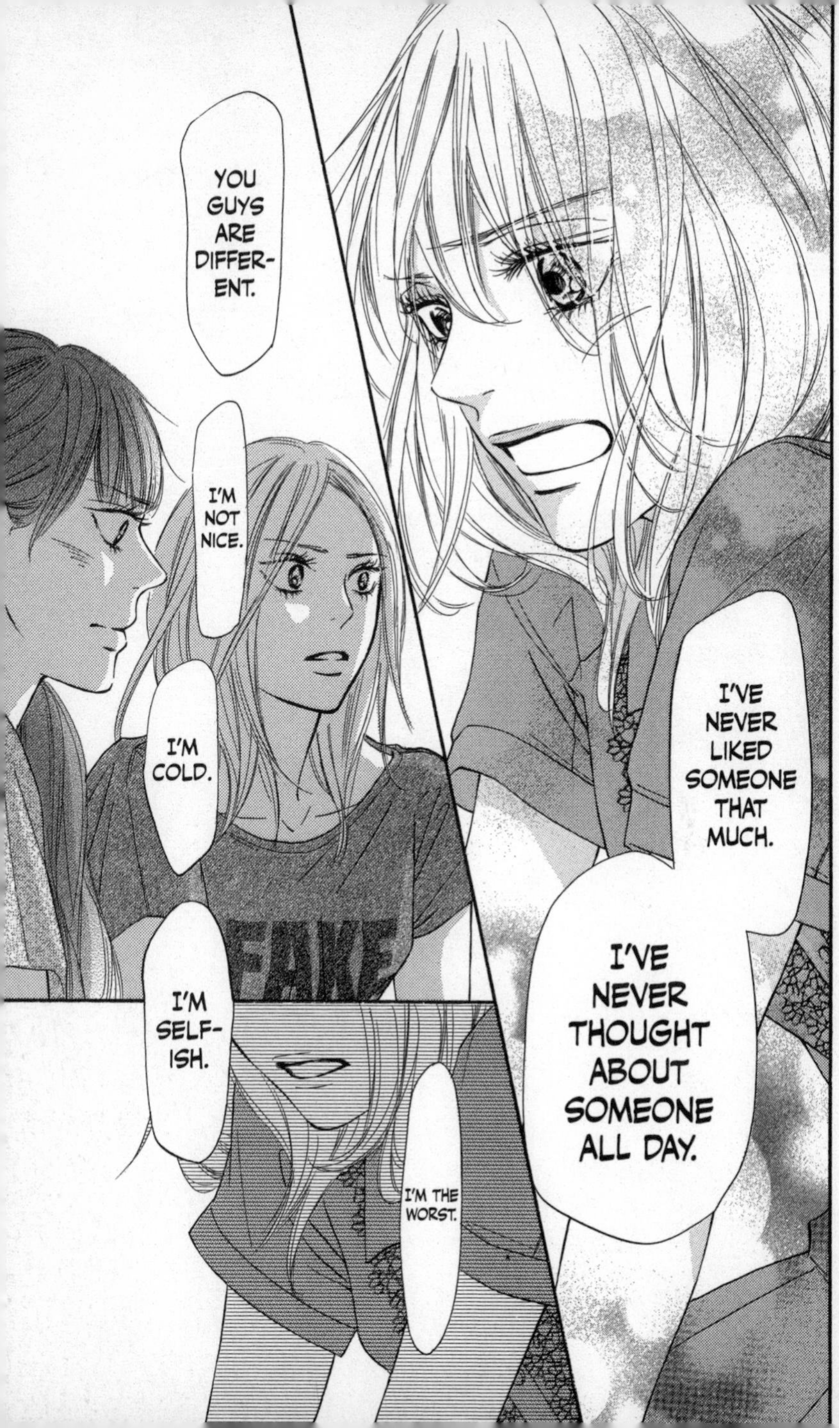
I'VE NEVER LIKED SOMEONE THAT MUCH.
I'VE NEVER THOUGHT ABOUT SOMEONE ALL DAY.
YOU GUYS ARE DIFFER-ENT.
I'M NOT NICE.
I'M COLD.
FAKE
I'M SELF-ISH.
I'M THE WORST.

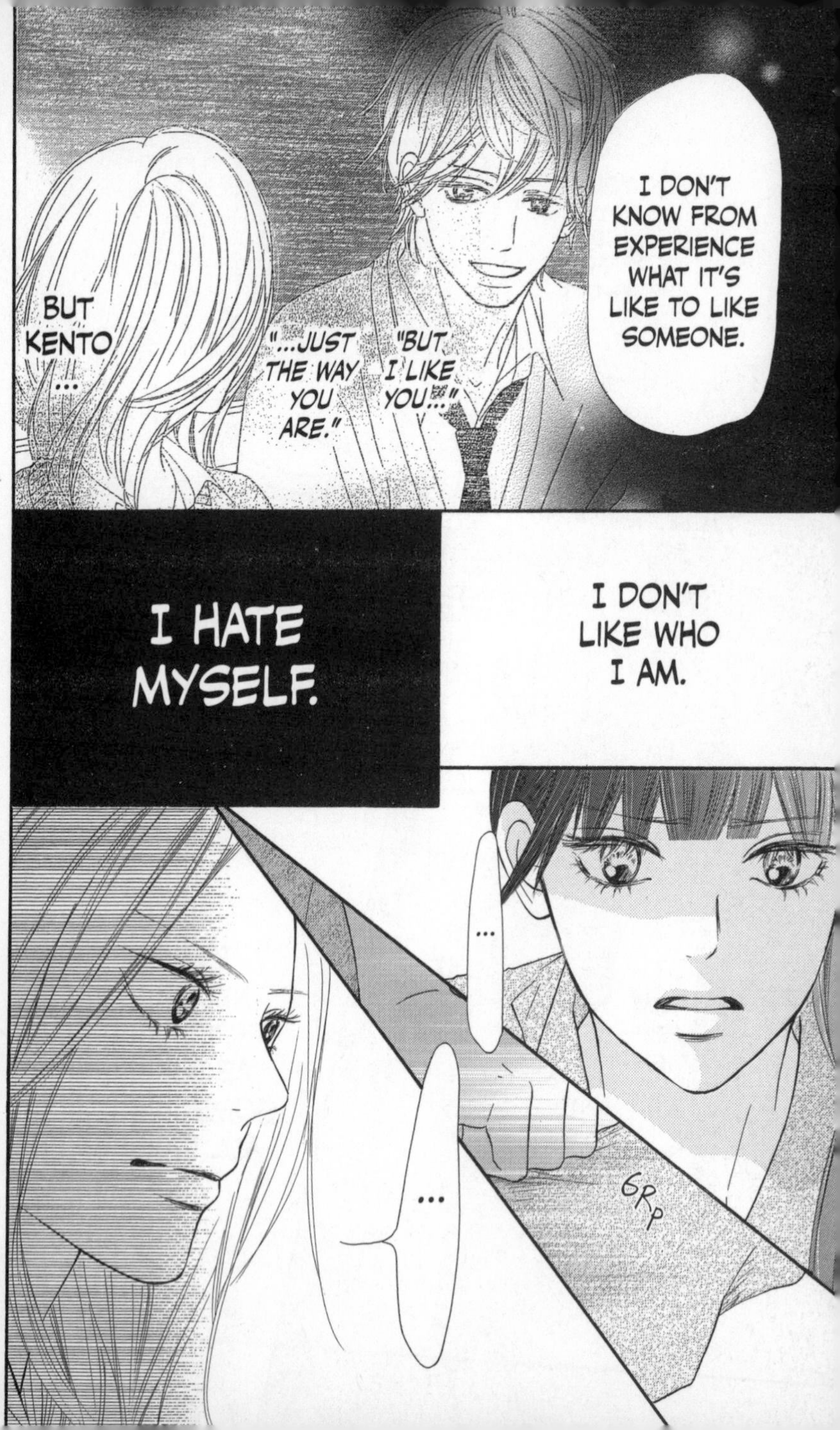
I DON'T KNOW FROM EXPERIENCE WHAT IT'S LIKE TO LIKE SOMEONE.
"BUT I LIKE YOU..."
"...JUST THE WAY YOU ARE."
BUT KENTO...
I DON'T LIKE WHO I AM.
I HATE MYSELF.
...
GRP
...

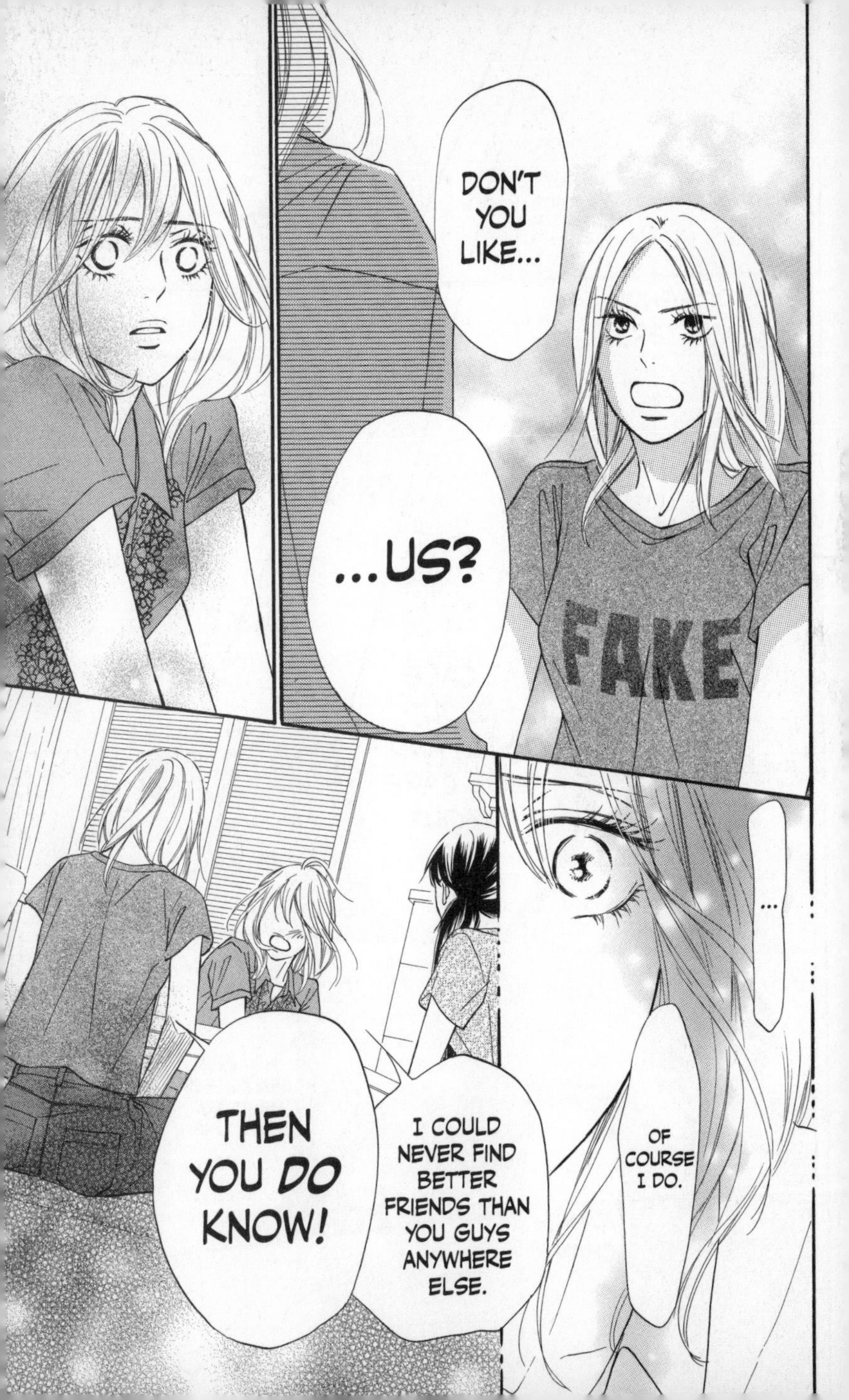
DON'T YOU LIKE...
...US?
...
OF COURSE I DO.
I COULD NEVER FIND BETTER FRIENDS THAN YOU GUYS ANYWHERE ELSE.
THEN YOU *DO* KNOW!
FAKE

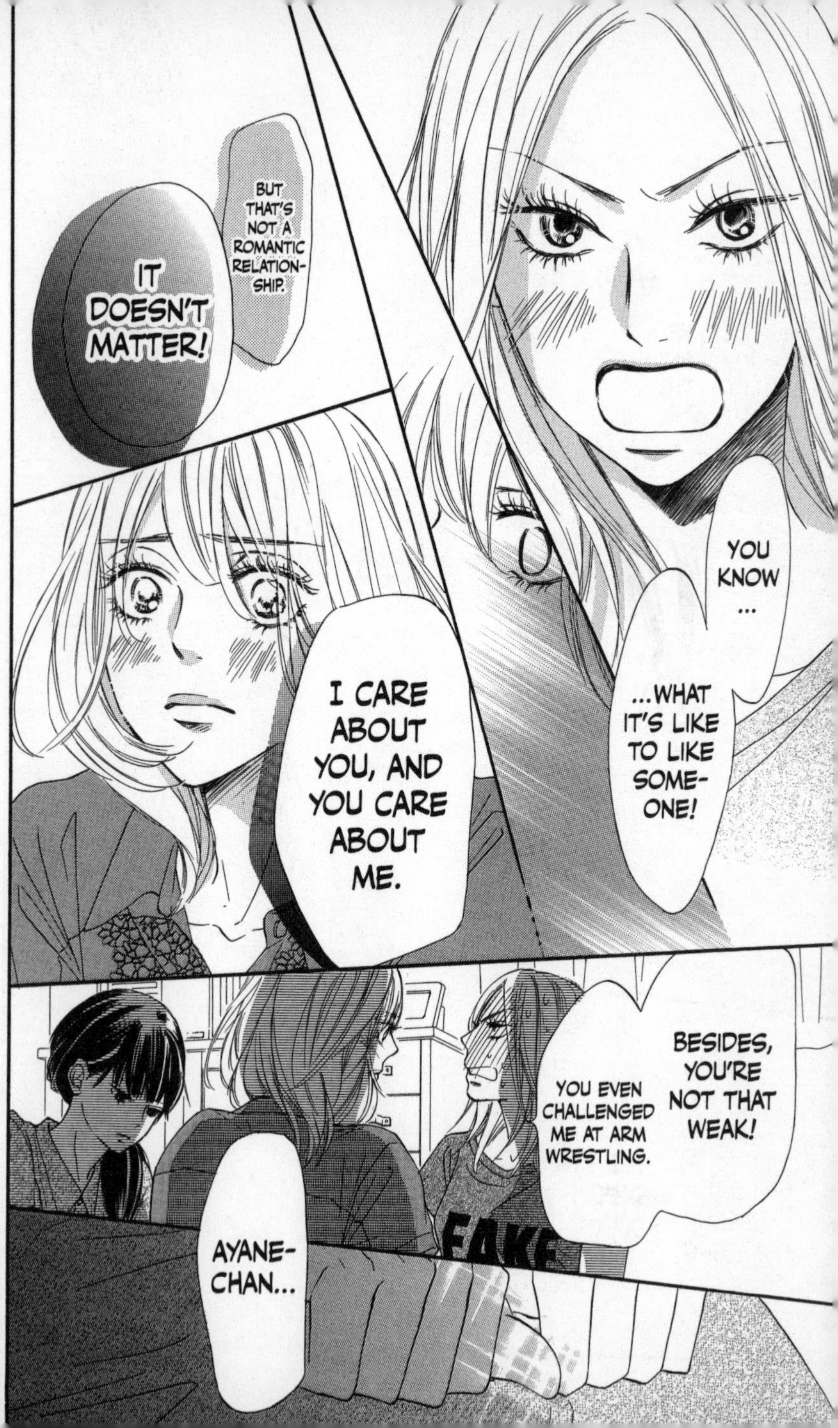
BUT THAT'S NOT A ROMANTIC RELATION-SHIP.
IT DOESN'T MATTER!
YOU KNOW...
...WHAT IT'S LIKE TO LIKE SOME-ONE!
I CARE ABOUT YOU, AND YOU CARE ABOUT ME.
BESIDES, YOU'RE NOT THAT WEAK!
YOU EVEN CHALLENGED ME AT ARM WRESTLING.
FAKE
AYANE-CHAN...

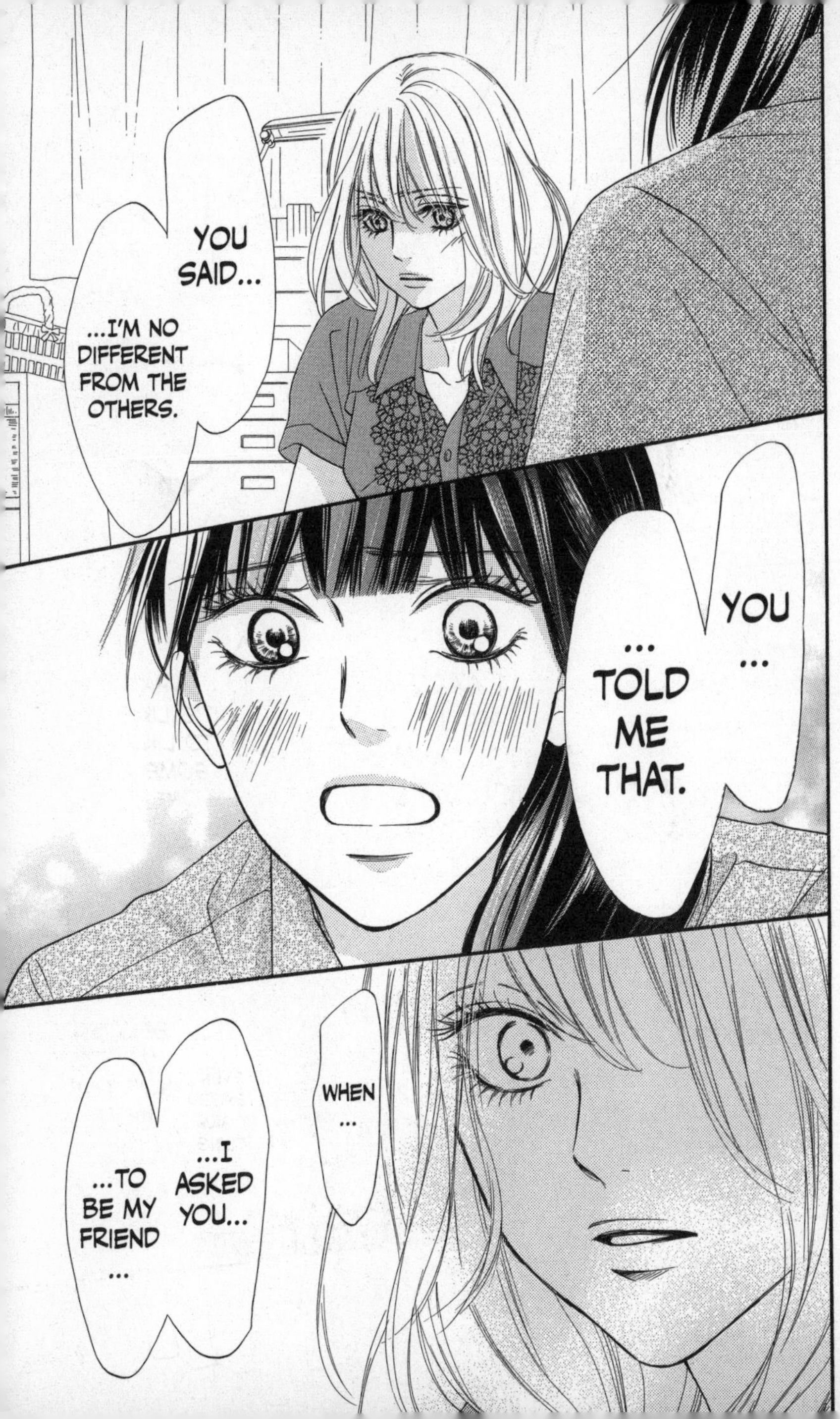
YOU SAID...
...I'M NO DIFFERENT FROM THE OTHERS.
YOU ... ... TOLD ME THAT.
WHEN ...
...I ASKED YOU...
...TO BE MY FRIEND ...

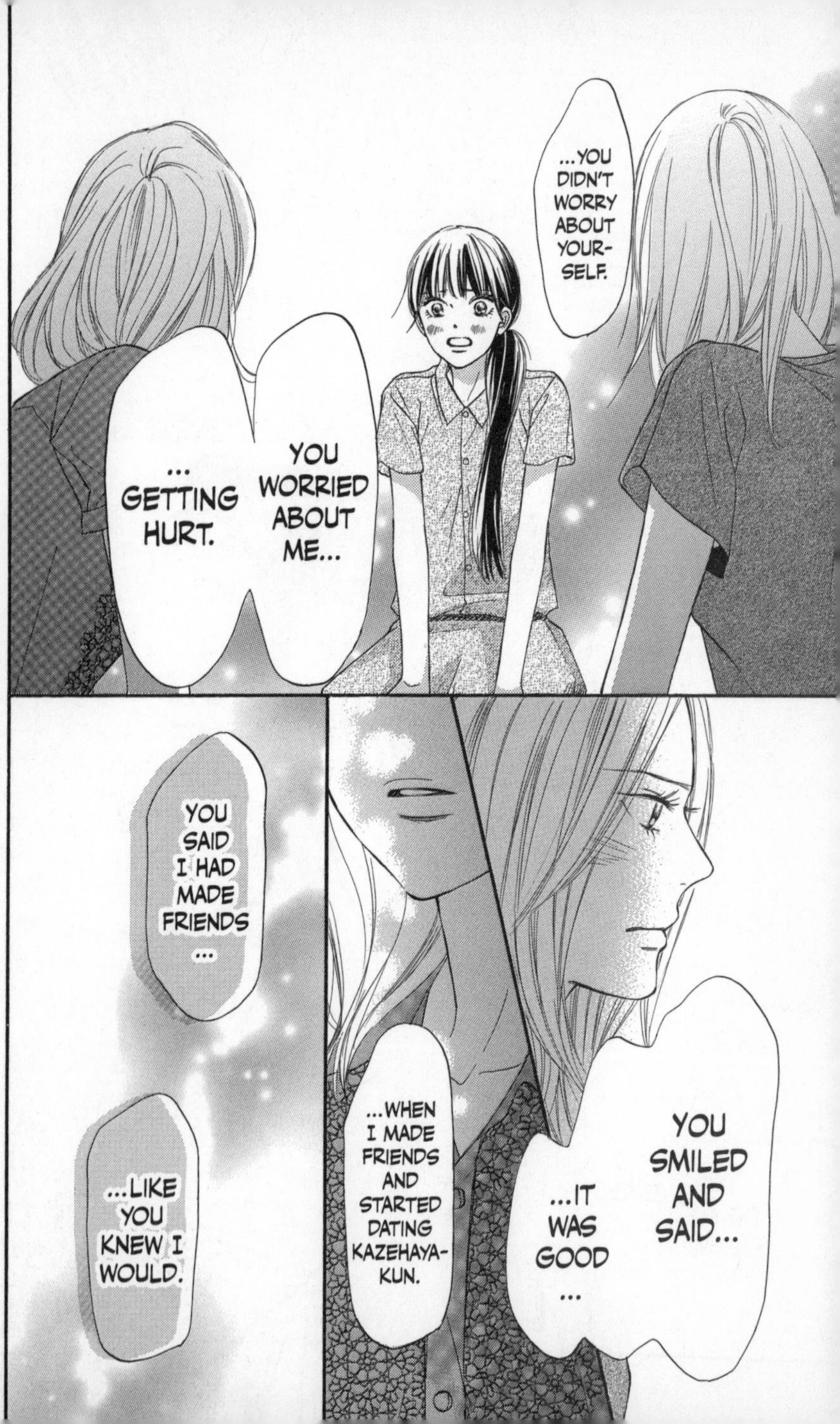
...YOU DIDN'T WORRY ABOUT YOUR-SELF.
YOU WORRIED ABOUT ME...
...GETTING HURT.
YOU SMILED AND SAID...
...IT WAS GOOD...
...WHEN I MADE FRIENDS AND STARTED DATING KAZEHAYA-KUN.
YOU SAID I HAD MADE FRIENDS...
...LIKE YOU KNEW I WOULD.

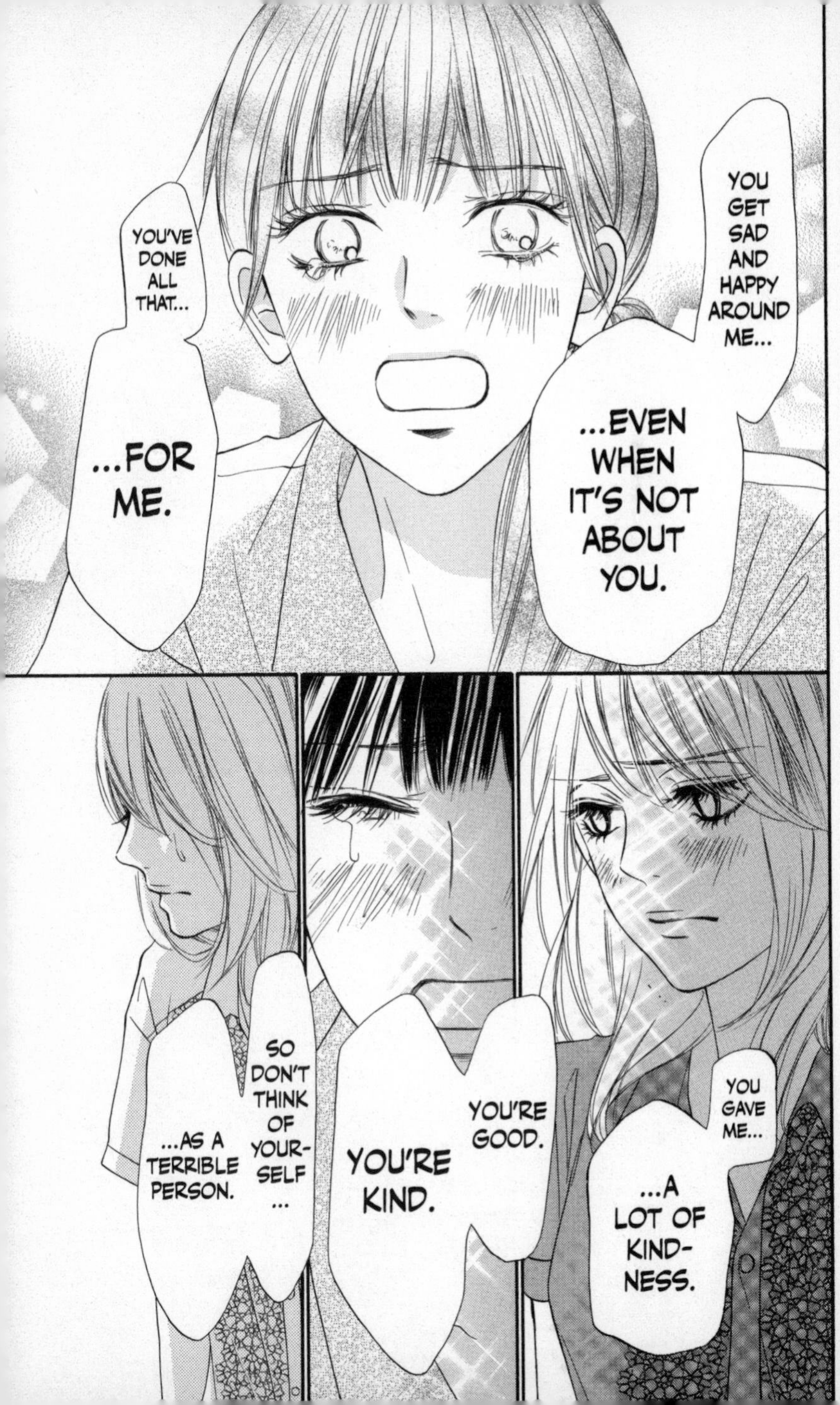
YOU GET SAD AND HAPPY AROUND ME...
...EVEN WHEN IT'S NOT ABOUT YOU.
YOU'VE DONE ALL THAT...
...FOR ME.
YOU GAVE ME...
...A LOT OF KIND-NESS.
YOU'RE GOOD.
YOU'RE KIND.
SO DON'T THINK OF YOUR-SELF ...
...AS A TERRIBLE PERSON.

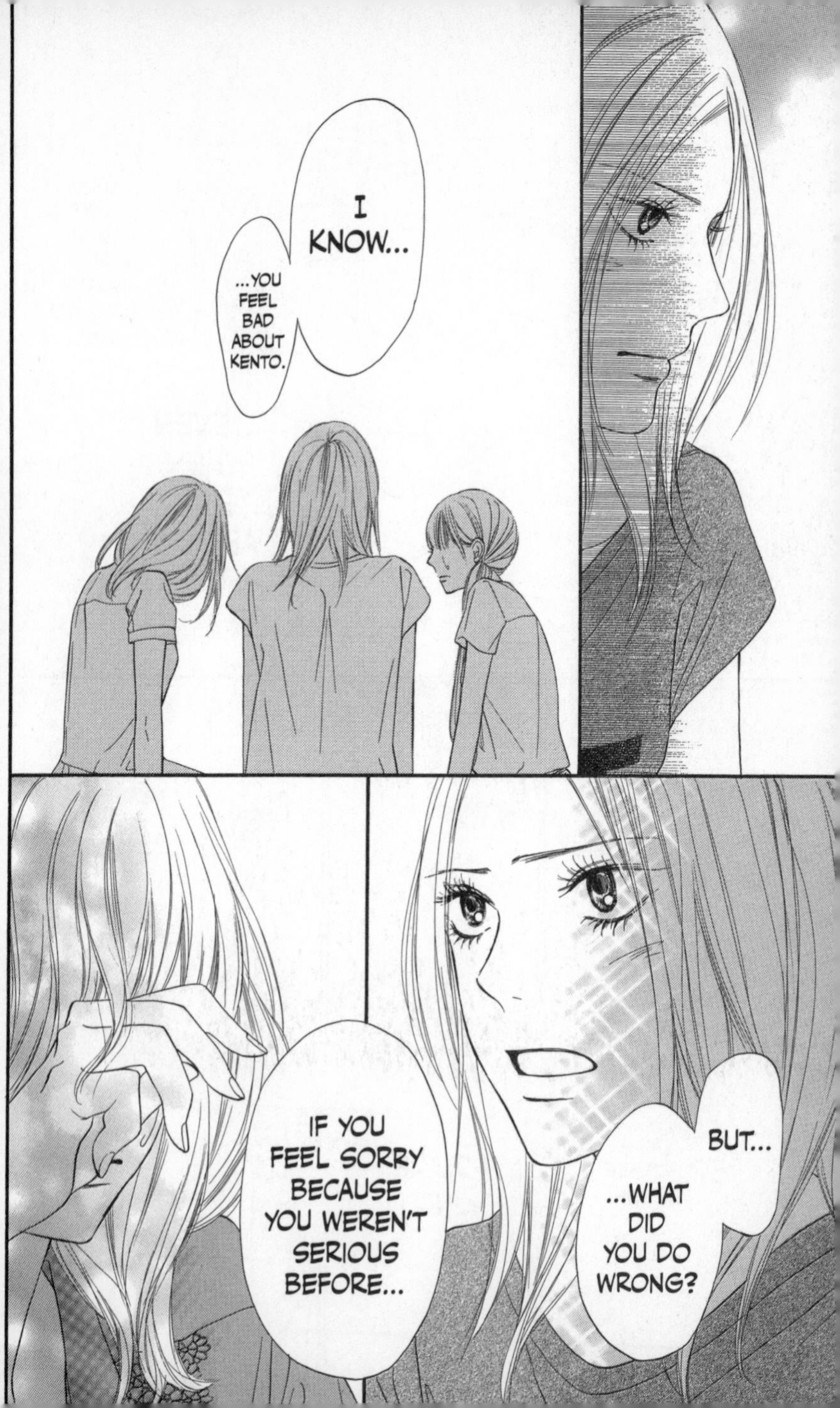
I KNOW...
...YOU FEEL BAD ABOUT KENTO.
IF YOU FEEL SORRY BECAUSE YOU WEREN'T SERIOUS BEFORE...
BUT...
...WHAT DID YOU DO WRONG?

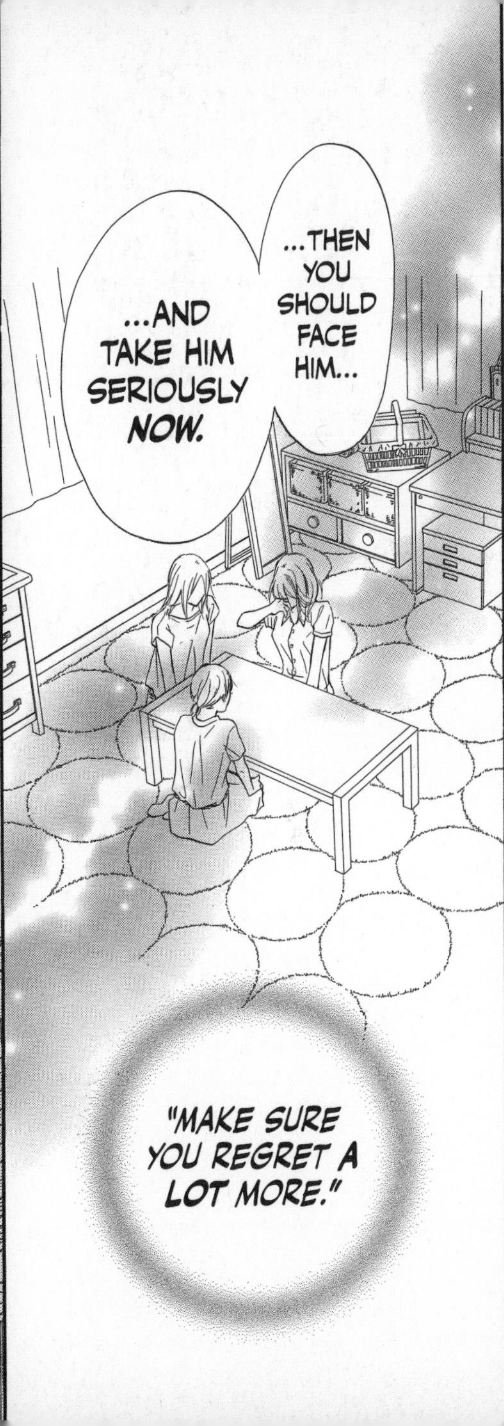
...THEN YOU SHOULD FACE HIM...
...AND TAKE HIM SERIOUSLY NOW.
"MAKE SURE YOU REGRET A LOT MORE."

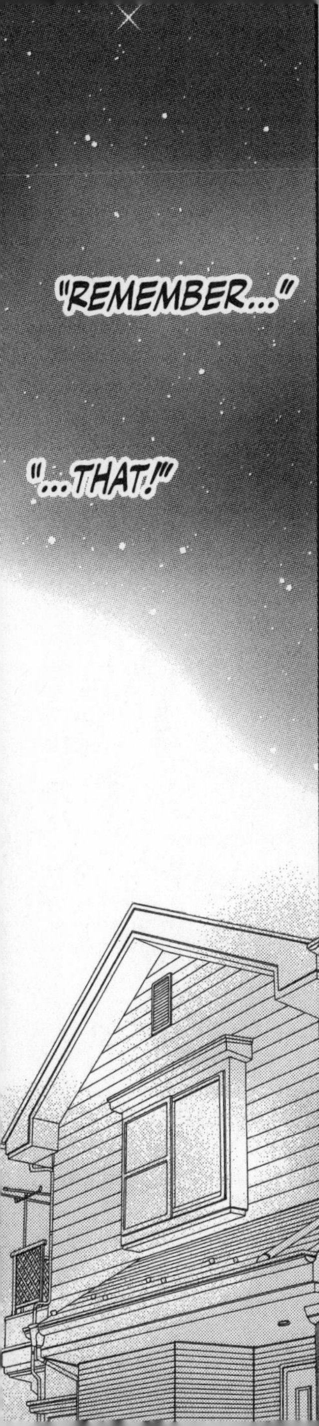
"REMEMBER..."
"...THAT!"

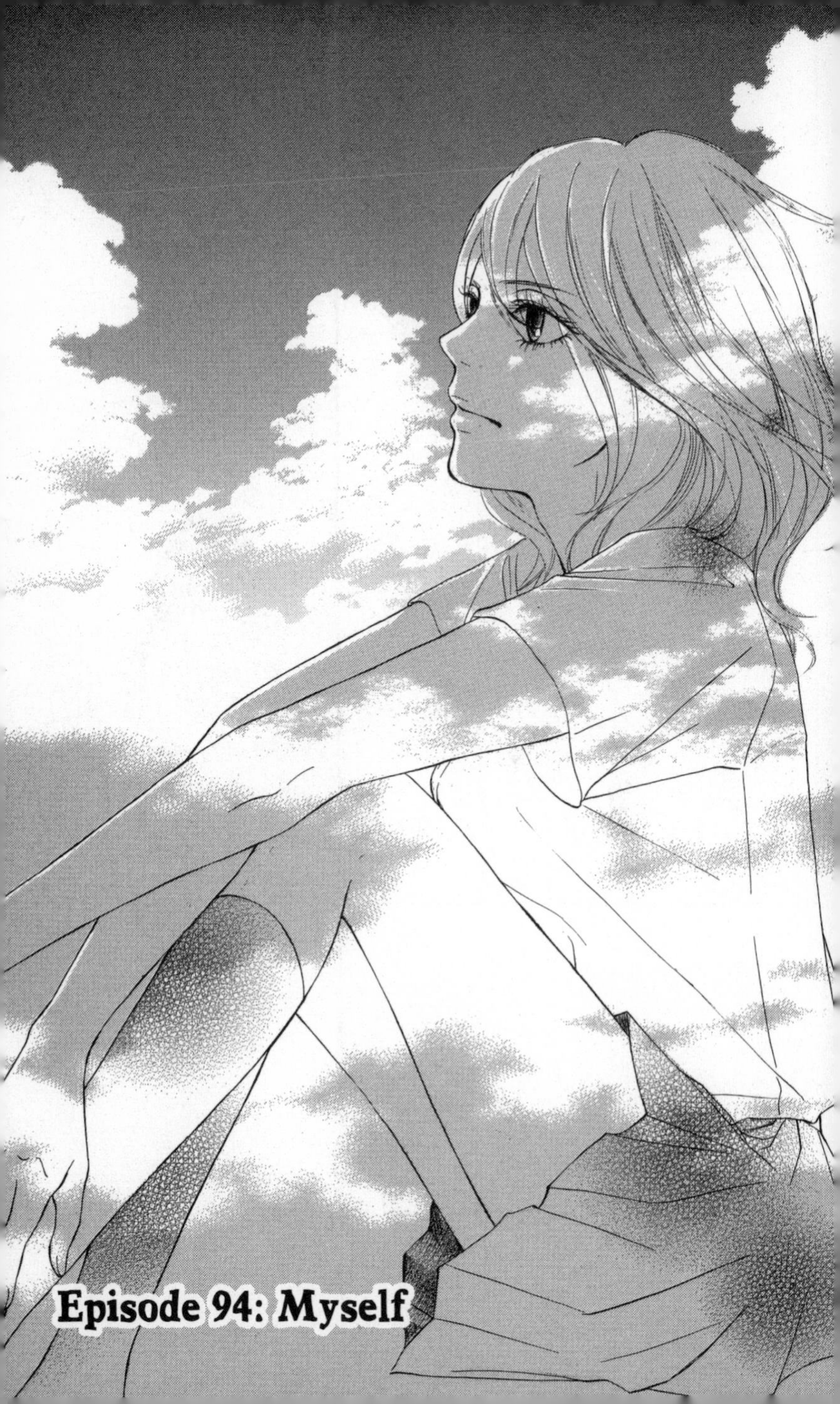
Episode 94: Myself

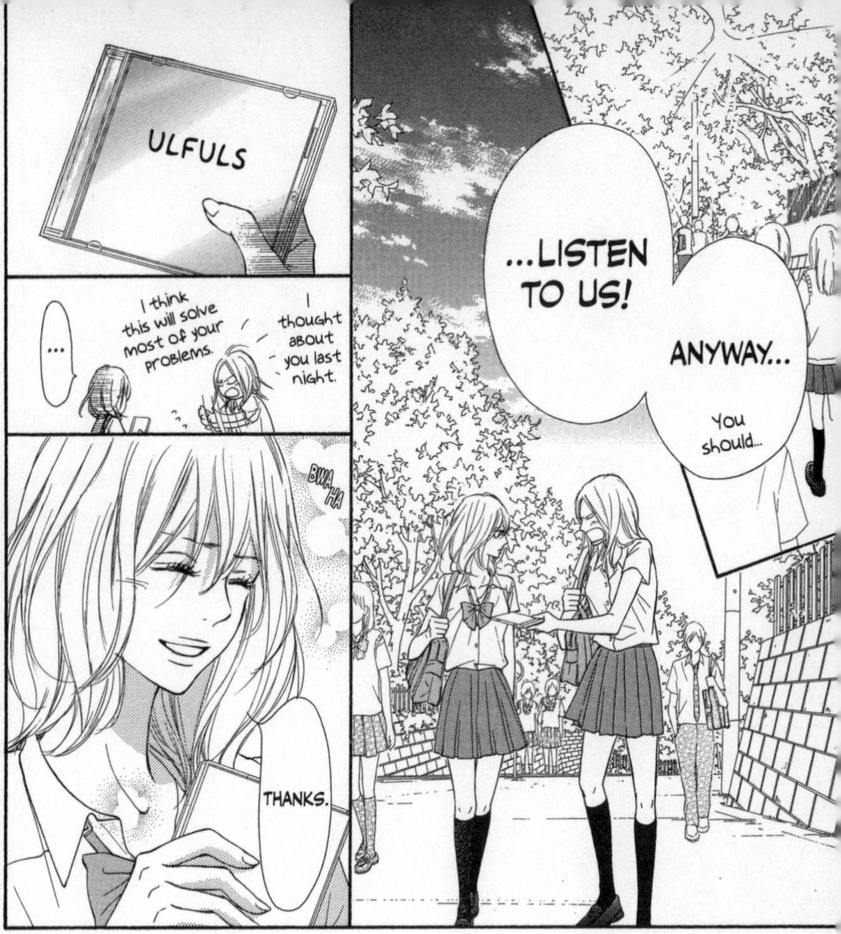
ANYWAY...
You should...
...LISTEN TO US!
ULFULS
I thought about you last night.
I think this will solve most of your problems.
...
BWAHA
THANKS.

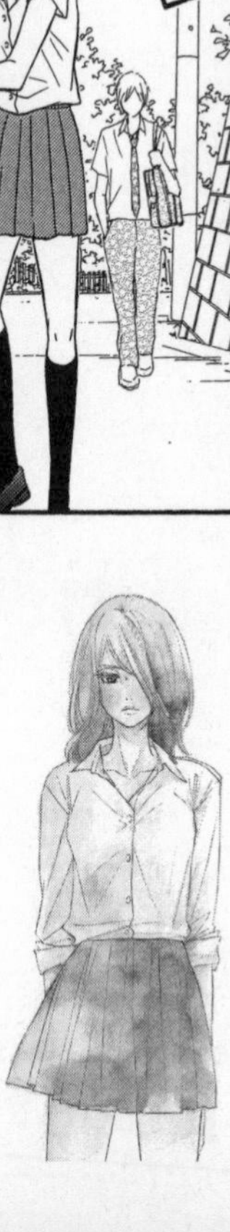

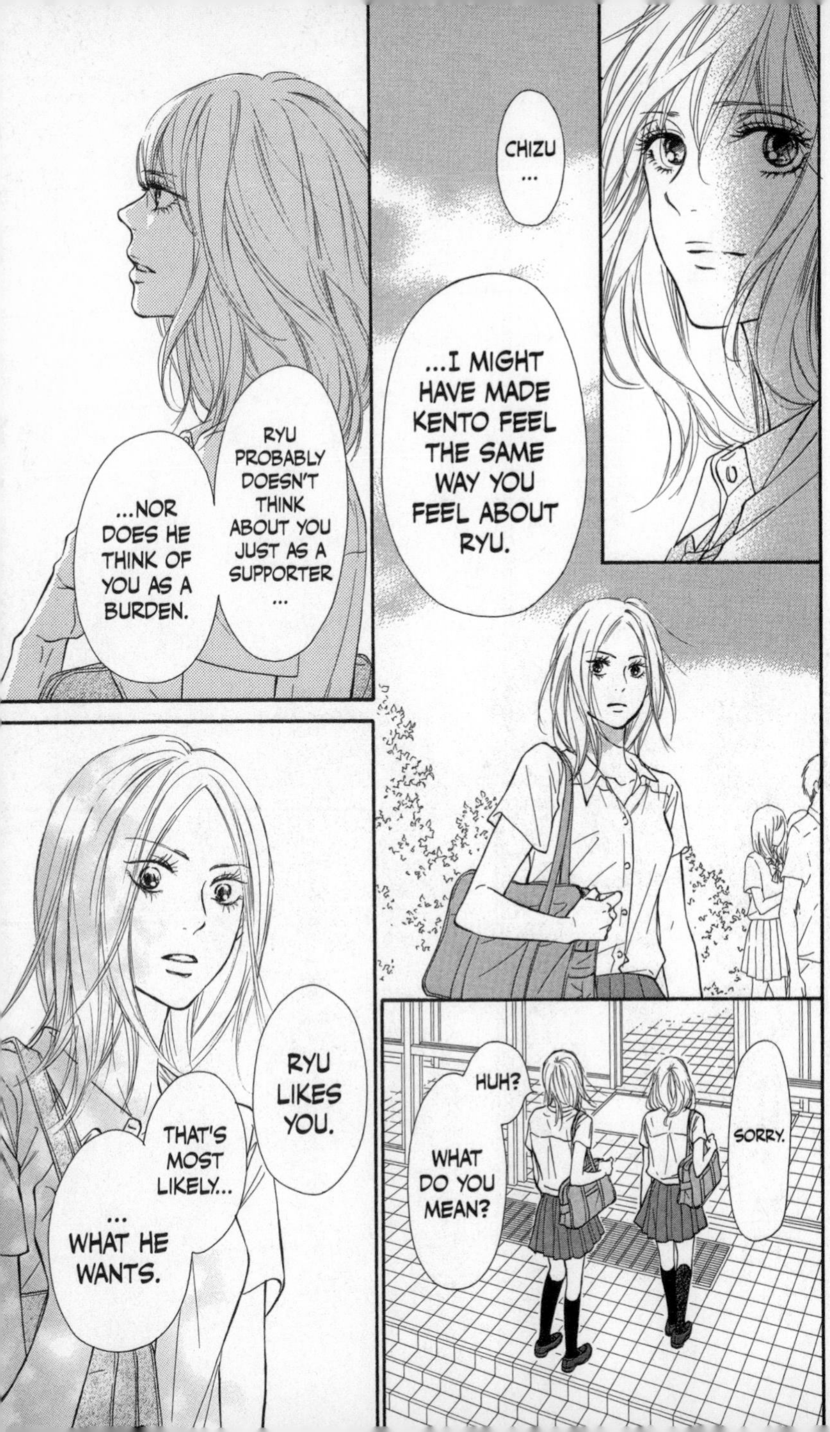
CHIZU ...
...I MIGHT HAVE MADE KENTO FEEL THE SAME WAY YOU FEEL ABOUT RYU.
RYU PROBABLY DOESN'T THINK ABOUT YOU JUST AS A SUPPORTER ...
...NOR DOES HE THINK OF YOU AS A BURDEN.
SORRY.
HUH?
WHAT DO YOU MEAN?
RYU LIKES YOU.
THAT'S MOST LIKELY...
... WHAT HE WANTS.

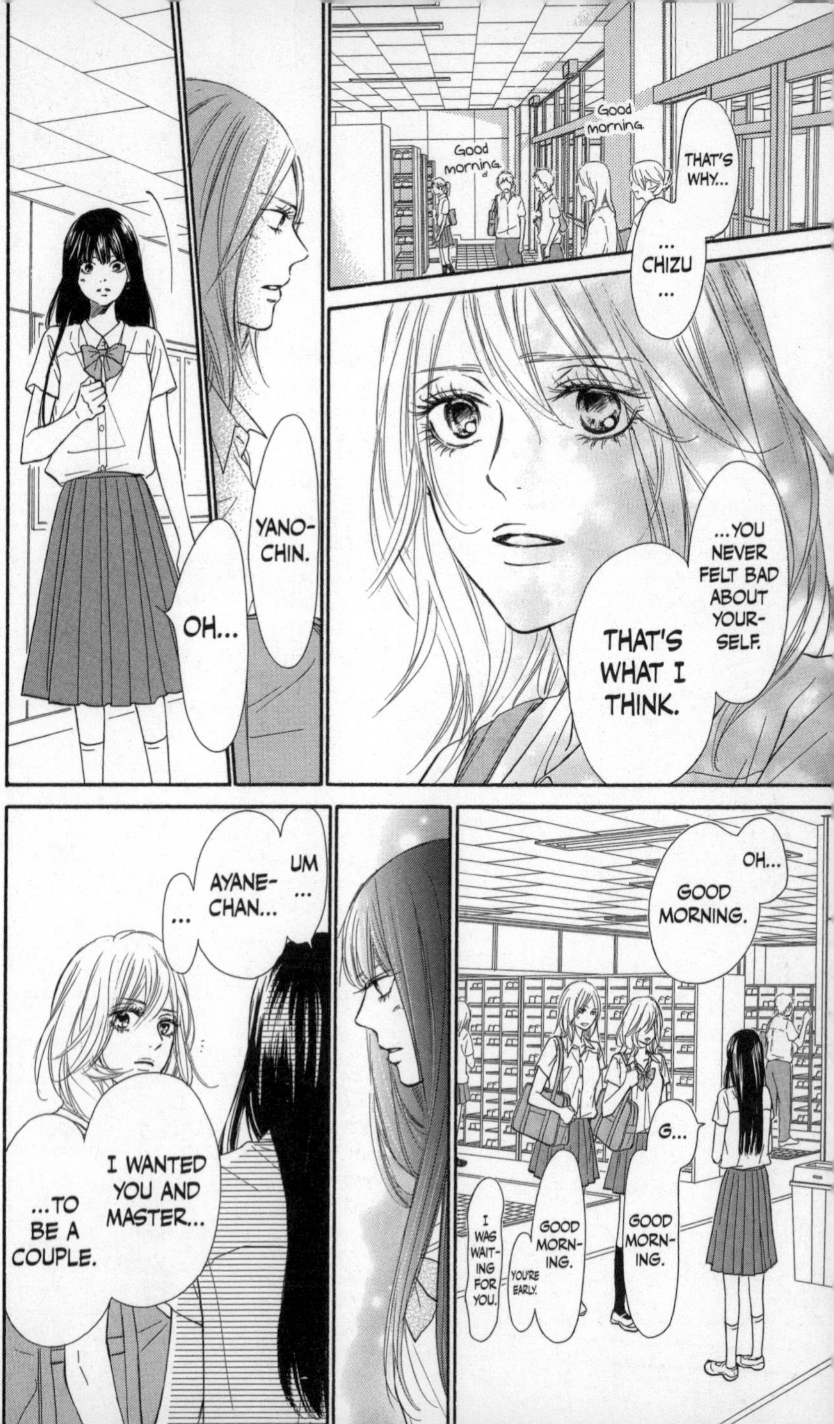
Good morning.
Good morning.
THAT'S WHY...
...CHIZU...
...YOU NEVER FELT BAD ABOUT YOURSELF.
THAT'S WHAT I THINK.
YANO-CHIN.
OH...
OH... GOOD MORNING.
G...
GOOD MORNING.
GOOD MORNING.
YOU'RE EARLY.
I WAS WAITING FOR YOU.
UM...
AYANE-CHAN...
...
I WANTED YOU AND MASTER...
...TO BE A COUPLE.

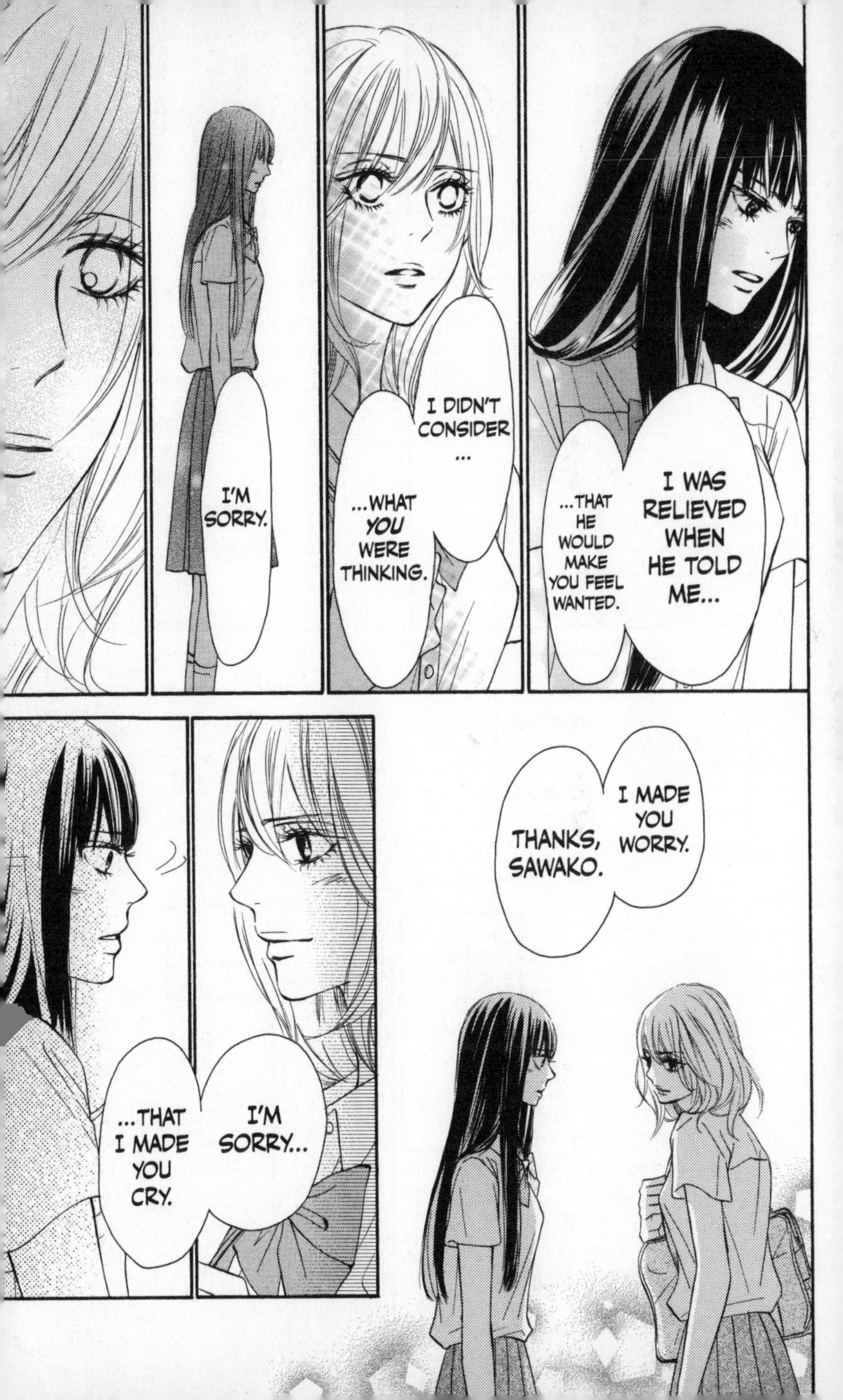
I WAS RELIEVED WHEN HE TOLD ME...
...THAT HE WOULD MAKE YOU FEEL WANTED.
I DIDN'T CONSIDER ...
...WHAT *YOU* WERE THINKING.
I'M SORRY.
I MADE YOU WORRY.
THANKS, SAWAKO.
I'M SORRY...
...THAT I MADE YOU CRY.

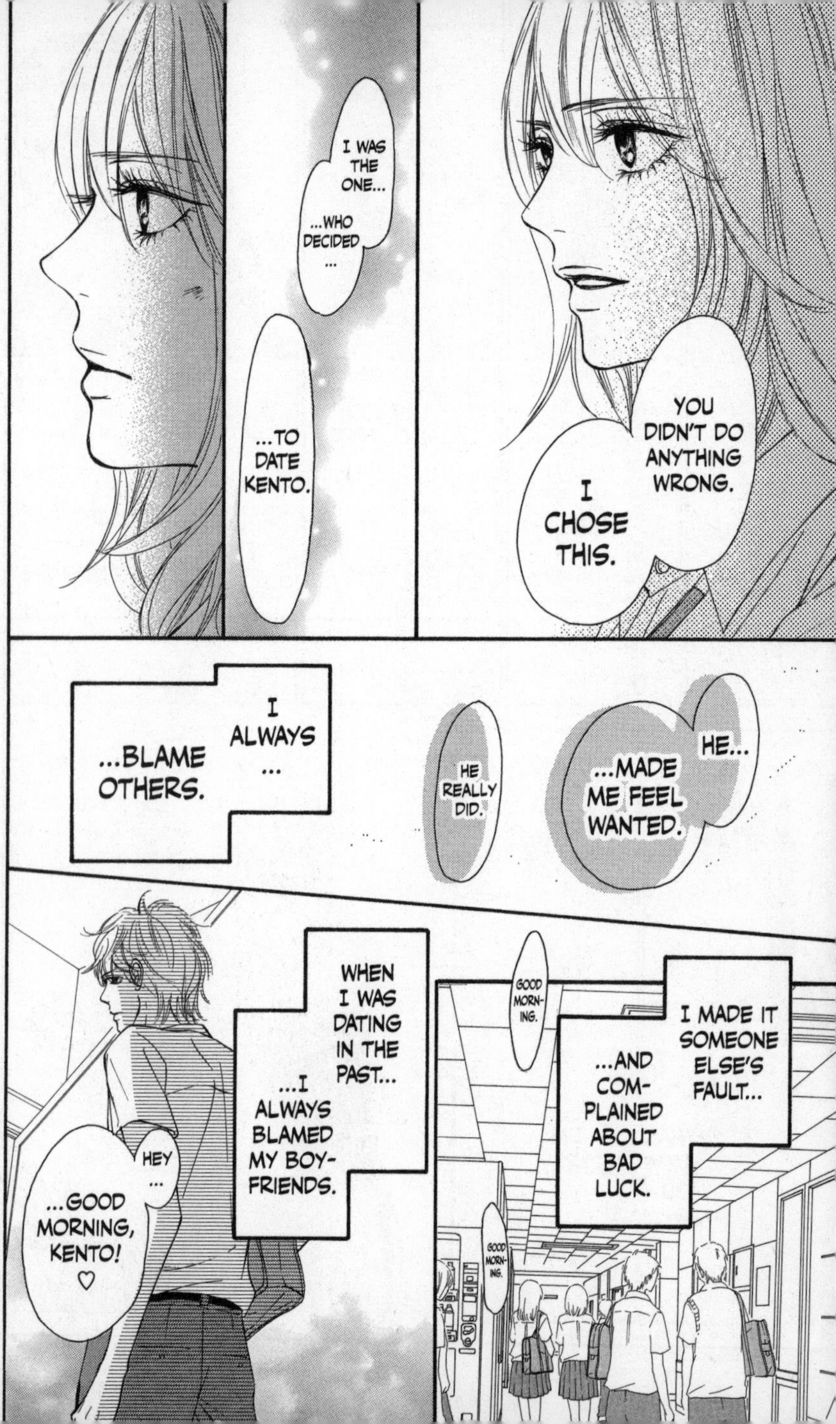
YOU DIDN'T DO ANYTHING WRONG.
I CHOSE THIS.
I WAS THE ONE...
...WHO DECIDED ...
...TO DATE KENTO.
HE...
...MADE ME FEEL WANTED.
HE REALLY DID.
I ALWAYS ...
...BLAME OTHERS.
I MADE IT SOMEONE ELSE'S FAULT...
...AND COM-PLAINED ABOUT BAD LUCK.
GOOD MORN-ING.
GOOD MORN-ING.
WHEN I WAS DATING IN THE PAST...
...I ALWAYS BLAMED MY BOY-FRIENDS.
HEY ...
...GOOD MORNING, KENTO! ♡

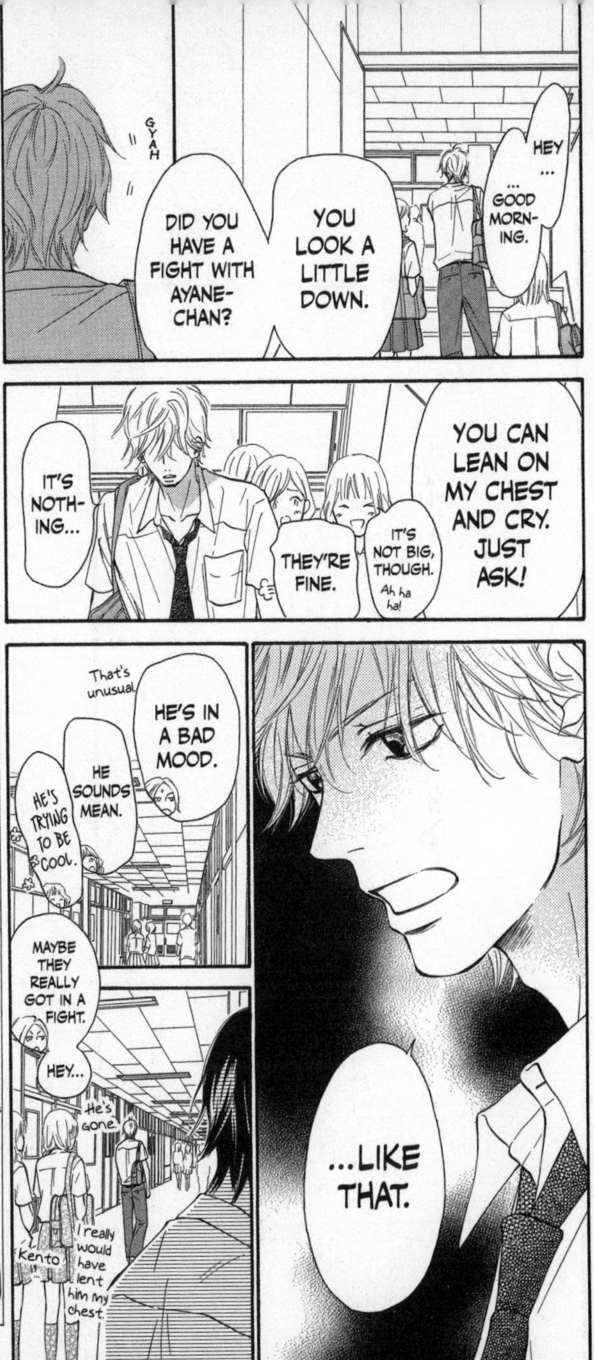
HEY ... ...GOOD MORNING.
YOU LOOK A LITTLE DOWN.
DID YOU HAVE A FIGHT WITH AYANE-CHAN?
GYAH
YOU CAN LEAN ON MY CHEST AND CRY. JUST ASK!
IT'S NOT BIG, THOUGH.
Ah ha ha!
THEY'RE FINE.
IT'S NOTHING...
...LIKE THAT.
HE'S IN A BAD MOOD.
That's unusual.
HE SOUNDS MEAN.
HE'S TRYING TO BE COOL.
MAYBE THEY REALLY GOT IN A FIGHT.
HEY...
He's Gone.
I really would have lent him my chest.
Kento...

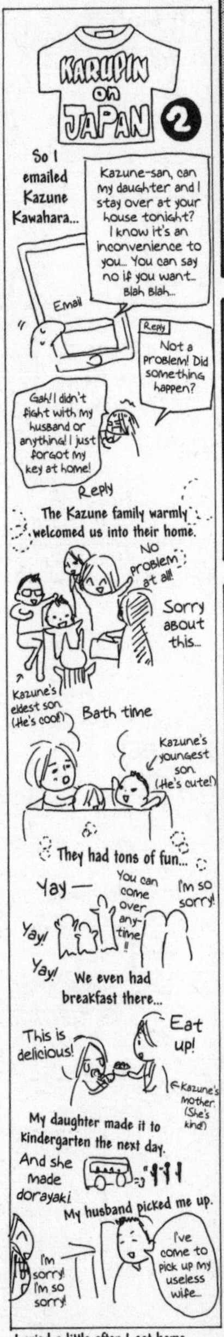
KARUPIN on JAPAN 2
So I emailed Kazune Kawahara...
Kazune-san, can my daughter and I stay over at your house tonight? I know it's an inconvenience to you... You can say no if you want... Blah Blah...
Email
Reply
Not a problem! Did something happen?
Gah! I didn't fight with my husband or anything! I just forgot my key at home!
Reply
The Kazune family warmly welcomed us into their home.
No problem at all!
Sorry about this...
Kazune's eldest son. (He's cool!)
Bath time
Kazune's youngest son. (He's cute!)
They had tons of fun...
Yay —
Yay!
Yay!
You can come over any-time!
I'm so sorry!
We even had breakfast there...
This is delicious!
Eat up!
Kazune's mother. (She's kind!)
My daughter made it to kindergarten the next day.
And she made dorayaki.
My husband picked me up.
I'm sorry! I'm so sorry!
I've come to pick up my useless wife...

I cried a little after I got home. Sorry, everyone...and thank you!

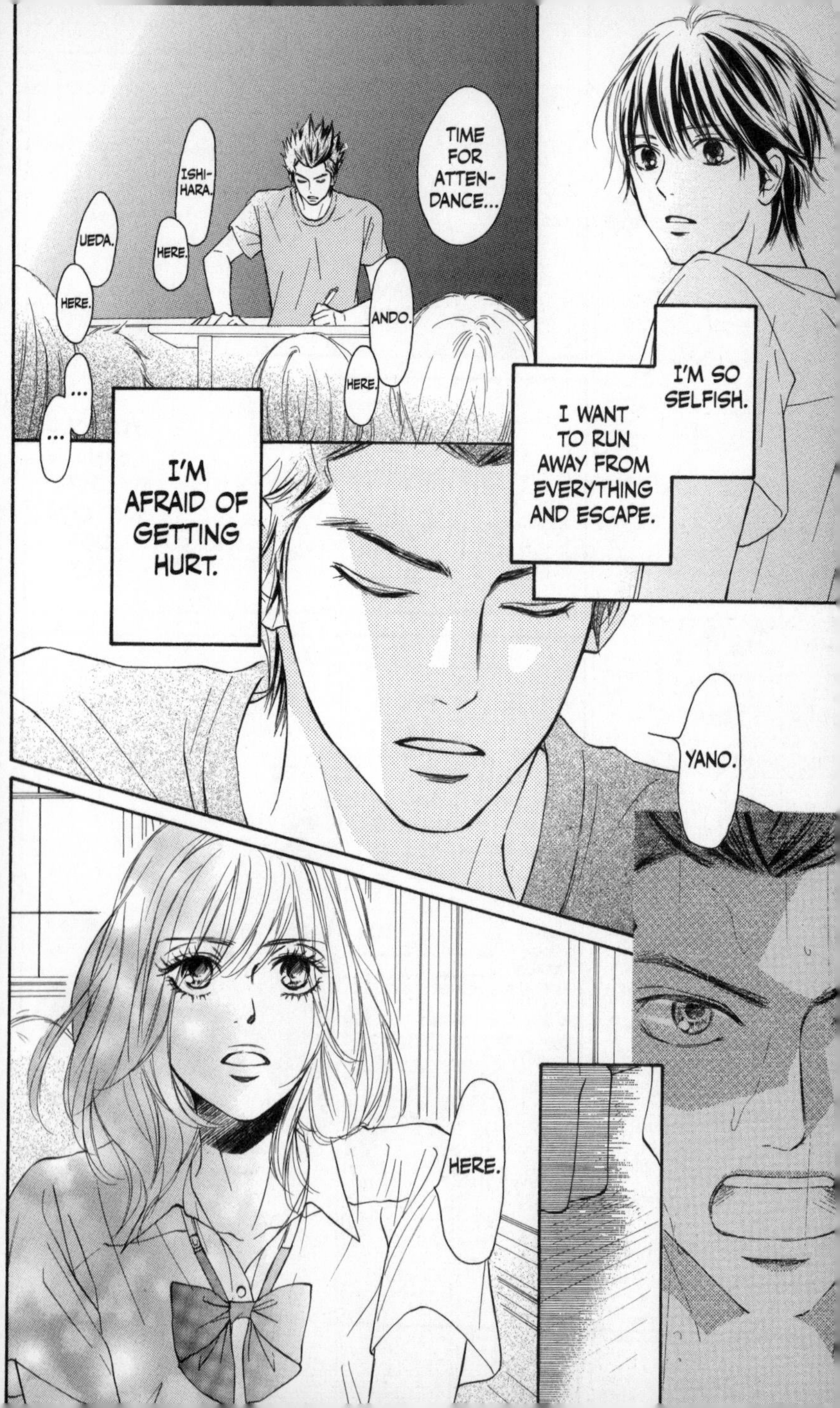
I'M SO SELFISH.
I WANT TO RUN AWAY FROM EVERYTHING AND ESCAPE.
TIME FOR ATTEN-DANCE...
ANDO.
HERE.
ISHI-HARA.
HERE.
UEDA.
HERE.
...
...
I'M AFRAID OF GETTING HURT.
YANO.
HERE.

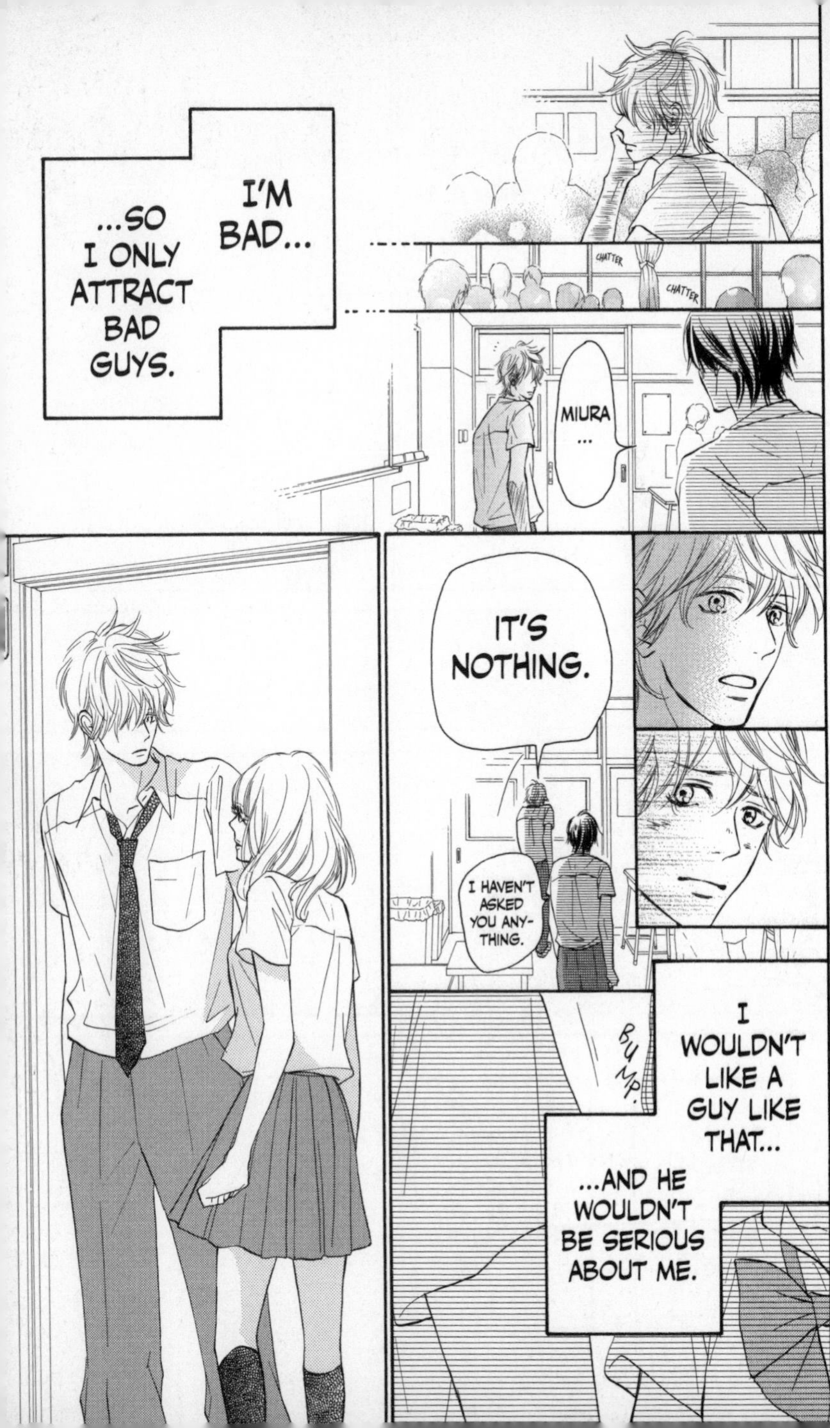
CHATTER
CHATTER
MIURA ...
I'M BAD...
...SO I ONLY ATTRACT BAD GUYS.
IT'S NOTHING.
I HAVEN'T ASKED YOU ANY-THING.
BUMP
I WOULDN'T LIKE A GUY LIKE THAT...
...AND HE WOULDN'T BE SERIOUS ABOUT ME.

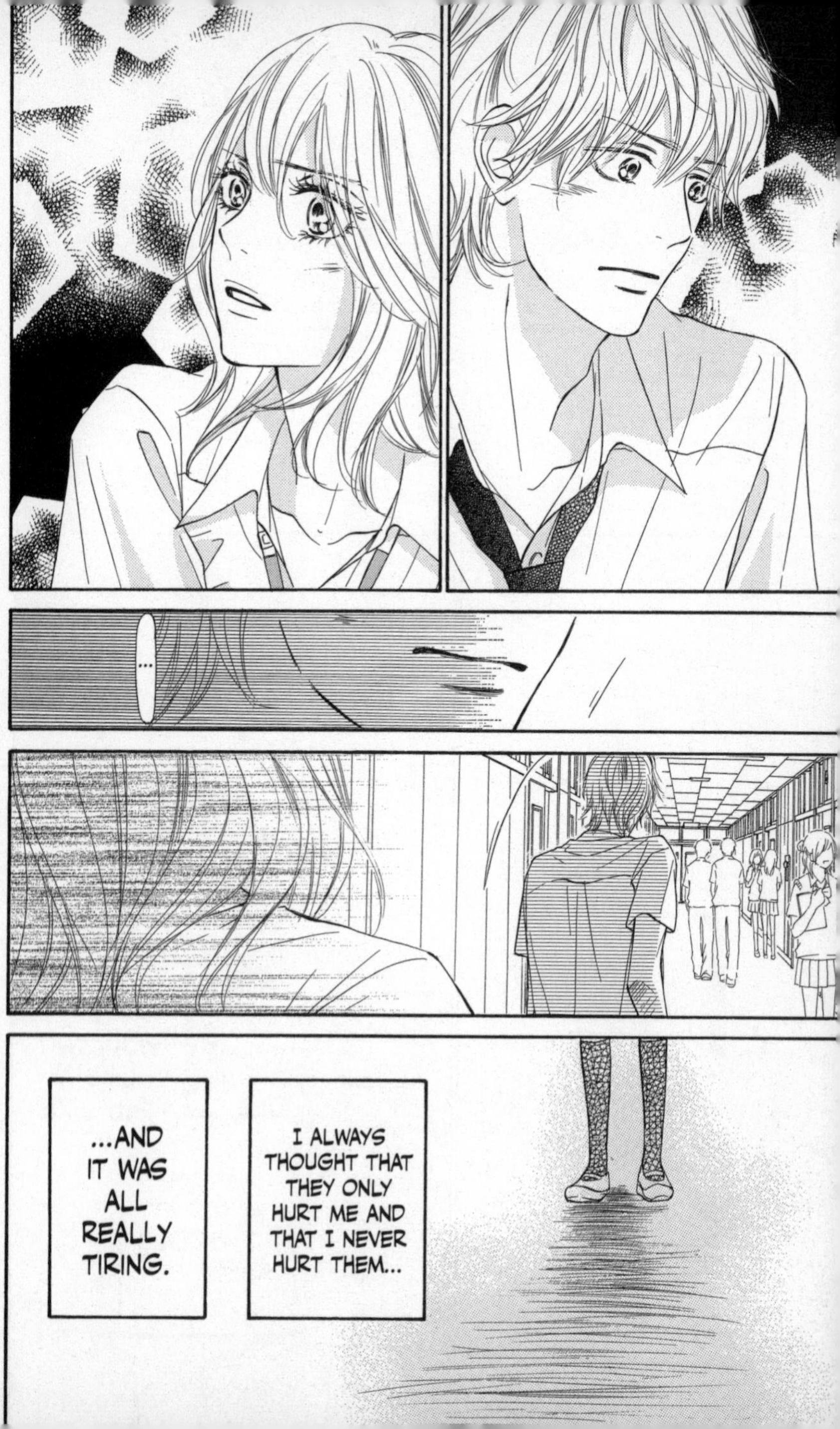
...
I ALWAYS THOUGHT THAT THEY ONLY HURT ME AND THAT I NEVER HURT THEM...
...AND IT WAS ALL REALLY TIRING.

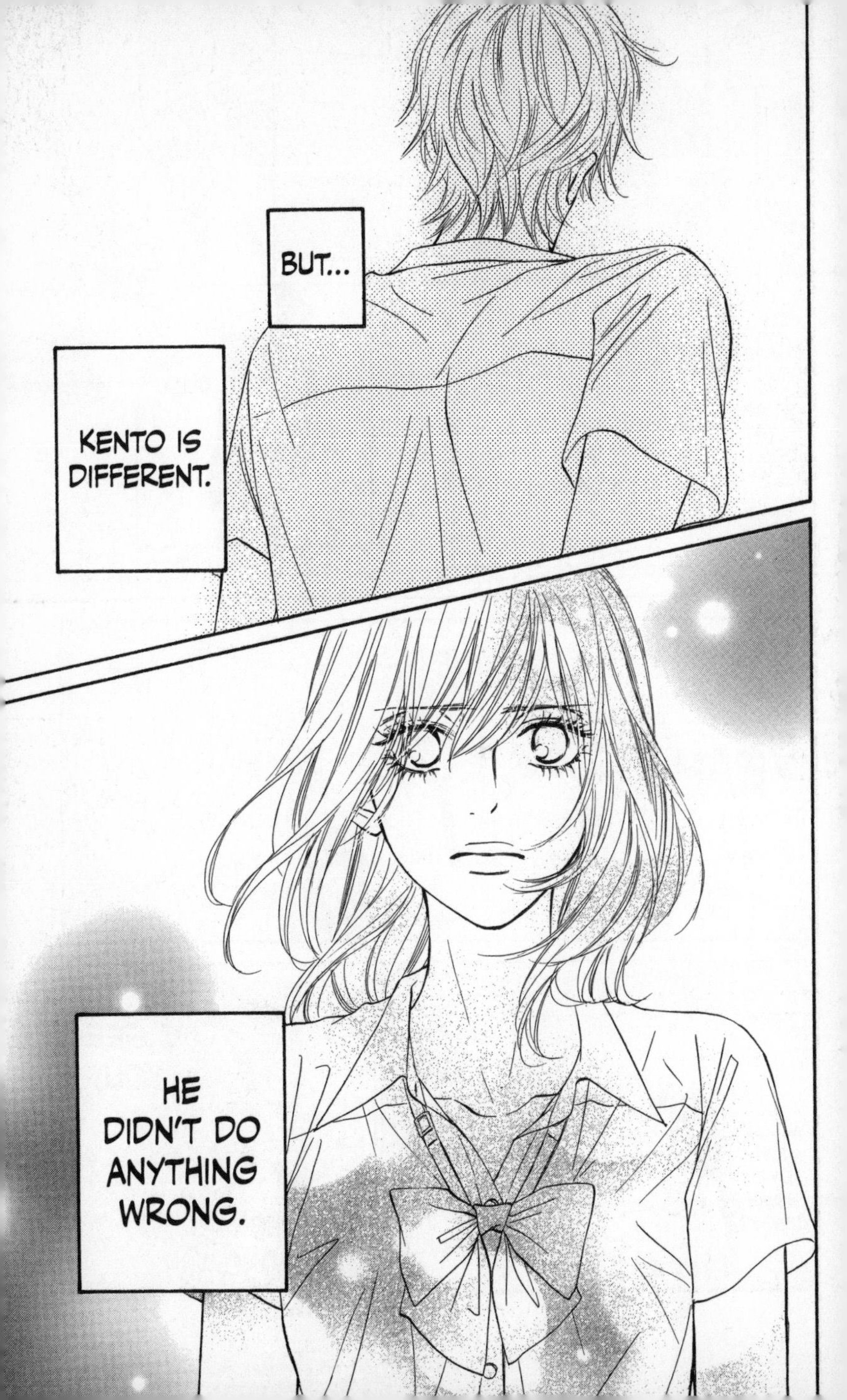
BUT...
KENTO IS DIFFERENT.
HE DIDN'T DO ANYTHING WRONG.

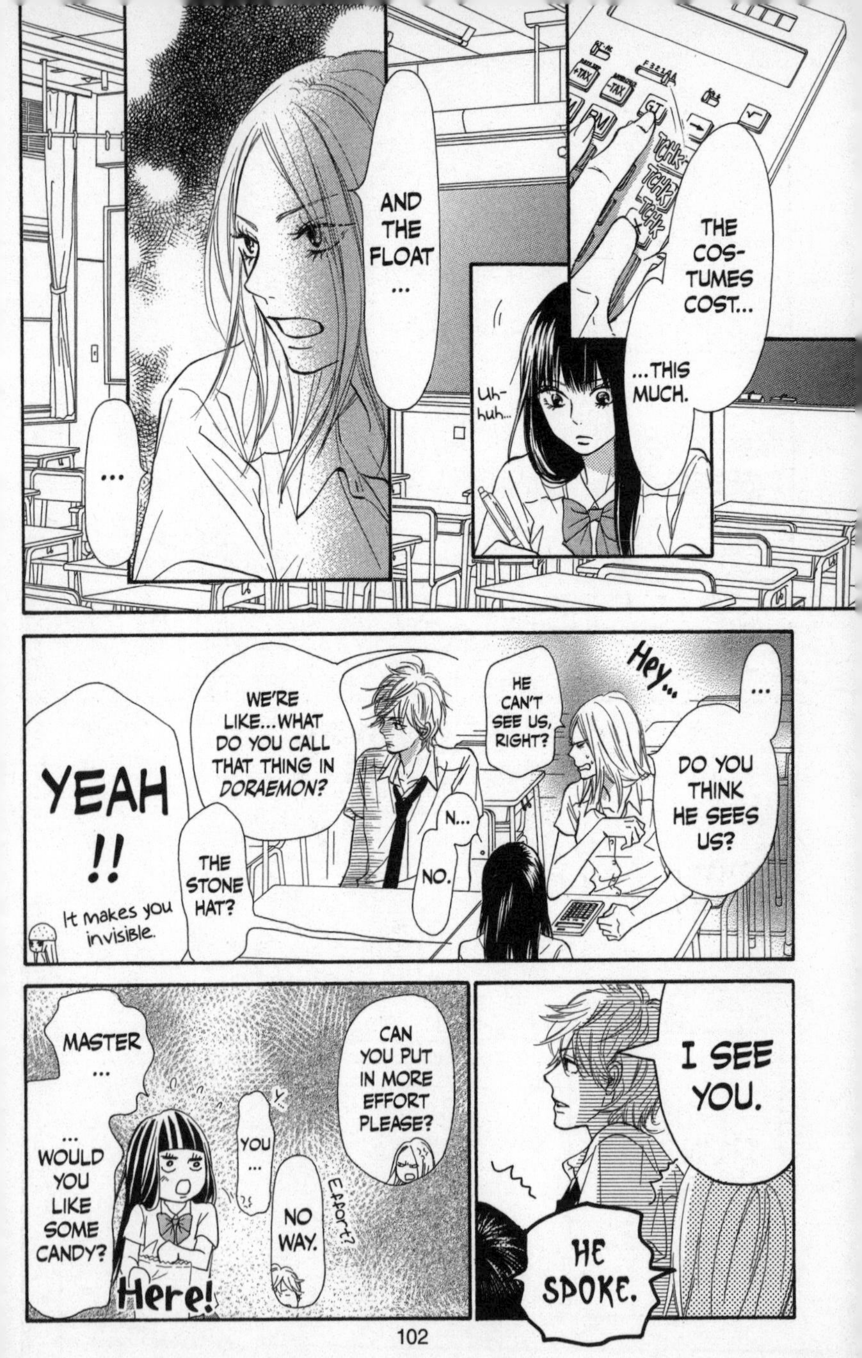
TCHK TCHK TCHK
THE COSTUMES COST...
...THIS MUCH.
Uh-huh...
AND THE FLOAT ...
...
Hey...
...
DO YOU THINK HE SEES US?
HE CAN'T SEE US, RIGHT?
N...
NO.
WE'RE LIKE...WHAT DO YOU CALL THAT THING IN *DORAEMON*?
THE STONE HAT?
YEAH !!
It makes you invisible.
I SEE YOU.
HE SPOKE.
CAN YOU PUT IN MORE EFFORT PLEASE?
Effort?
Y... YOU ...
NO WAY.
MASTER ...
... WOULD YOU LIKE SOME CANDY?
Here!

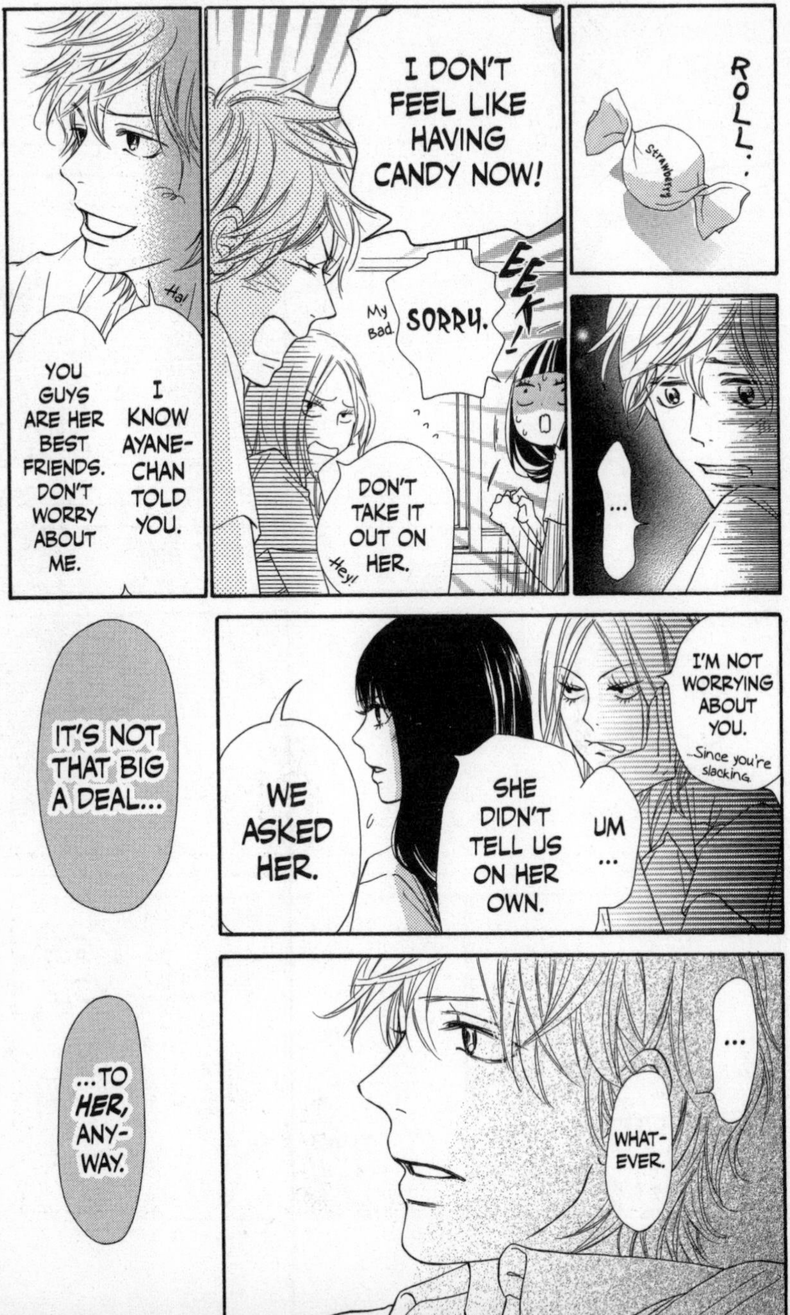
ROLL..
Strawberry
...
I DON'T FEEL LIKE HAVING CANDY NOW!
EEK!
SORRY.
My Bad.
DON'T TAKE IT OUT ON HER.
Hey!
I KNOW AYANE-CHAN TOLD YOU.
YOU GUYS ARE HER BEST FRIENDS. DON'T WORRY ABOUT ME.
Ha!
I'M NOT WORRYING ABOUT YOU.
...Since you're slacking.
UM...
SHE DIDN'T TELL US ON HER OWN.
WE ASKED HER.
IT'S NOT THAT BIG A DEAL...
...
WHAT-EVER.
...TO HER, ANYWAY.

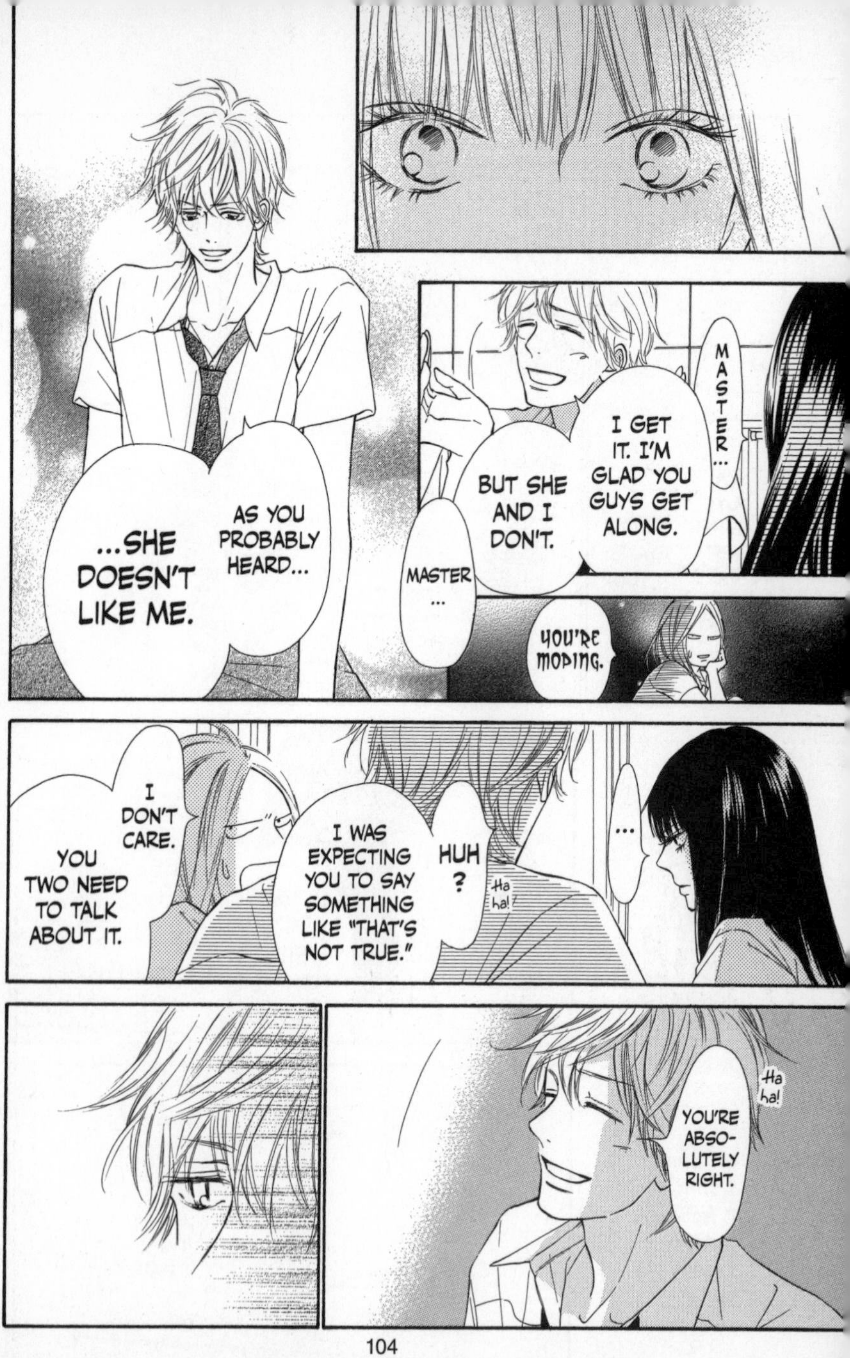
MASTER...
I GET IT. I'M GLAD YOU GUYS GET ALONG.
BUT SHE AND I DON'T.
YOU'RE MOPING.
MASTER...
AS YOU PROBABLY HEARD...
...SHE DOESN'T LIKE ME.
...
Ha ha!
HUH?
I WAS EXPECTING YOU TO SAY SOMETHING LIKE "THAT'S NOT TRUE."
I DON'T CARE.
YOU TWO NEED TO TALK ABOUT IT.
Ha ha!
YOU'RE ABSO-LUTELY RIGHT.

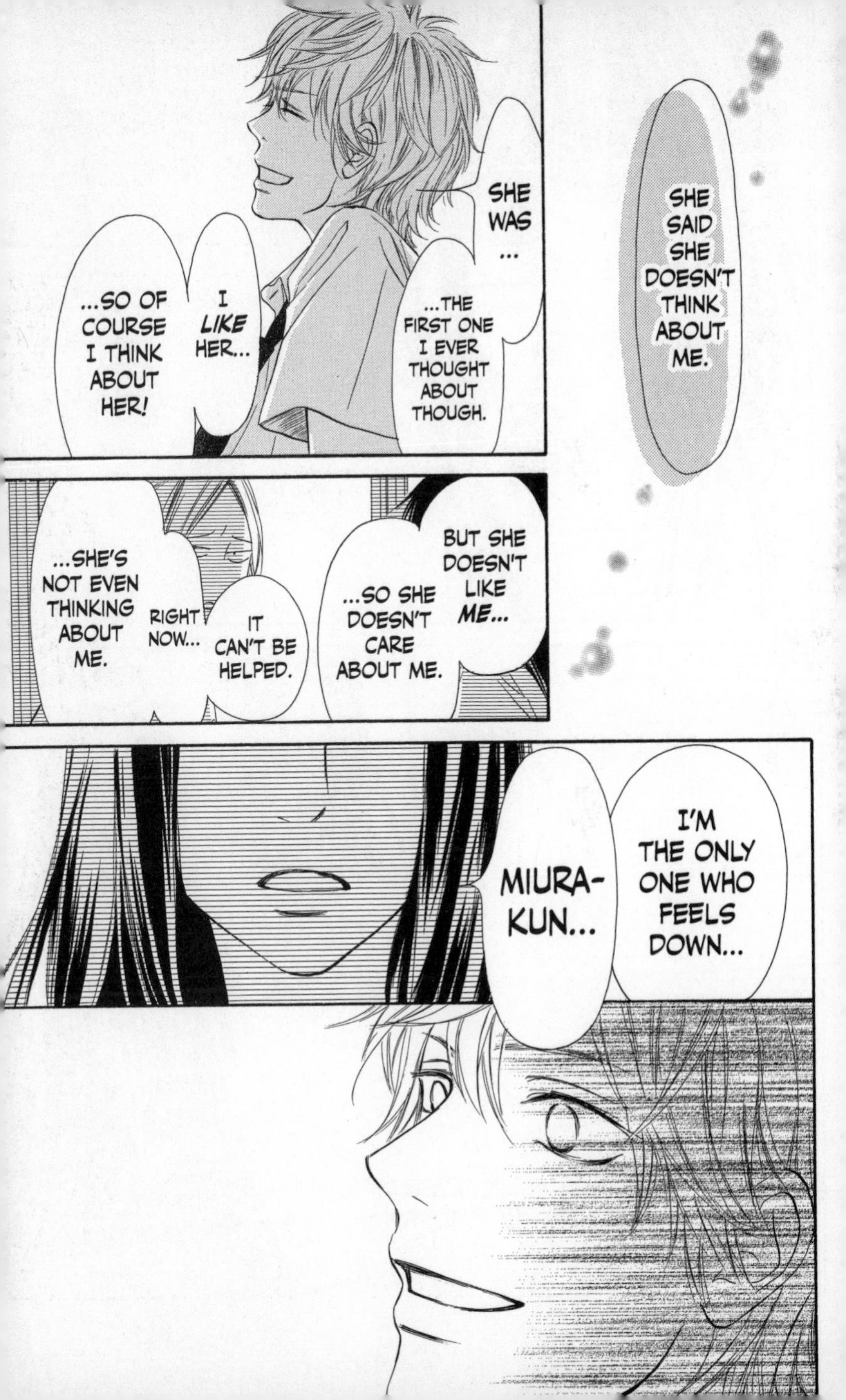
SHE SAID SHE DOESN'T THINK ABOUT ME.
SHE WAS ...
...THE FIRST ONE I EVER THOUGHT ABOUT THOUGH.
I *LIKE* HER...
...SO OF COURSE I THINK ABOUT HER!
BUT SHE DOESN'T LIKE *ME*...
...SO SHE DOESN'T CARE ABOUT ME.
IT CAN'T BE HELPED.
RIGHT NOW...
...SHE'S NOT EVEN THINKING ABOUT ME.
I'M THE ONLY ONE WHO FEELS DOWN...
MIURA-KUN...

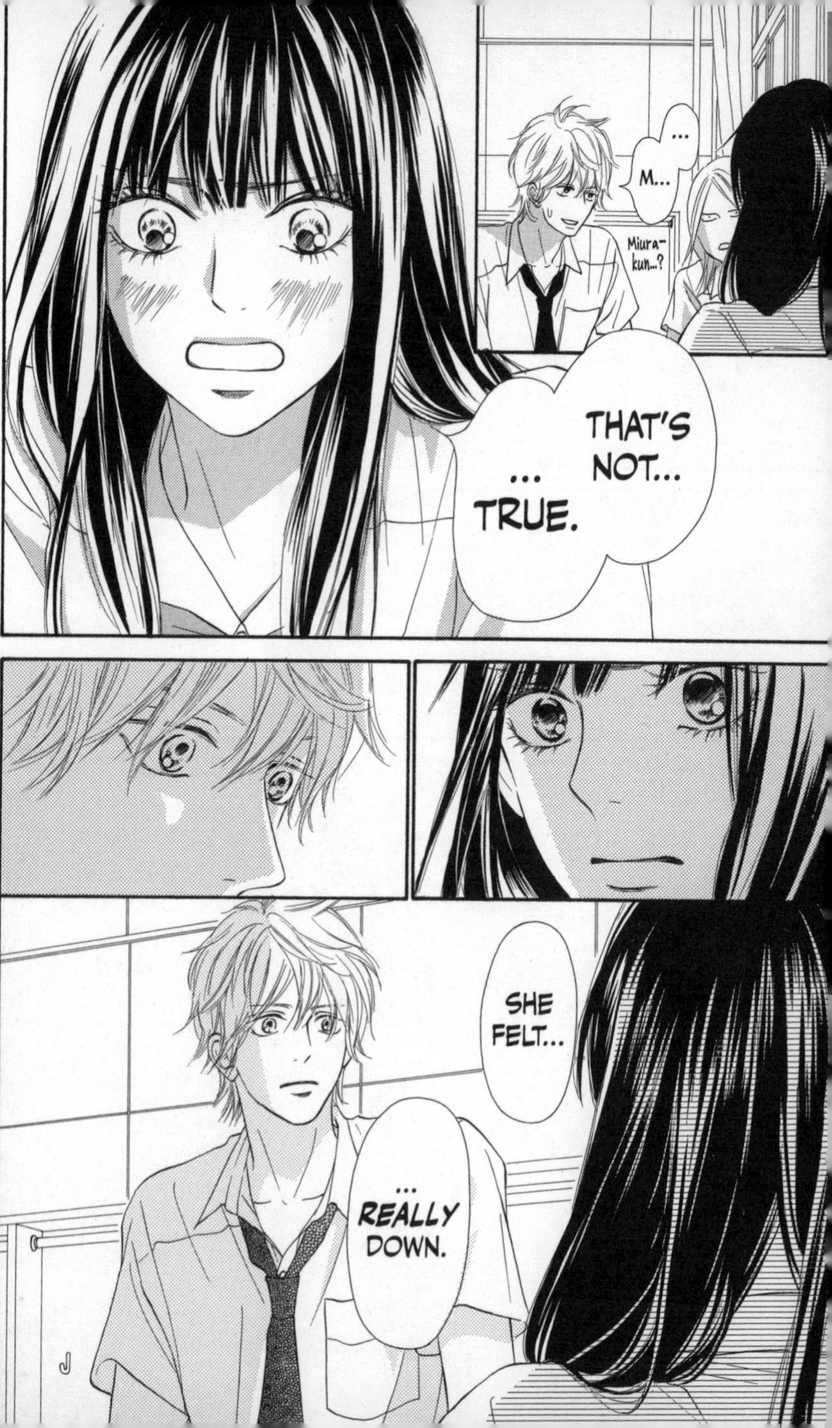
...
M...
Miura-kun...?
THAT'S NOT... ... TRUE.
SHE FELT...
... REALLY DOWN.

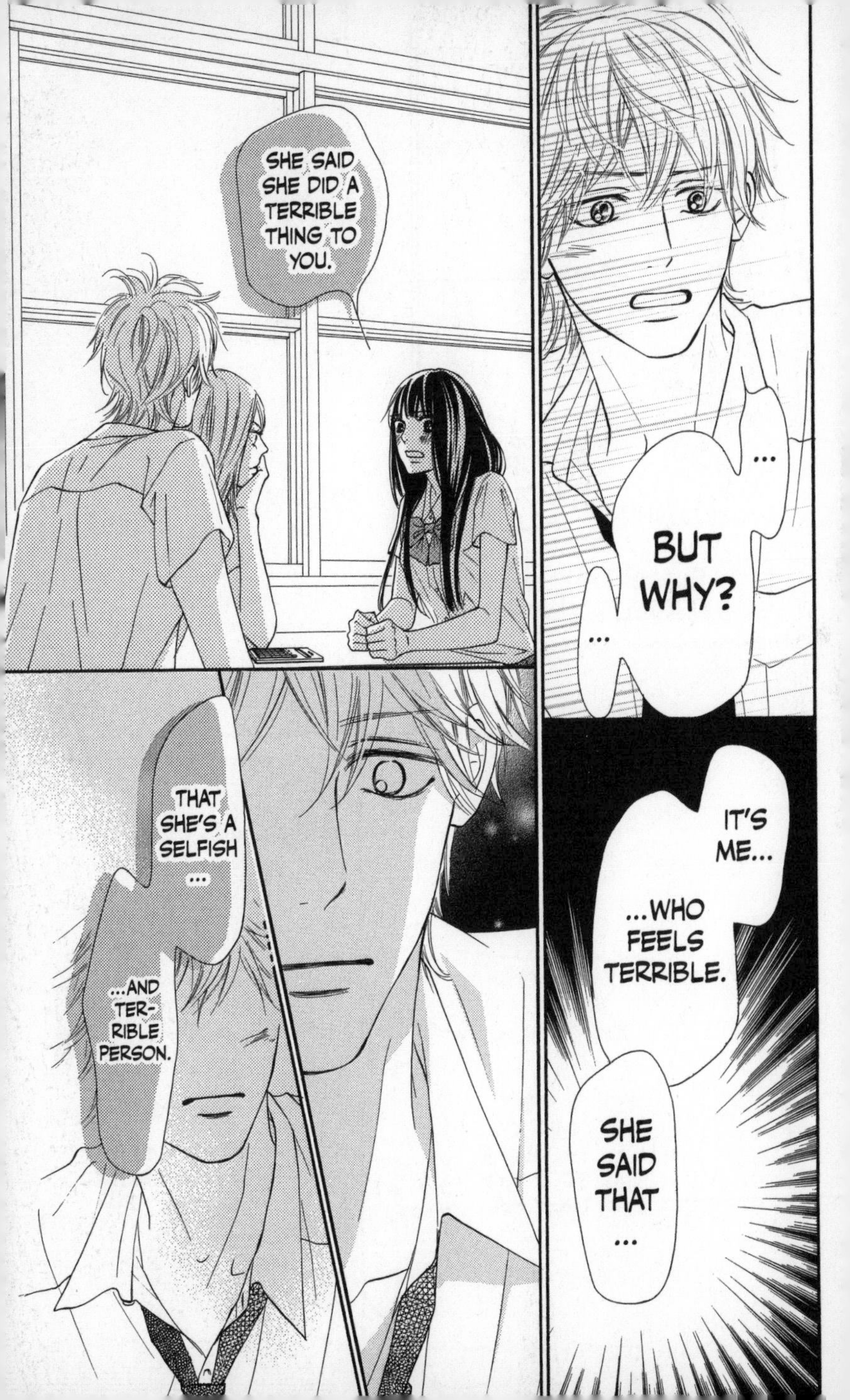
SHE SAID SHE DID A TERRIBLE THING TO YOU.
... BUT WHY? ...
THAT SHE'S A SELFISH ...
...AND TERRIBLE PERSON.
IT'S ME...
...WHO FEELS TERRIBLE.
SHE SAID THAT ...

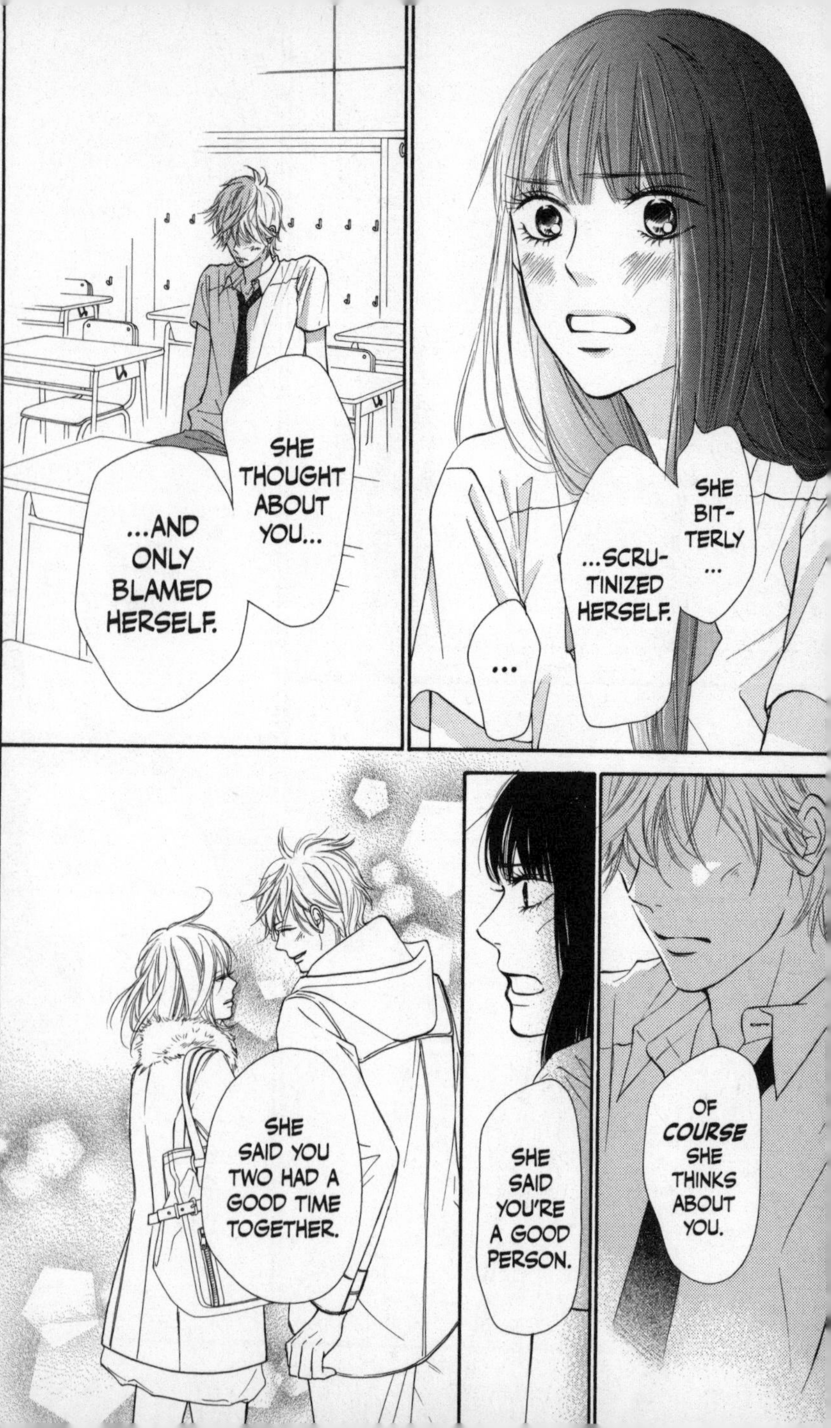
SHE BITTERLY...
...SCRUTINIZED HERSELF.
...
SHE THOUGHT ABOUT YOU...
...AND ONLY BLAMED HERSELF.
OF *COURSE* SHE THINKS ABOUT YOU.
SHE SAID YOU'RE A GOOD PERSON.
SHE SAID YOU TWO HAD A GOOD TIME TOGETHER.

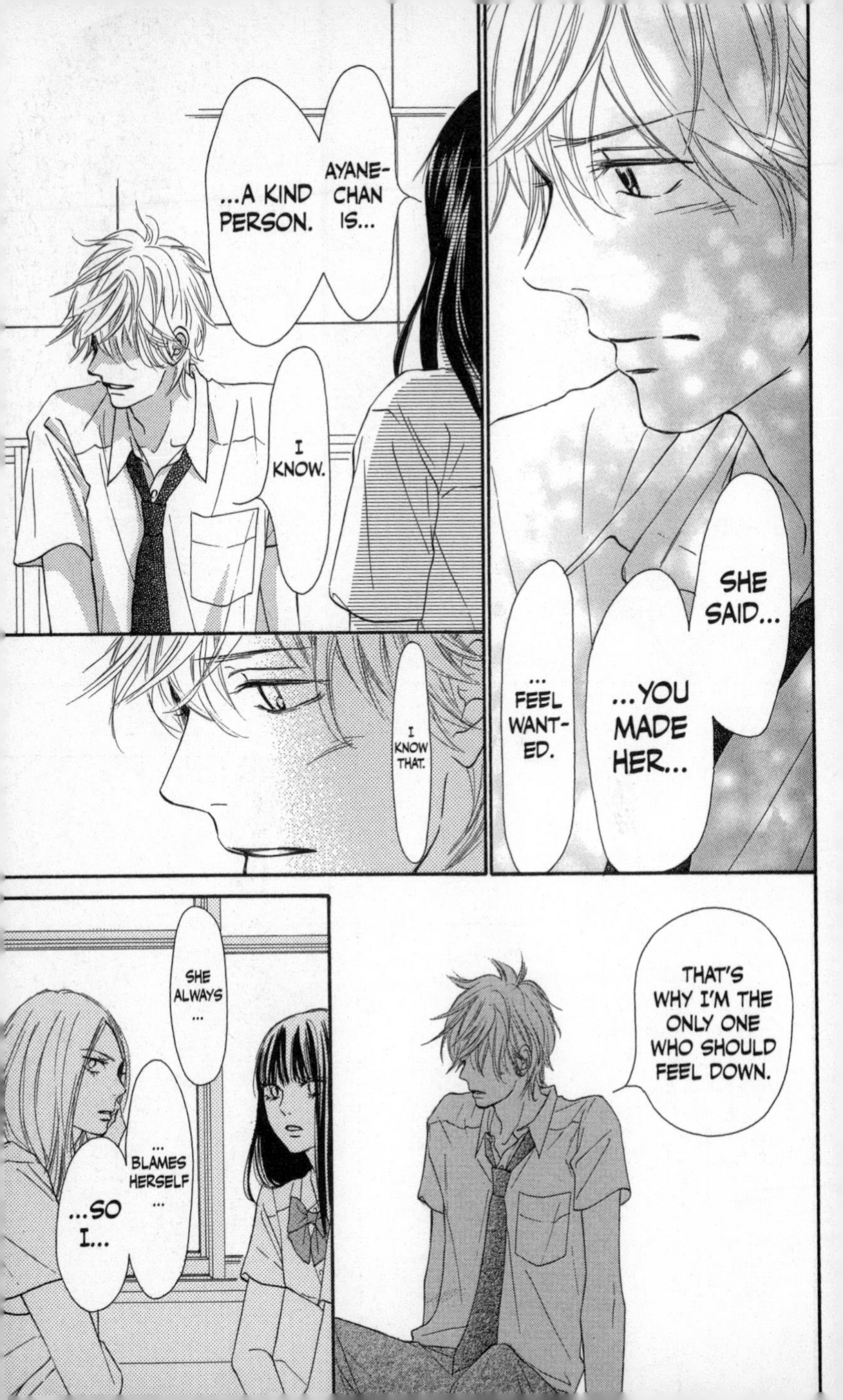
AYANE-CHAN IS...
...A KIND PERSON.
I KNOW.
SHE SAID...
...YOU MADE HER...
...FEEL WANTED.
I KNOW THAT.
THAT'S WHY I'M THE ONLY ONE WHO SHOULD FEEL DOWN.
SHE ALWAYS...
...BLAMES HERSELF...
...SO I...

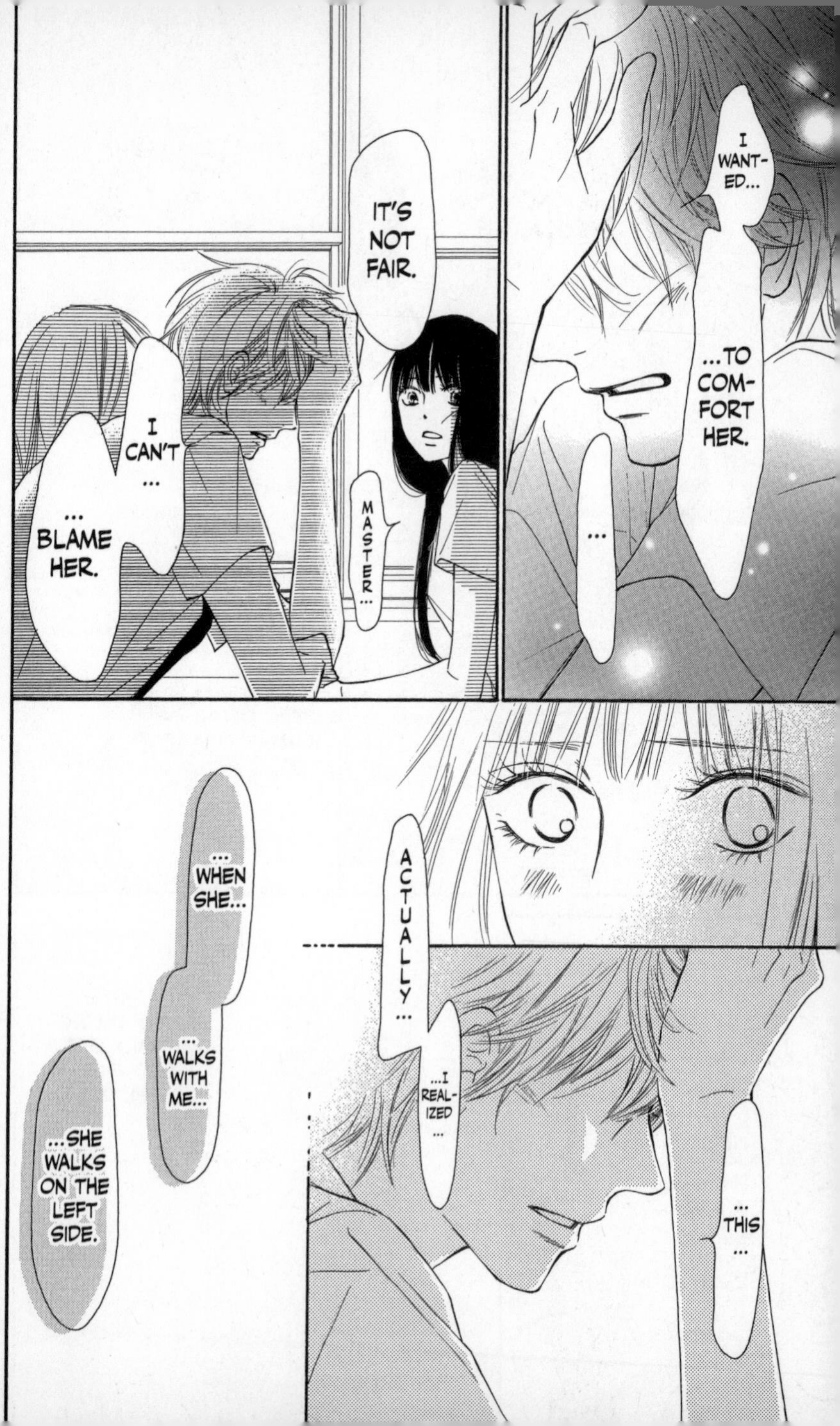
I WANTED...
...TO COMFORT HER.
...
IT'S NOT FAIR.
MASTER...
I CAN'T...
...BLAME HER.
ACTUALLY...
...I REALIZED...
...THIS...
...WHEN SHE...
...WALKS WITH ME...
...SHE WALKS ON THE LEFT SIDE.

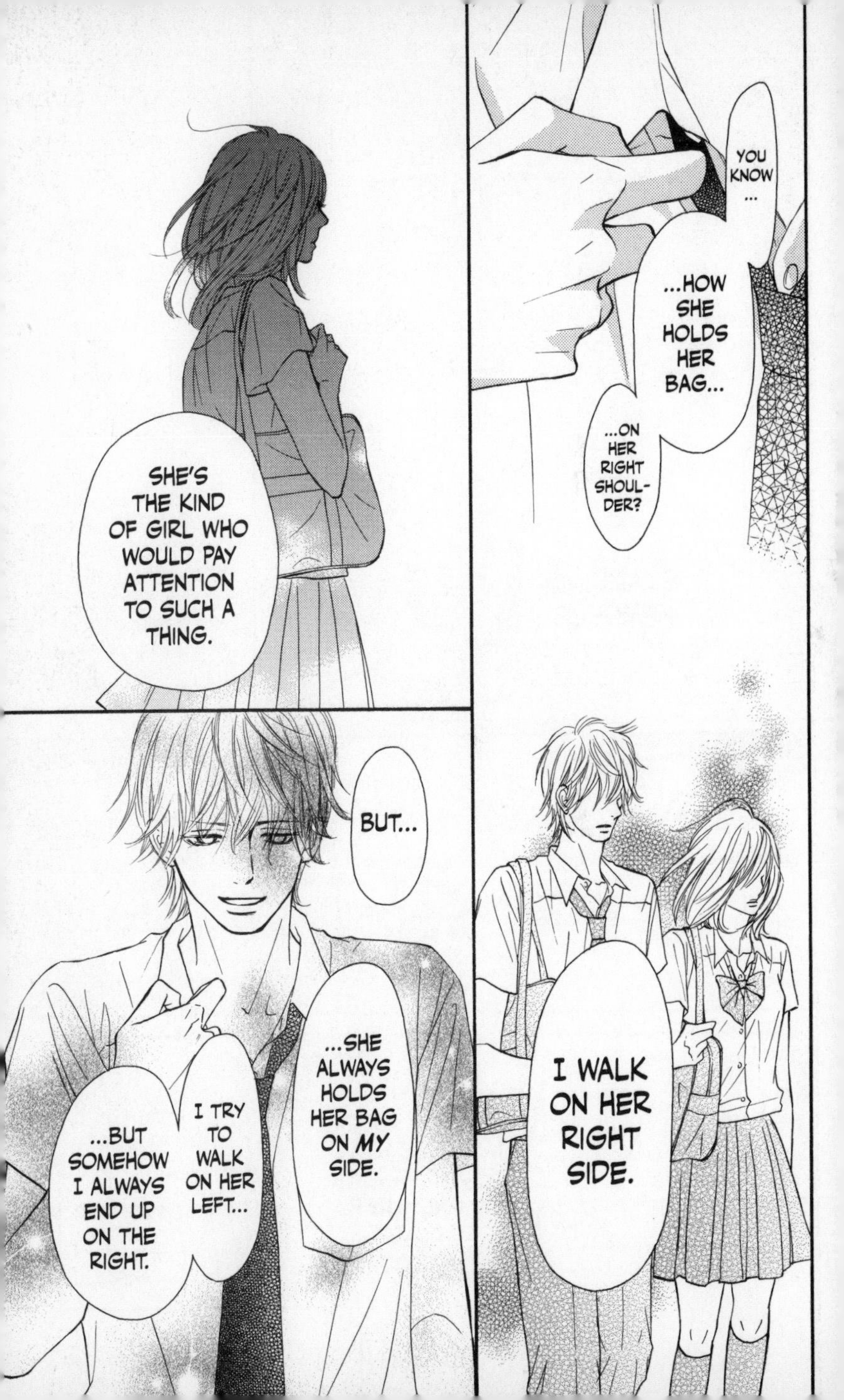
YOU KNOW ...
...HOW SHE HOLDS HER BAG...
...ON HER RIGHT SHOUL-DER?
I WALK ON HER RIGHT SIDE.
SHE'S THE KIND OF GIRL WHO WOULD PAY ATTENTION TO SUCH A THING.
BUT...
...SHE ALWAYS HOLDS HER BAG ON *MY* SIDE.
I TRY TO WALK ON HER LEFT...
...BUT SOMEHOW I ALWAYS END UP ON THE RIGHT.

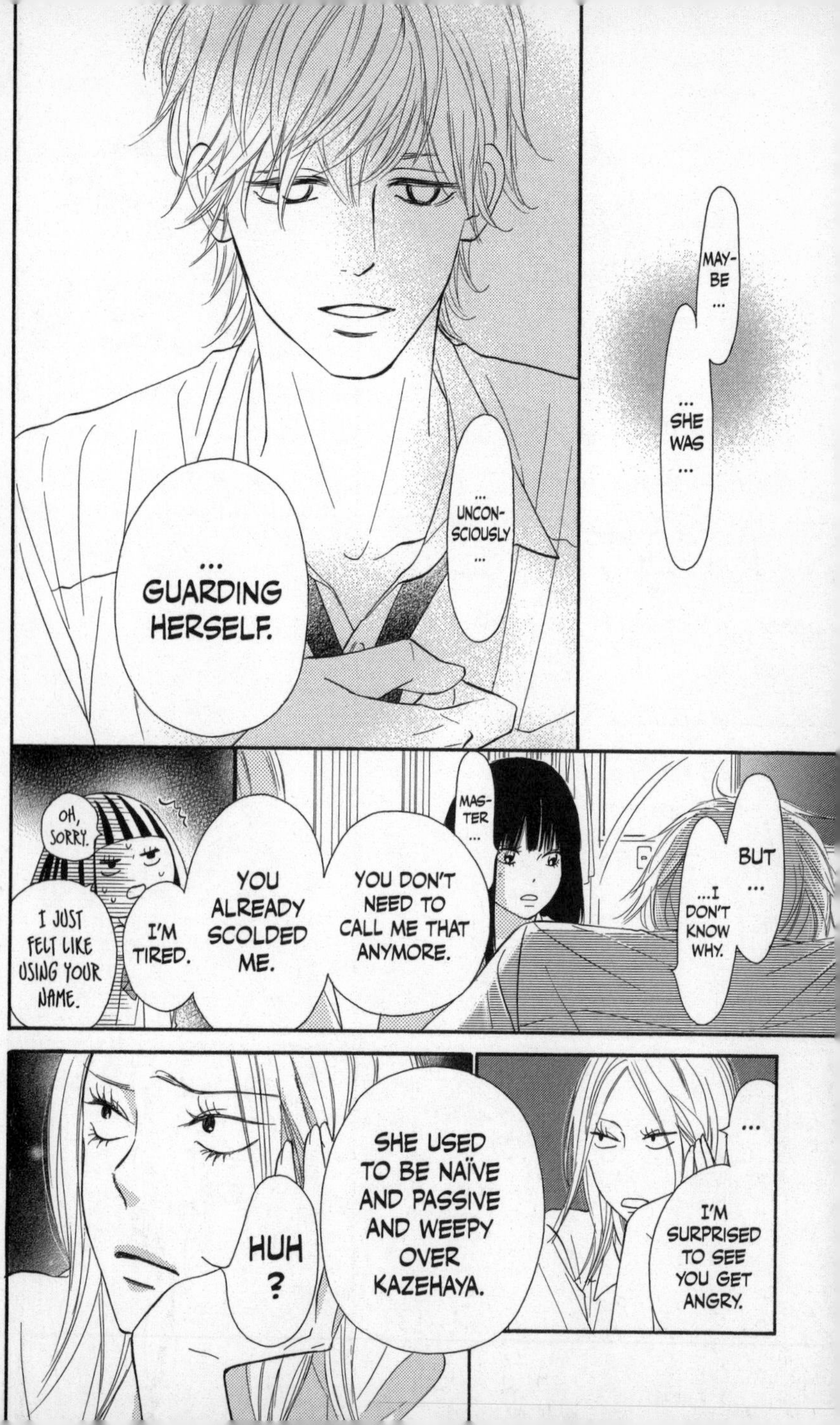
MAY-BE ...
... SHE WAS ...
... UNCON-SCIOUSLY ...
... GUARDING HERSELF.
BUT ...
...I DON'T KNOW WHY.
MAS-TER ...
YOU DON'T NEED TO CALL ME THAT ANYMORE.
YOU ALREADY SCOLDED ME.
I'M TIRED.
OH, SORRY.
I JUST FELT LIKE USING YOUR NAME.
...
I'M SURPRISED TO SEE YOU GET ANGRY.
SHE USED TO BE NAÏVE AND PASSIVE AND WEEPY OVER KAZEHAYA.
HUH?

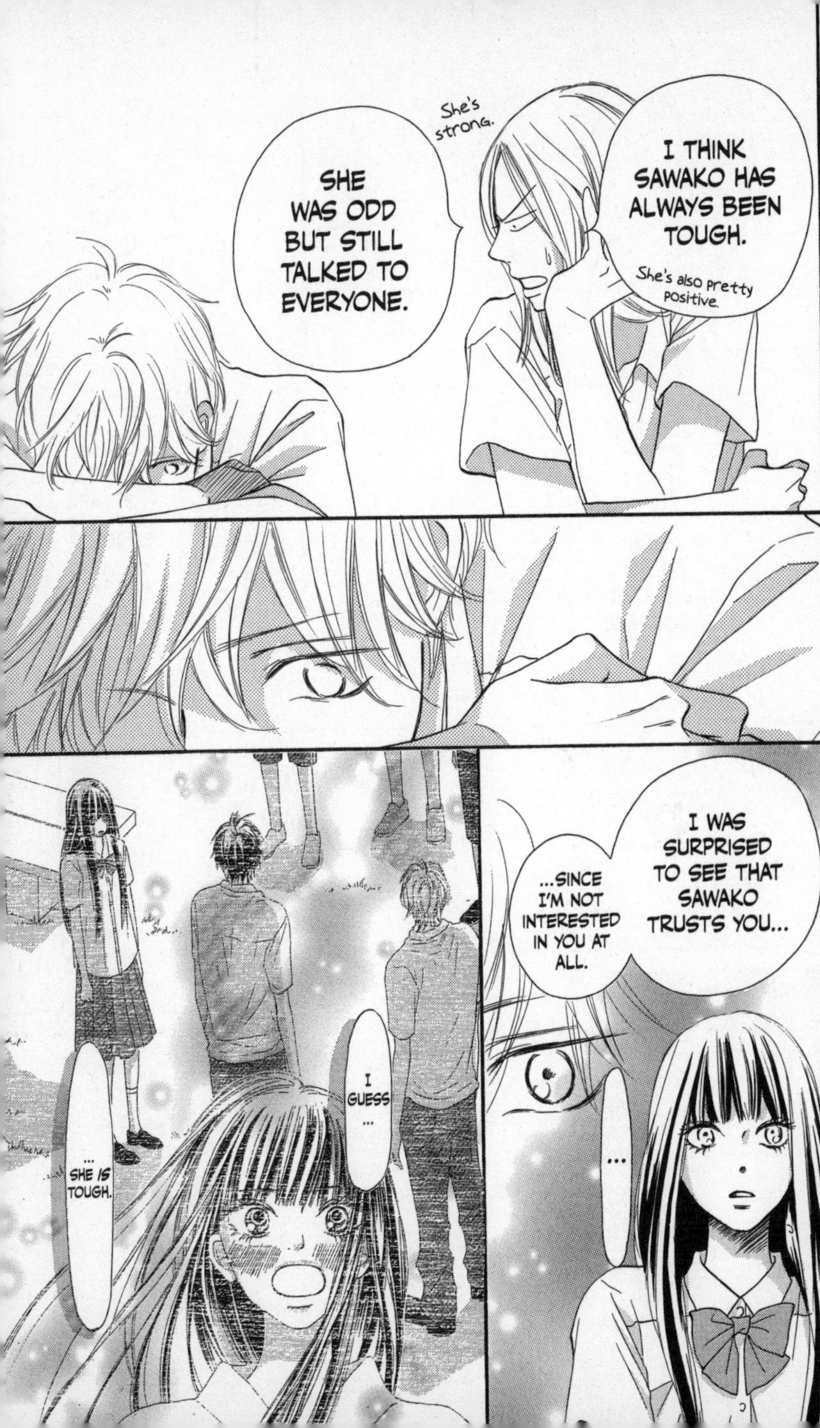
I THINK SAWAKO HAS ALWAYS BEEN TOUGH.
She's also pretty positive.
She's strong.
SHE WAS ODD BUT STILL TALKED TO EVERYONE.
I WAS SURPRISED TO SEE THAT SAWAKO TRUSTS YOU...
...SINCE I'M NOT INTERESTED IN YOU AT ALL.
...
I GUESS...
...SHE *IS* TOUGH.

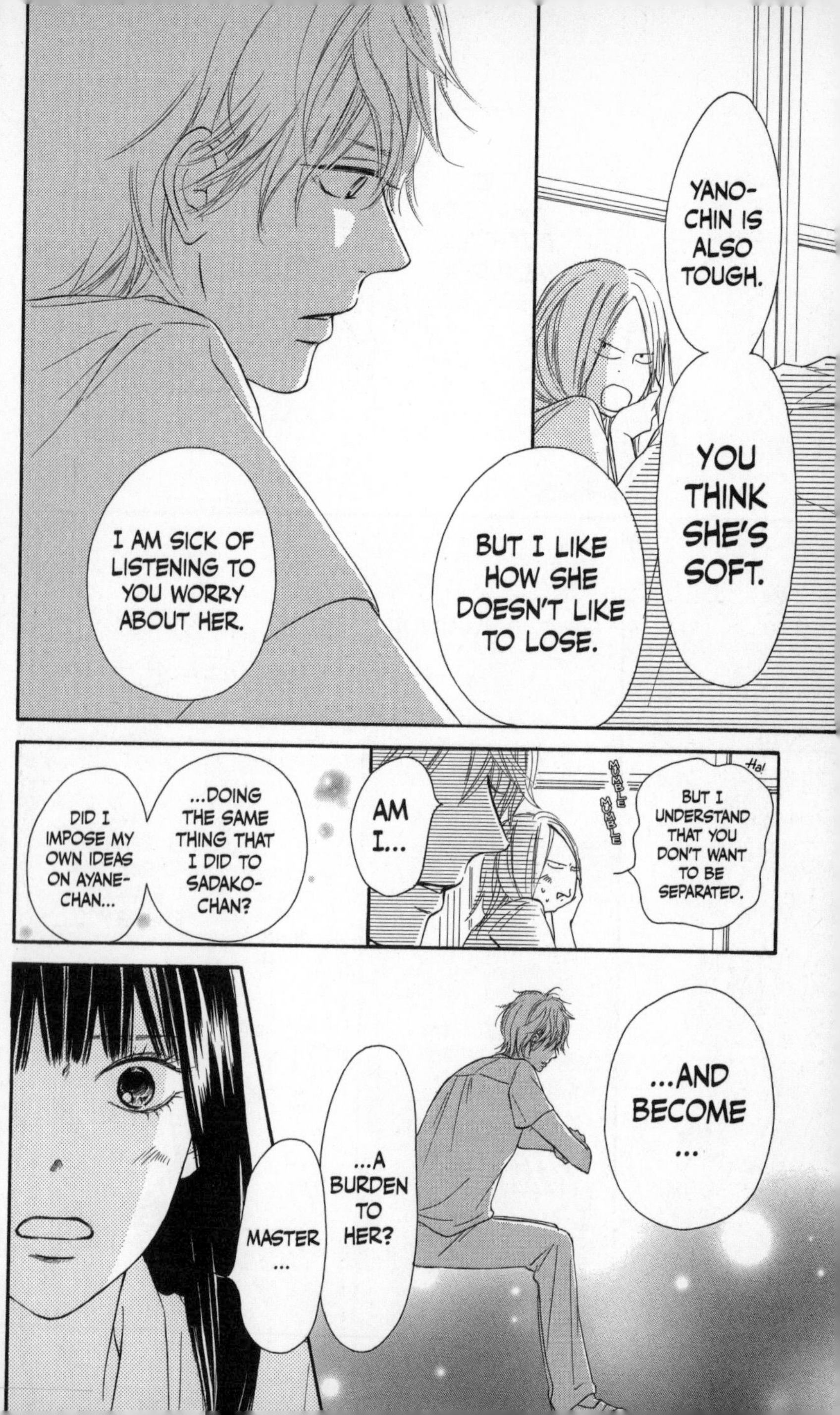
YANO-CHIN IS ALSO TOUGH.
YOU THINK SHE'S SOFT.
BUT I LIKE HOW SHE DOESN'T LIKE TO LOSE.
I AM SICK OF LISTENING TO YOU WORRY ABOUT HER.
Ha!
MUMBLE MUMBLE
BUT I UNDERSTAND THAT YOU DON'T WANT TO BE SEPARATED.
AM I...
...DOING THE SAME THING THAT I DID TO SADAKO-CHAN?
DID I IMPOSE MY OWN IDEAS ON AYANE-CHAN...
...AND BECOME ...
...A BURDEN TO HER?
MASTER ...

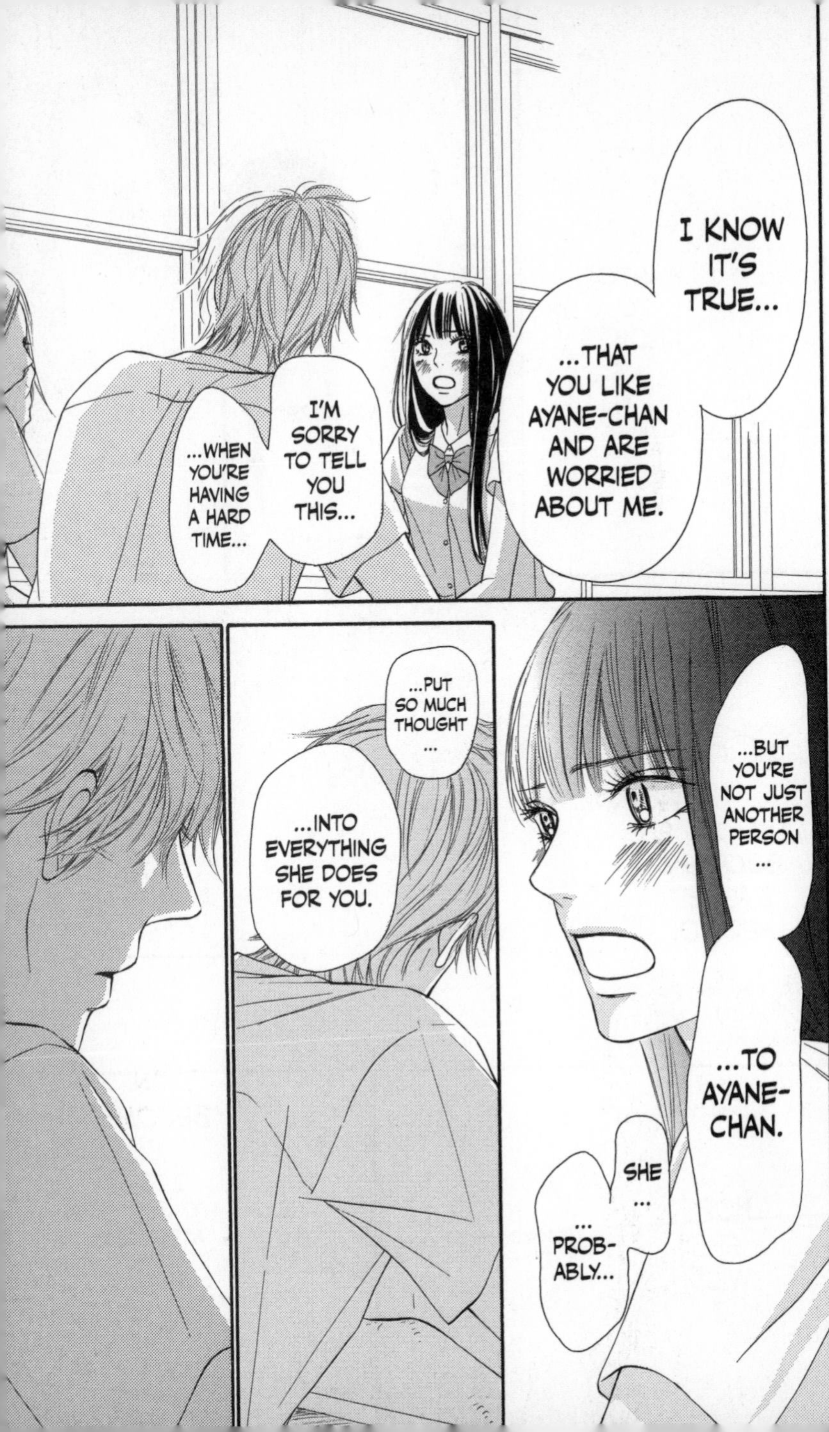
I KNOW IT'S TRUE...
...THAT YOU LIKE AYANE-CHAN AND ARE WORRIED ABOUT ME.
I'M SORRY TO TELL YOU THIS...
...WHEN YOU'RE HAVING A HARD TIME...
...BUT YOU'RE NOT JUST ANOTHER PERSON...
...TO AYANE-CHAN.
SHE... ...PROBABLY...
...PUT SO MUCH THOUGHT...
...INTO EVERYTHING SHE DOES FOR YOU.

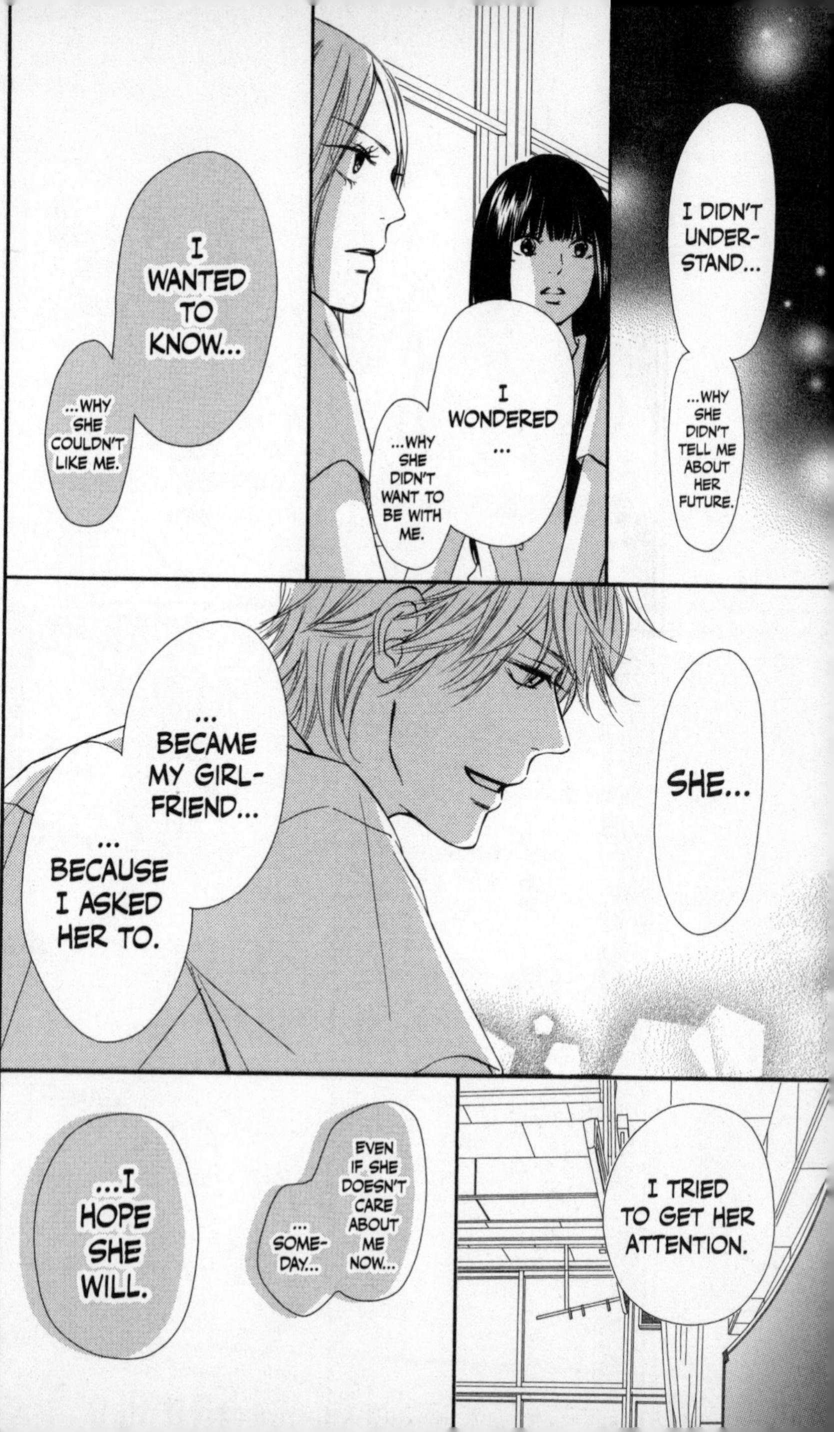
I DIDN'T UNDER-STAND...
...WHY SHE DIDN'T TELL ME ABOUT HER FUTURE.
I WONDERED...
...WHY SHE DIDN'T WANT TO BE WITH ME.
I WANTED TO KNOW...
...WHY SHE COULDN'T LIKE ME.
SHE...
...BECAME MY GIRL-FRIEND...
...BECAUSE I ASKED HER TO.
I TRIED TO GET HER ATTENTION.
EVEN IF SHE DOESN'T CARE ABOUT ME NOW...
...SOME-DAY...
...I HOPE SHE WILL.

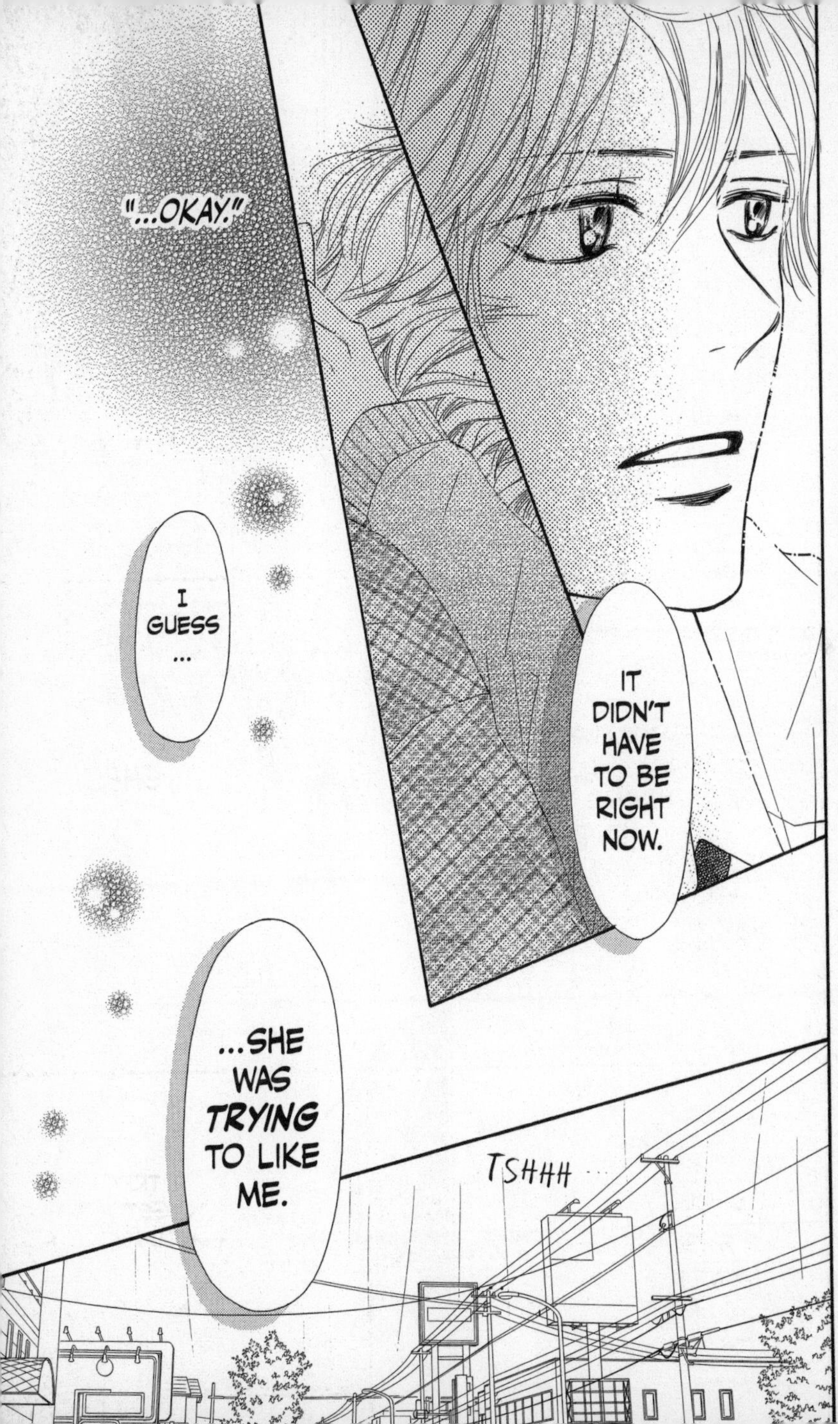
IT DIDN'T HAVE TO BE RIGHT NOW.
"...OKAY."
I GUESS ...
...SHE WAS *TRYING* TO LIKE ME.
TSHHH

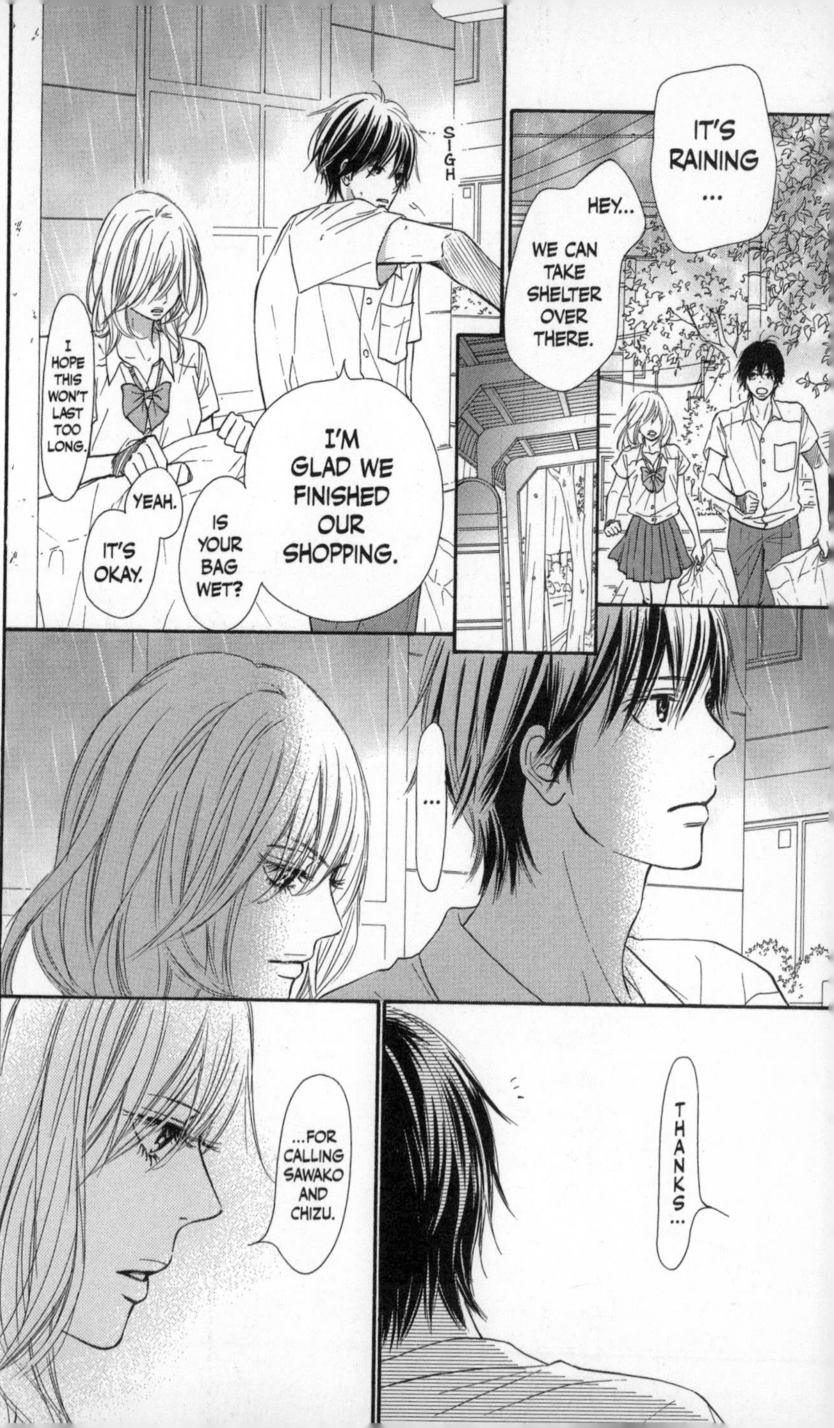
IT'S RAINING ...
HEY...
WE CAN TAKE SHELTER OVER THERE.
SIGH
I'M GLAD WE FINISHED OUR SHOPPING.
IS YOUR BAG WET?
YEAH.
IT'S OKAY.
I HOPE THIS WON'T LAST TOO LONG.
...
THANKS...
...FOR CALLING SAWAKO AND CHIZU.

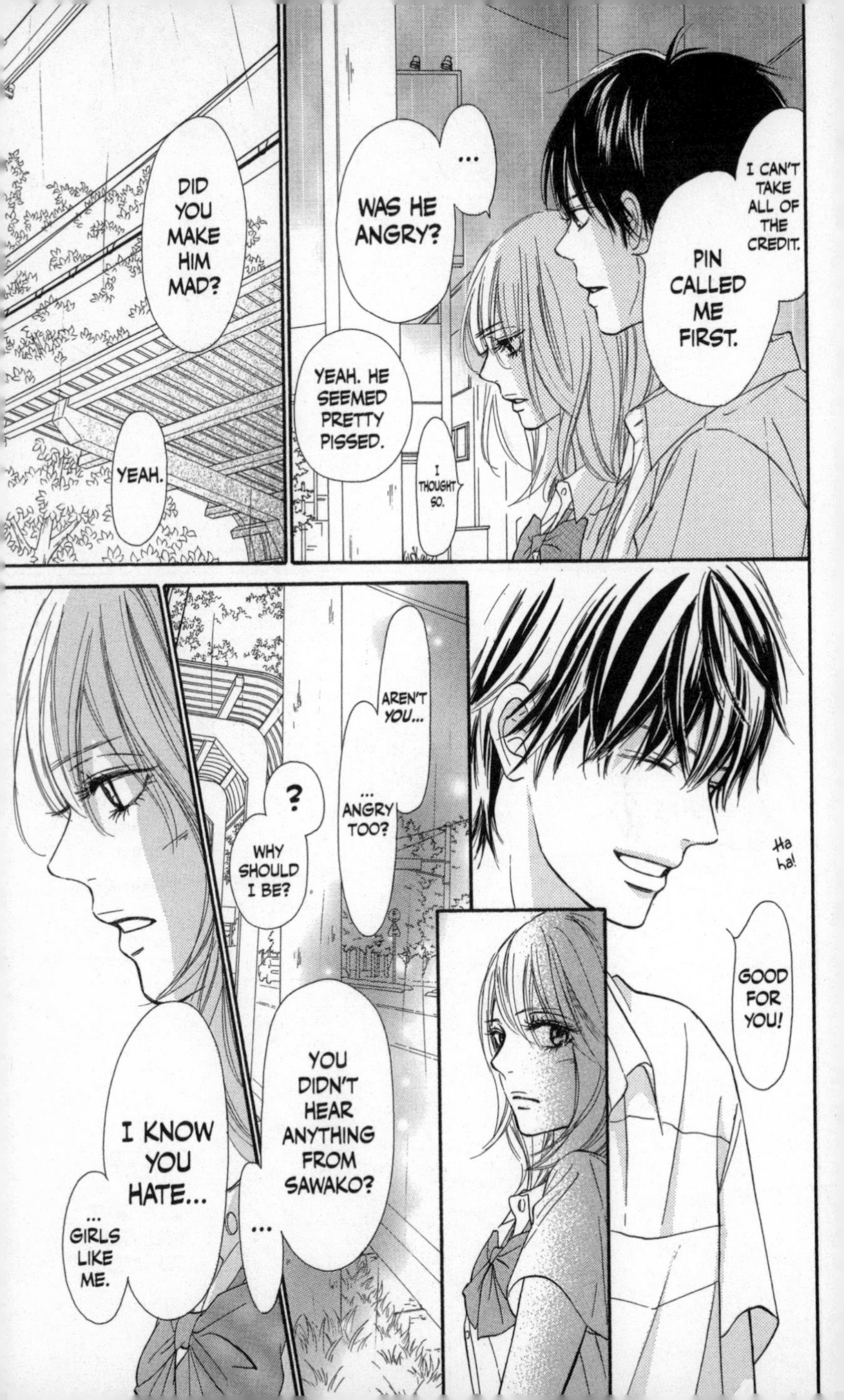
I CAN'T TAKE ALL OF THE CREDIT.
PIN CALLED ME FIRST.
...
WAS HE ANGRY?
YEAH. HE SEEMED PRETTY PISSED.
I THOUGHT SO.
DID YOU MAKE HIM MAD?
YEAH.
Ha ha!
GOOD FOR YOU!
AREN'T YOU...
... ANGRY TOO?
?
WHY SHOULD I BE?
YOU DIDN'T HEAR ANYTHING FROM SAWAKO?
...
I KNOW YOU HATE...
... GIRLS LIKE ME.

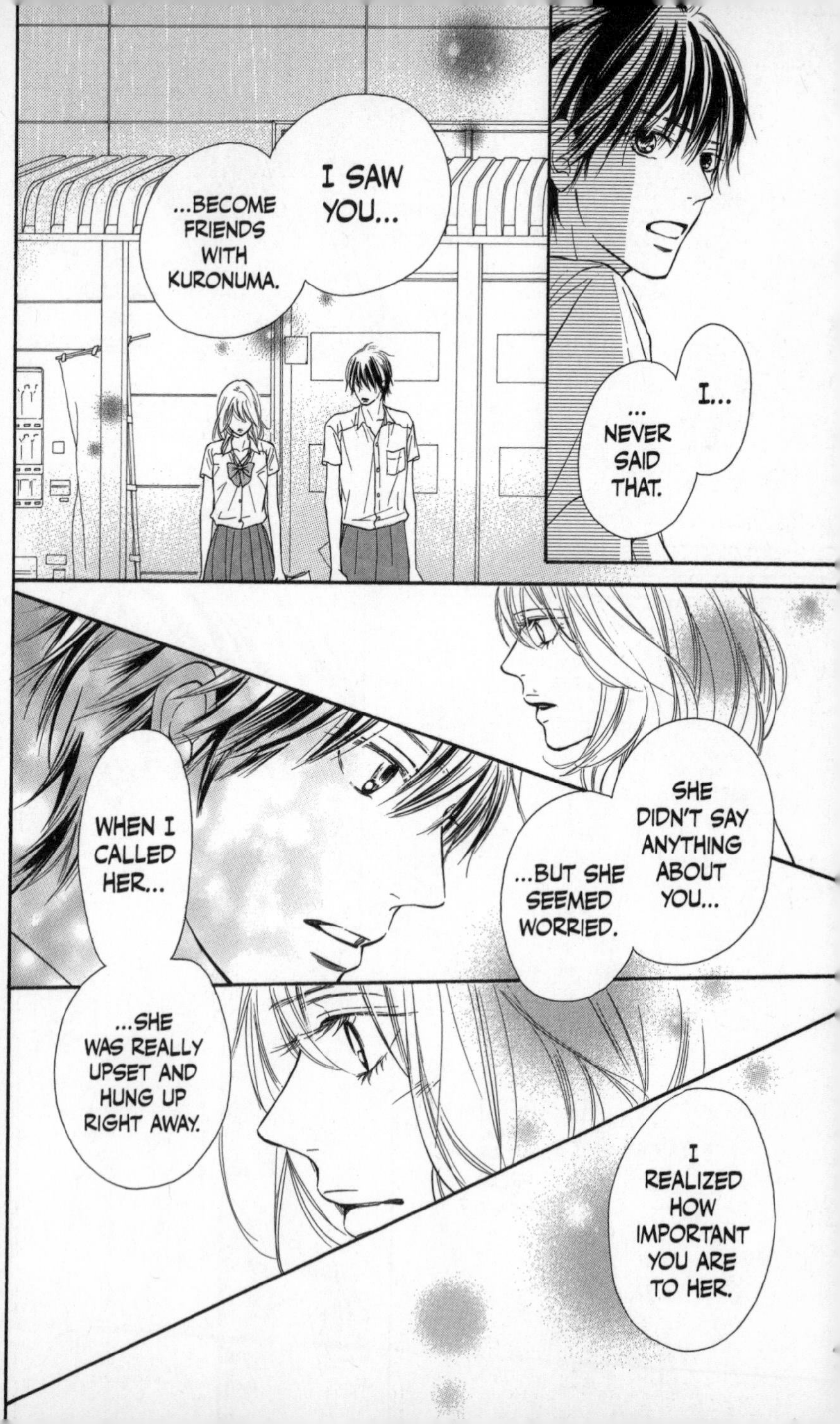
I... ...NEVER SAID THAT.
I SAW YOU...
...BECOME FRIENDS WITH KURONUMA.
SHE DIDN'T SAY ANYTHING ABOUT YOU...
...BUT SHE SEEMED WORRIED.
WHEN I CALLED HER...
...SHE WAS REALLY UPSET AND HUNG UP RIGHT AWAY.
I REALIZED HOW IMPORTANT YOU ARE TO HER.

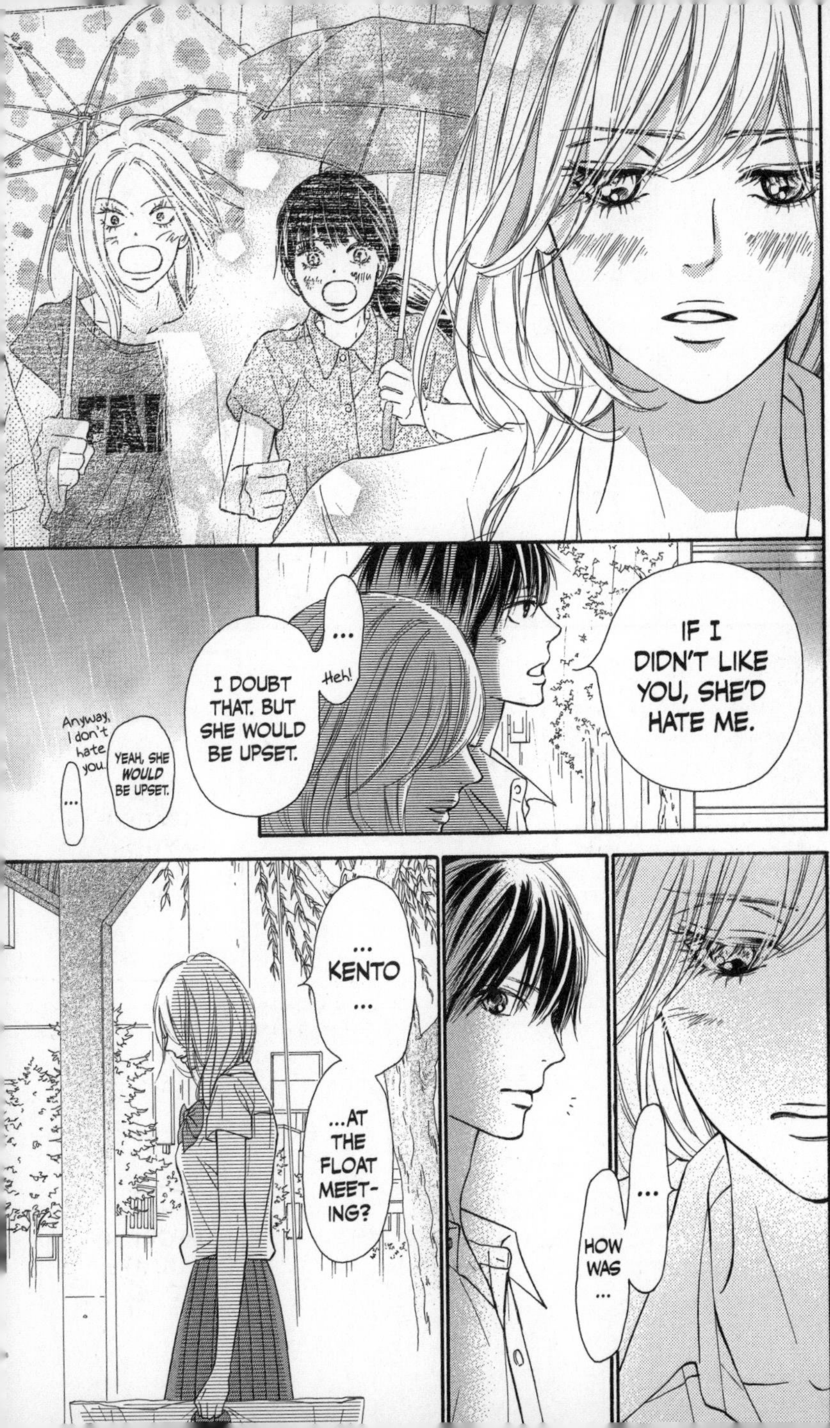
IF I DIDN'T LIKE YOU, SHE'D HATE ME.
...
Heh!
I DOUBT THAT. BUT SHE WOULD BE UPSET.
YEAH, SHE *WOULD* BE UPSET.
Anyway, I don't hate you.
...
...
HOW WAS ...
... KENTO ...
...AT THE FLOAT MEET-ING?

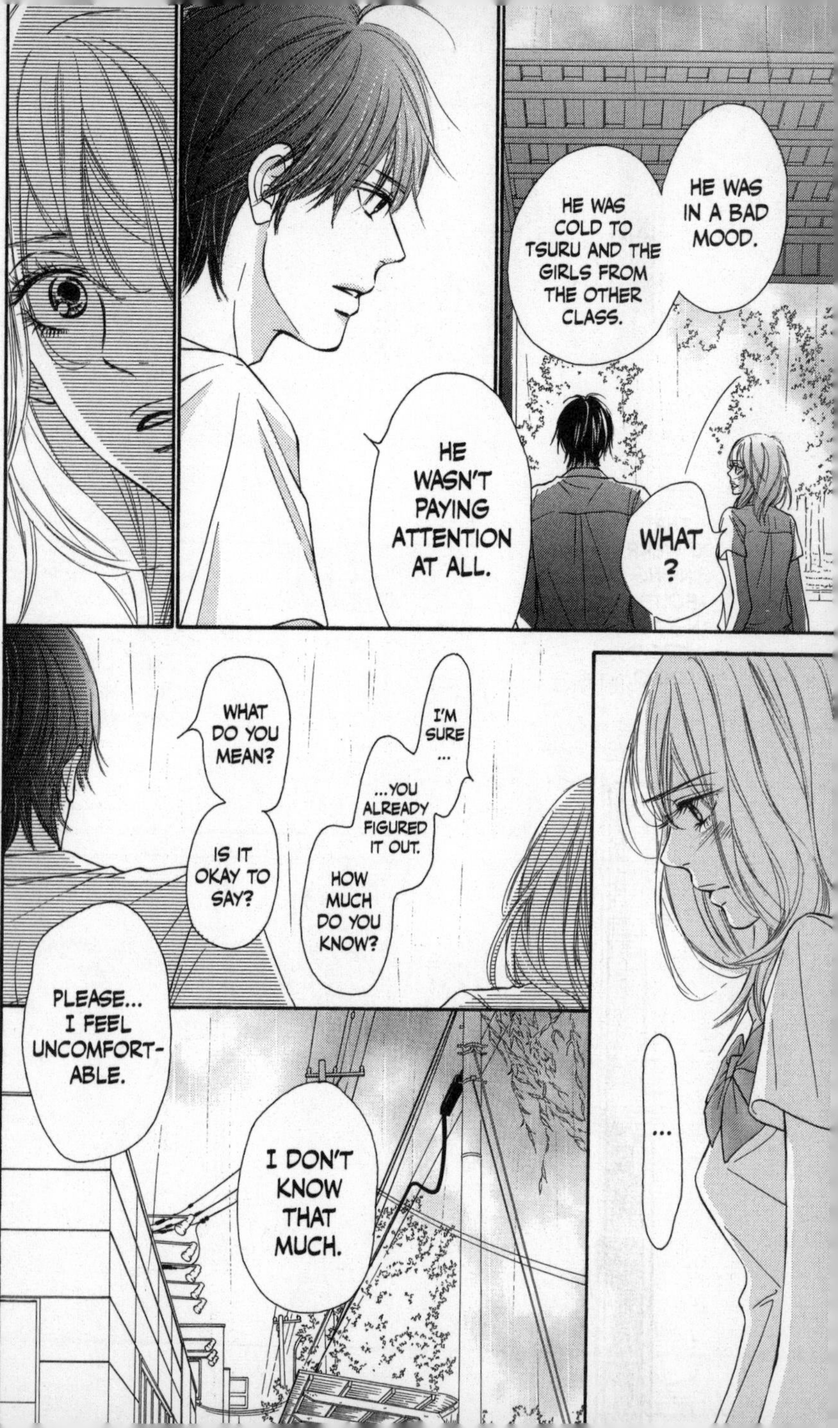
HE WAS IN A BAD MOOD.
HE WAS COLD TO TSURU AND THE GIRLS FROM THE OTHER CLASS.
HE WASN'T PAYING ATTENTION AT ALL.
WHAT?
...
I'M SURE ...
...YOU ALREADY FIGURED IT OUT.
WHAT DO YOU MEAN?
HOW MUCH DO YOU KNOW?
IS IT OKAY TO SAY?
I DON'T KNOW THAT MUCH.
PLEASE... I FEEL UNCOMFORT-ABLE.

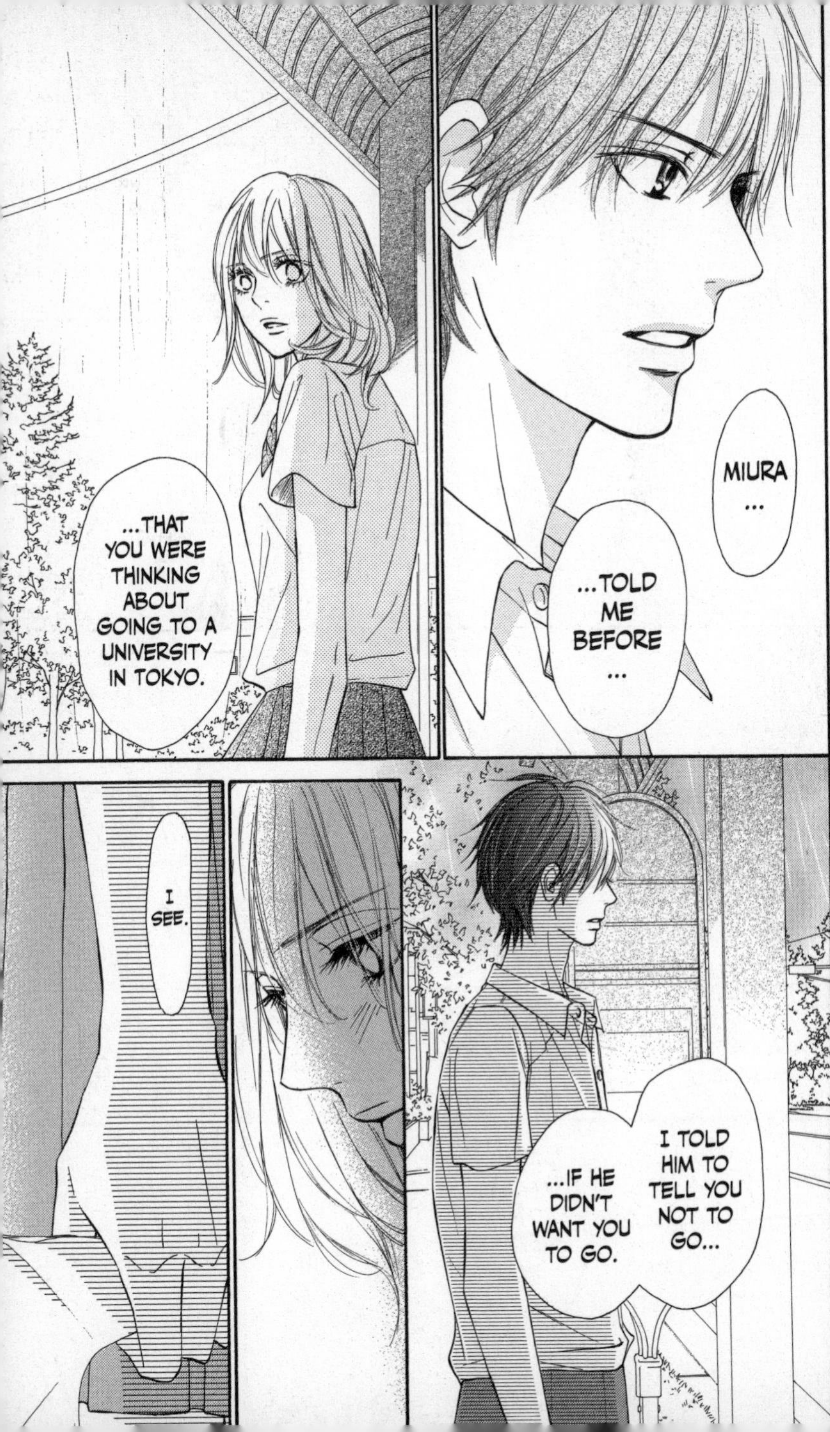
MIURA ...
...TOLD ME BEFORE ...
...THAT YOU WERE THINKING ABOUT GOING TO A UNIVERSITY IN TOKYO.
I TOLD HIM TO TELL YOU NOT TO GO...
...IF HE DIDN'T WANT YOU TO GO.
I SEE.

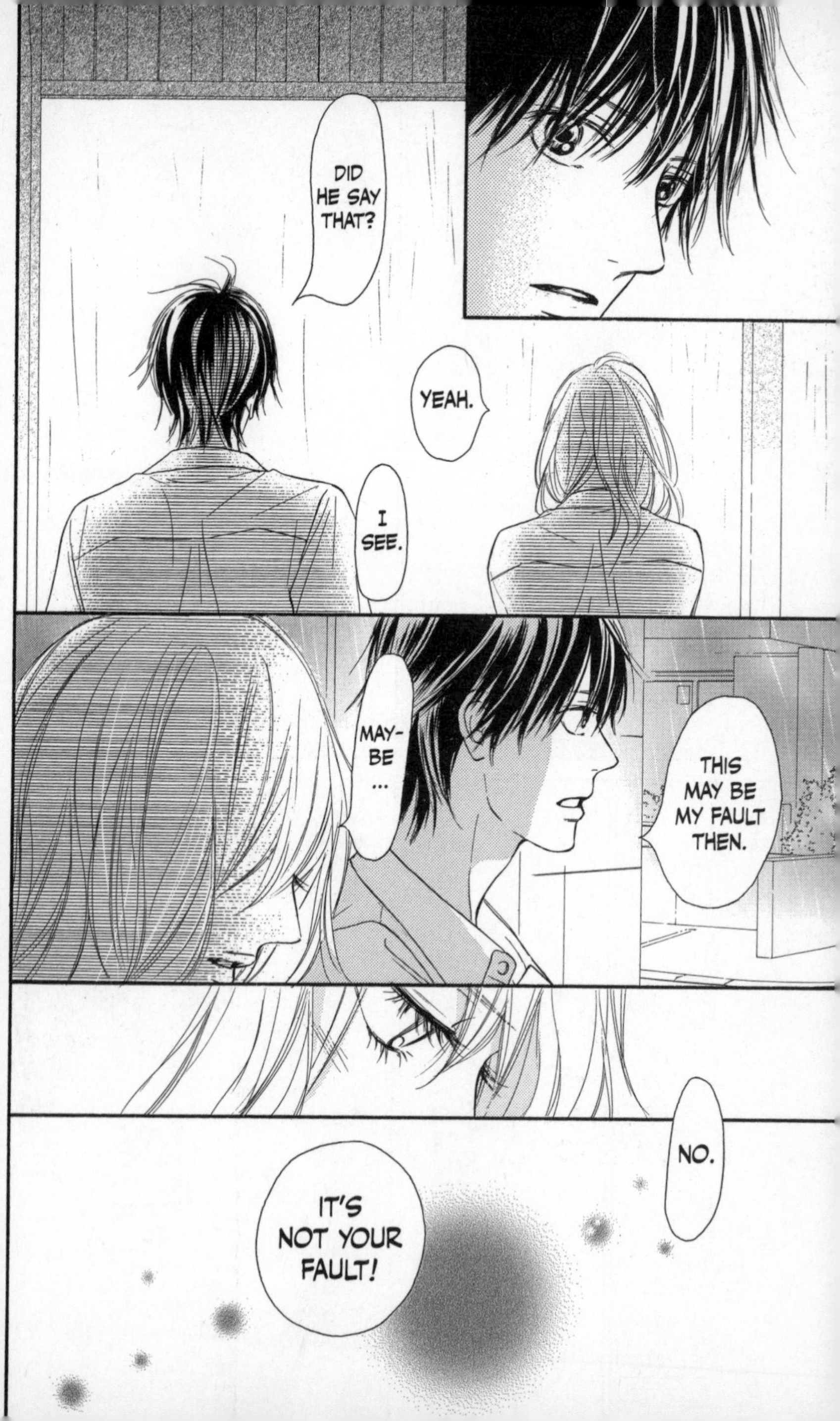
DID HE SAY THAT?
YEAH.
I SEE.
MAY-BE ...
THIS MAY BE MY FAULT THEN.
NO.
IT'S NOT YOUR FAULT!

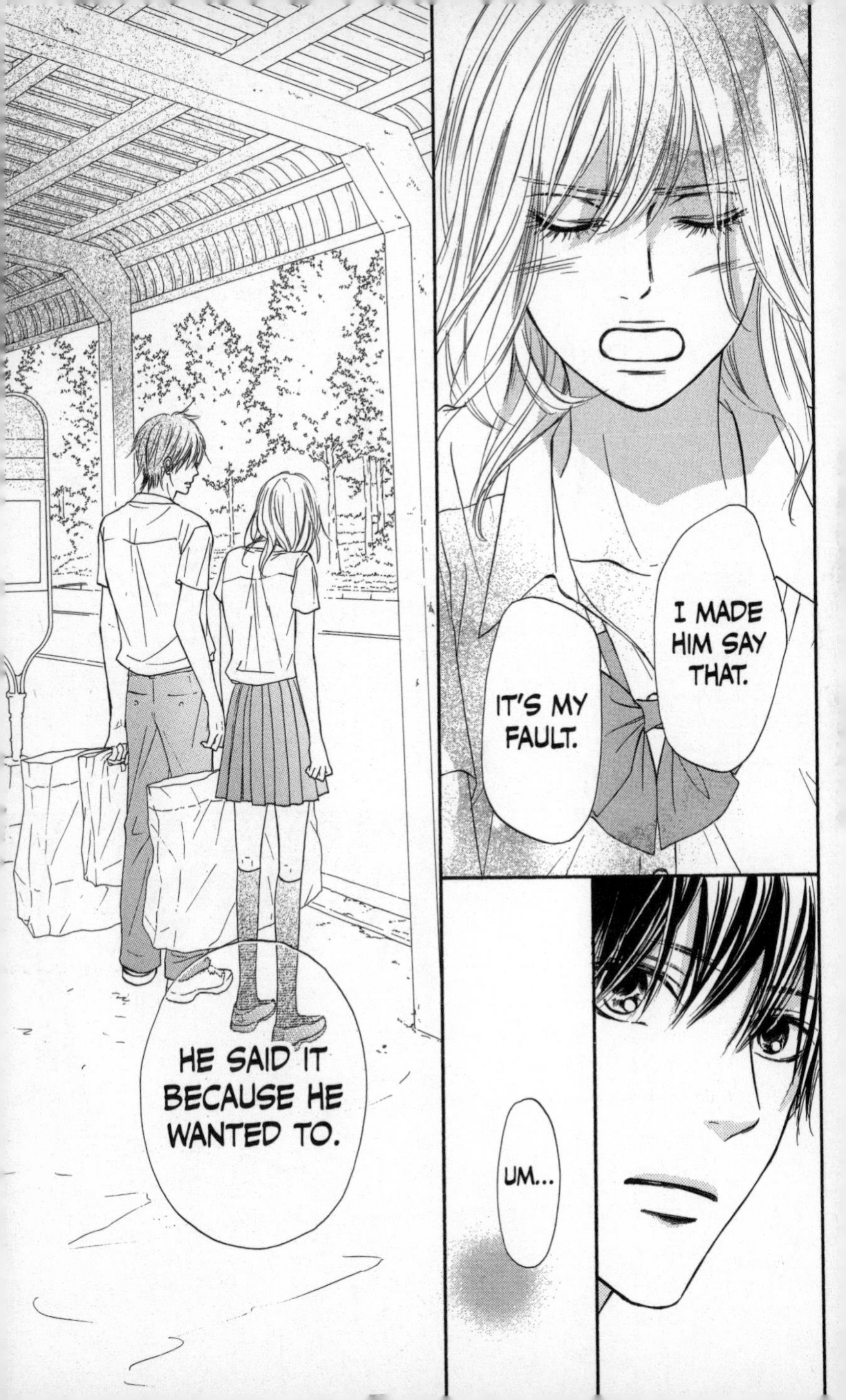
I MADE HIM SAY THAT.
IT'S MY FAULT.
UM...
HE SAID IT BECAUSE HE WANTED TO.

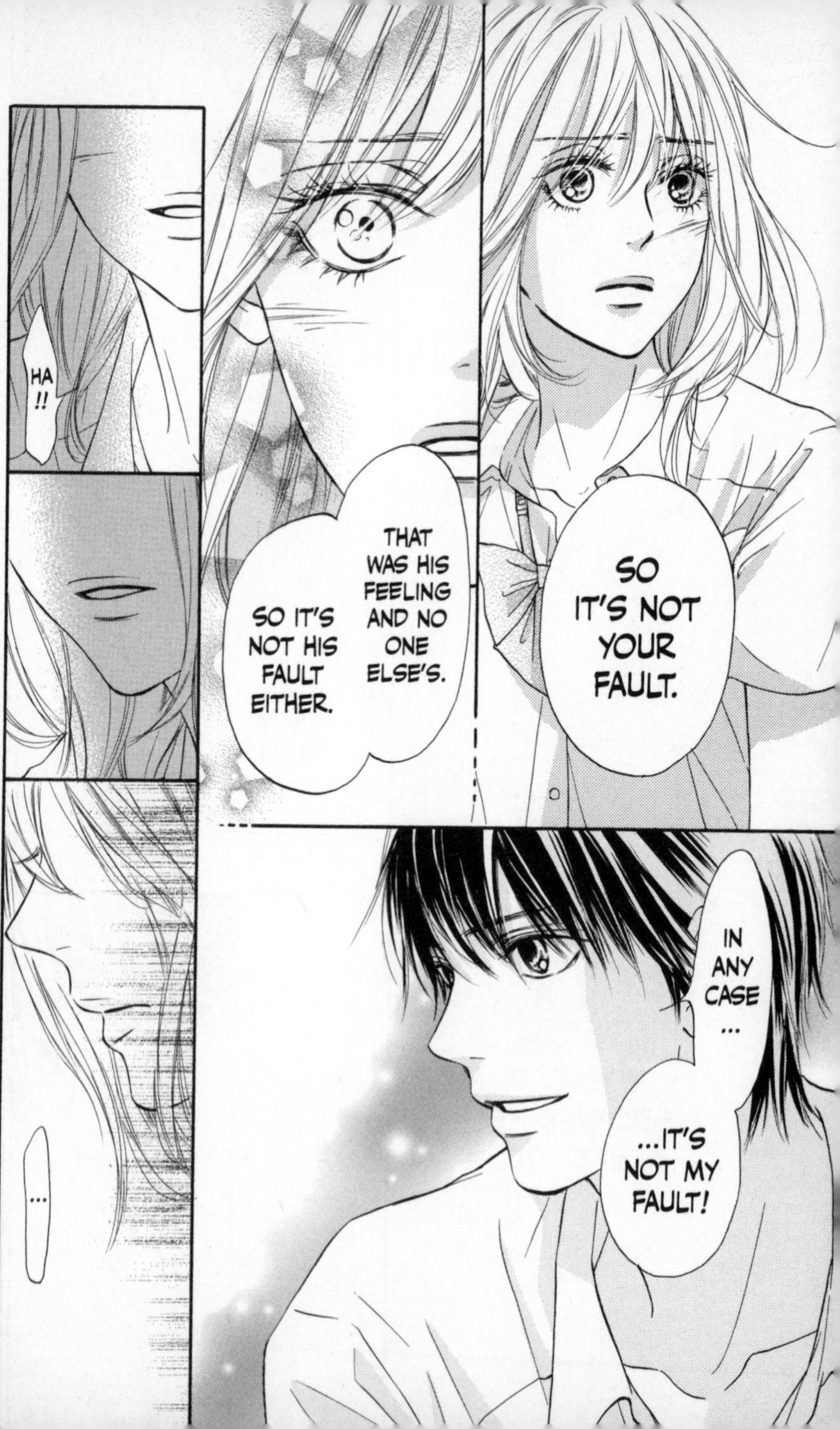
SO IT'S NOT YOUR FAULT.
THAT WAS HIS FEELING AND NO ONE ELSE'S.
SO IT'S NOT HIS FAULT EITHER.
HA!!
IN ANY CASE...
...IT'S NOT MY FAULT!
...

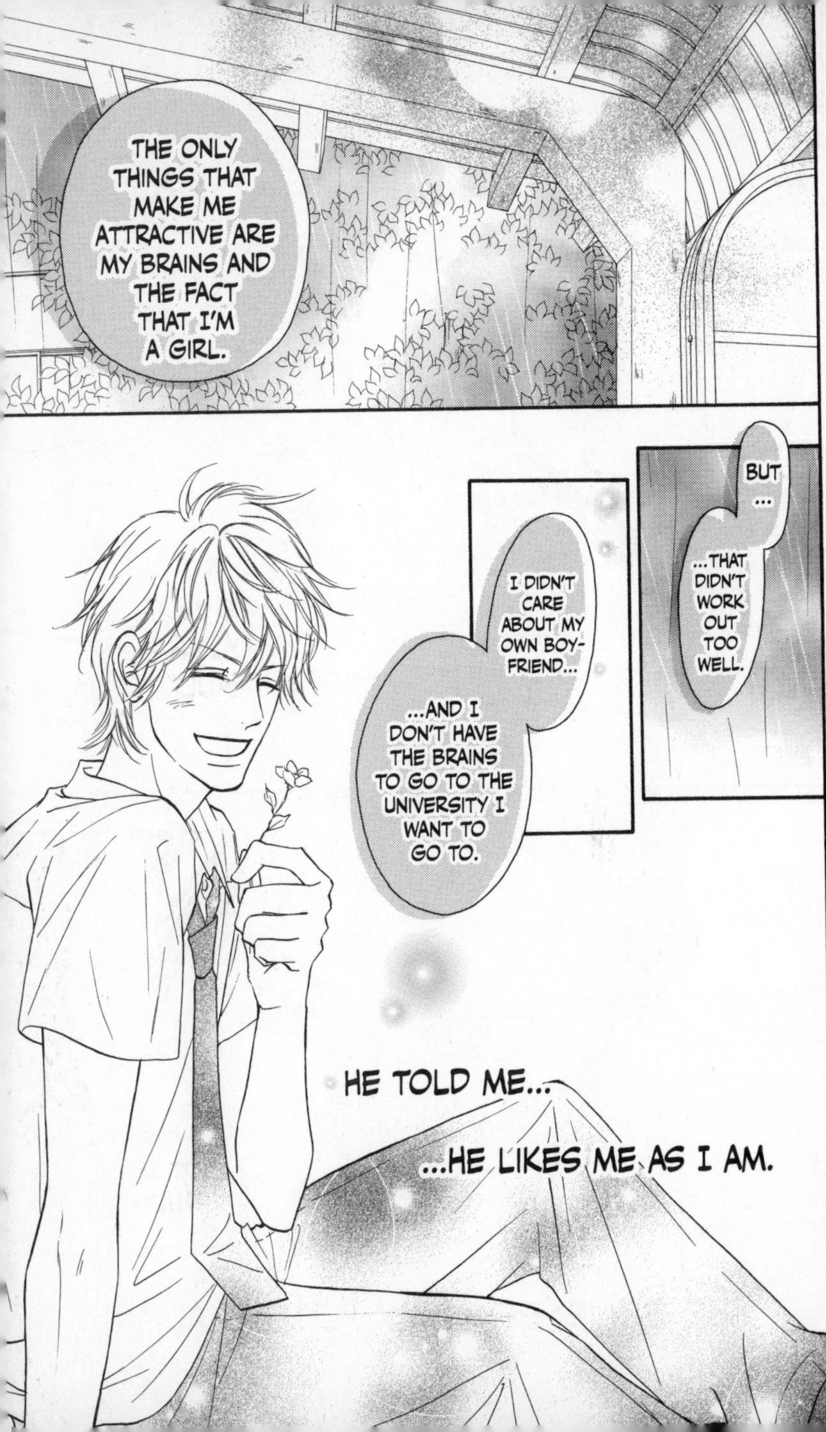
THE ONLY THINGS THAT MAKE ME ATTRACTIVE ARE MY BRAINS AND THE FACT THAT I'M A GIRL.
BUT...
...THAT DIDN'T WORK OUT TOO WELL.
I DIDN'T CARE ABOUT MY OWN BOY-FRIEND...
...AND I DON'T HAVE THE BRAINS TO GO TO THE UNIVERSITY I WANT TO GO TO.
HE TOLD ME...
...HE LIKES ME AS I AM.

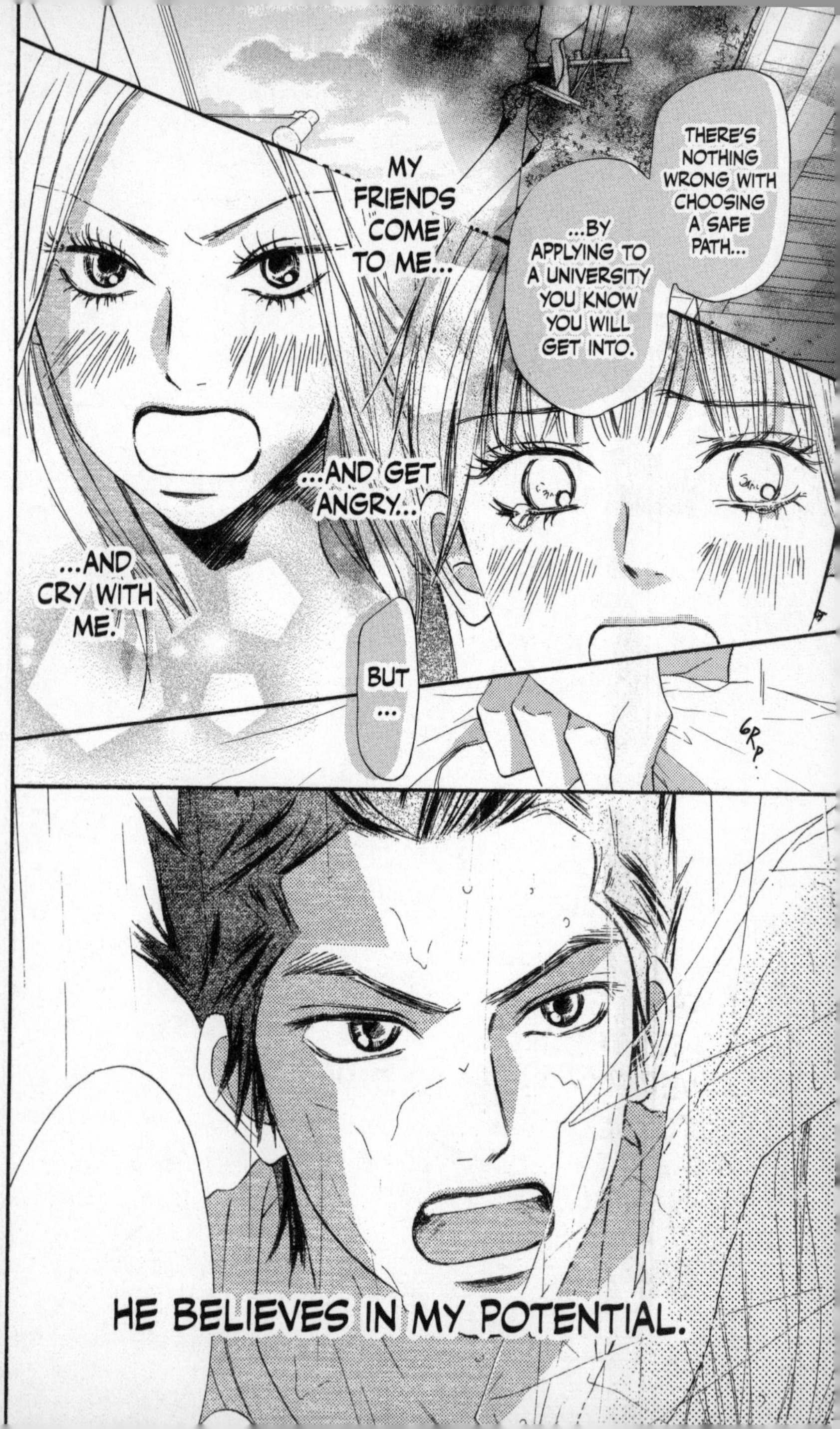
THERE'S NOTHING WRONG WITH CHOOSING A SAFE PATH...
...BY APPLYING TO A UNIVERSITY YOU KNOW YOU WILL GET INTO.
MY FRIENDS COME TO ME...
...AND GET ANGRY...
...AND CRY WITH ME.
BUT ...
HE BELIEVES IN MY POTENTIAL.

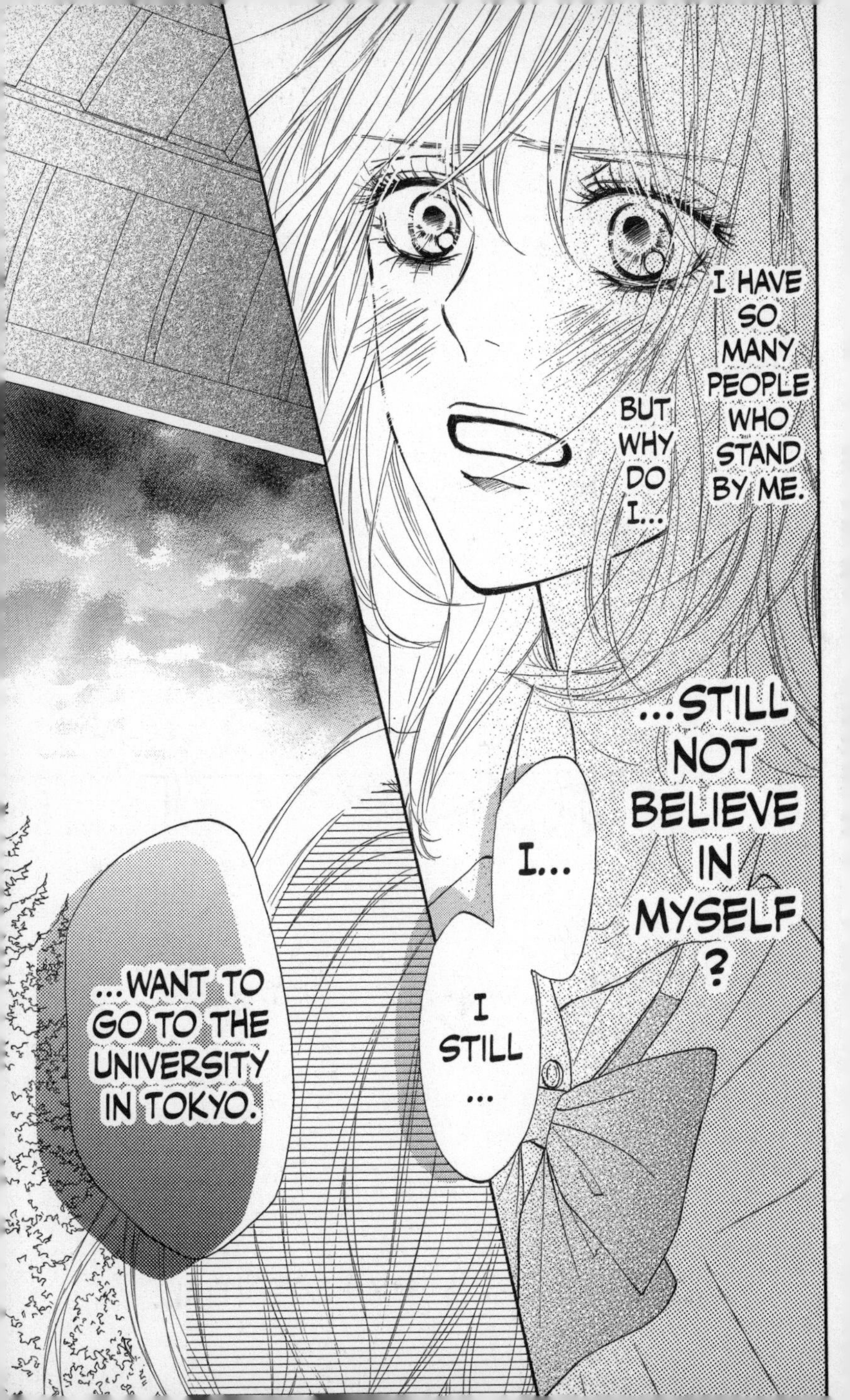
I HAVE SO MANY PEOPLE WHO STAND BY ME.
BUT WHY DO I...
...STILL NOT BELIEVE IN MYSELF?
I...
I STILL ...
...WANT TO GO TO THE UNIVERSITY IN TOKYO.

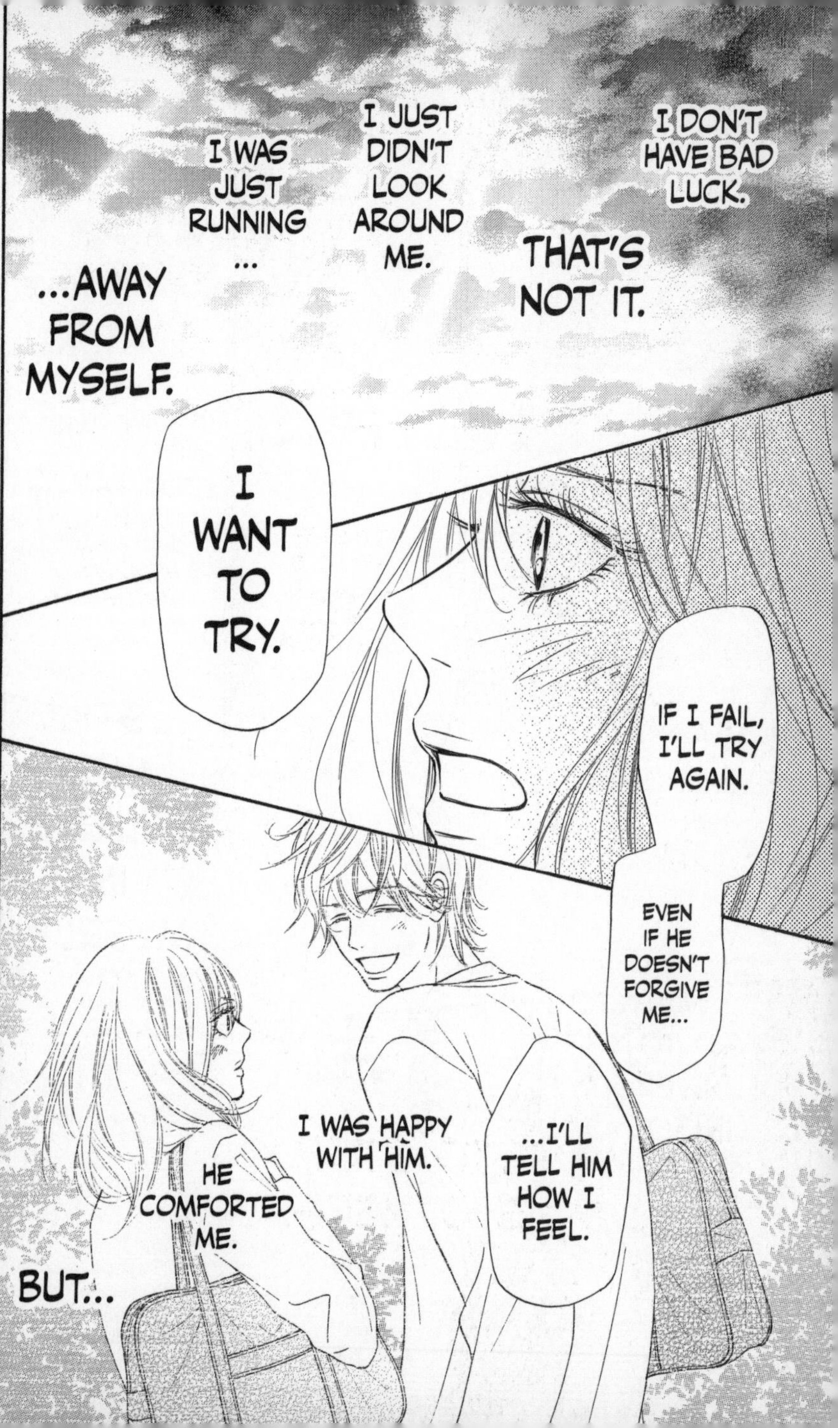
I DON'T HAVE BAD LUCK.
THAT'S NOT IT.
I JUST DIDN'T LOOK AROUND ME.
I WAS JUST RUNNING...
...AWAY FROM MYSELF.
I WANT TO TRY.
IF I FAIL, I'LL TRY AGAIN.
EVEN IF HE DOESN'T FORGIVE ME...
...I'LL TELL HIM HOW I FEEL.
I WAS HAPPY WITH HIM.
HE COMFORTED ME.
BUT...

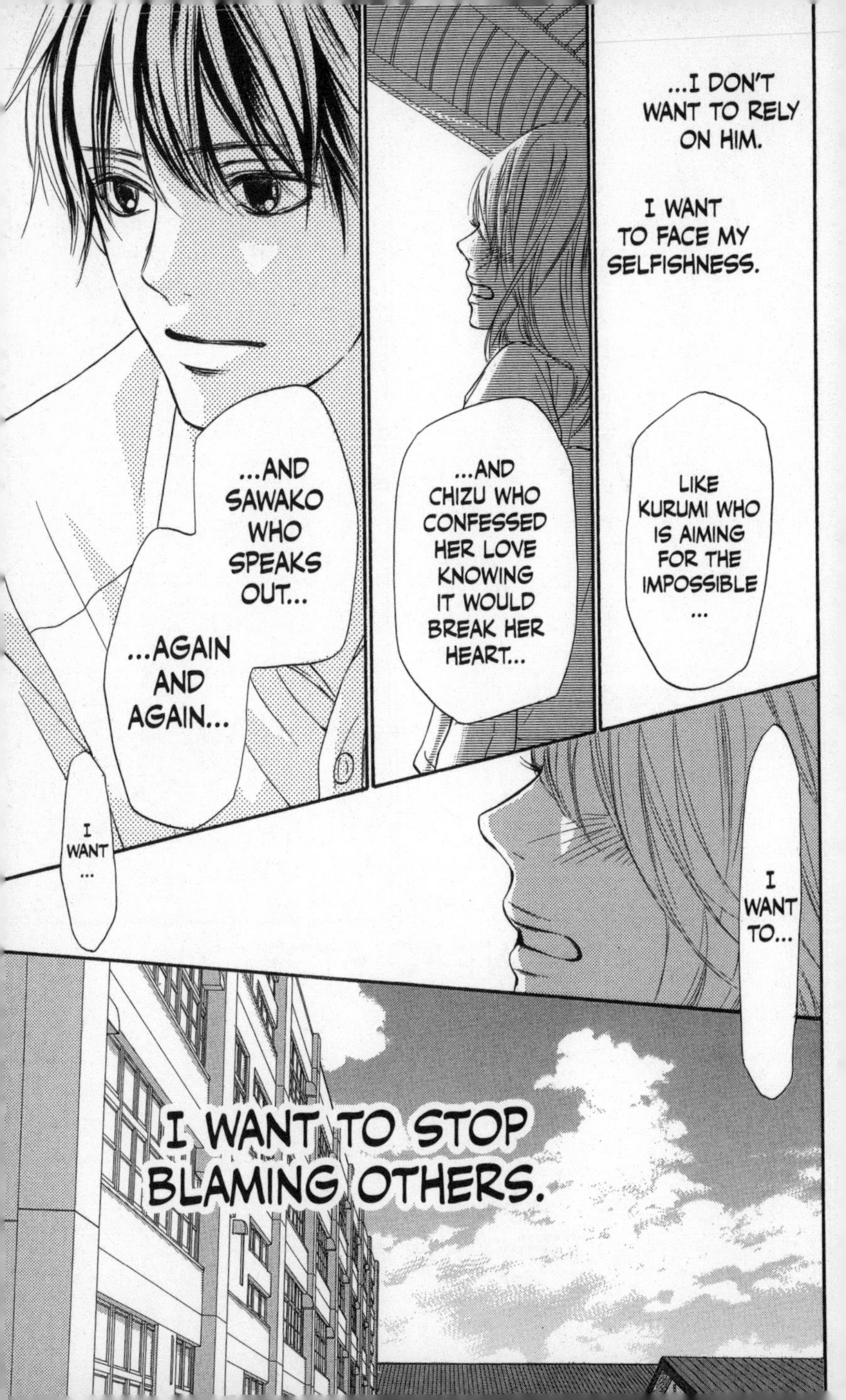
...I DON'T WANT TO RELY ON HIM.
I WANT TO FACE MY SELFISHNESS.
LIKE KURUMI WHO IS AIMING FOR THE IMPOSSIBLE...
...AND CHIZU WHO CONFESSED HER LOVE KNOWING IT WOULD BREAK HER HEART...
...AND SAWAKO WHO SPEAKS OUT...
...AGAIN AND AGAIN...
I WANT TO...
I WANT...
I WANT TO STOP BLAMING OTHERS.

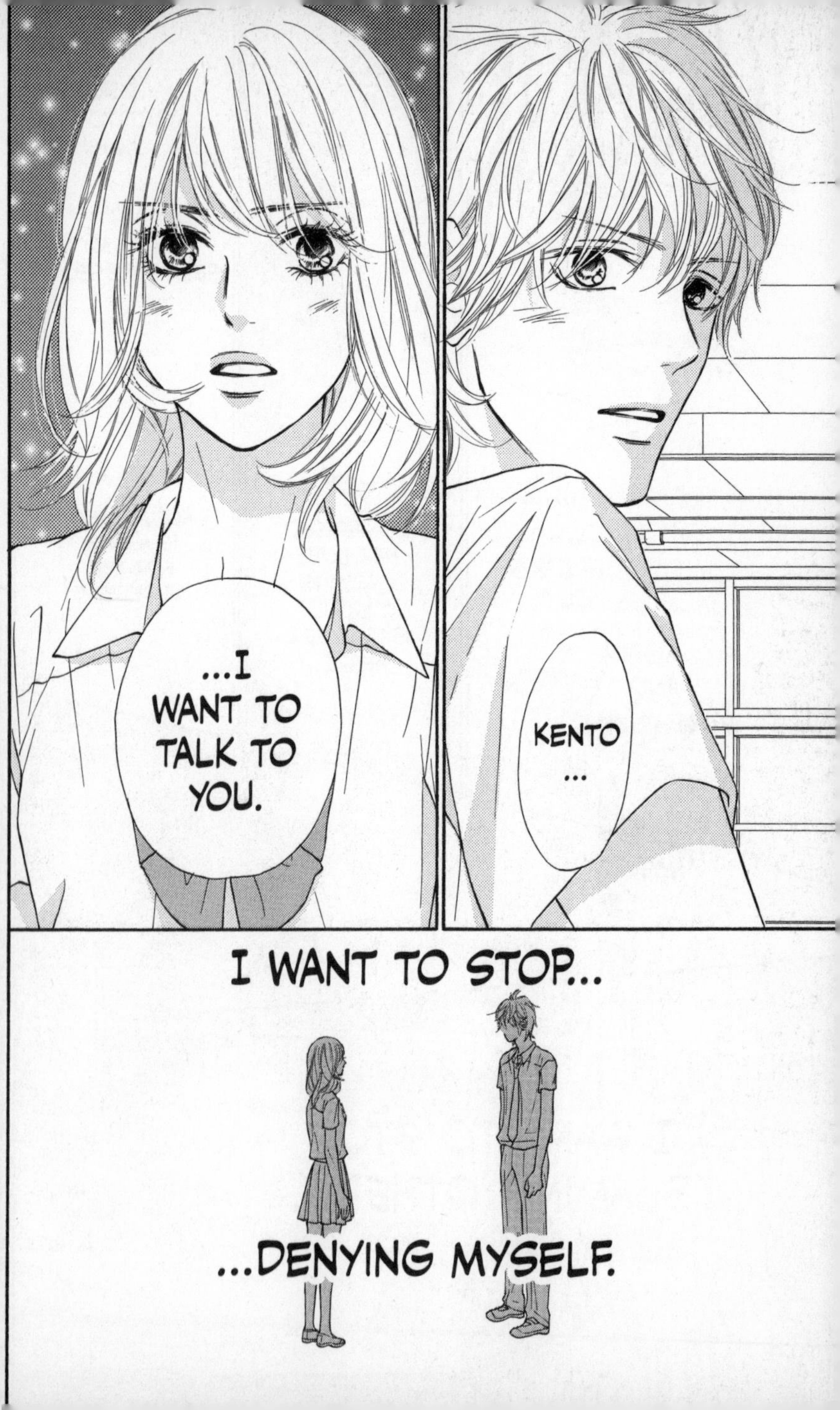
KENTO ...
...I WANT TO TALK TO YOU.
I WANT TO STOP...
...DENYING MYSELF.

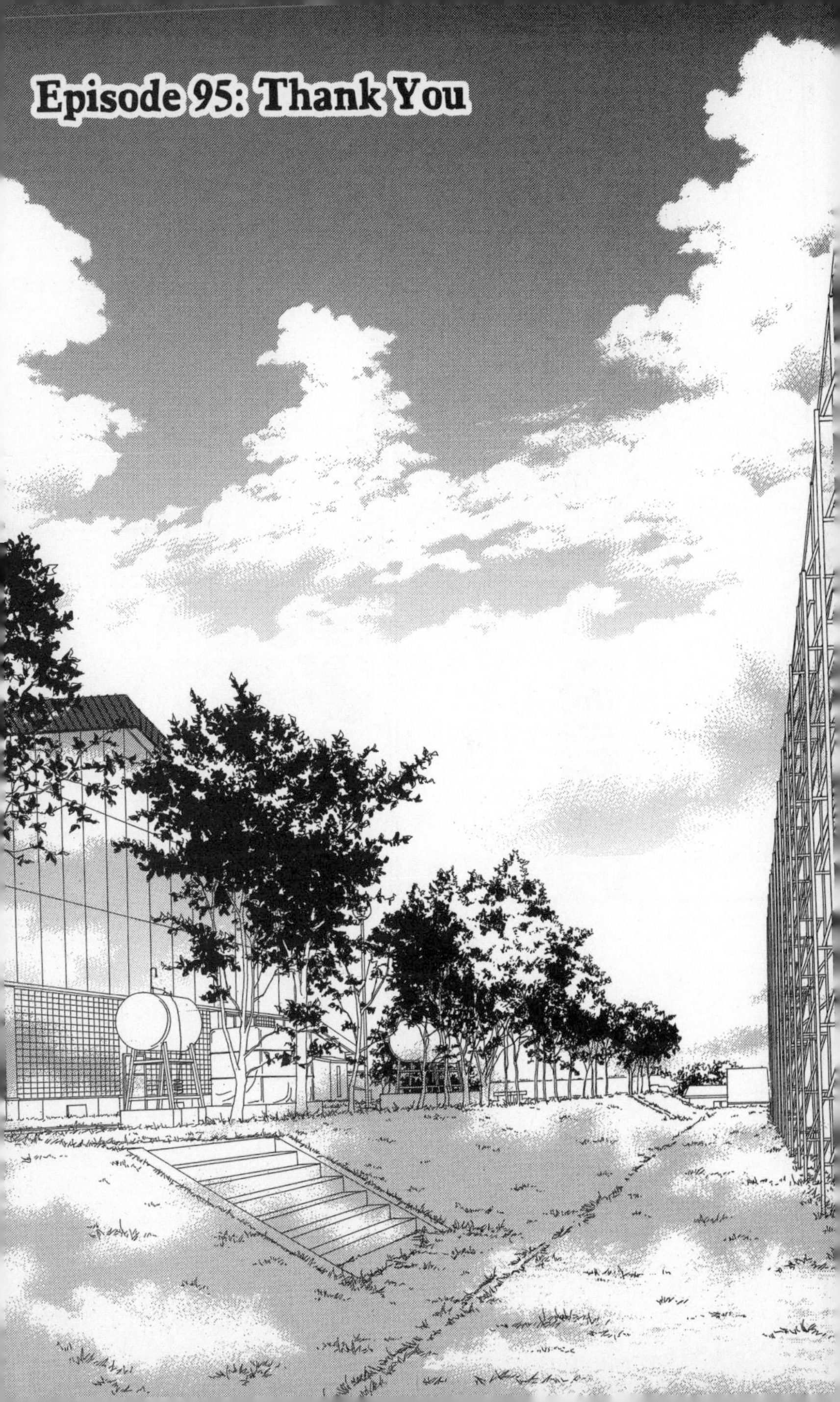
Episode 95: Thank You

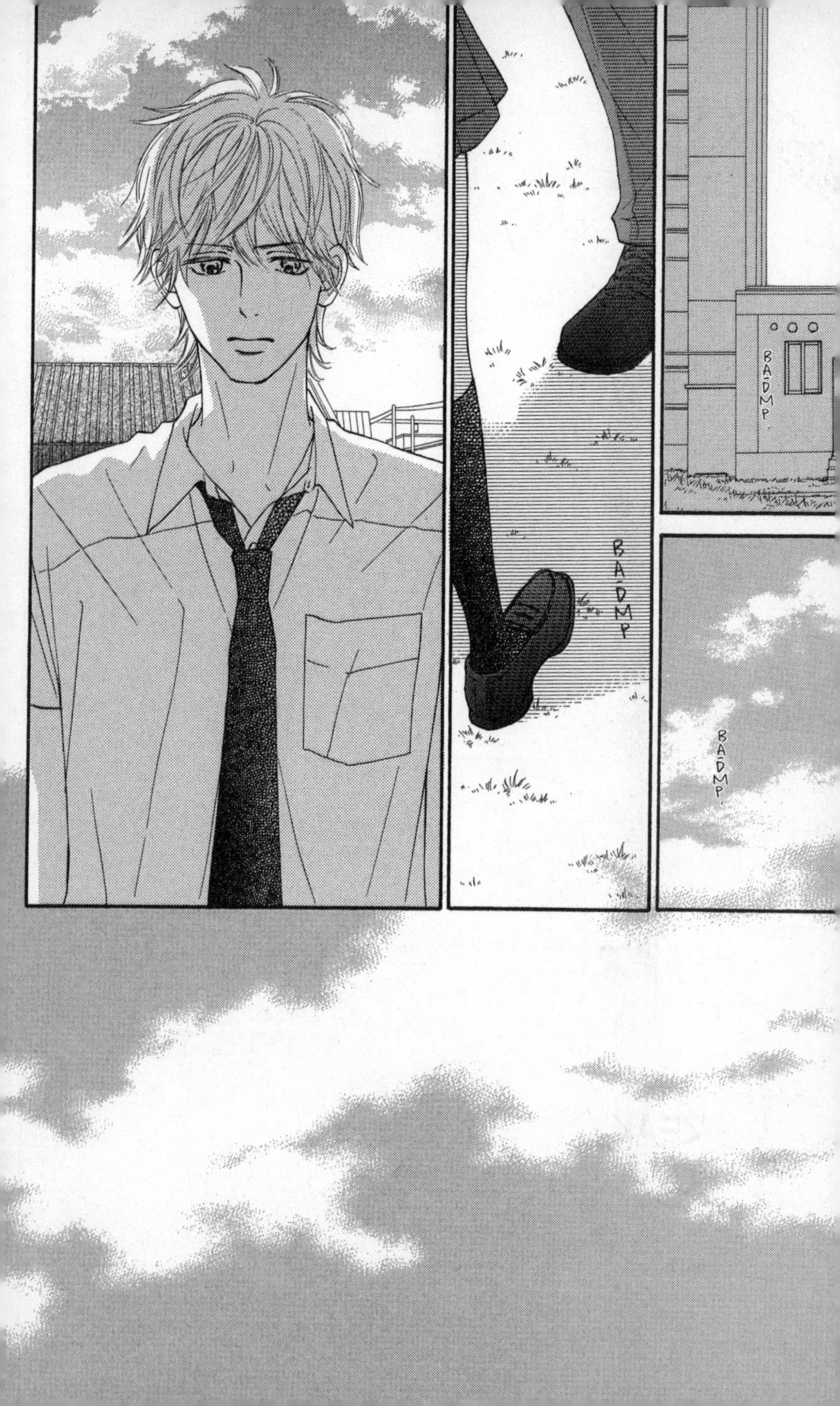
BA-DMP
BA-DMP
BA-DMP

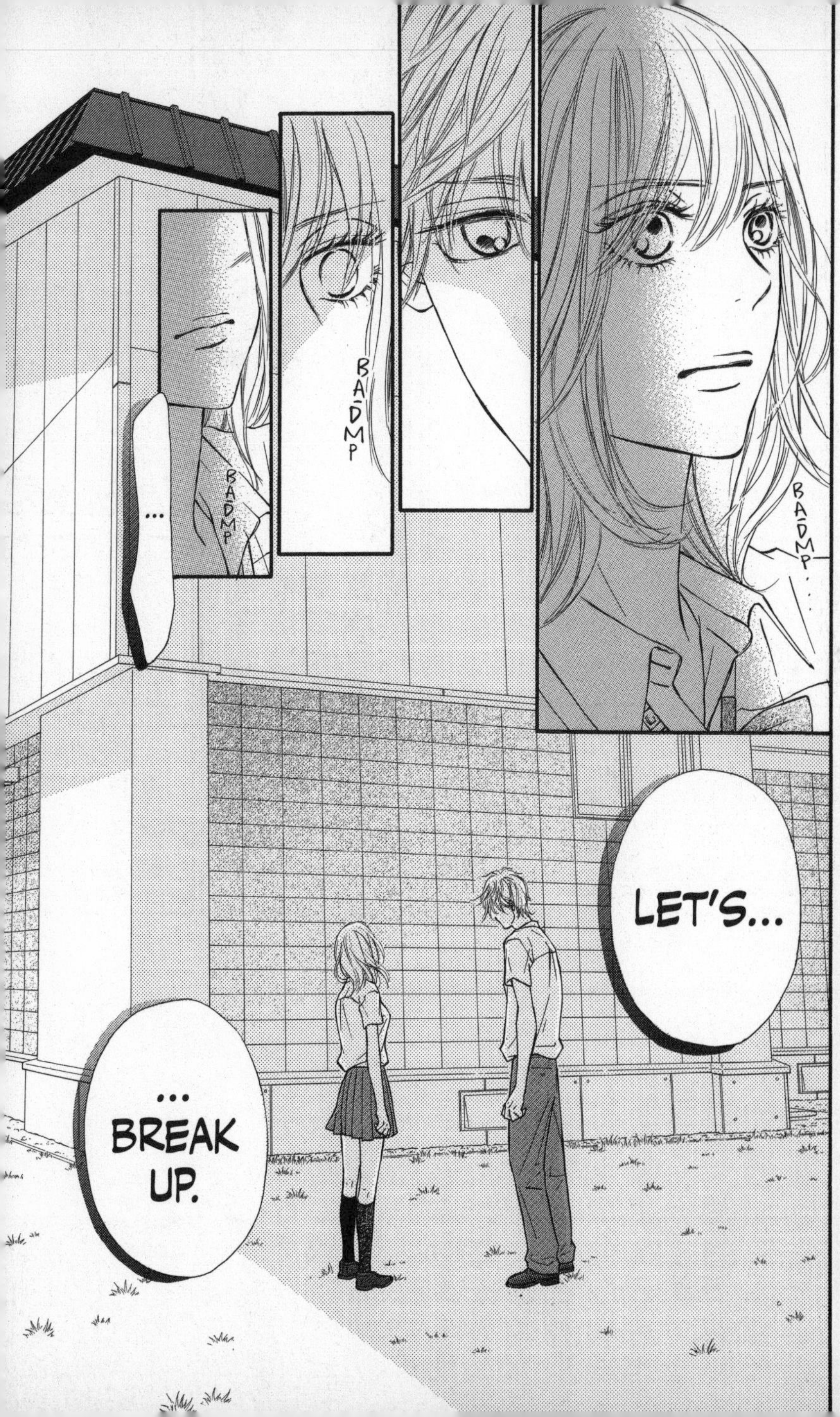
BA-DMP...
BA-DMP
BA-DMP
...
LET'S...
...BREAK UP.

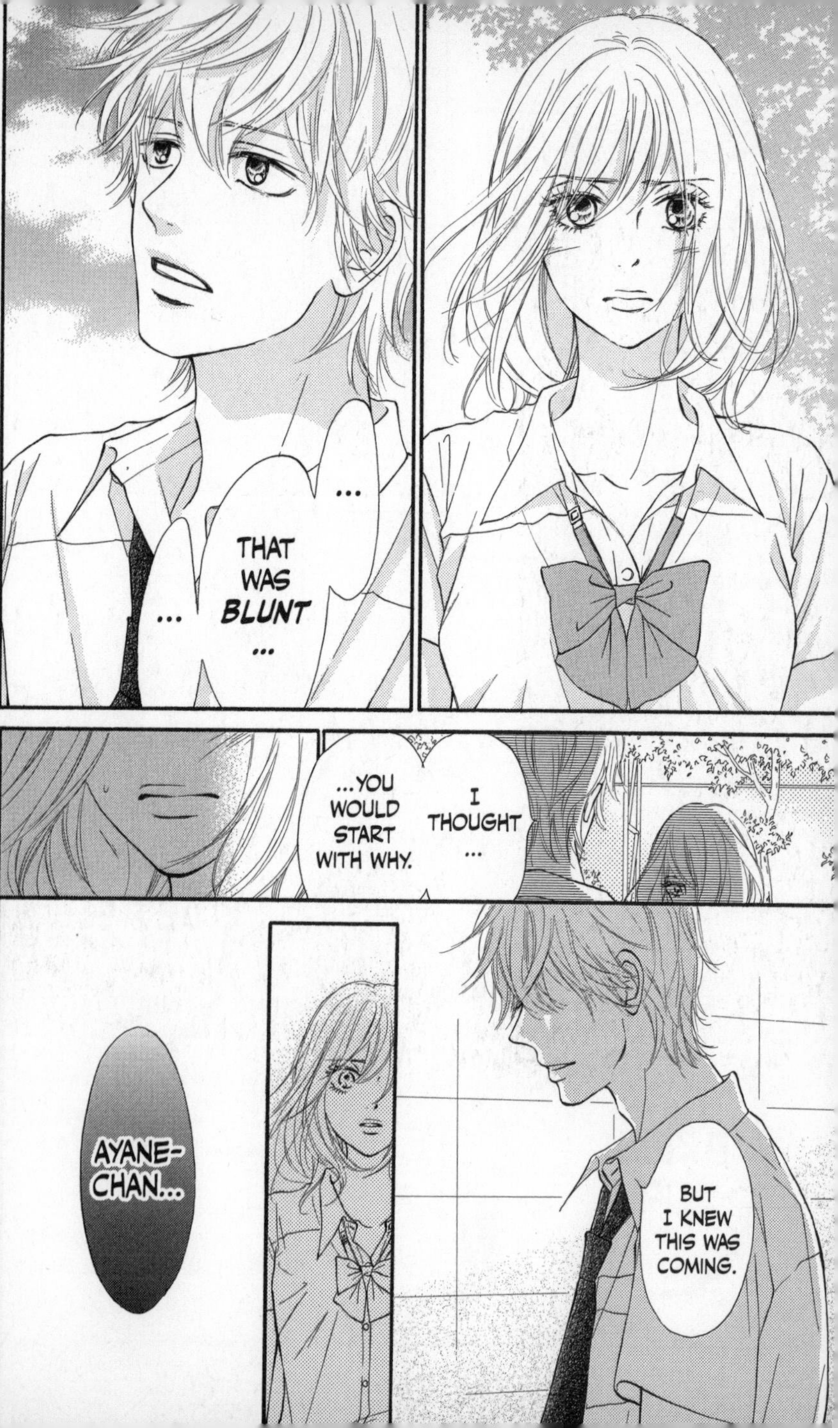
...
... THAT WAS BLUNT ...
I THOUGHT ...
...YOU WOULD START WITH WHY.
BUT I KNEW THIS WAS COMING.
AYANE-CHAN...

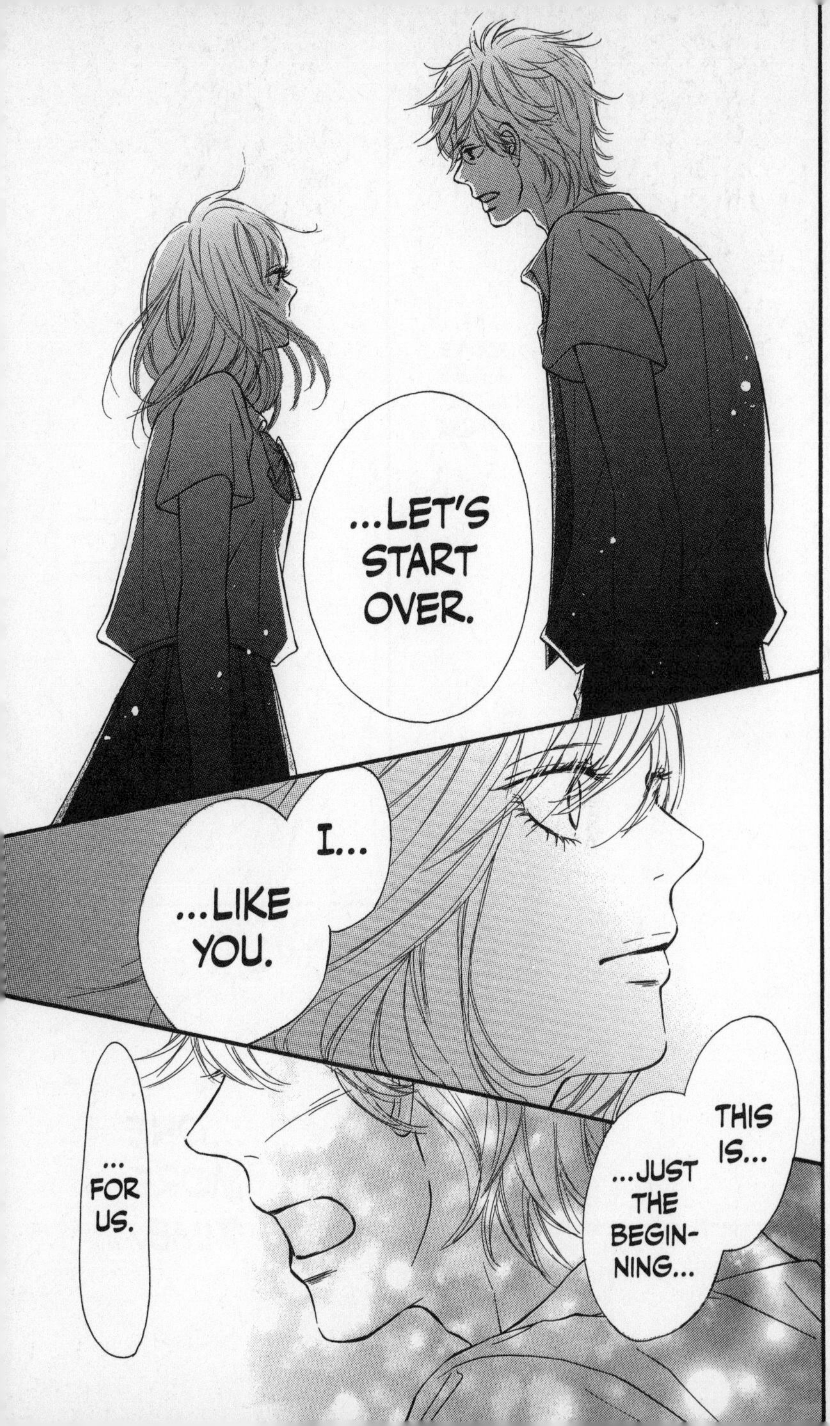
...LET'S START OVER.
I... ...LIKE YOU.
THIS IS... ...JUST THE BEGIN-NING...
...FOR US.

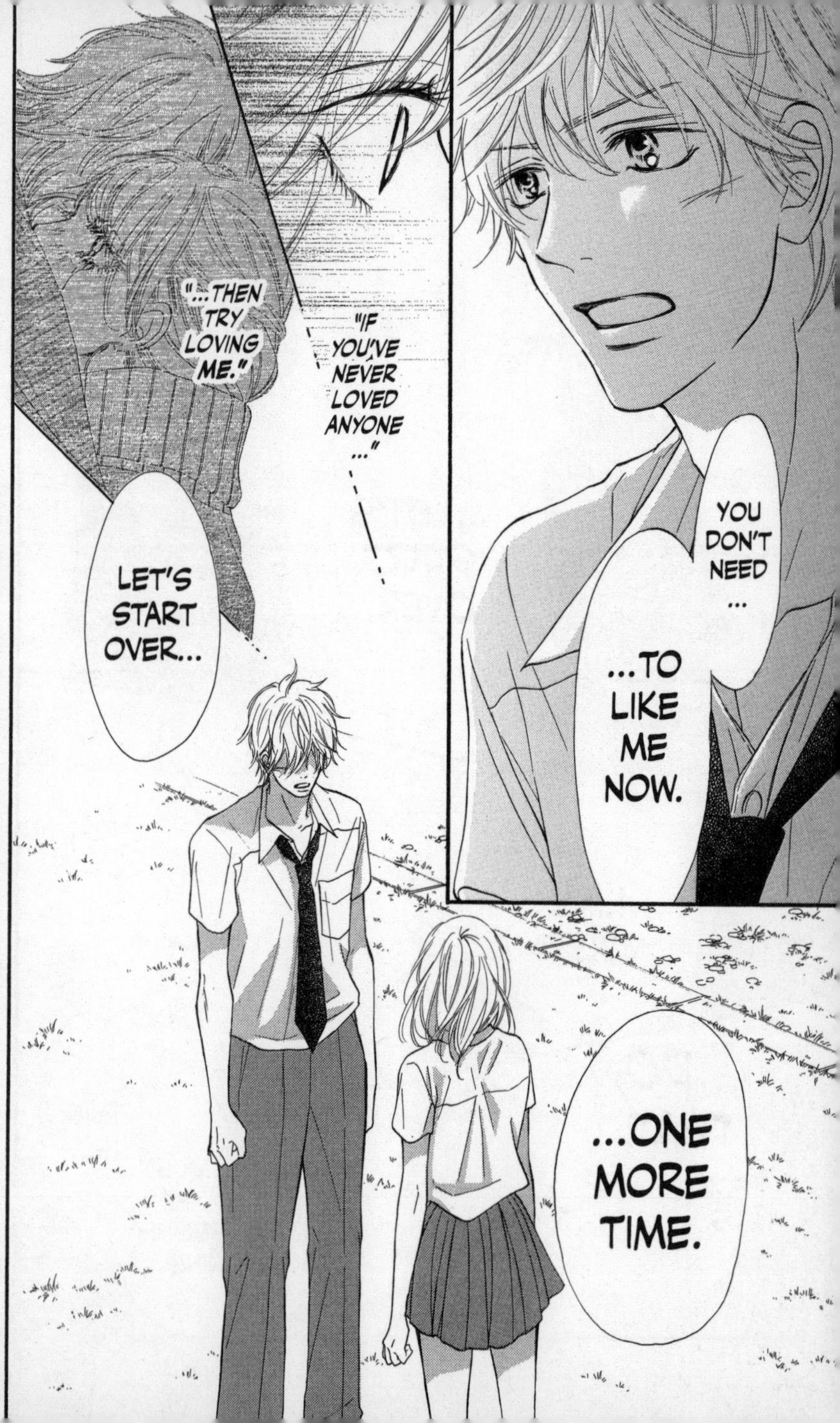
YOU DON'T NEED ...
...TO LIKE ME NOW.
"IF YOU'VE NEVER LOVED ANYONE ..."
"...THEN TRY LOVING ME."
LET'S START OVER...
...ONE MORE TIME.

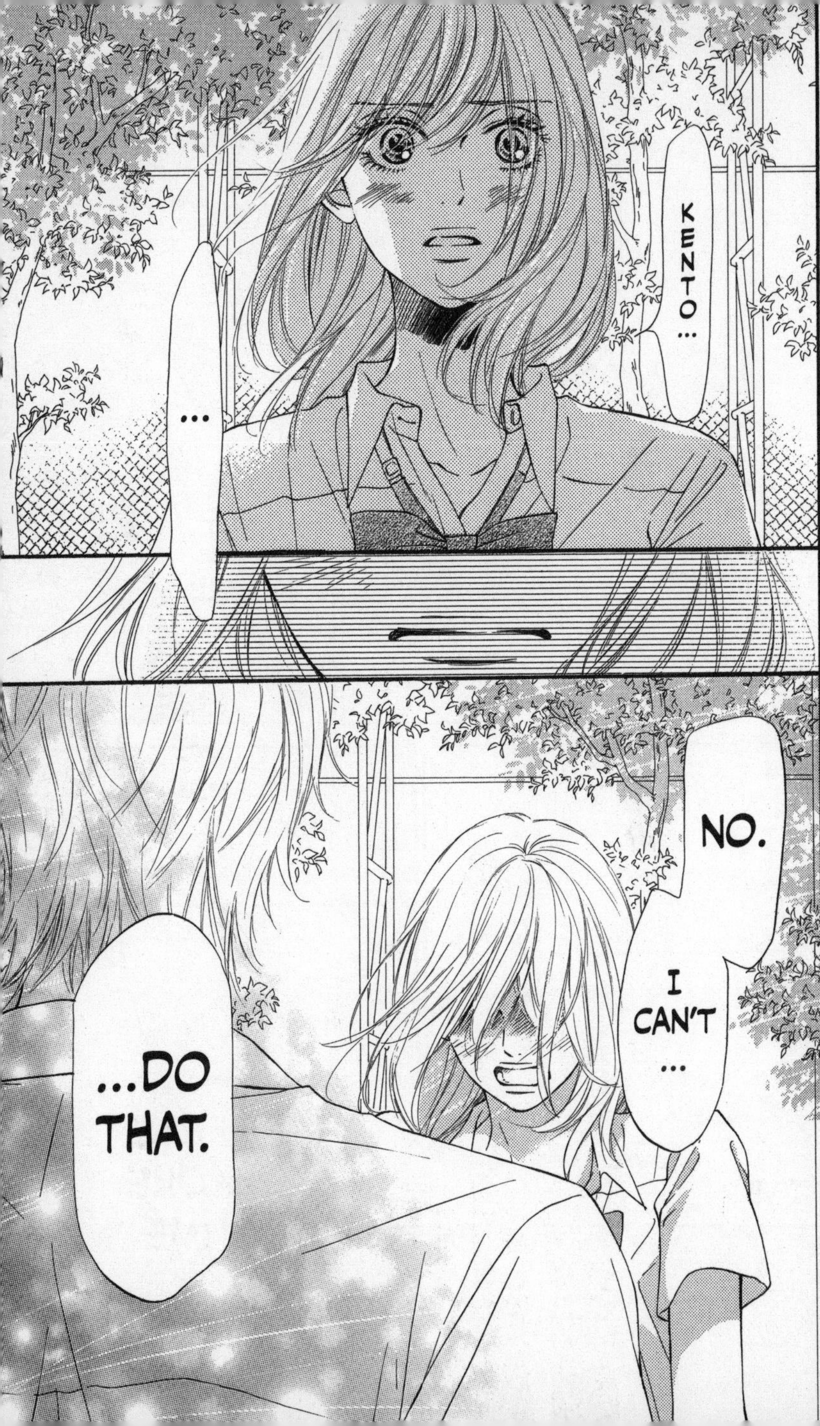
KENTO...
...
NO.
I CAN'T...
...DO THAT.

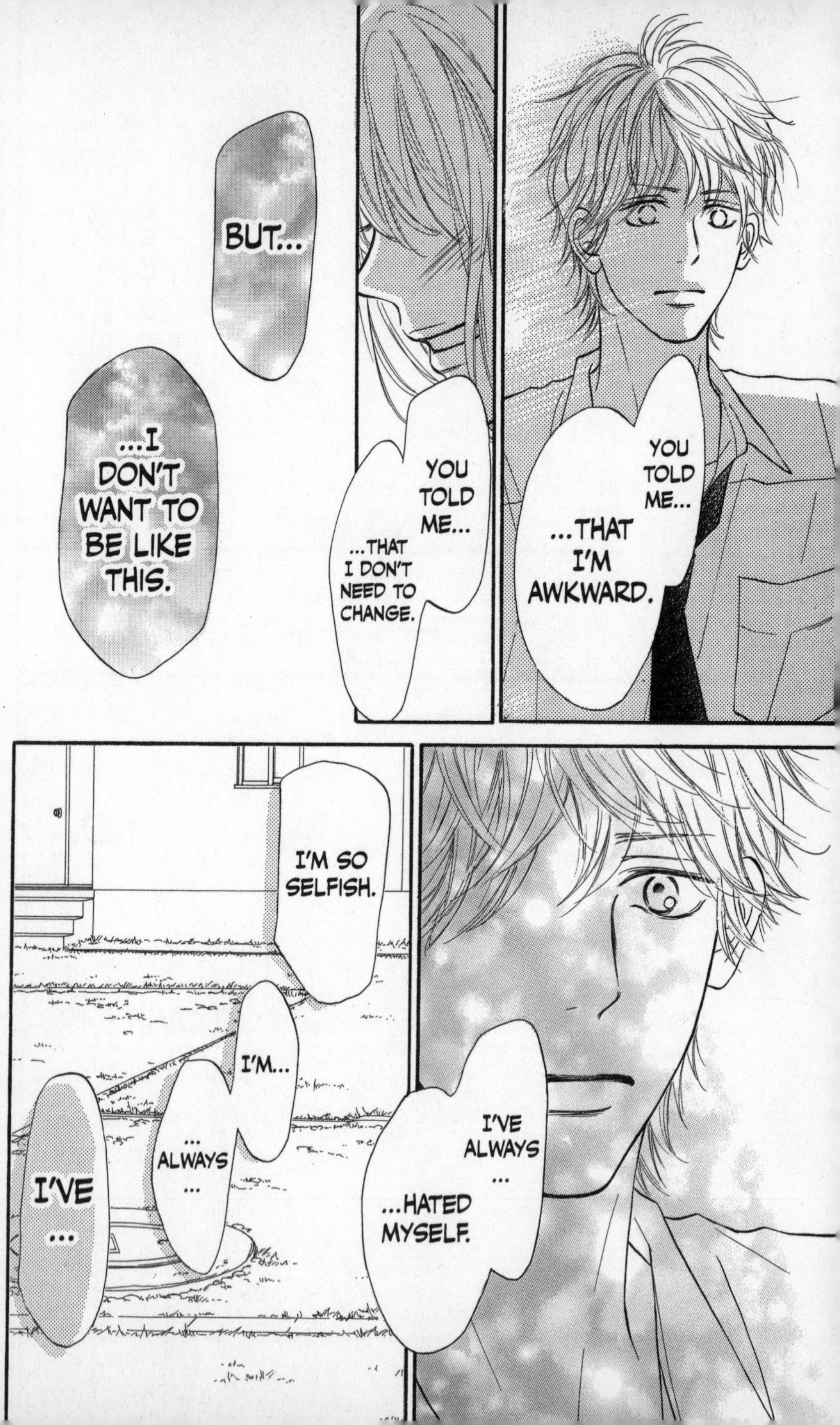
YOU TOLD ME...
...THAT I'M AWKWARD.
YOU TOLD ME...
...THAT I DON'T NEED TO CHANGE.
BUT...
...I DON'T WANT TO BE LIKE THIS.
I'VE ALWAYS...
...HATED MYSELF.
I'M SO SELFISH.
I'M...
...ALWAYS...
I'VE...

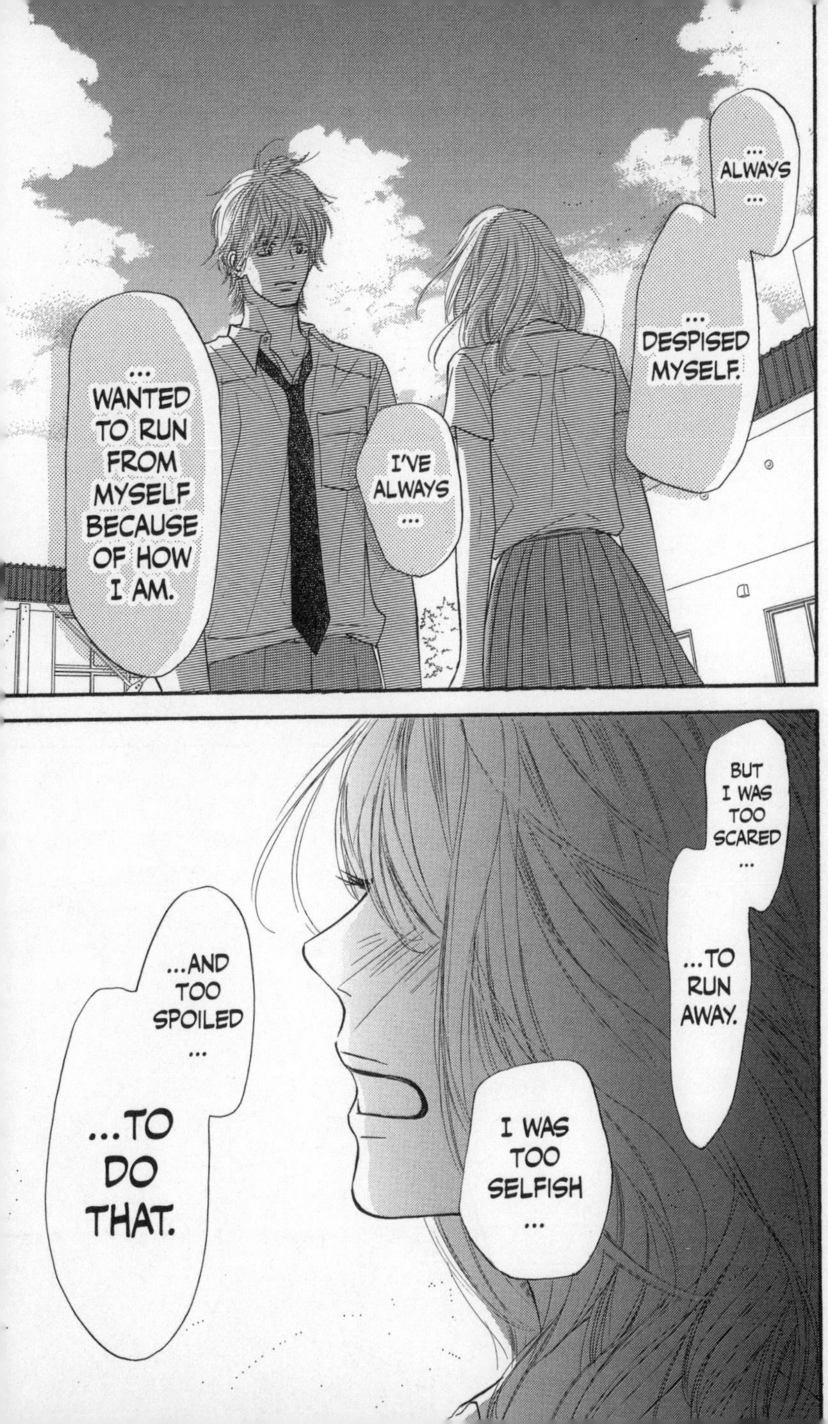
... ALWAYS ...
... DESPISED MYSELF.
I'VE ALWAYS ...
... WANTED TO RUN FROM MYSELF BECAUSE OF HOW I AM.
BUT I WAS TOO SCARED ...
...TO RUN AWAY.
I WAS TOO SELFISH ...
...AND TOO SPOILED ...
...TO DO THAT.

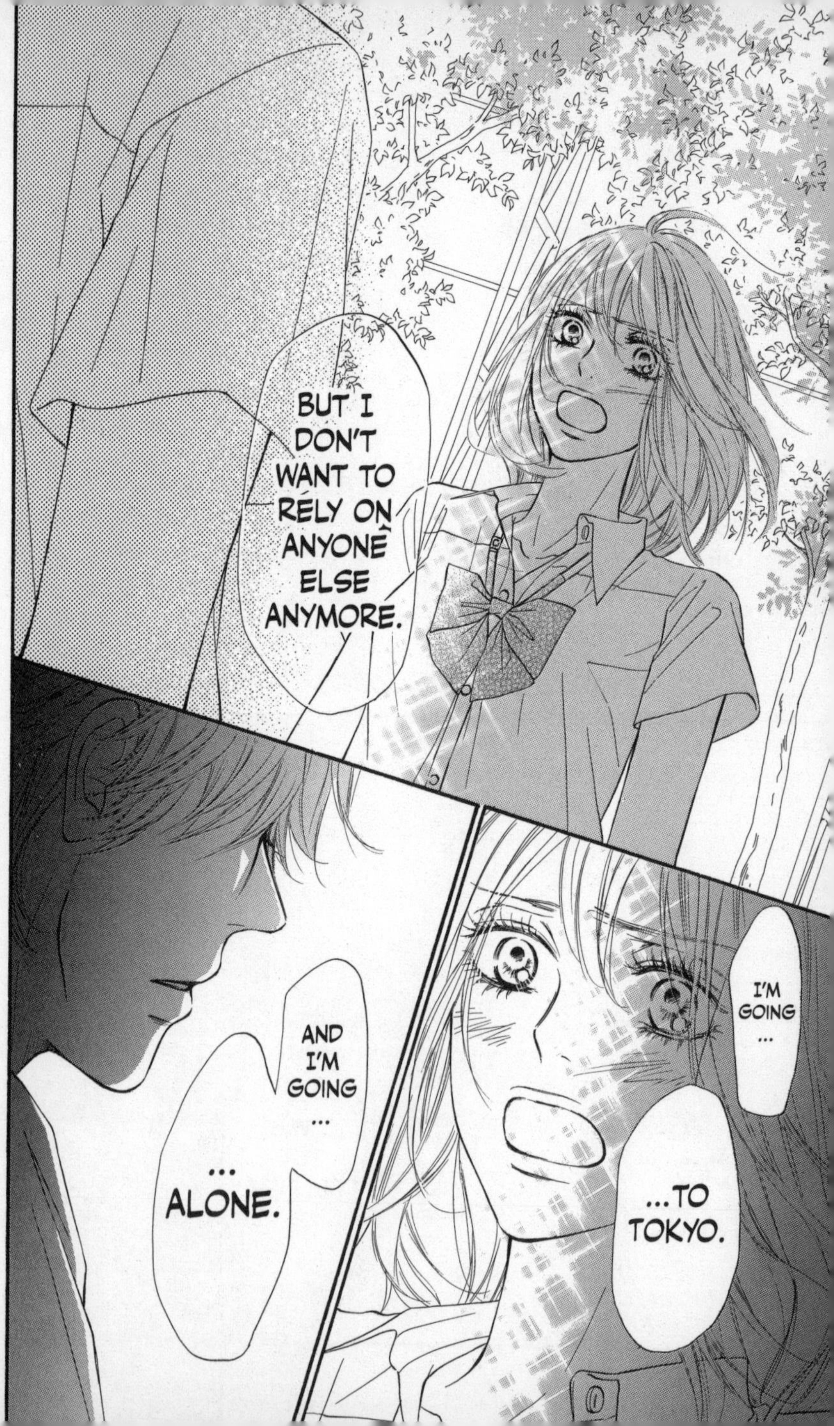
BUT I DON'T WANT TO RELY ON ANYONE ELSE ANYMORE.
I'M GOING ...
...TO TOKYO.
AND I'M GOING ...
... ALONE.

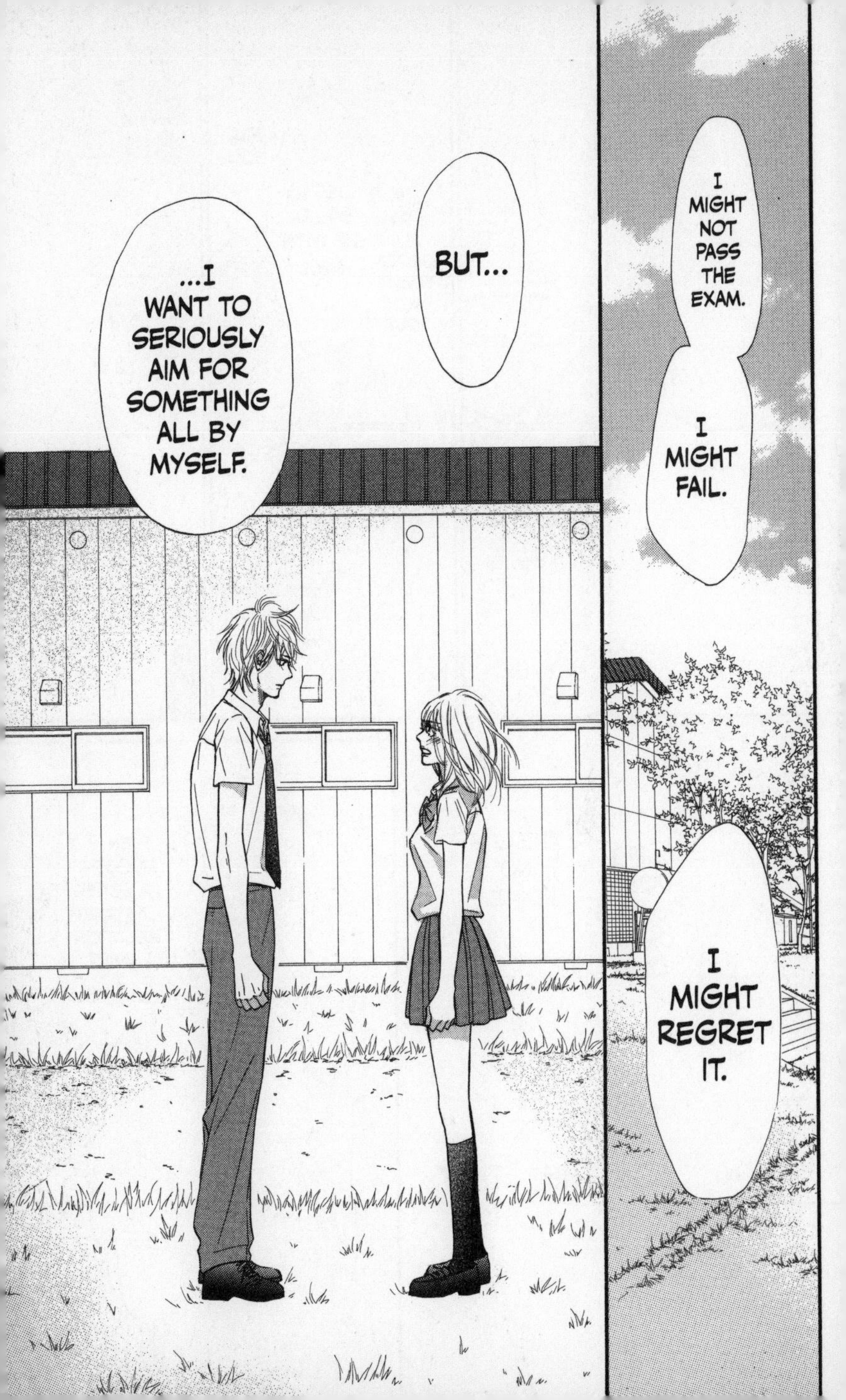
I MIGHT NOT PASS THE EXAM.
I MIGHT FAIL.
I MIGHT REGRET IT.
BUT...
...I WANT TO SERIOUSLY AIM FOR SOMETHING ALL BY MYSELF.

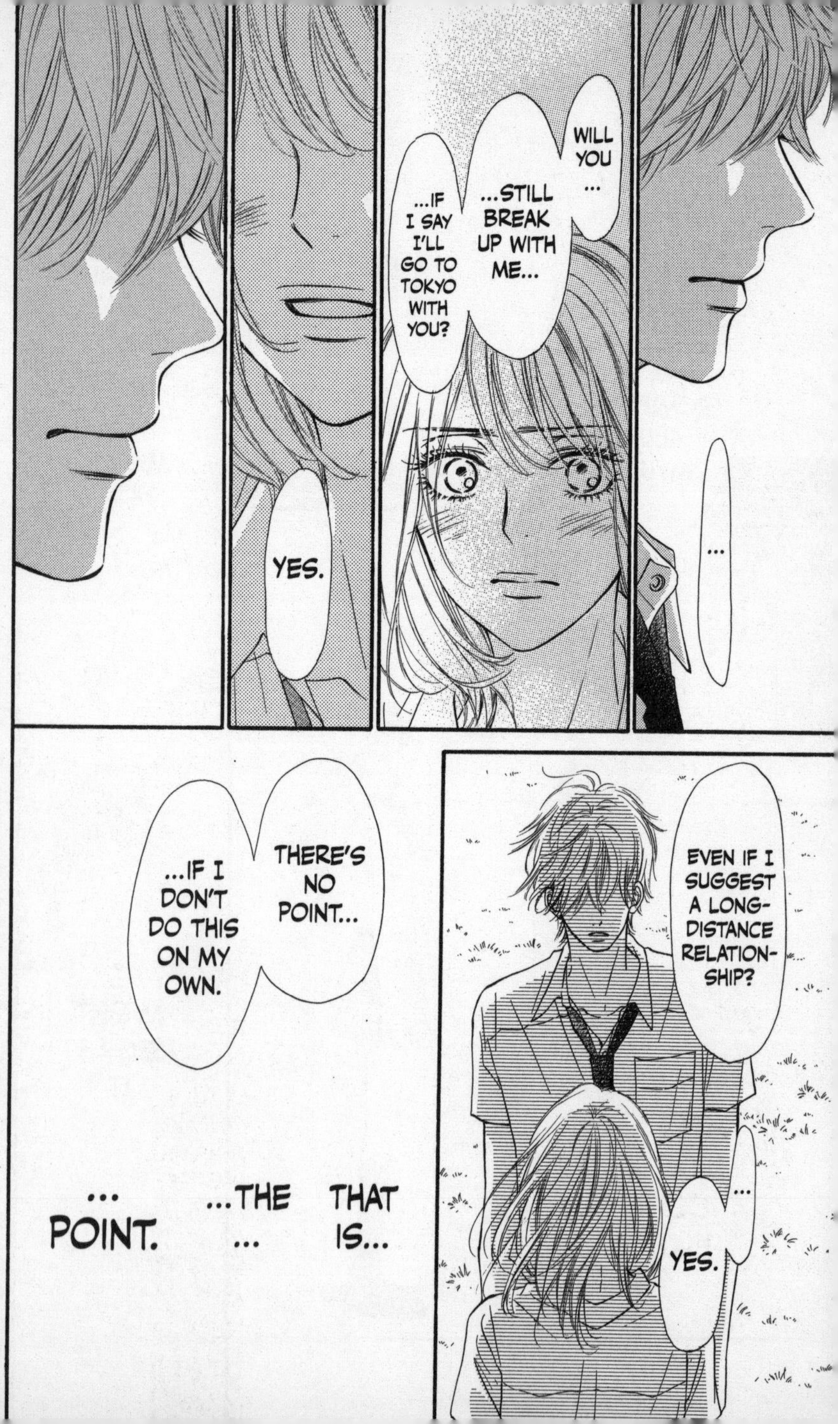
...
WILL YOU ...
...STILL BREAK UP WITH ME...
...IF I SAY I'LL GO TO TOKYO WITH YOU?
YES.
EVEN IF I SUGGEST A LONG-DISTANCE RELATIONSHIP?
...
YES.
THERE'S NO POINT...
...IF I DON'T DO THIS ON MY OWN.
THAT IS...
...THE ...
... POINT.

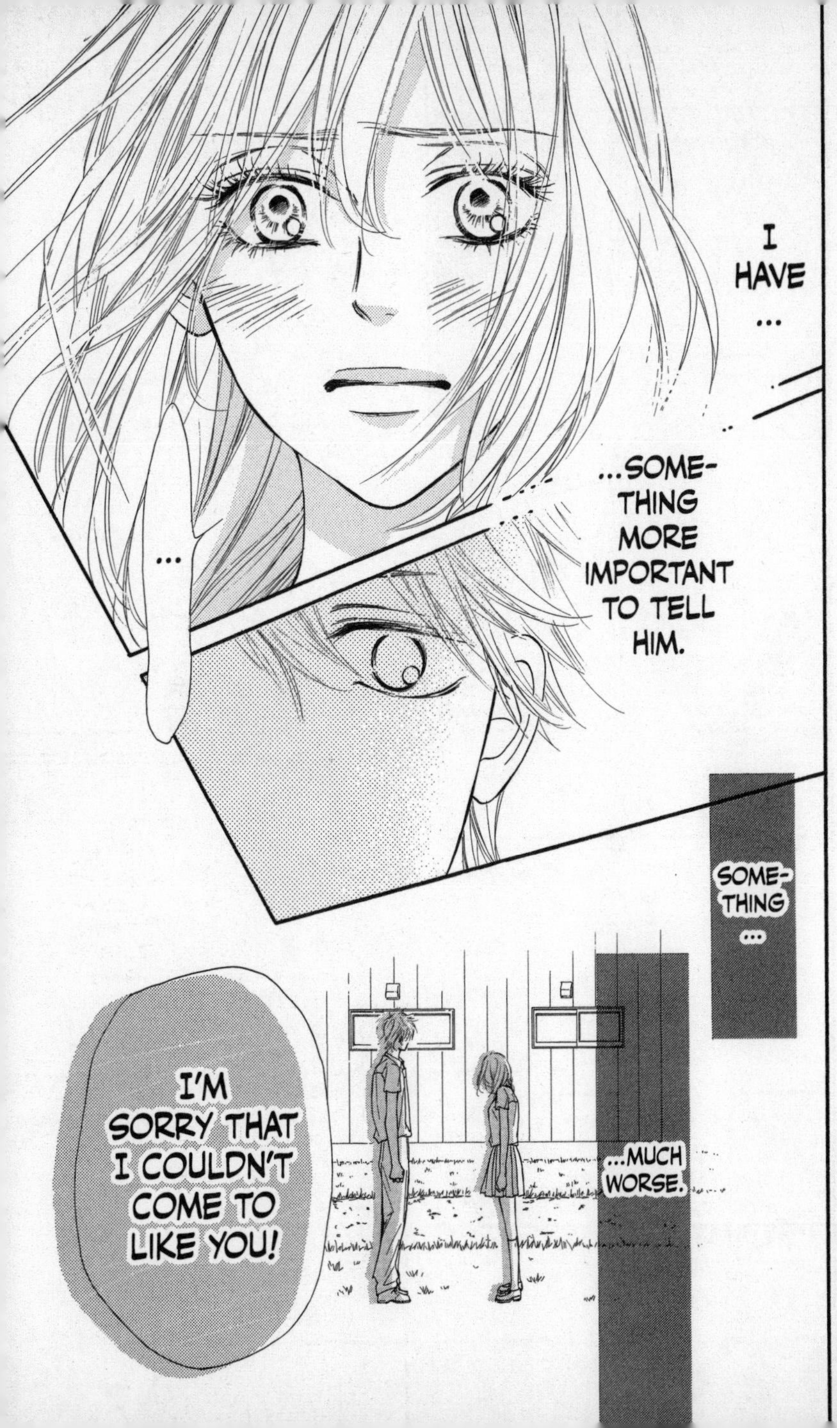
I HAVE ...
...SOME-THING MORE IMPORTANT TO TELL HIM.
...
SOME-THING ...
...MUCH WORSE.
I'M SORRY THAT I COULDN'T COME TO LIKE YOU!

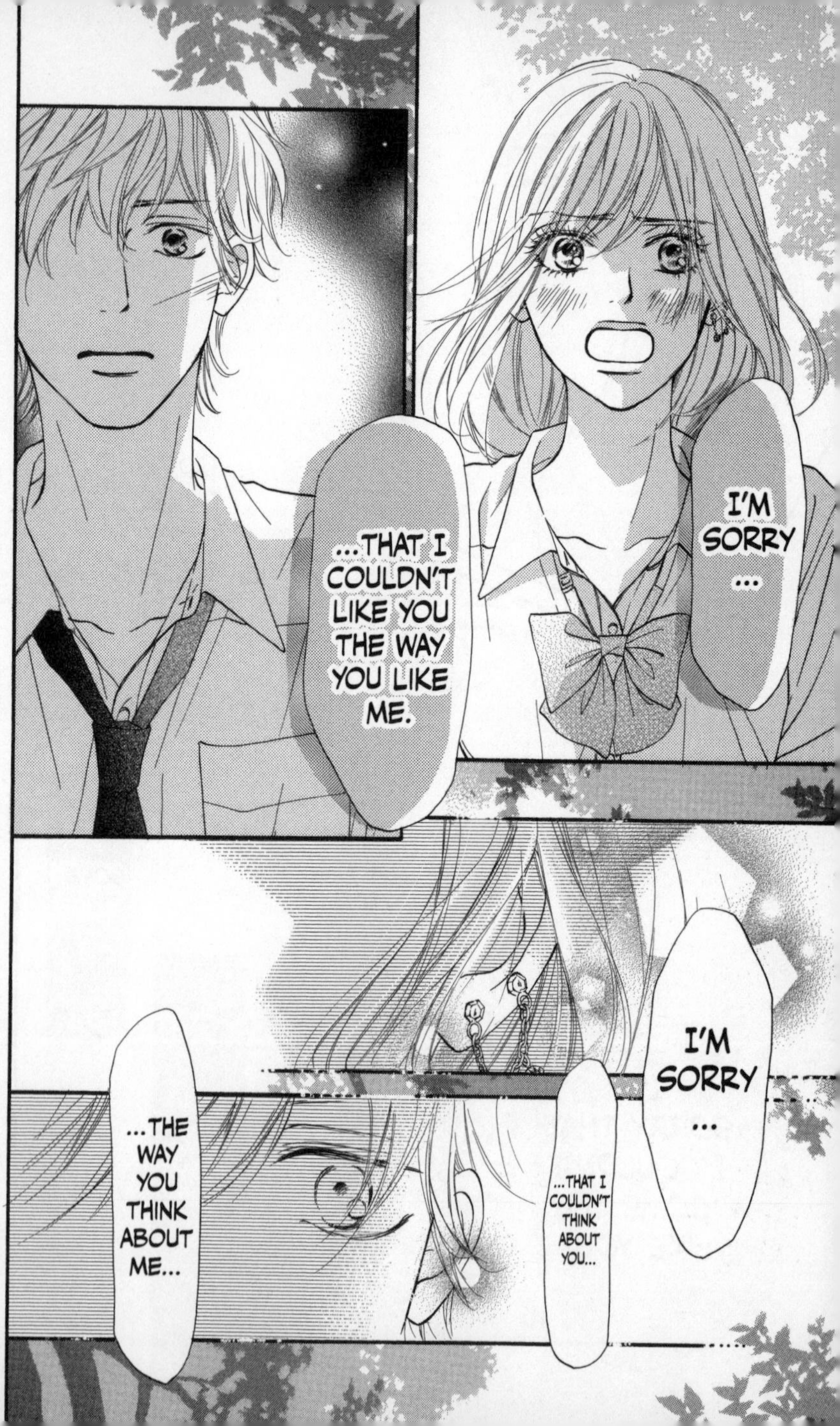
I'M SORRY ...
...THAT I COULDN'T LIKE YOU THE WAY YOU LIKE ME.
I'M SORRY ...
...THAT I COULDN'T THINK ABOUT YOU...
...THE WAY YOU THINK ABOUT ME...

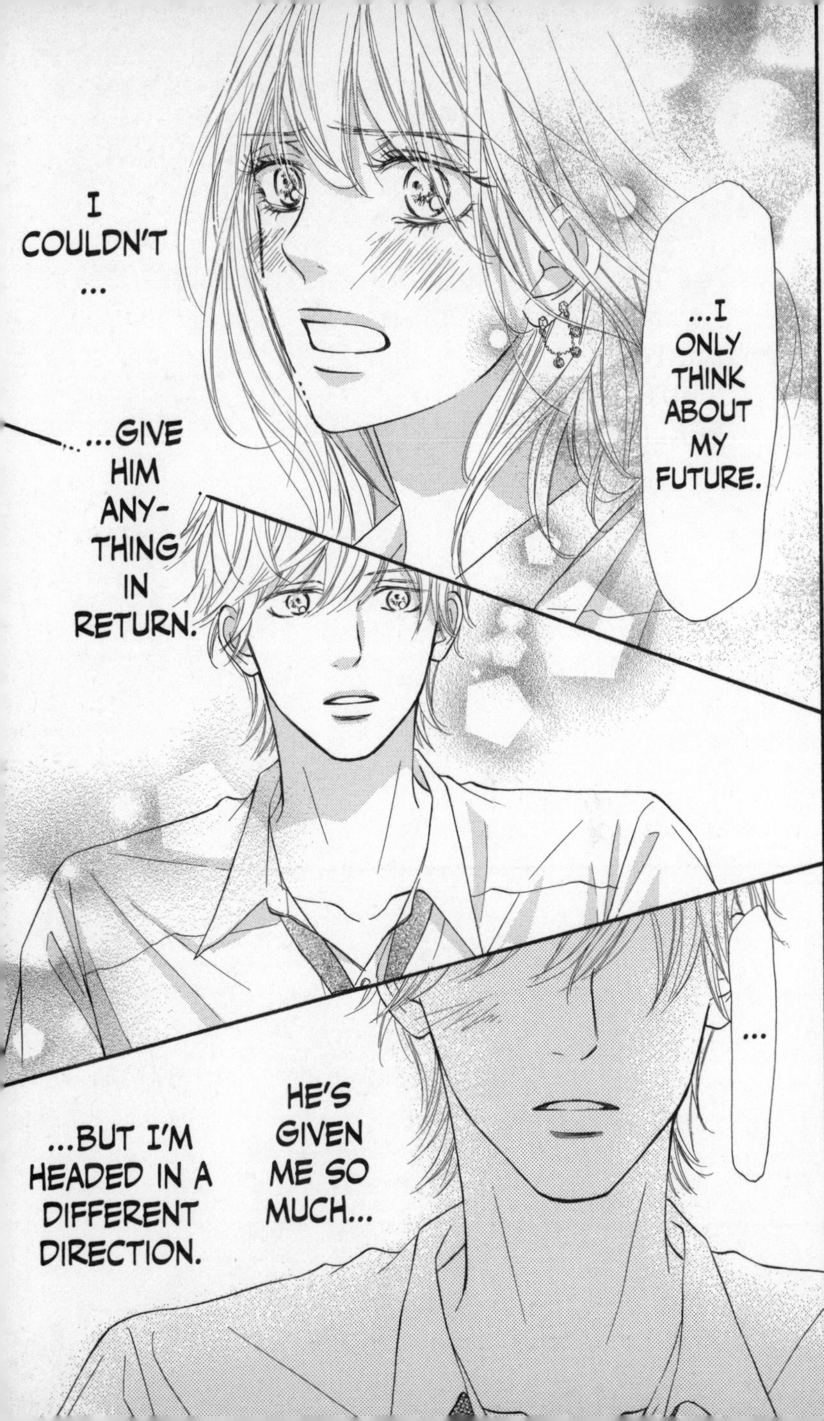
...I ONLY THINK ABOUT MY FUTURE.
I COULDN'T ...
...GIVE HIM ANY-THING IN RETURN.
...
HE'S GIVEN ME SO MUCH...
...BUT I'M HEADED IN A DIFFERENT DIRECTION.

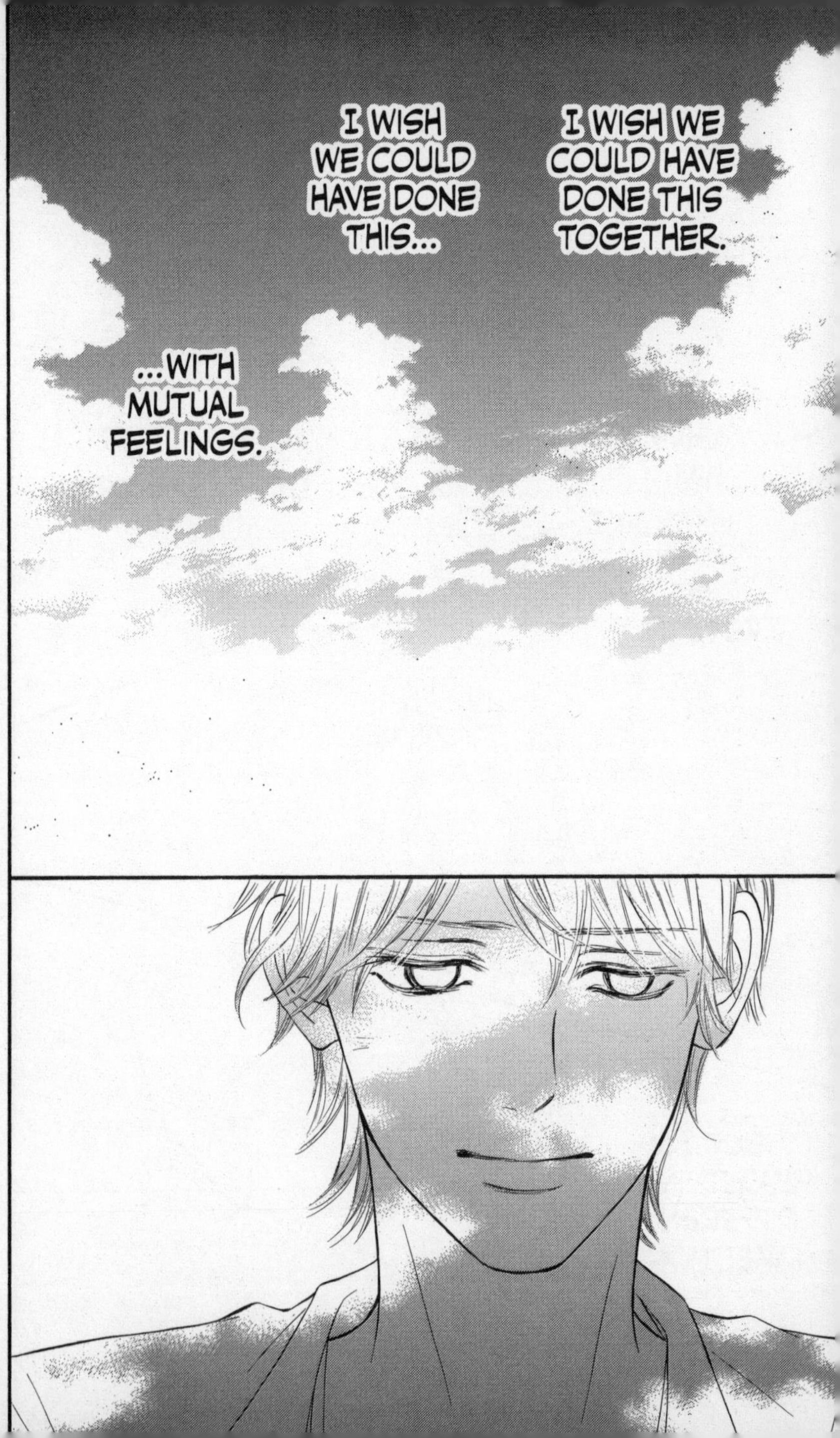
I WISH WE COULD HAVE DONE THIS TOGETHER.
I WISH WE COULD HAVE DONE THIS...
...WITH MUTUAL FEELINGS.

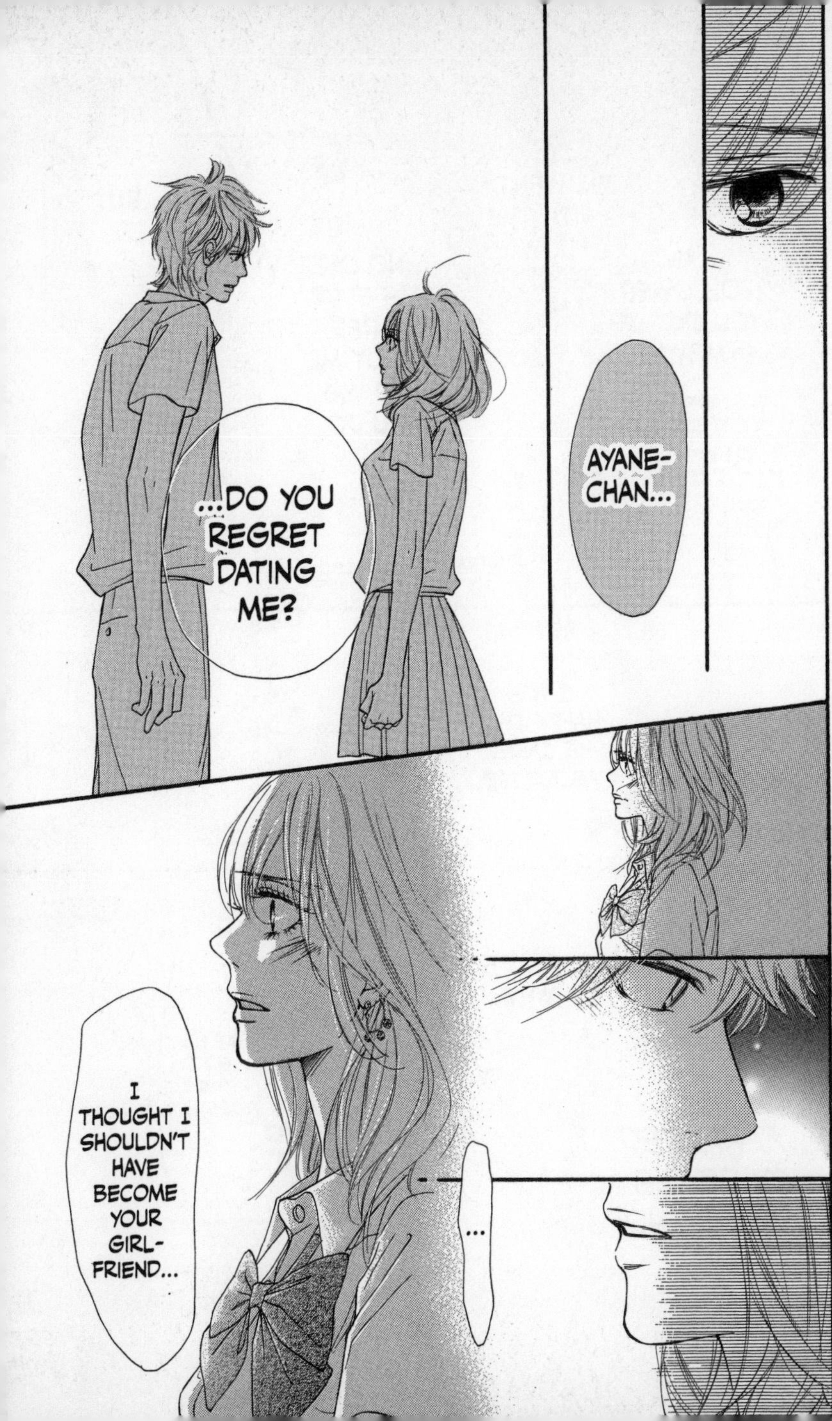
AYANE-CHAN...
...DO YOU REGRET DATING ME?
...
I THOUGHT I SHOULDN'T HAVE BECOME YOUR GIRLFRIEND...

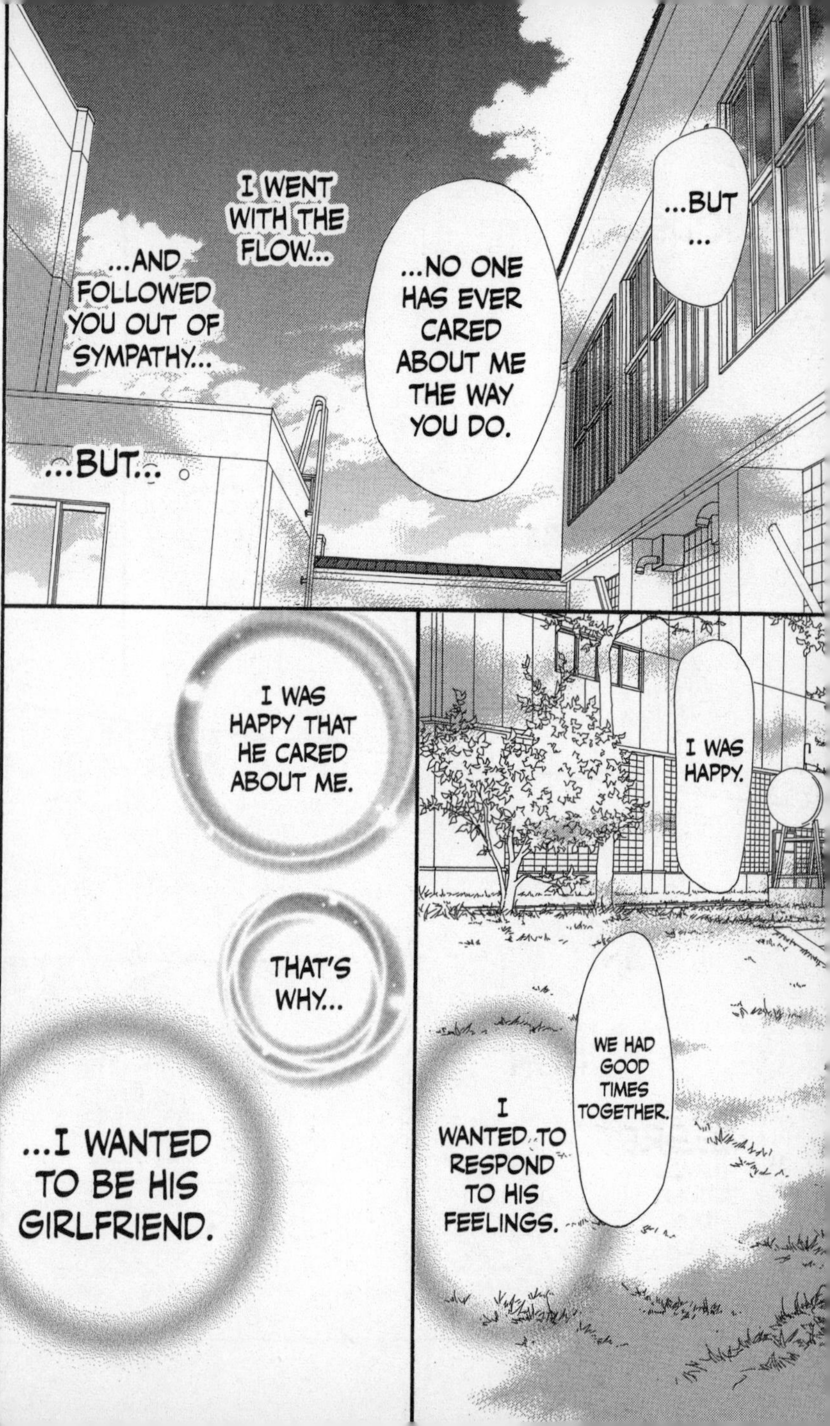
...BUT ...
...NO ONE HAS EVER CARED ABOUT ME THE WAY YOU DO.
I WENT WITH THE FLOW...
...AND FOLLOWED YOU OUT OF SYMPATHY...
...BUT...
I WAS HAPPY.
WE HAD GOOD TIMES TOGETHER.
I WANTED TO RESPOND TO HIS FEELINGS.
I WAS HAPPY THAT HE CARED ABOUT ME.
THAT'S WHY...
...I WANTED TO BE HIS GIRLFRIEND.

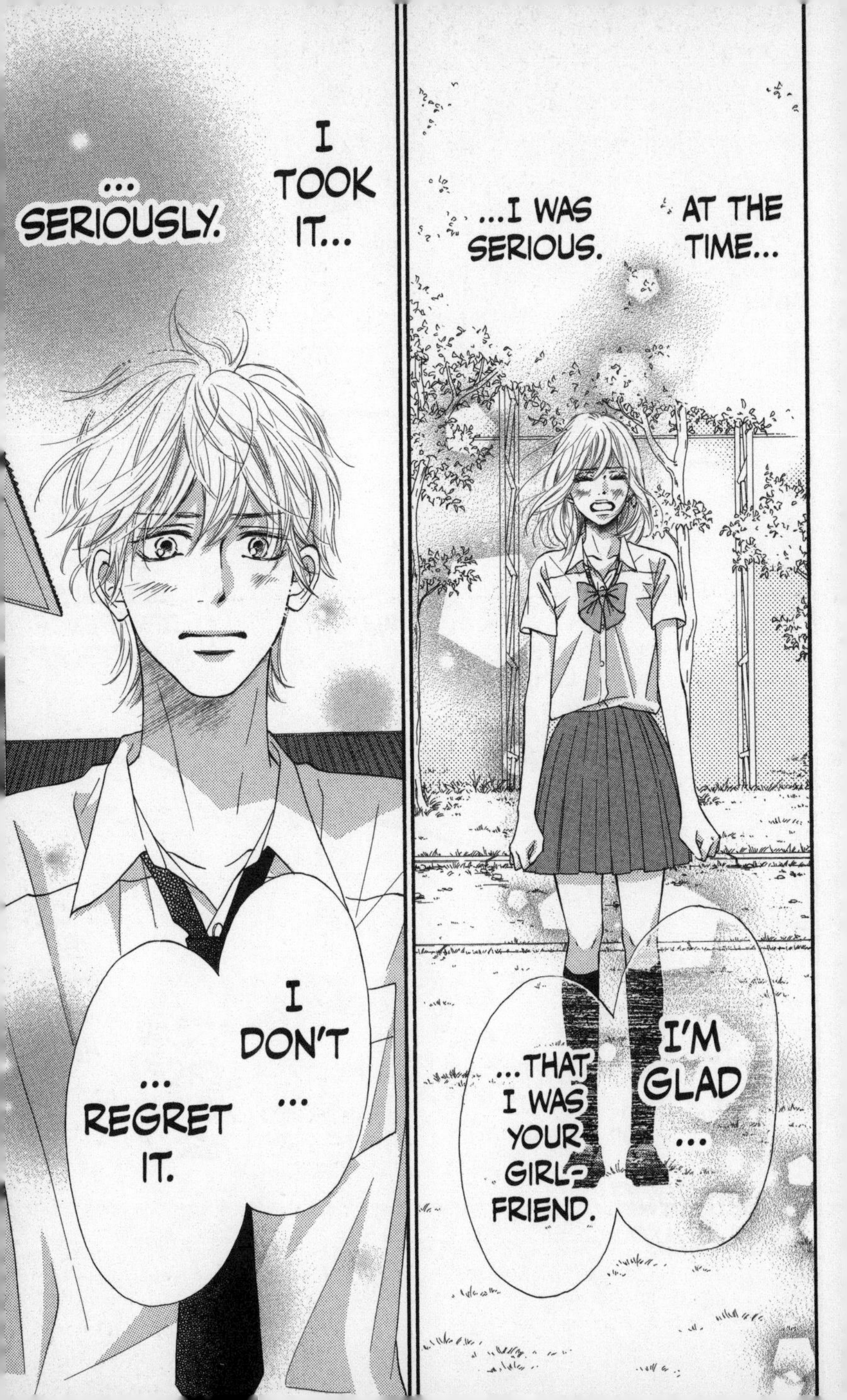
AT THE TIME...
...I WAS SERIOUS.
I'M GLAD ... ...THAT I WAS YOUR GIRL-FRIEND.
I TOOK IT...
...SERIOUSLY.
I DON'T ... ...REGRET IT.

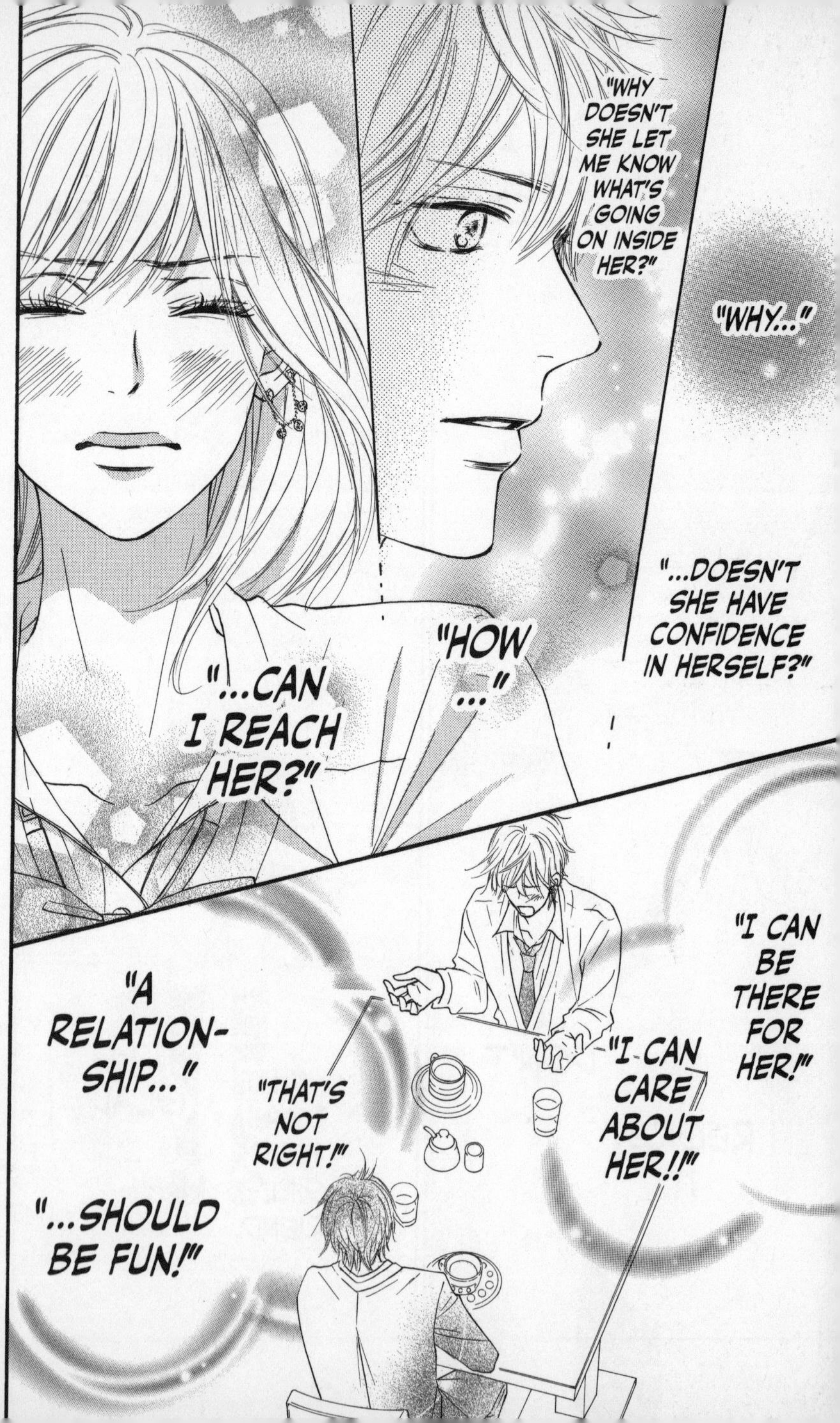
"WHY DOESN'T SHE LET ME KNOW WHAT'S GOING ON INSIDE HER?"
"WHY..."
"...DOESN'T SHE HAVE CONFIDENCE IN HERSELF?"
"HOW ..."
"...CAN I REACH HER?"
"I CAN BE THERE FOR HER!"
"I CAN CARE ABOUT HER!!"
"THAT'S NOT RIGHT!"
"A RELATION-SHIP..."
"...SHOULD BE FUN!"

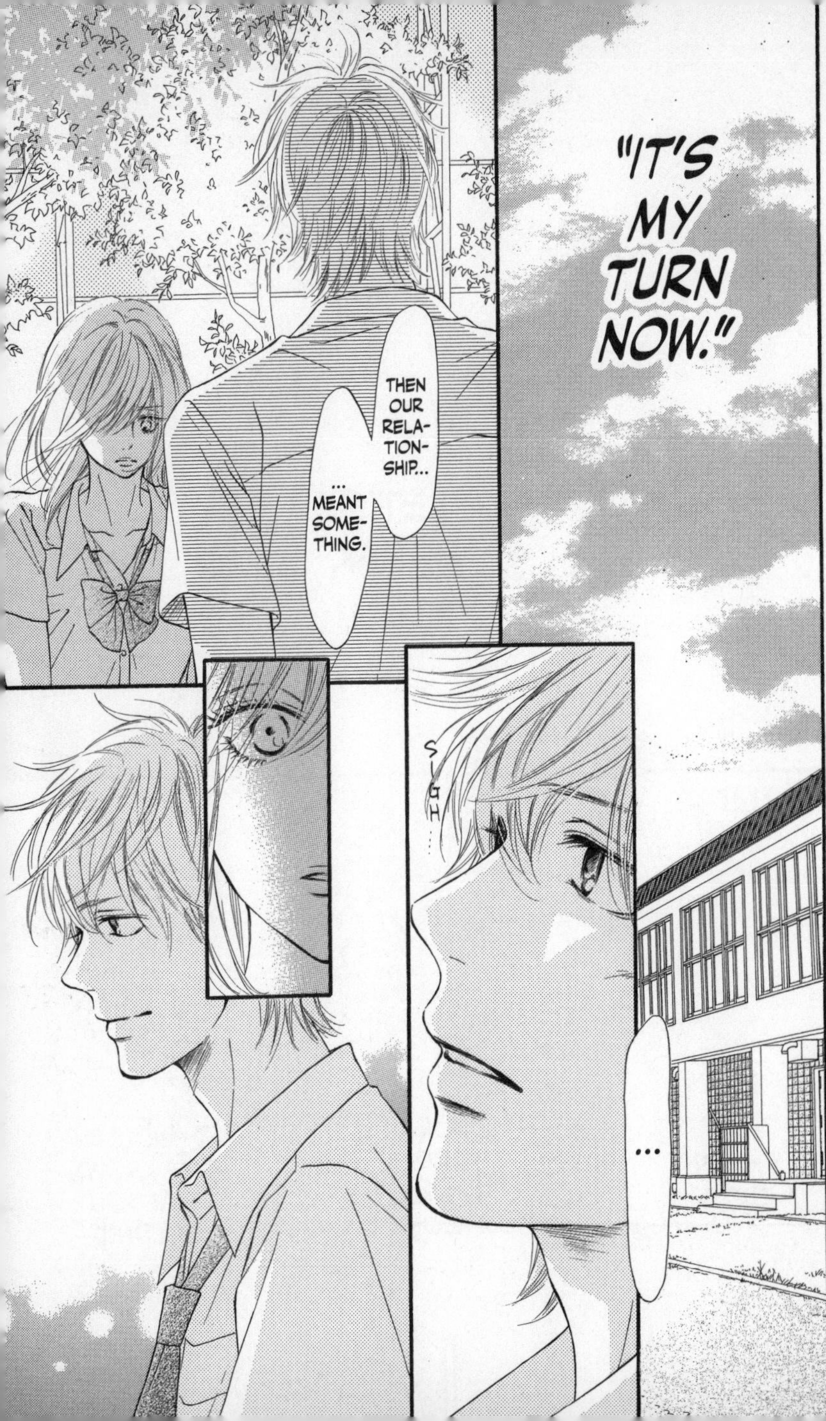
"IT'S MY TURN NOW."
THEN OUR RELATIONSHIP...
... MEANT SOMETHING.
SIGH...
...

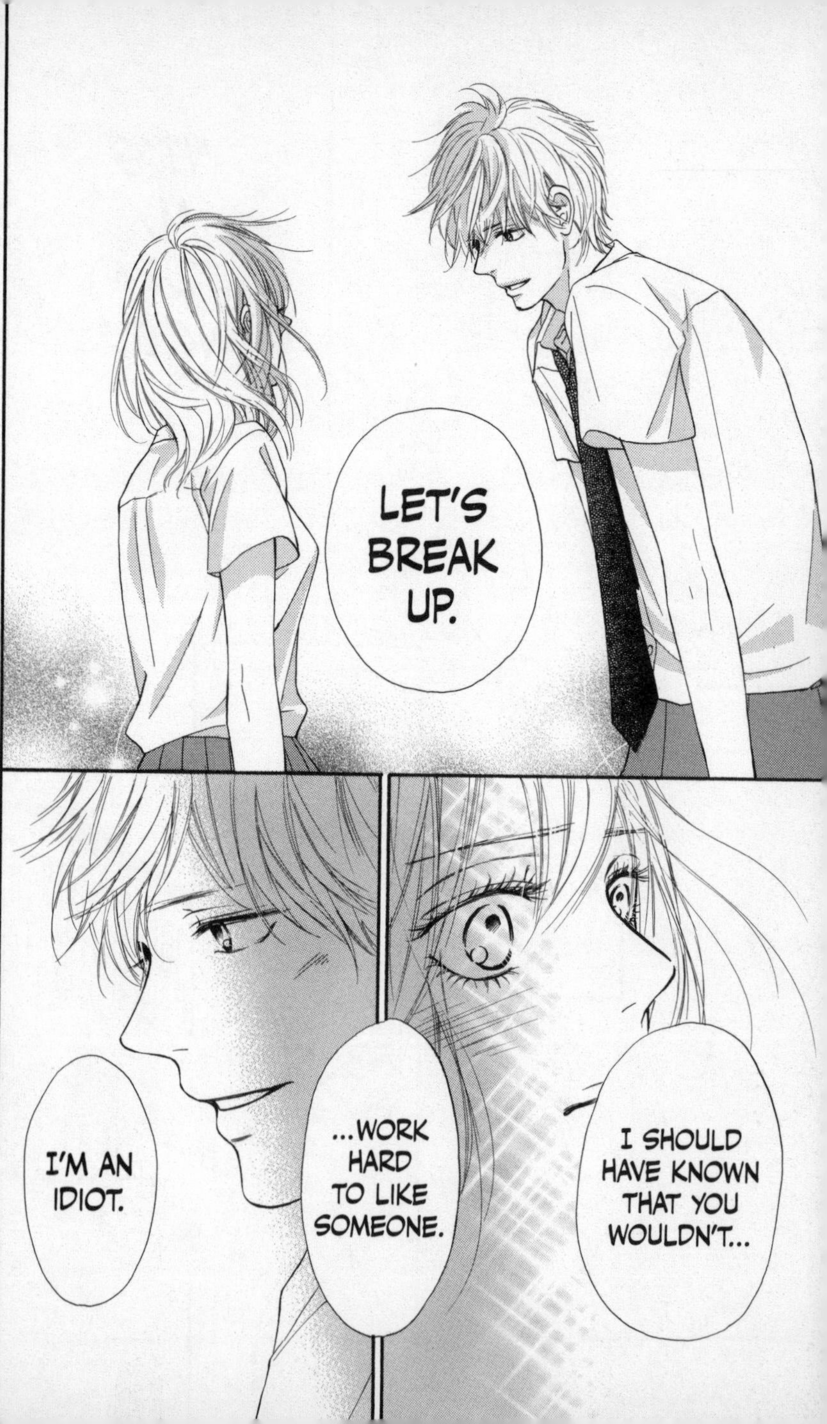
LET'S BREAK UP.
I SHOULD HAVE KNOWN THAT YOU WOULDN'T...
...WORK HARD TO LIKE SOMEONE.
I'M AN IDIOT.

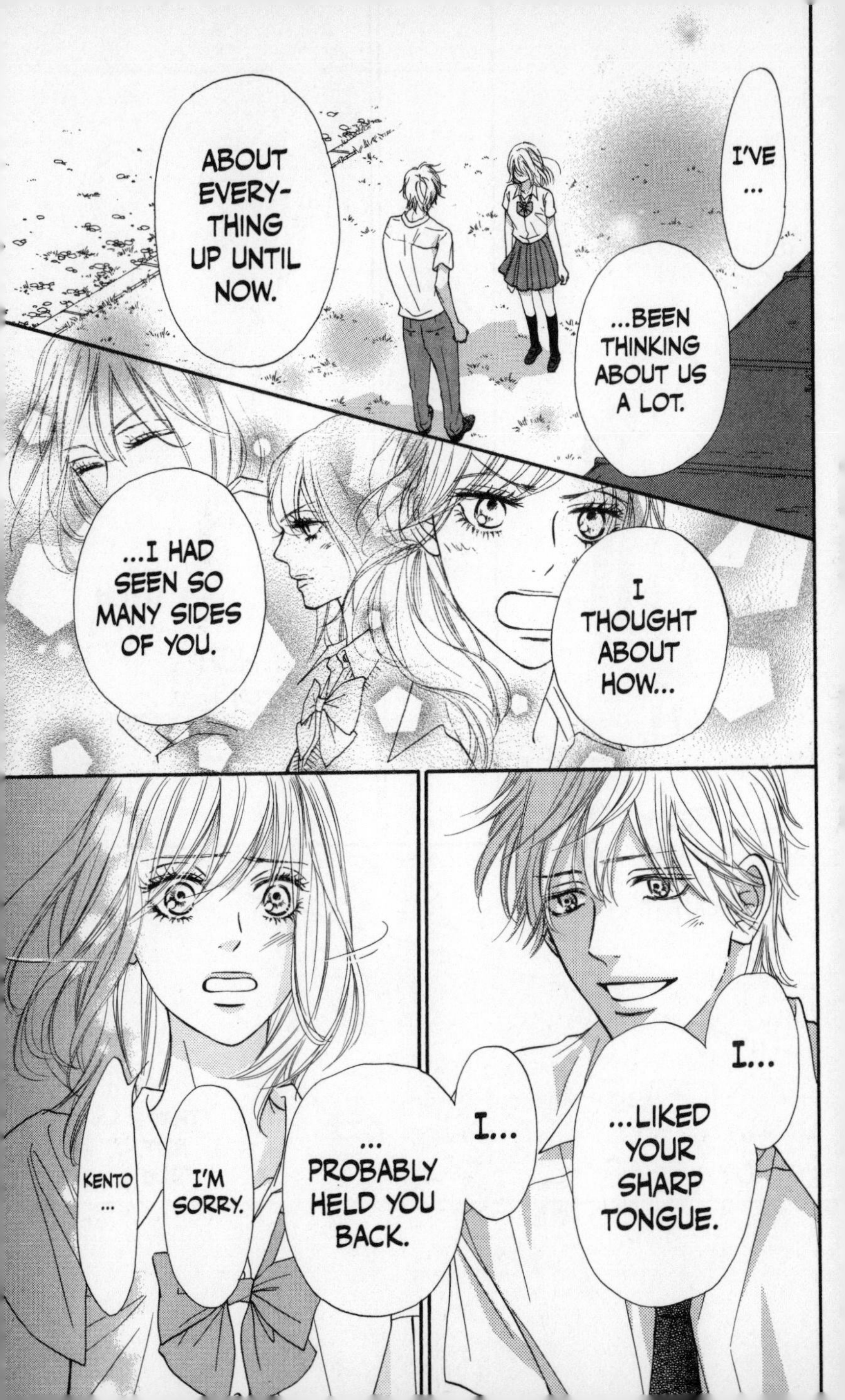
I'VE ...
...BEEN THINKING ABOUT US A LOT.
ABOUT EVERY-THING UP UNTIL NOW.
I THOUGHT ABOUT HOW...
...I HAD SEEN SO MANY SIDES OF YOU.
I...
...LIKED YOUR SHARP TONGUE.
I...
...PROBABLY HELD YOU BACK.
I'M SORRY.
KENTO ...

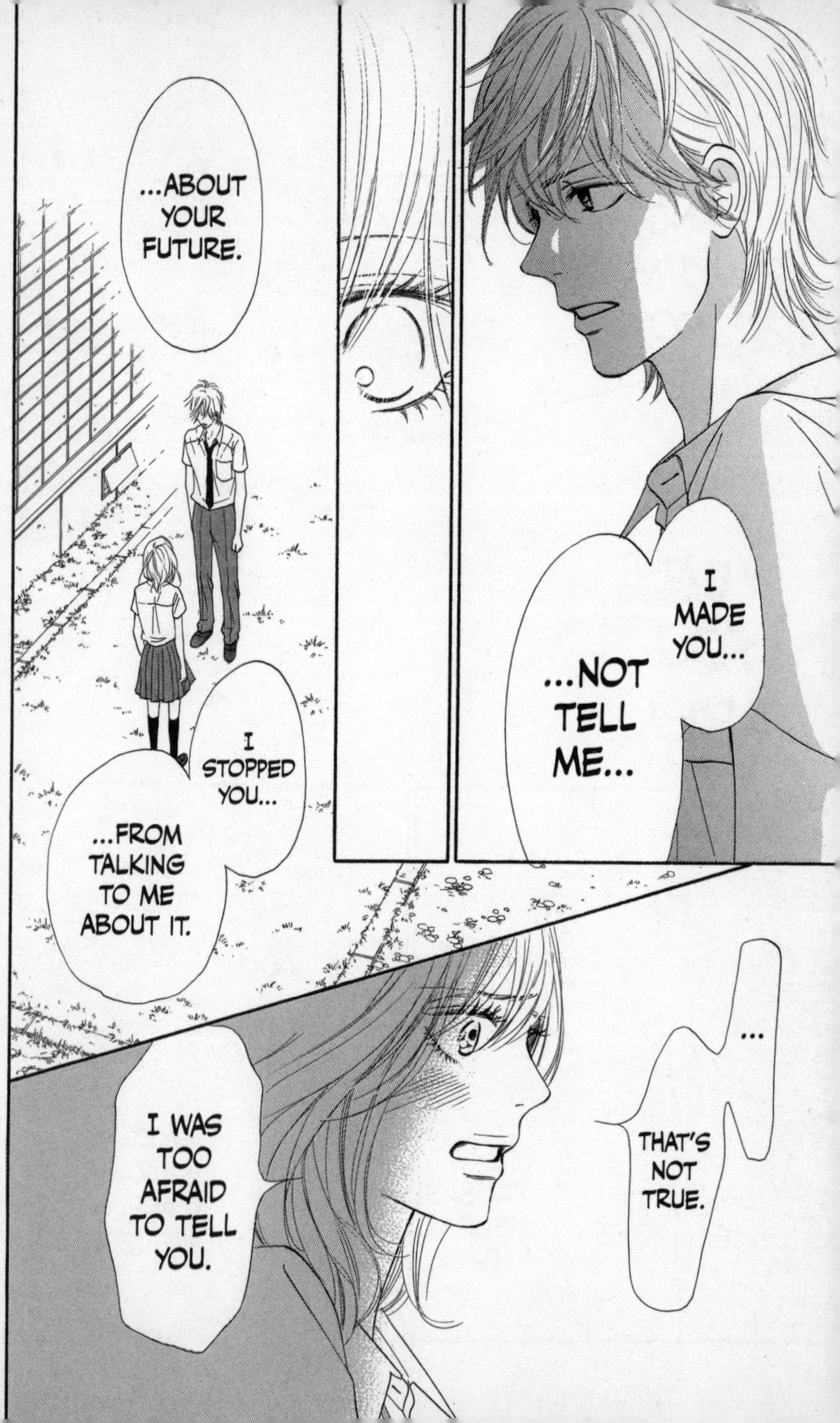
I MADE YOU...
...NOT TELL ME...
...ABOUT YOUR FUTURE.
I STOPPED YOU...
...FROM TALKING TO ME ABOUT IT.
...
THAT'S NOT TRUE.
I WAS TOO AFRAID TO TELL YOU.

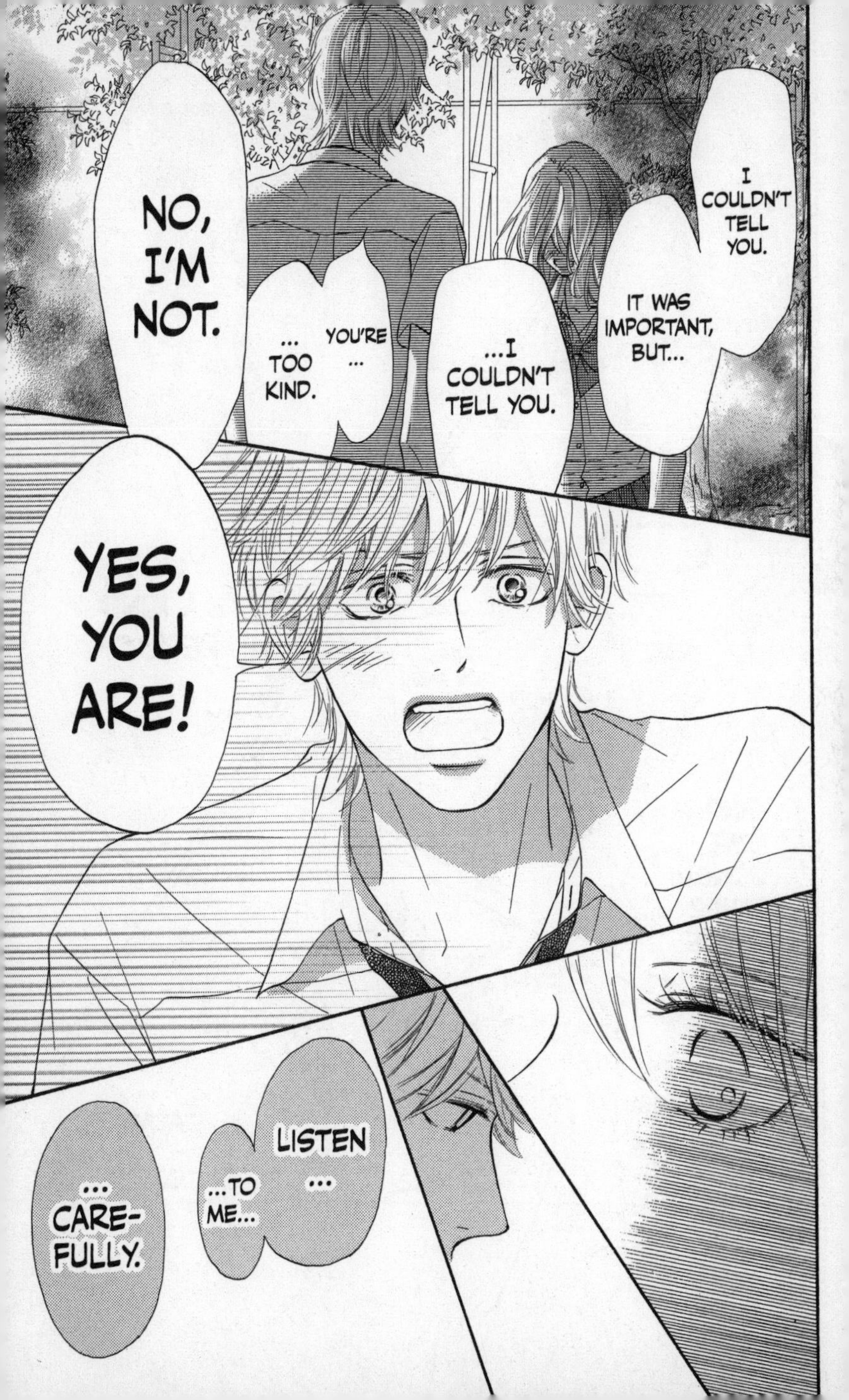
I COULDN'T TELL YOU.
IT WAS IMPORTANT, BUT...
...I COULDN'T TELL YOU.
YOU'RE ... ... TOO KIND.
NO, I'M NOT.
YES, YOU ARE!
LISTEN ...
...TO ME...
... CARE-FULLY.

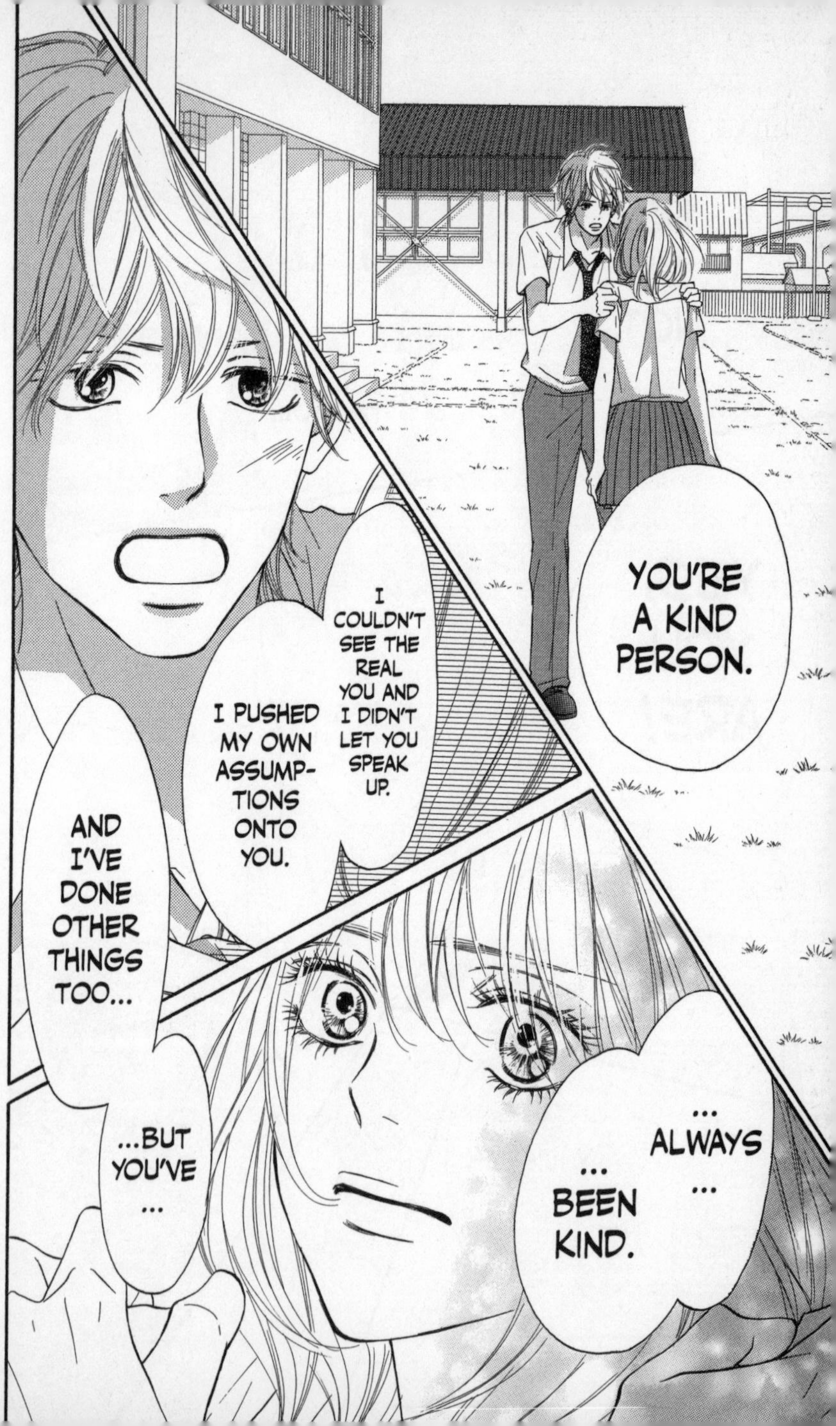
YOU'RE A KIND PERSON.
I COULDN'T SEE THE REAL YOU AND I DIDN'T LET YOU SPEAK UP.
I PUSHED MY OWN ASSUMPTIONS ONTO YOU.
AND I'VE DONE OTHER THINGS TOO...
...BUT YOU'VE ...
... ALWAYS ... ... BEEN KIND.

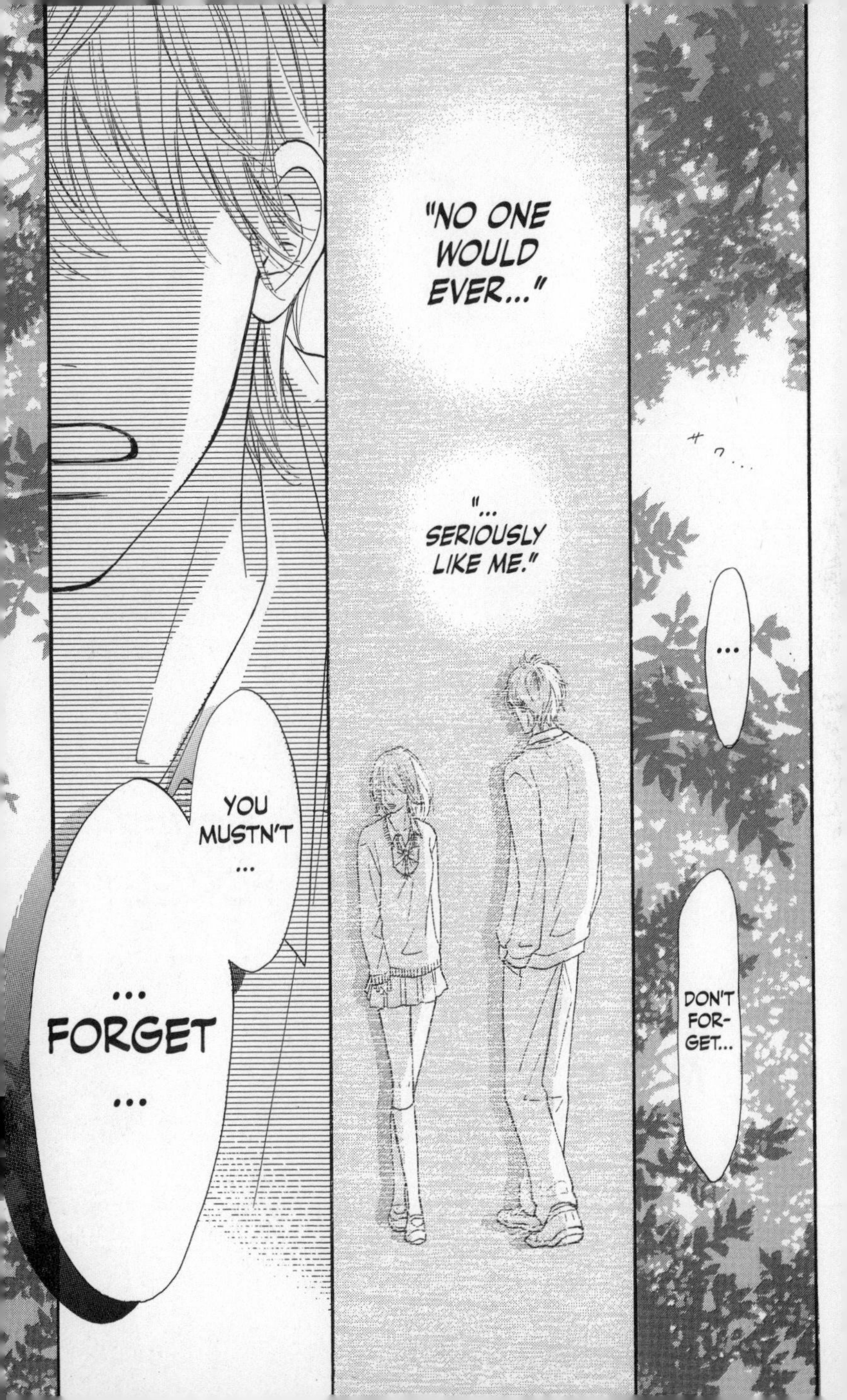
...
DON'T FOR-GET...
"NO ONE WOULD EVER..."
"...SERIOUSLY LIKE ME."
YOU MUSTN'T ...
...FORGET ...

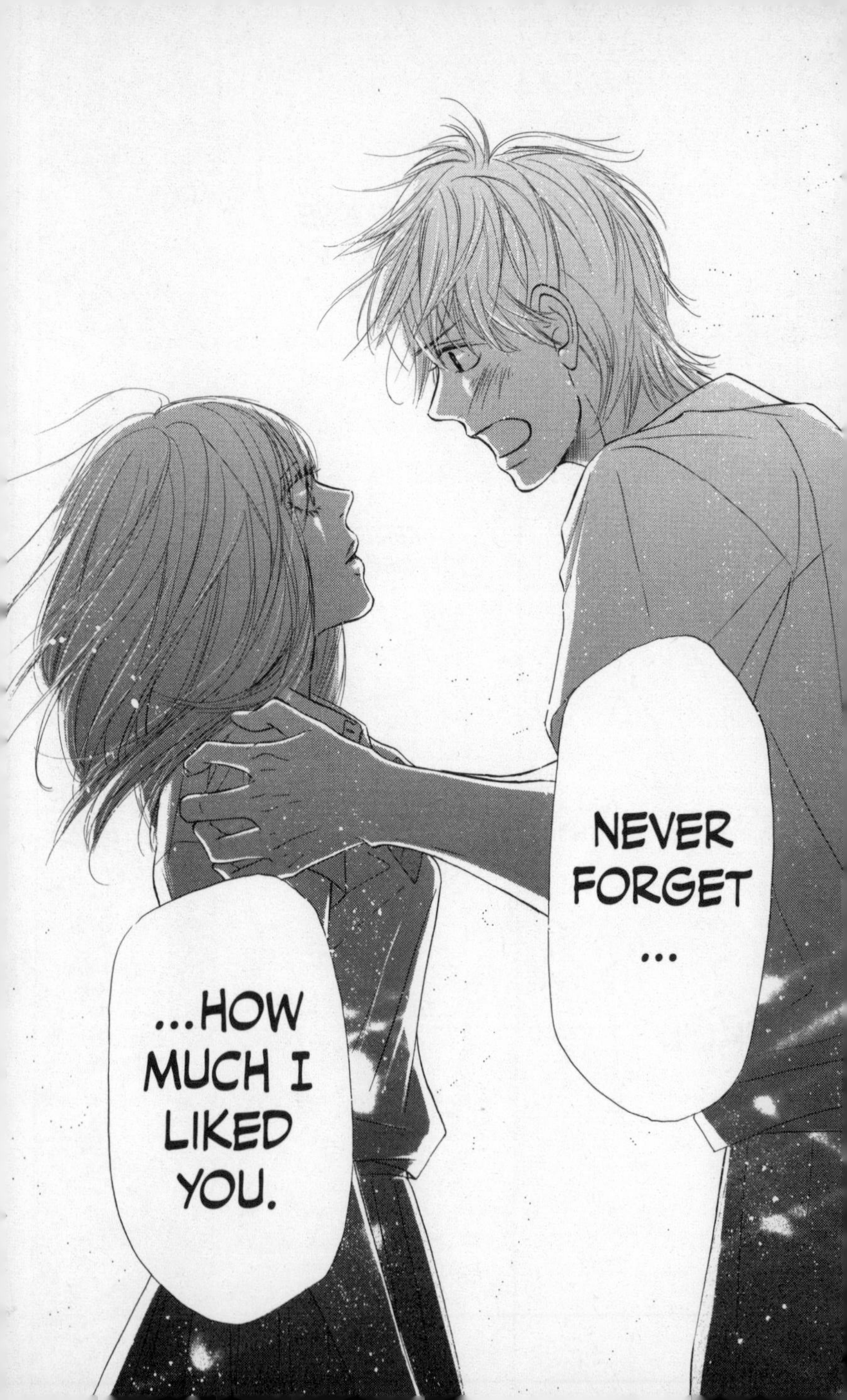
NEVER FORGET ...
...HOW MUCH I LIKED YOU.

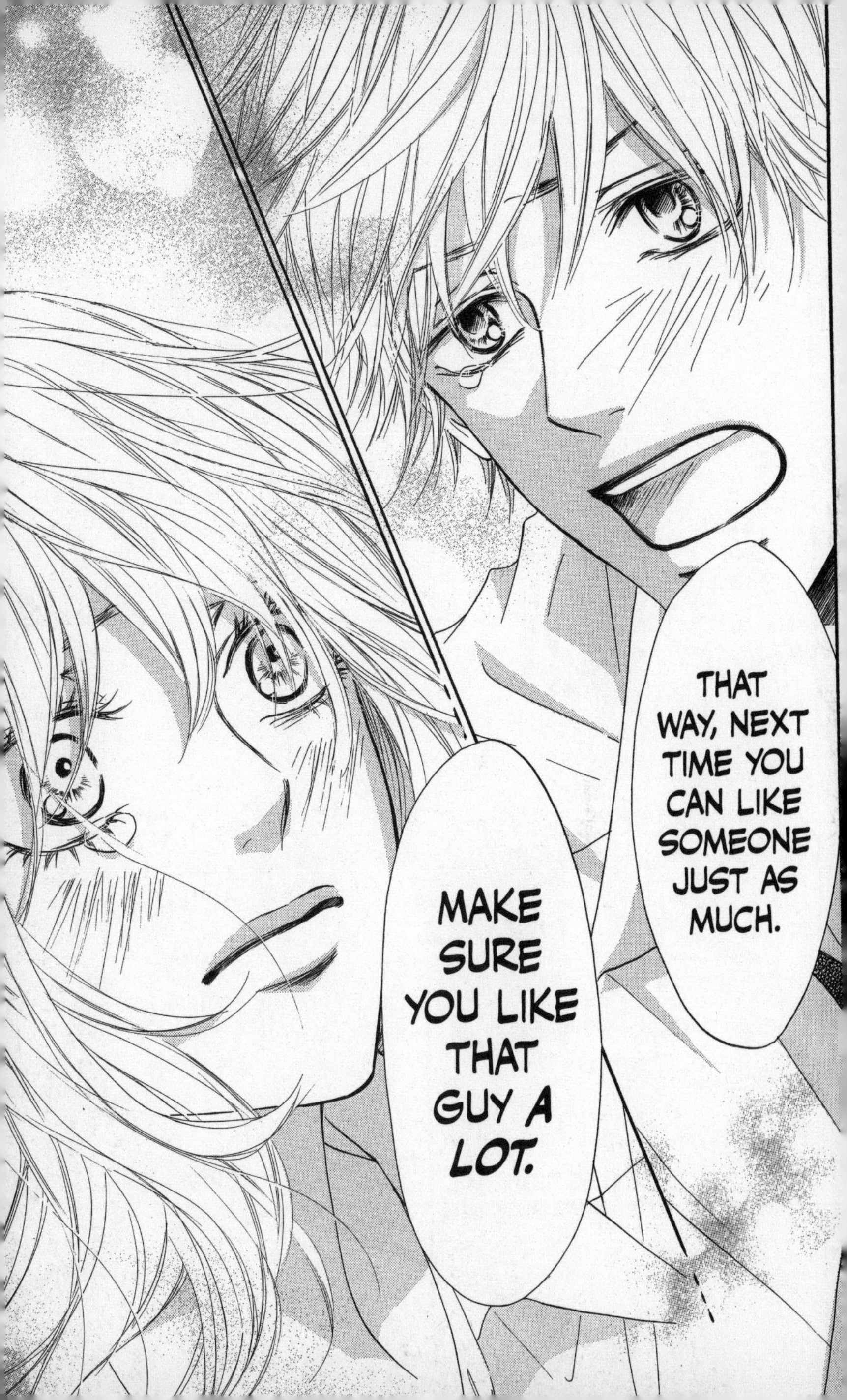
THAT WAY, NEXT TIME YOU CAN LIKE SOMEONE JUST AS MUCH.
MAKE SURE YOU LIKE THAT GUY A LOT.

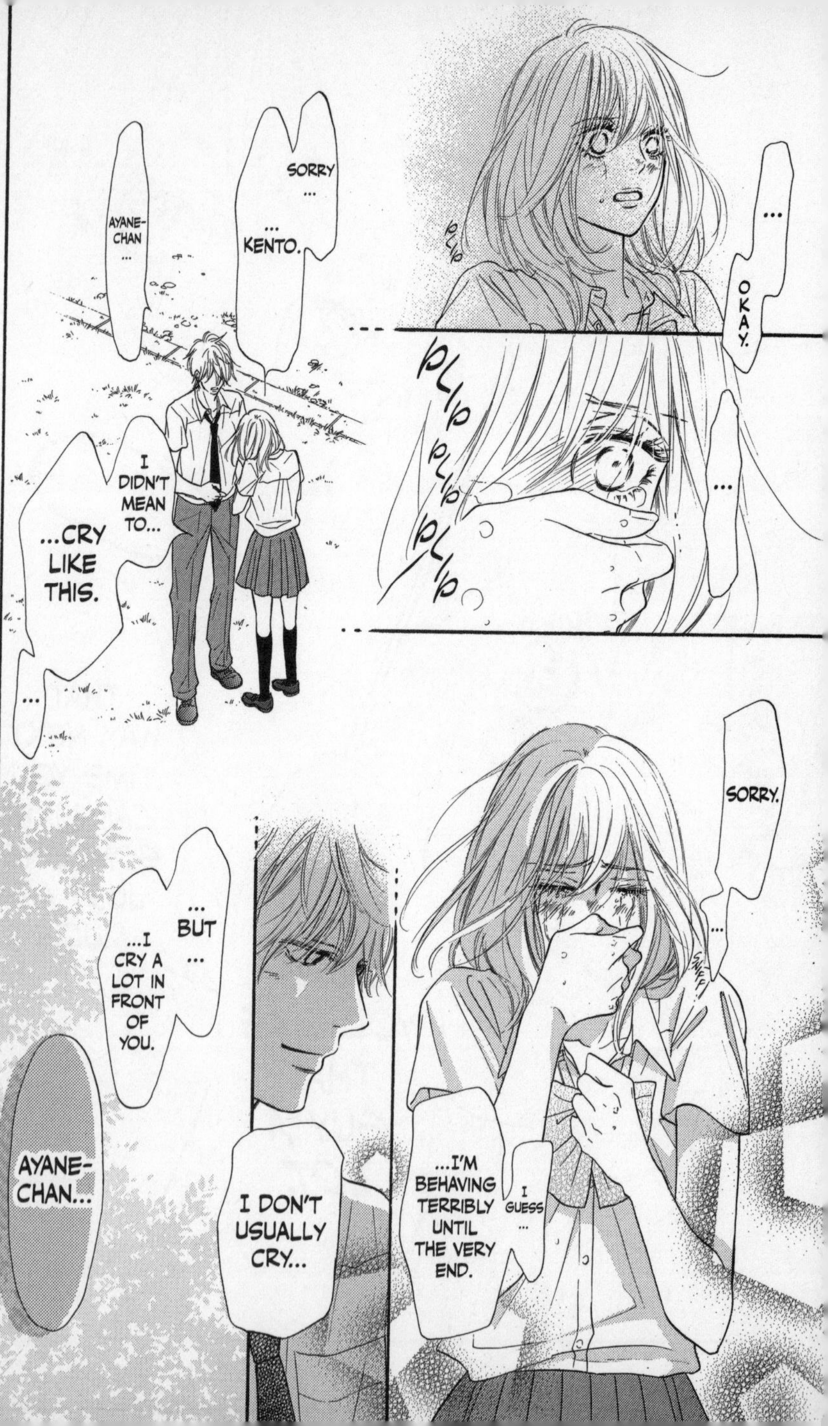
...
OKAY.
PLIP
PLIP PLIP PLIP PLIP
...
SORRY ...
... KENTO.
AYANE-CHAN ...
I DIDN'T MEAN TO...
...CRY LIKE THIS.
...
SORRY.
...
SNIFF
...I'M BEHAVING TERRIBLY UNTIL THE VERY END.
I GUESS ...
I DON'T USUALLY CRY...
... BUT ...
...I CRY A LOT IN FRONT OF YOU.
AYANE-CHAN...

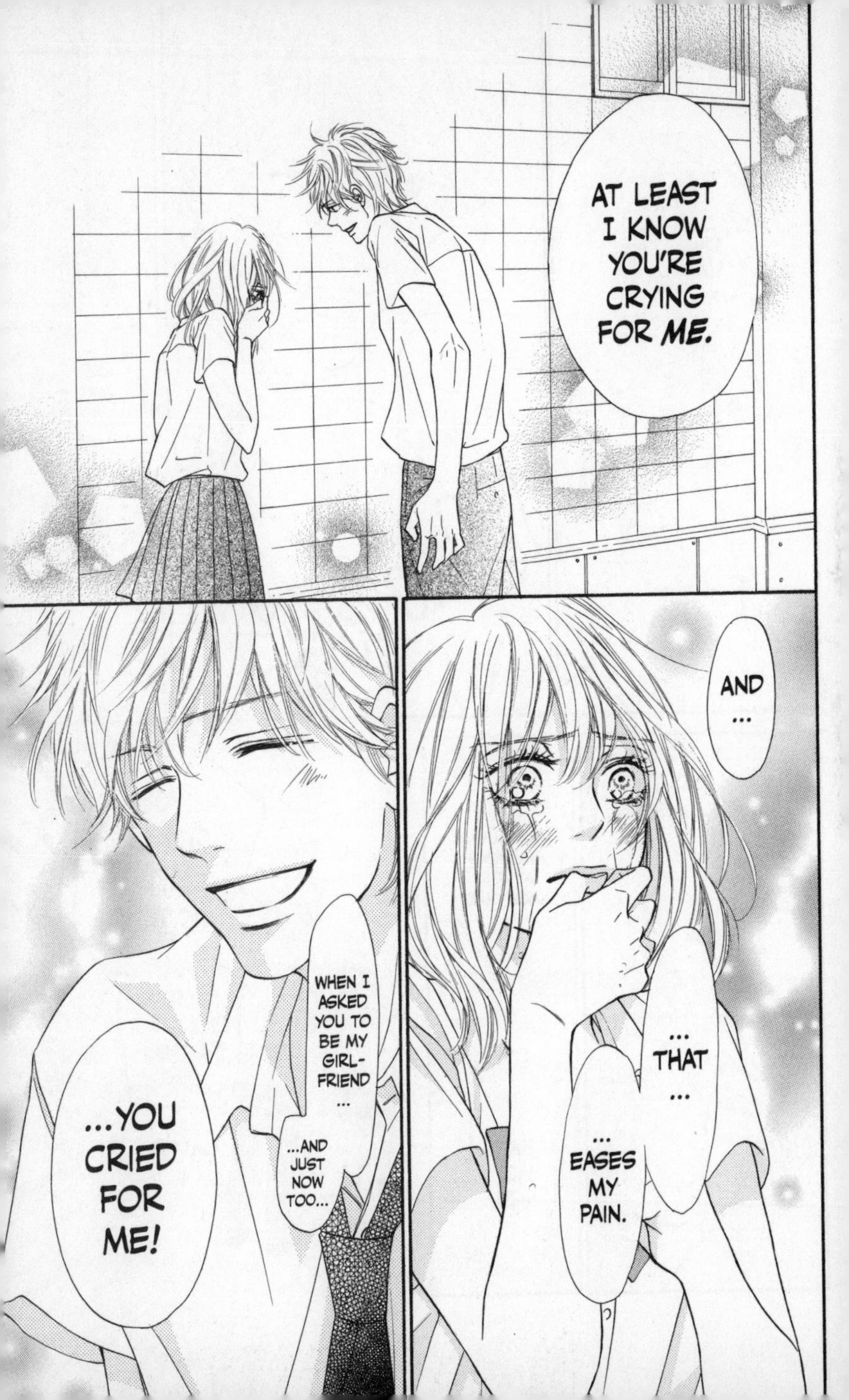
AT LEAST I KNOW YOU'RE CRYING FOR *ME.*
AND ...
... THAT ...
... EASES MY PAIN.
WHEN I ASKED YOU TO BE MY GIRL-FRIEND ...
...AND JUST NOW TOO...
...YOU CRIED FOR ME!

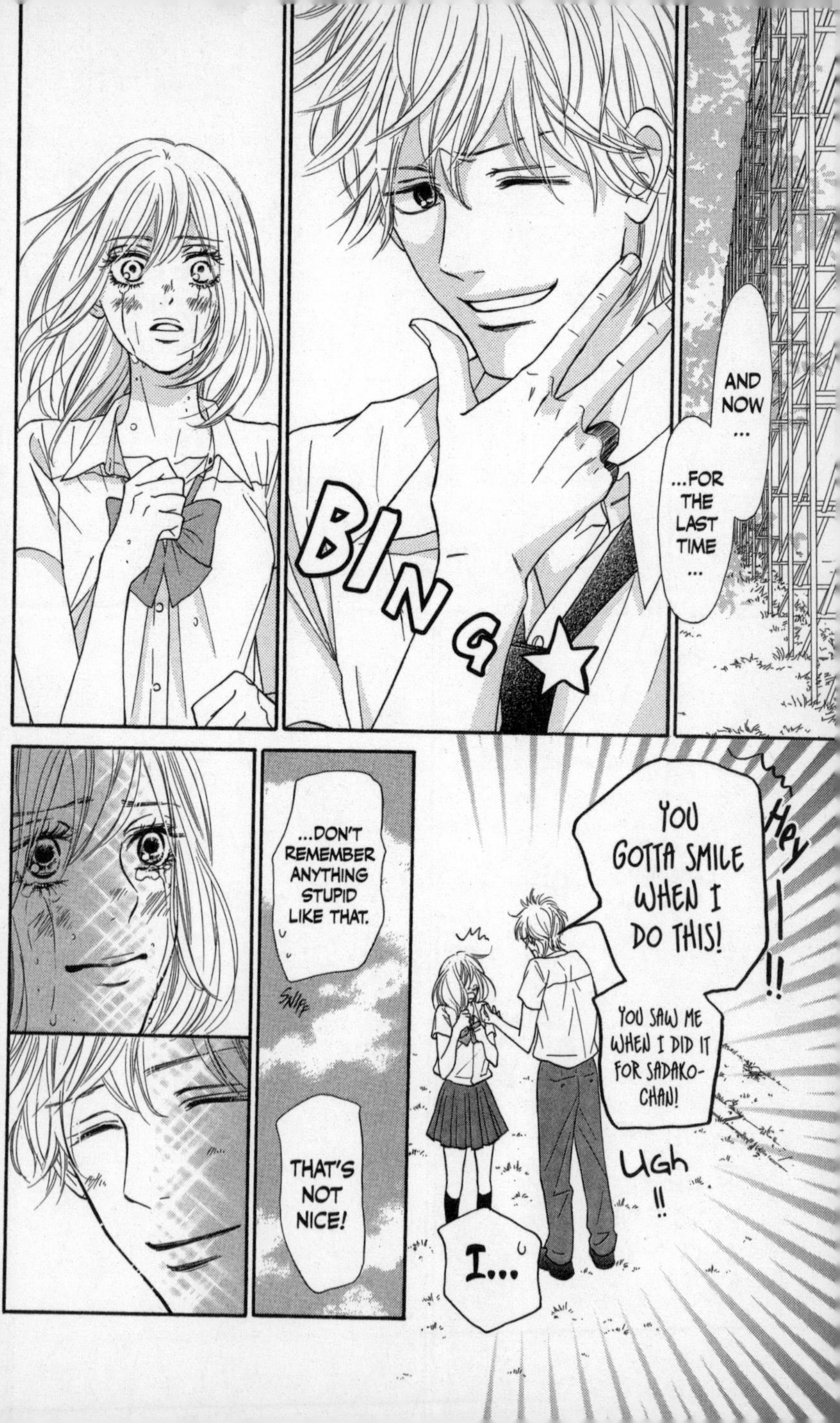
AND NOW ...
...FOR THE LAST TIME ...
BING
Hey—!!
YOU GOTTA SMILE WHEN I DO THIS!
YOU SAW ME WHEN I DID IT FOR SADAKO-CHAN!
Ugh!!
I...
...DON'T REMEMBER ANYTHING STUPID LIKE THAT.
SNIFF
THAT'S NOT NICE!

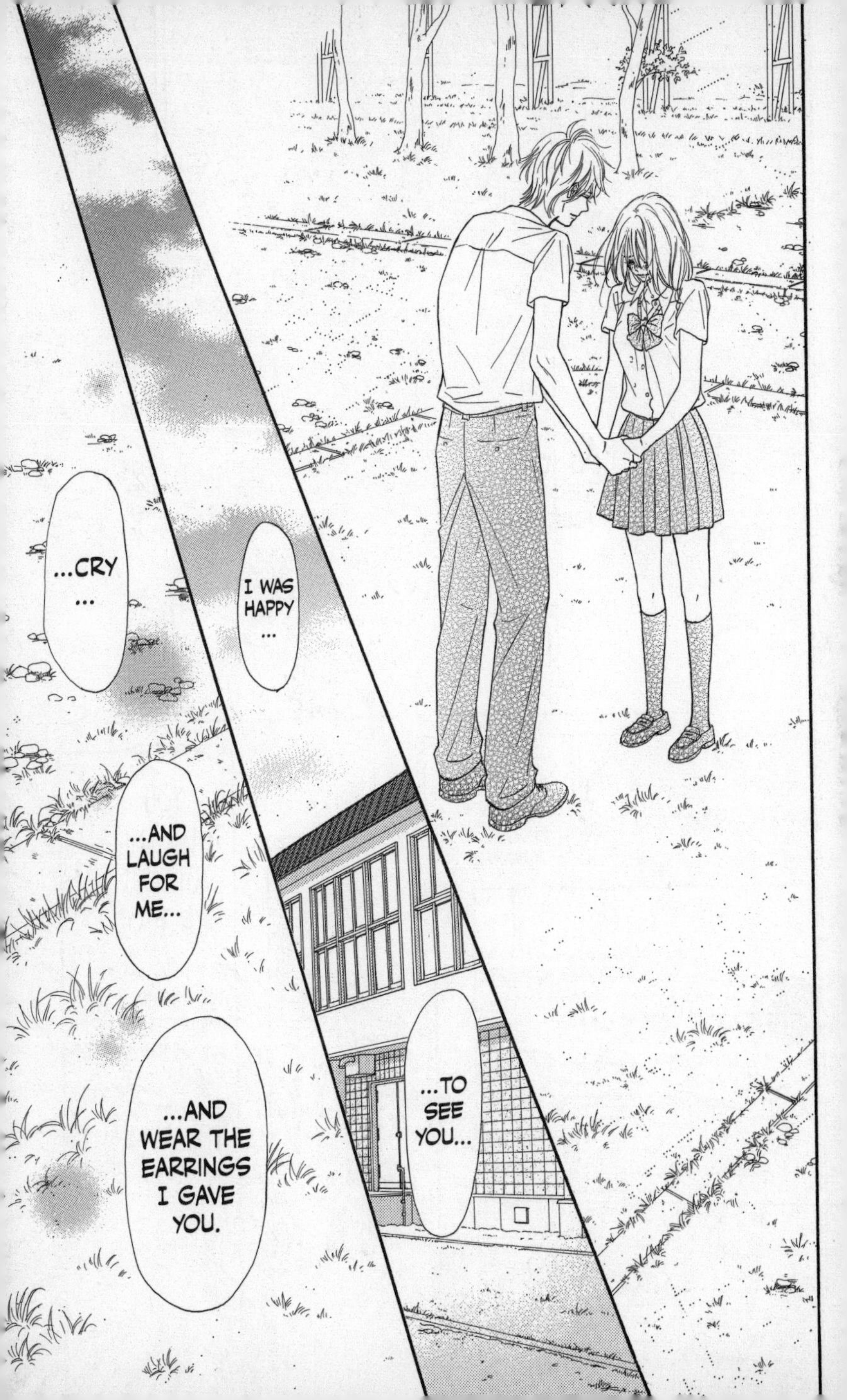
I WAS HAPPY...
...TO SEE YOU...
...CRY...
...AND LAUGH FOR ME...
...AND WEAR THE EARRINGS I GAVE YOU.

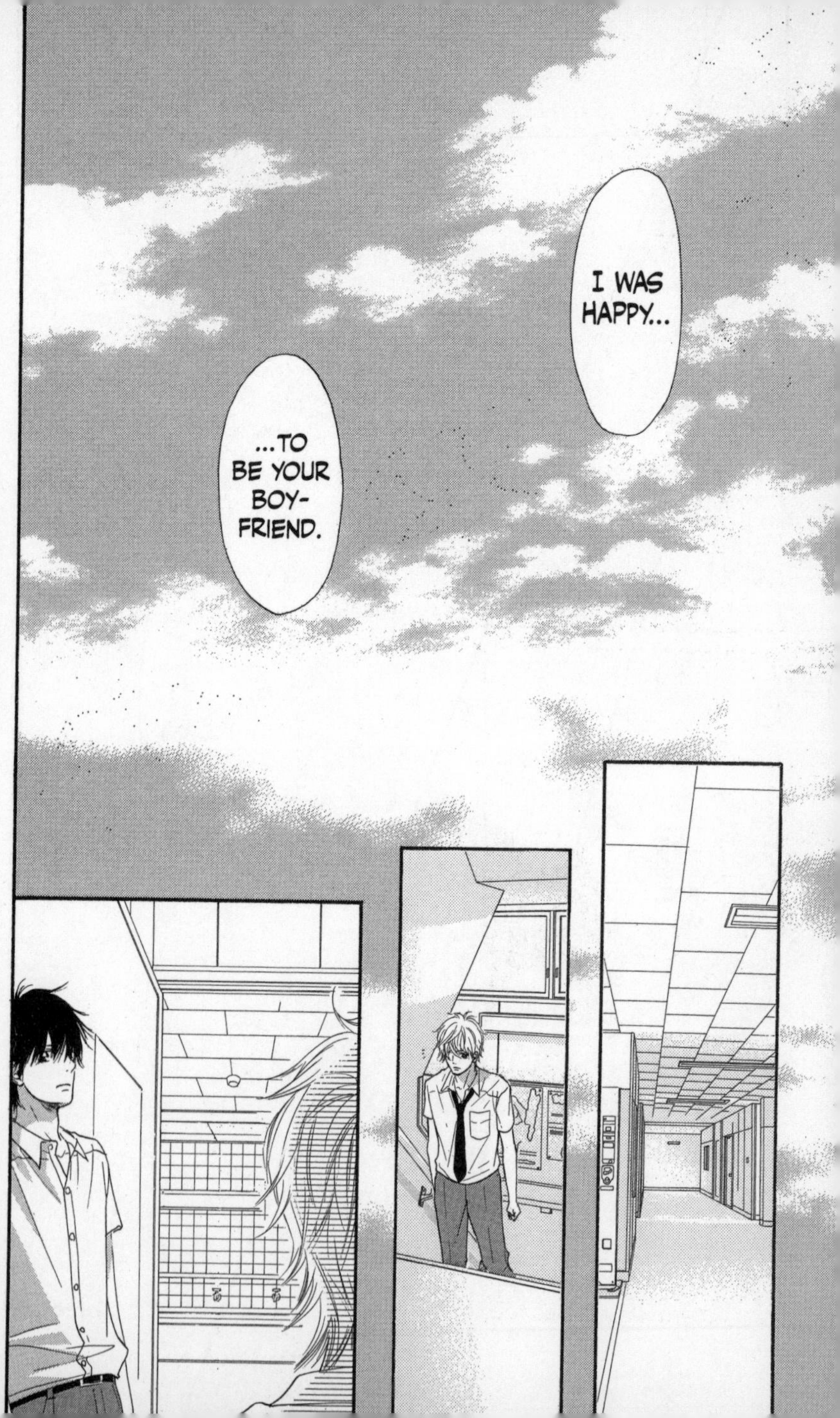
I WAS HAPPY...
...TO BE YOUR BOY-FRIEND.

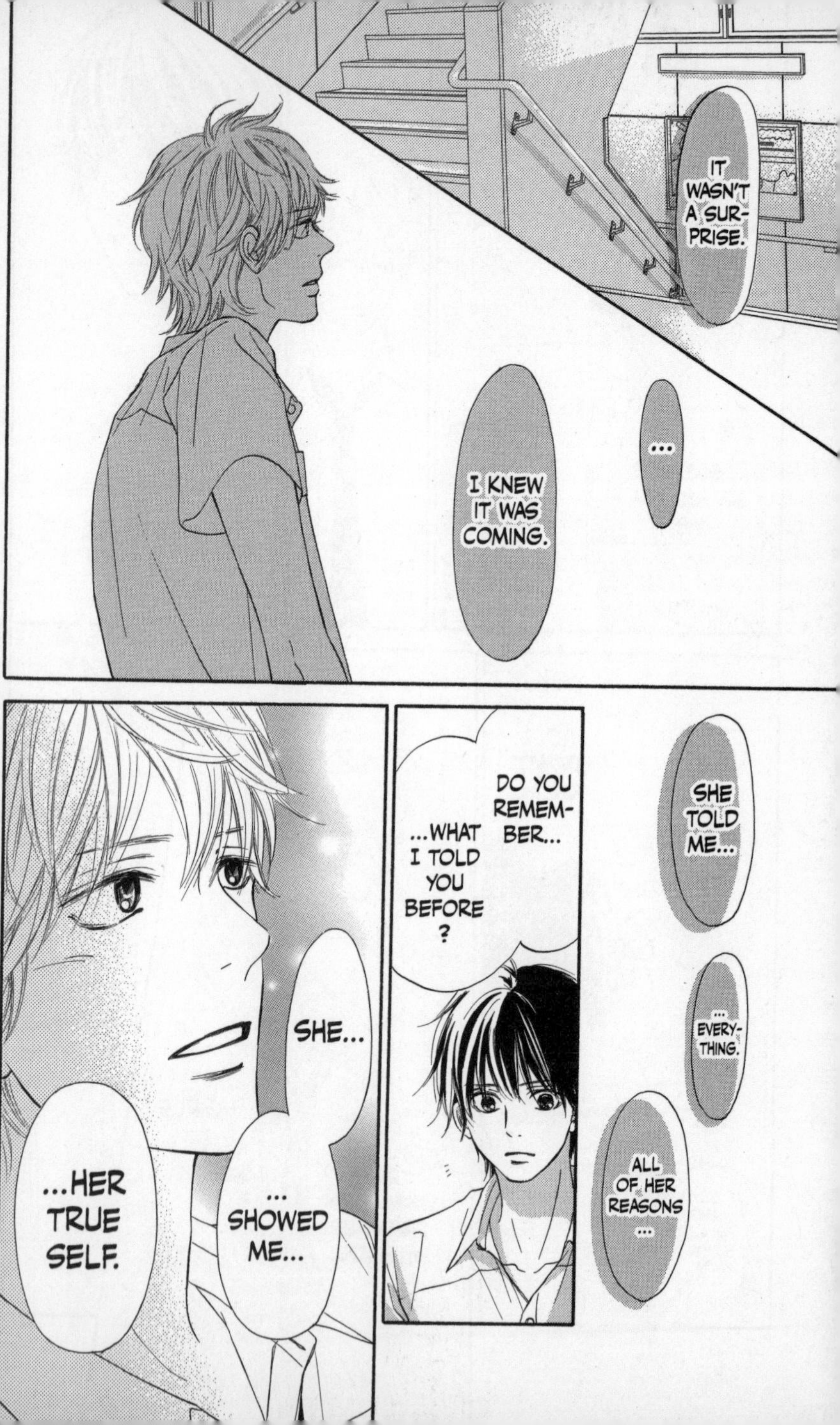
IT WASN'T A SUR-PRISE.
...
I KNEW IT WAS COMING.
SHE TOLD ME...
...EVERY-THING.
ALL OF HER REASONS ...
DO YOU REMEM-BER...
...WHAT I TOLD YOU BEFORE?
SHE...
...SHOWED ME...
...HER TRUE SELF.

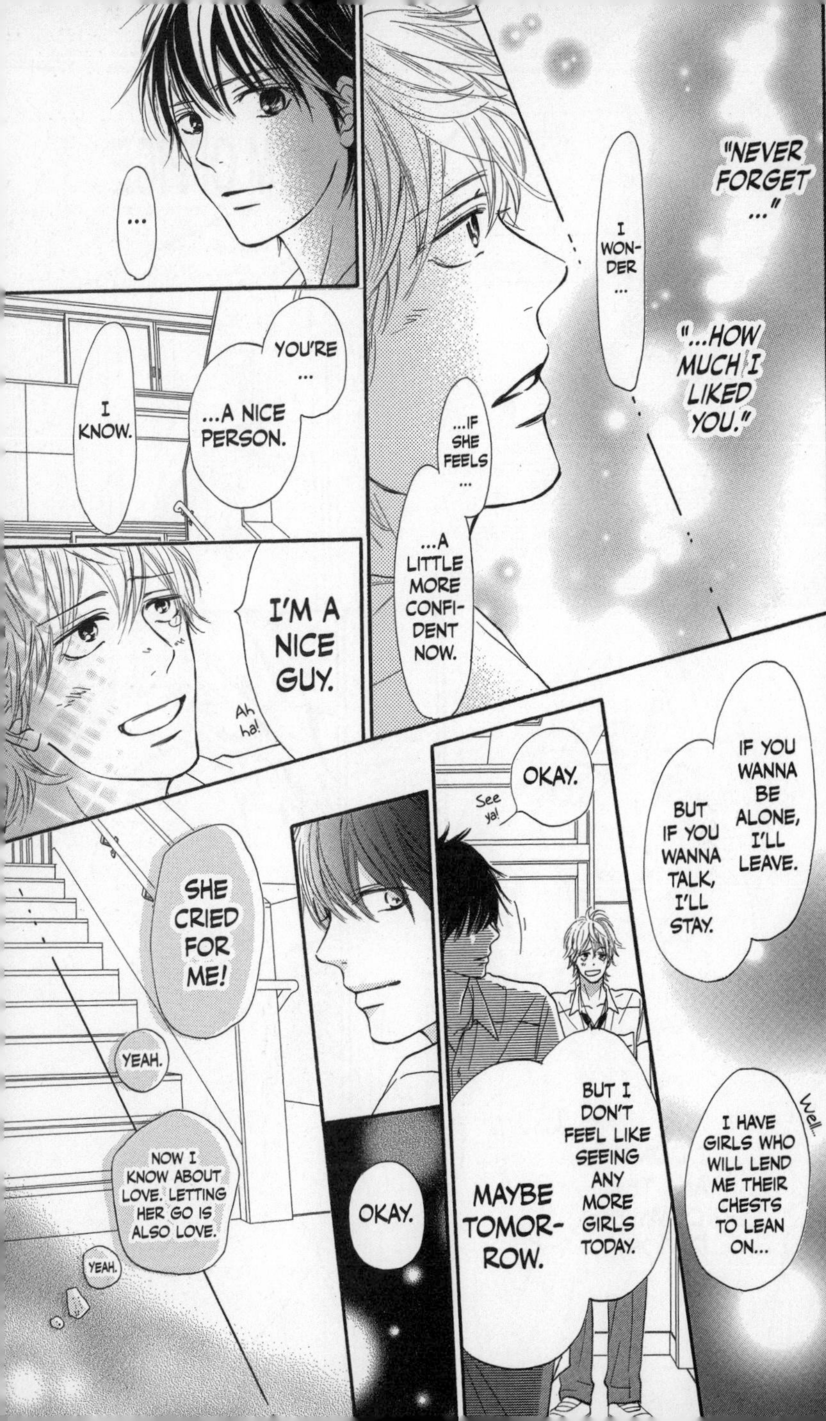
"NEVER FORGET..."
"...HOW MUCH I LIKED YOU."
I WONDER...
...IF SHE FEELS...
...A LITTLE MORE CONFIDENT NOW.
...
YOU'RE...
...A NICE PERSON.
I KNOW.
I'M A NICE GUY.
Ah ha!
OKAY.
See ya!
IF YOU WANNA BE ALONE, I'LL LEAVE.
BUT IF YOU WANNA TALK, I'LL STAY.
Well...
I HAVE GIRLS WHO WILL LEND ME THEIR CHESTS TO LEAN ON...
BUT I DON'T FEEL LIKE SEEING ANY MORE GIRLS TODAY.
MAYBE TOMORROW.
OKAY.
SHE CRIED FOR ME!
YEAH.
NOW I KNOW ABOUT LOVE. LETTING HER GO IS ALSO LOVE.
YEAH.

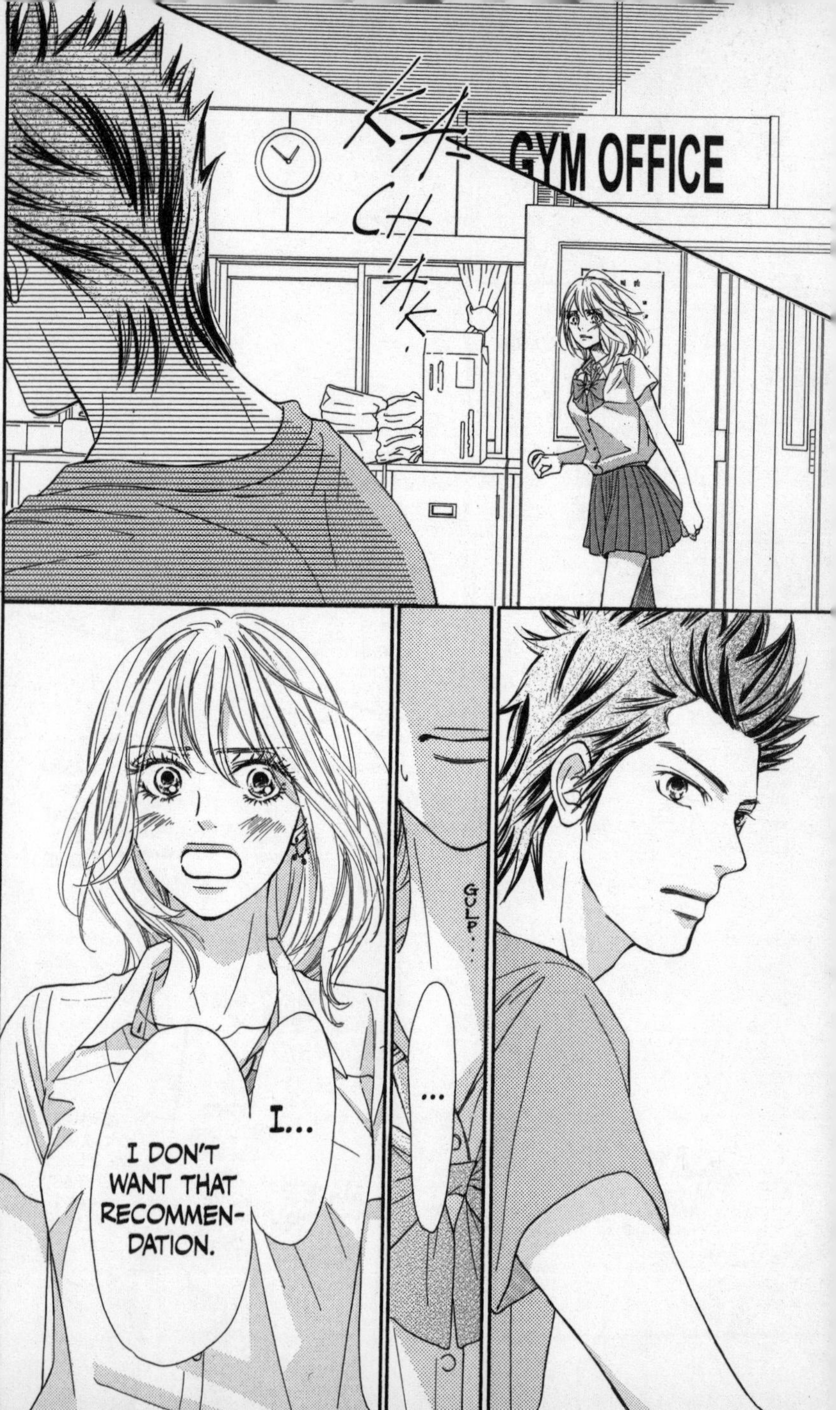
GYM OFFICE
KA-CHAK.
GULP...
...
I...
I DON'T WANT THAT RECOMMEN-DATION.

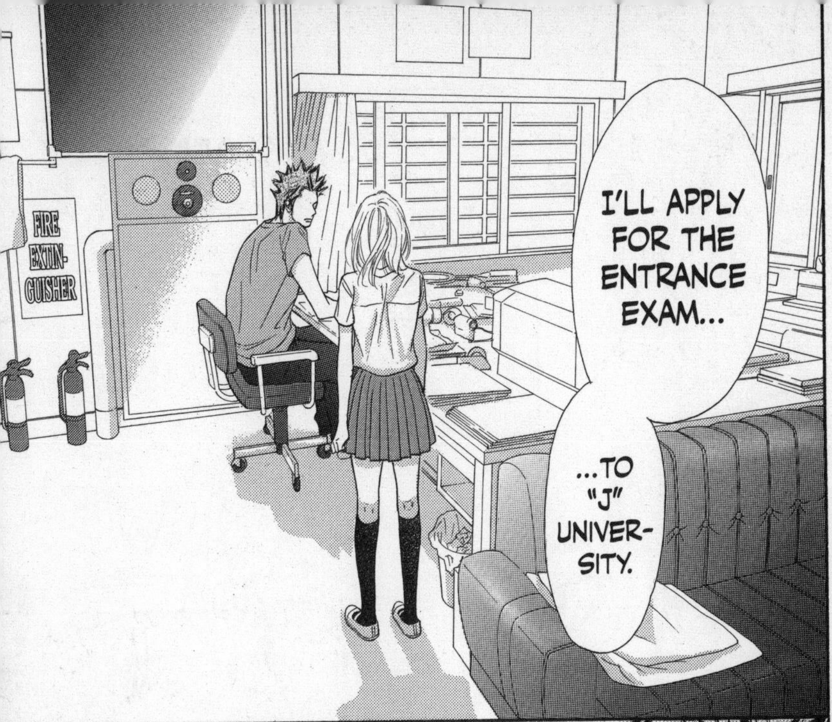
FIRE EXTIN-GUISHER
I'LL APPLY FOR THE ENTRANCE EXAM...
...TO "J" UNIVER-SITY.
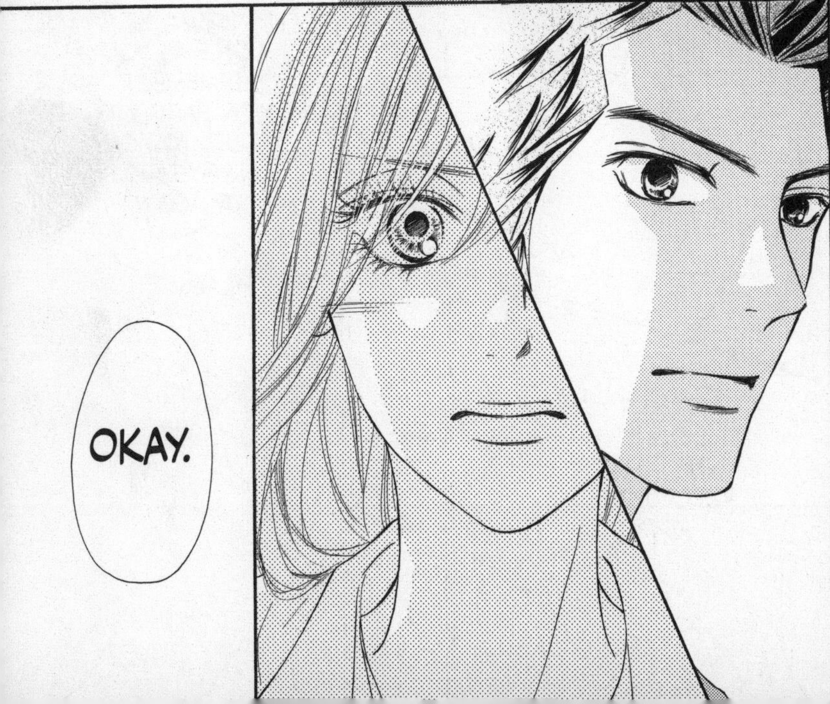
OKAY.

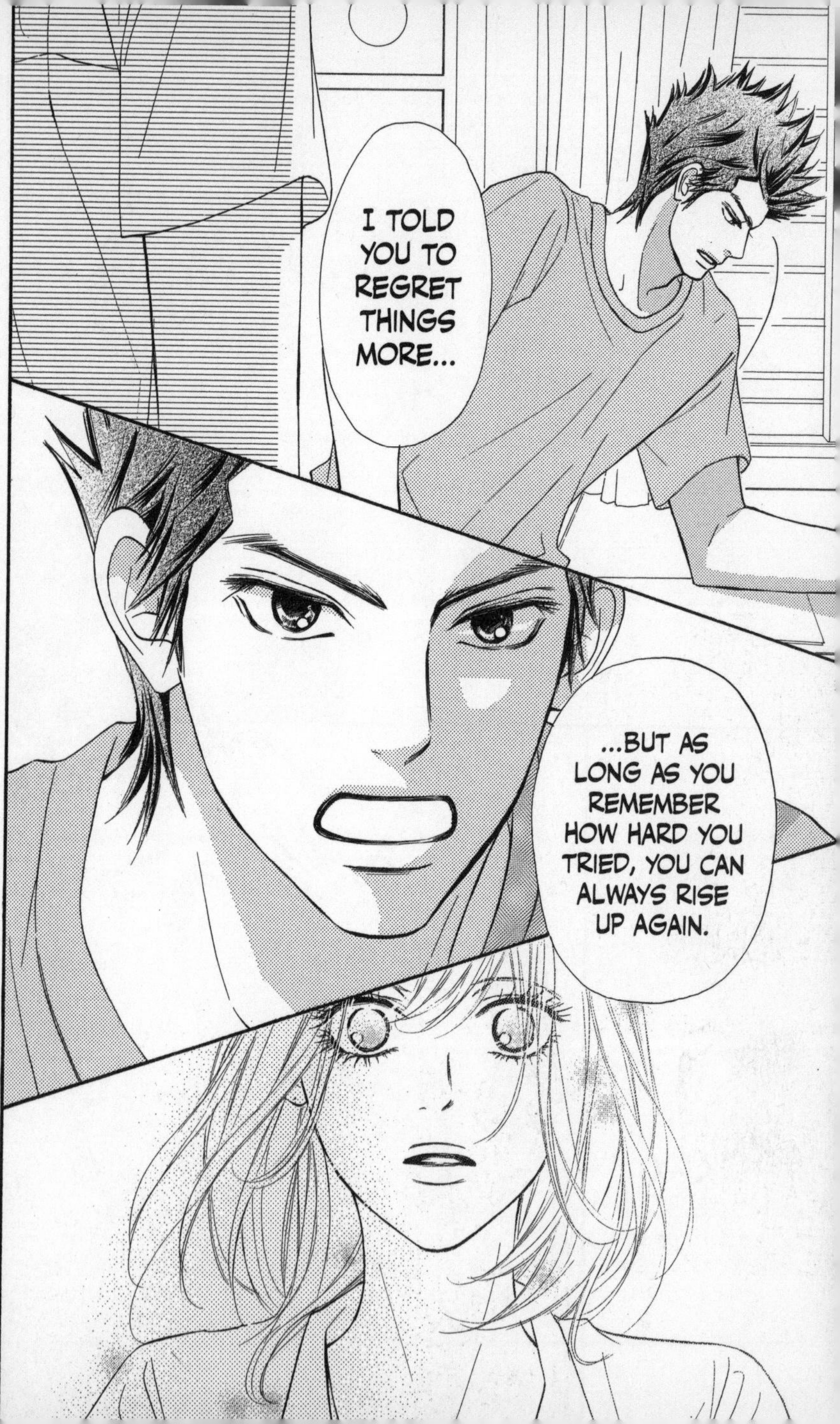
I TOLD YOU TO REGRET THINGS MORE...
...BUT AS LONG AS YOU REMEMBER HOW HARD YOU TRIED, YOU CAN ALWAYS RISE UP AGAIN.

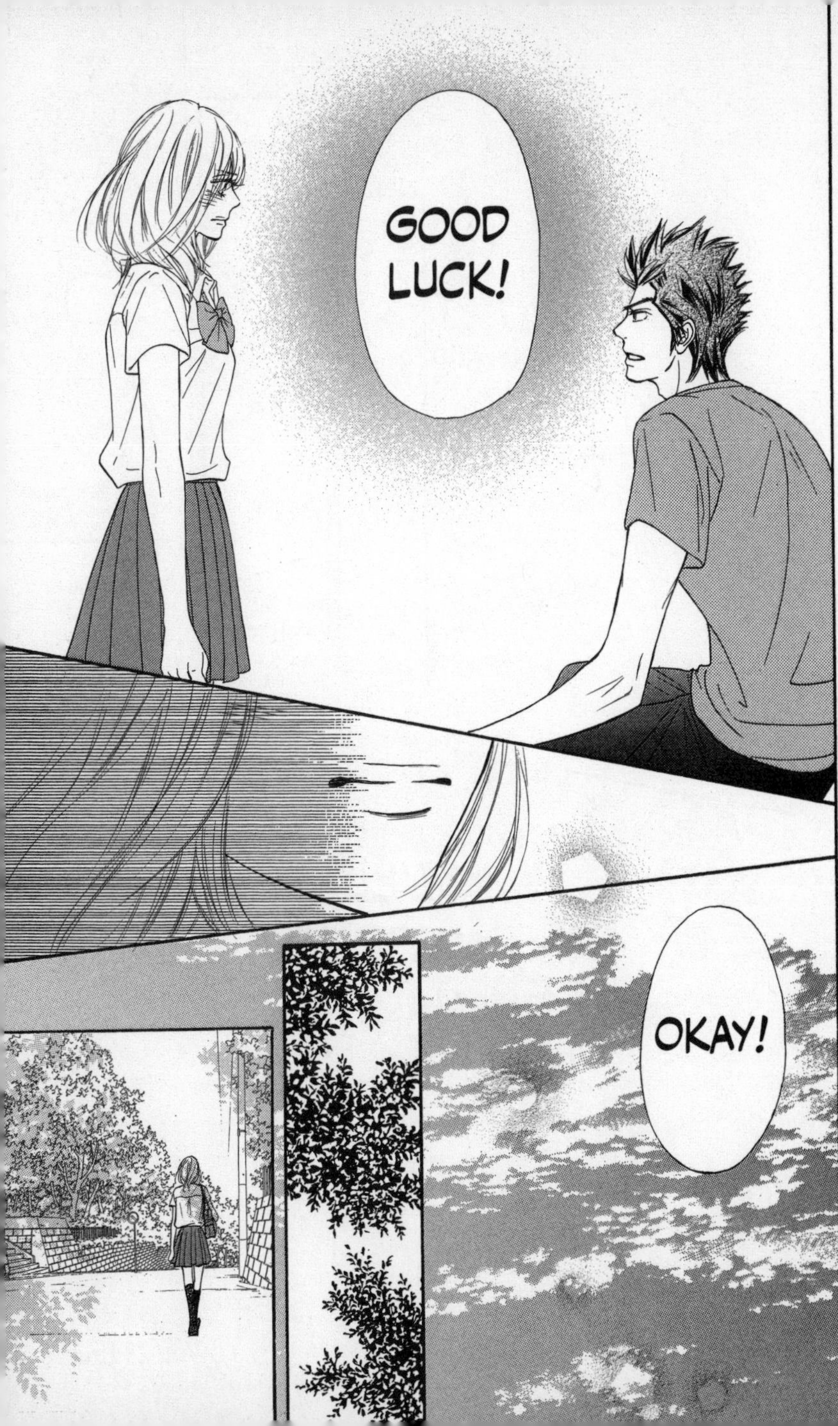
GOOD LUCK!
OKAY!

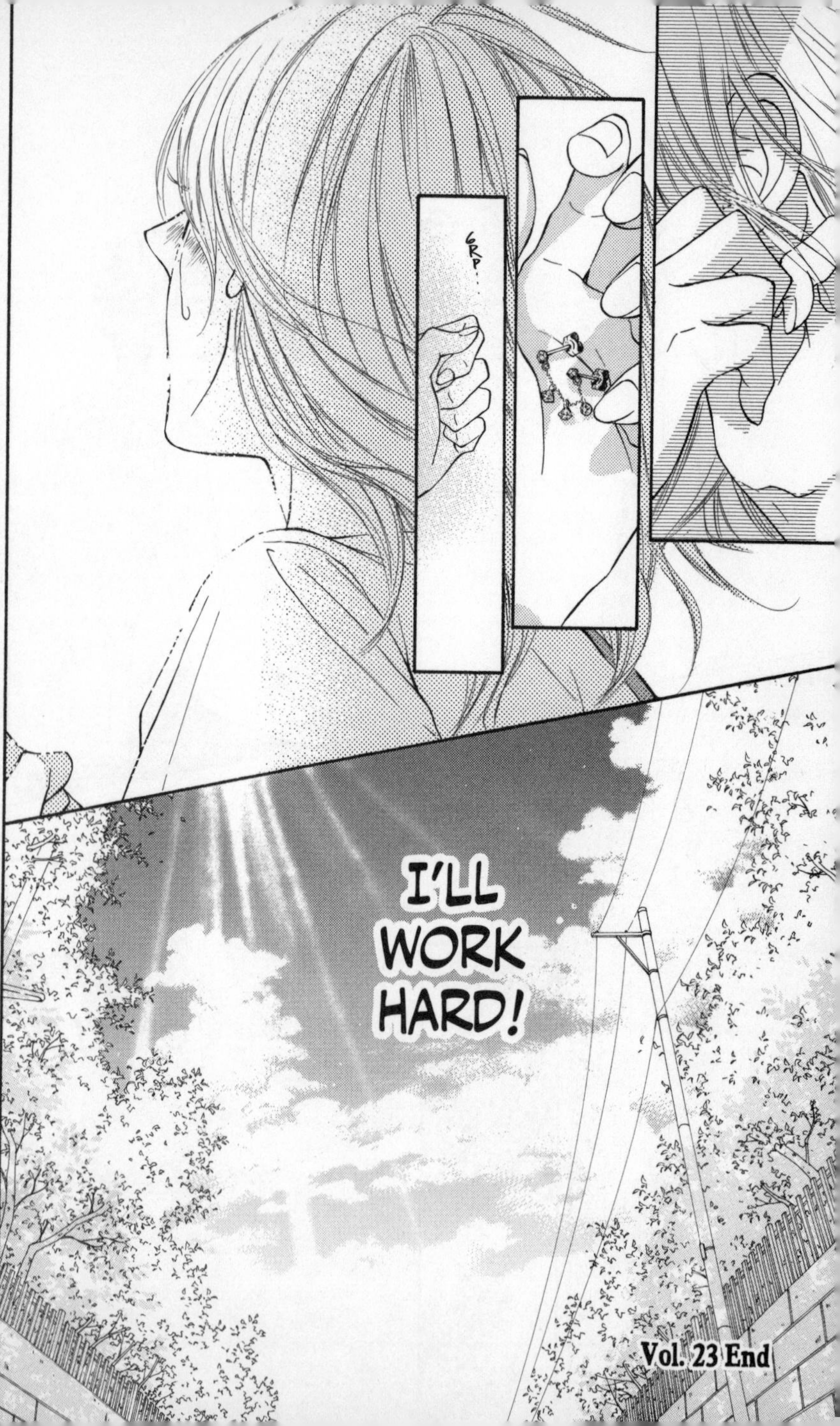
GRP...
I'LL WORK HARD!
Vol. 23 End

From me (the editor) to you (the reader).

Here are some Japanese culture explanations that will help you better understand the references in the _Kimi ni Todoke_ world.

Honorifics:
When saying someone's name in Japanese, a suffix is often attached to indicate how familiar the speaker is with the person. Some are more polite and respectful, while others are endearing. Calling someone by just their first name is the most informal.
-kun is used for young men or boys, usually someone you are familiar with.
-chan is used for young women, girls or young children and can be used as a term of endearment.
-san is used for someone you respect or are not close to, or to be polite.

Page 9, dorayaki:
A Japanese confection. It is usually made with a pancake-like exterior and filled with red bean jam.

Page 9, Aeon:
A shopping center chain in Japan.. It contains a department store and a grocery store.

Page 92, ULFULS:
A real Japanese rock band from Osaka that debuted in 1992. The name comes from a member misreading the word "soulful" on the cover of one of the band member's favorite records.

Page 102, Doraemon:
A popular children's anime and manga. In one episode, Doraemon gives a child, Nobita, a stone hat to turn himself invisible so he can do anything he wants without people complaining about his actions.

This is volume 23! Most of it is about Ayane. Sorry the main heroine doesn't show up that much. I've been thinking about this part of the story for years, and I can finally draw it! I put the episodes that I thought about earlier in a scrapbook. It's a little sad to see them gradually disappearing.

--Karuho Shiina

Karuho Shiina was born and raised in Hokkaido, Japan. Though *Kimi ni Todoke* is only her second series following many one-shot stories, it has already racked up accolades from various "Best Manga of the Year" lists. Winner of the 2008 Kodansha Manga Award for the shojo category, *Kimi ni Todoke* also placed fifth in the first-ever Manga Taisho (Cartoon Grand Prize) contest in 2008. In Japan, an animated TV series debuted in October 2009, and a live-action film was released in 2010.

Kimi ni Todoke
VOL. 23

Shojo Beat Edition

STORY AND ART BY
KARUHO SHIINA

Translation/Ari Yasuda, HC Language Solutions, Inc.
Touch-up Art & Lettering/Vanessa Satone
Design/Nozomi Akashi
Editor/Marlene First

Printed in the U.S.A.

Published by VIZ Media, LLC
P.O. Box 77010
San Francisco, CA 94107

10 9 8 7 6 5 4 3 2 1
First printing, January 2016

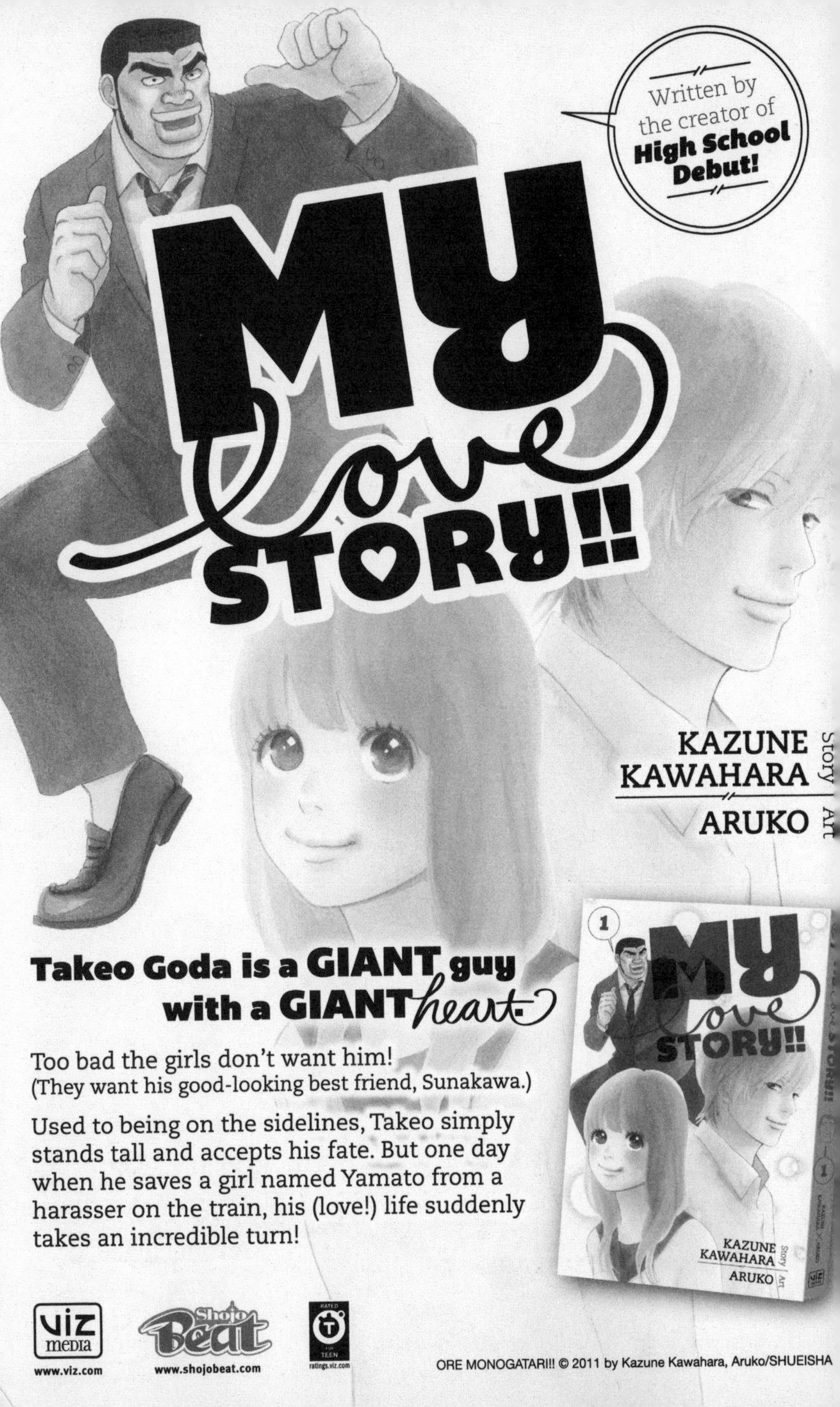
Written by the creator of High School Debut!
MY love STORY!!
KAZUNE KAWAHARA Story
ARUKO Art
Takeo Goda is a GIANT guy with a GIANT heart.
Too bad the girls don't want him! (They want his good-looking best friend, Sunakawa.)
Used to being on the sidelines, Takeo simply stands tall and accepts his fate. But one day when he saves a girl named Yamato from a harasser on the train, his (love!) life suddenly takes an incredible turn!
1
MY love STORY!!
KAZUNE KAWAHARA Story
ARUKO Art
viz media
www.viz.com
Shojo Beat
www.shojobeat.com
RATED T FOR TEEN
ratings.viz.com
ORE MONOGATARI!! © 2011 by Kazune Kawahara, Aruko/SHUEISHA

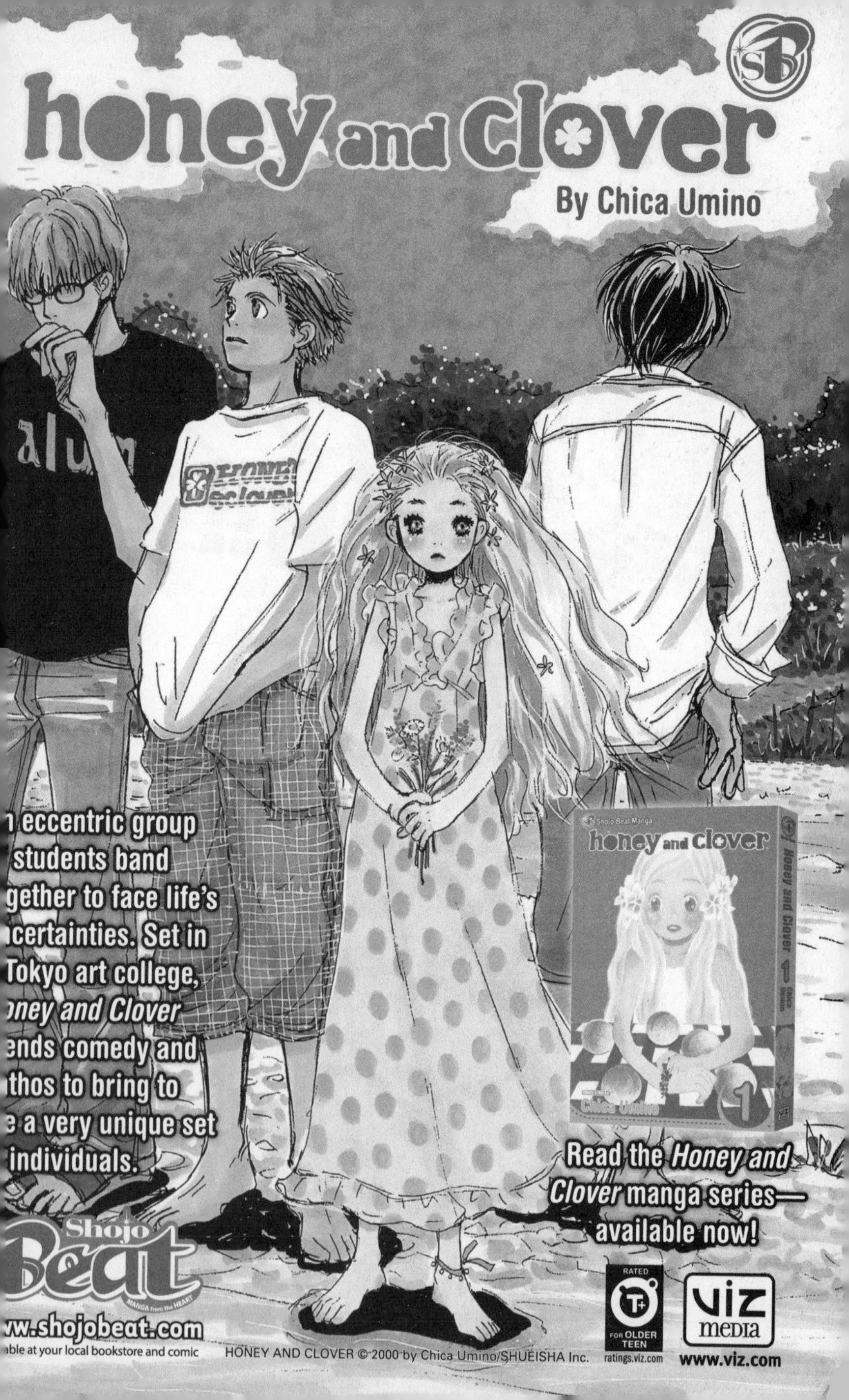

Is this girl a devil in disguise... or a misunderstood angel?

A Devil and Her Love Song

Story and Art by Miyoshi Tomori

Meet Maria Kawai—she's gorgeous and whip-smart, a girl who seems to have it all. But when she unleashes her sharp tongue, it's no wonder some consider her to be the very devil! Maria's difficult ways even get her kicked out of an elite school, but this particular fall may actually turn out to be her saving grace...

Only **$9.99 US / $12.99 CAN** each!

Vol. 1 ISBN: 978-1-4215-4164-8
Vol. 2 ISBN: 978-1-4215-4165-5
Vol. 3 ISBN: 978-1-4215-4166-2
Vol. 4 ISBN: 978-1-4215-4167-9

Check your local manga retailer for availability!

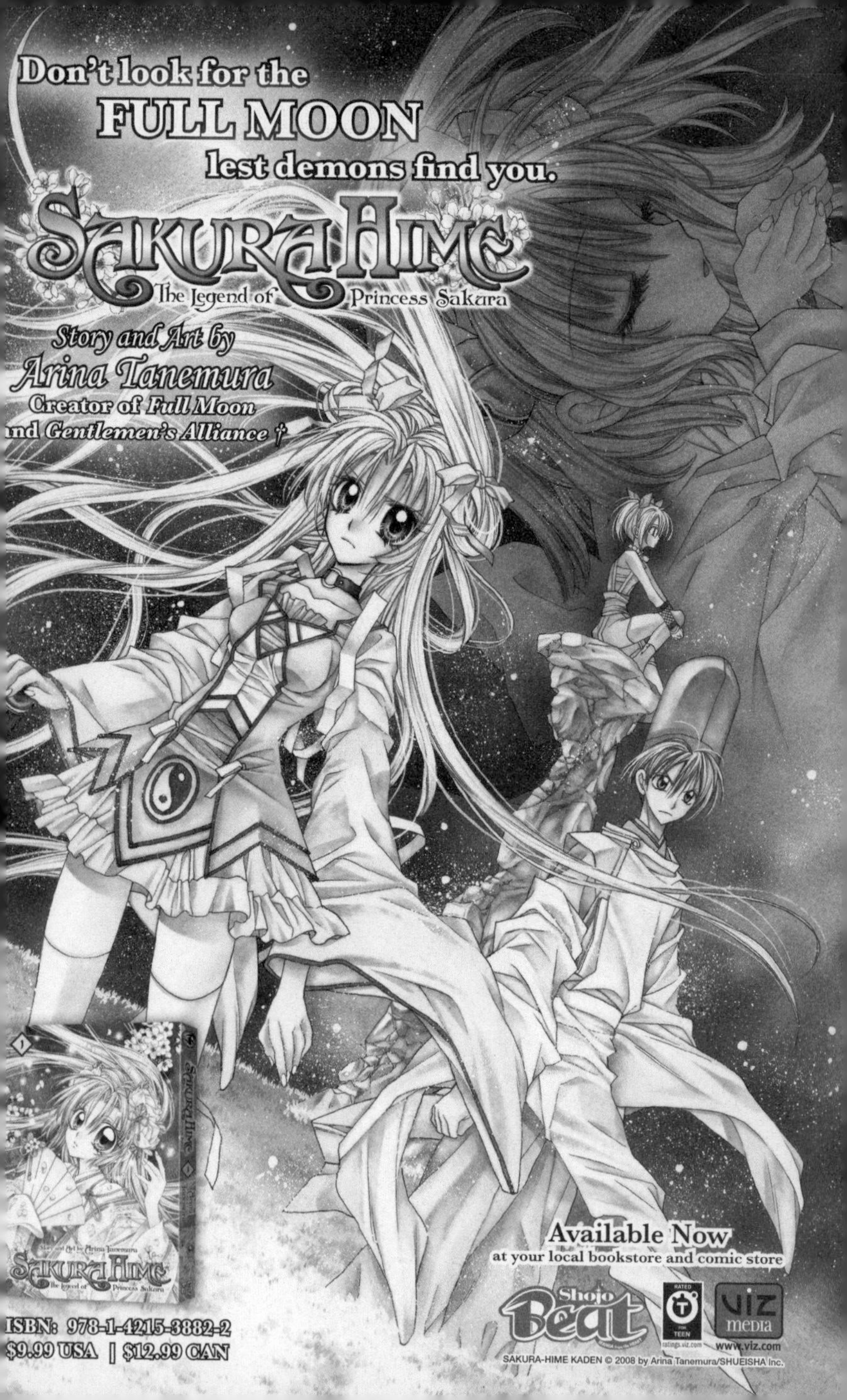
Don't look for the
FULL MOON
lest demons find you.
SAKURA HIME
The Legend of Princess Sakura
Story and Art by
Arina Tanemura
Creator of Full Moon
and Gentlemen's Alliance †
Available Now
at your local bookstore and comic store
ISBN: 978-1-4215-3882-2
$9.99 USA | $12.99 CAN
Shojo Beat
RATED T FOR TEEN
ratings.viz.com
VIZ media
www.viz.com
SAKURA-HIME KADEN © 2008 by Arina Tanemura/SHUEISHA Inc.

Surprise!

You may be reading the wrong way!

It's true: In keeping with the original Japanese comic format, this book reads from right to left—so action, sound effects, and word balloons are completely reversed. This preserves the orientation of the original artwork—plus, it's fun! Check out the diagram shown here to get the hang of things, and then turn to the other side of the book to get started!

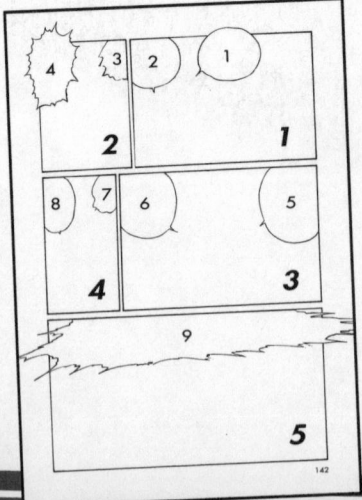